This Design by
Granderson Russell
of Cole and Redmayne

THE NORTHWEST JAZZ WORKSHOP PRESENTS

1956 SEAFAIR JAZZ FESTIVAL

MOORE THEATRE

Sunday, August 5th, 8:30 P.M.

ADMISSION	1.95
FED. TAX	.20
CITY TAX	.10
	2.25

No. 710

LOOK! LOOK! LOOK!

DANCE

Brotherhood of Sleeping Car Porters and Ladies' Auxiliary

Tuesday, July 31, 1945

9:00 p. m. to 1:00 a. m.

Presenting

AL PIERRE'S ORCHESTRA

Featuring That Mad Drummer

VERNON BROWN

and the Three Rhythm Jesters

W. O. W. HALL
28 S.W. 11th AVENUE

ADMISSION
$1.50 Inc. Tax

Jackson Street After Hours

Jackson Street After Hours

The Roots of Jazz in Seattle

SECOND EDITION

Paul de Barros

RESEARCH ASSISTANCE: THEO DZIELAK

University of Washington Press
Seattle

4 CULTURE The second edition of *Jackson Street After Hours* was made possible in part by a grant from the 4Culture Heritage Projects Program.

Support for this publication was also provided by a generous gift from William Donnelly.

Design by Katrina Noble Composed in Miller Text

30 29 28 27 26 5 4 3 2 1

Printed and bound in Canada

UNIVERSITY OF WASHINGTON PRESS
uwapress.uw.edu

LIBRARY OF CONGRESS CATALOGING-IN-PUBLICATION DATA
Names: De Barros, Paul author | Dzielak, Theo researcher
Title: Jackson Street after hours : the roots of jazz in Seattle / Paul de Barros ; research assistance: Theo Dzielak.
Description: Second edition. | Seattle : University of Washington Press, 2026. | Includes bibliographical references and index.
Identifiers: LCCN 2026024325 (print) | LCCN 2026024326 (ebook) | ISBN 9780295755243 hardcover | ISBN 9780295755250 ebook
Subjects: LCSH: Jazz—Washington (State)—Seattle—History and criticism | Jazz musicians—Washington (State)—Seattle | Jackson Street (Seattle, Wash.)
Classification: LCC ML3508.8.S4 D4 2026 (print) | LCC ML3508.8.S4 (ebook) | DDC 781.6509797—dc23/eng/20260507
LC record available at https://lccn.loc.gov/2026024325
LC ebook record available at https://lccn.loc.gov/2026024326

For EU product safety concerns please contact Easy Access System Europe Oü 16879218, Mustamäe tee 50, 10621, Tallinn, Estonia, gpsr.requests@easproject.com, +372 56 98939.

♾ This paper meets the requirements of ANSI/NISO Z39.48-1992 (Permanence of Paper).

Frontispiece: Betty Marshall and Billy Tolles competing as a jitterbug team, 1940s. Courtesy of MOHAI, Al Smith Collection. 2014.49.13.12.01.

CONTENTS

PREFACE TO THE SECOND EDITION

NOT LONG AFTER *JACKSON STREET AFTER HOURS* WAS PUBLISHED IN 1993, I was talking to a guy about Seattle music. Out of the blue he said, "You know, like the old Jackson Street scene." I was a bit taken aback. It wasn't just that he didn't seem to know I'd written a book about the subject, it was the way he said it, as if this were common knowledge in Seattle and always had been—like, say, the Sonics winning the NBA Championship in 1979.

When I wrote *Jackson Street*, I thought new ideas took years to be absorbed. But I was wrong. In a matter of months, the message I had wanted to send to Seattle—that there had been a robust, almost completely unacknowledged African American jazz culture in our city for most of the twentieth century—had not only sunk in, it had apparently become common knowledge.

That was a very pleasant surprise. So was the fact that older Black musicians who had played on Jackson Street, people like Floyd Standifer and Jabo Ward and Buddy Catlett, seemed to be getting a little more respect. Suddenly, instead of being thought of as random old guys who didn't quite fit in, they were now recognized properly as the city's jazz elders.

"*Jackson Street* changed everything," Floyd Standifer told me. That meant an awful lot. It's not an exaggeration to say that before *Jackson Street After Hours* was published, most local jazz fans and even most of the players didn't know much about Seattle jazz history. I know, because I was one of them. Back in 1984, when I was writing a cover story for the *Seattle Weekly* about jazz, I called Jabo to ask him for some background. He was a sweet man, but after a few questions that must have struck him as unforgivably stupid, he cut loose.

"You don't know anything about jazz in Seattle," he said. "Do you know who Bumps Blackwell is? What about Al Pierre? And Vernon Brown? Have you ever heard of Quincy Jones? All kinds of musicians came out of Seattle. Did you know Ray Charles lived here?"

Thanks, Jabo. I owe you, big-time. That conversation is what got me started on this book. Jabo wouldn't be the last person to give me a piece of his mind. When you do community history, you discover that when you finally finish your project, it's not the end. It's the beginning. Because that is when all the people you couldn't find, find you. When *Earshot* magazine published a photograph of Leon Vaughn's 1944 band at Basin Street and I couldn't identify all the players, a guy called from Anchorage, Alaska.

"Is this Paul de Barros?" he asked.

"Yes."

"Well, this here is 'Unidentified.'" That is how Milton Walton's name got into the book. Many others did not. For years, I've carried around a tattered copy of *Jackson Street After Hours* marked up in pencil with all the omissions and mistakes and new discoveries I wanted to add in a future edition. I am so grateful to the University of Washington Press for giving me a chance to convert those pencil marks to ink, not only to make corrections but also to take advantage of the avalanche of research that has come out since 1993.

The first was Quintard Taylor's monumental *The Forging of a Black Community: Seattle's Central District from 1870 through the Civil Rights Era*. The book was followed by other indispensable works, by David Keller, Christopher T. Bayley, Kurt E. Armbruster, Peter Blecha, Brad Holden, Mark Miller, Phil Pastras, Robert Dietsche, Sam Stephenson, and Phil Moore. Their books are all included in the Sources section if you want to know more, and so are the articles published by Ashley Harrison, Desmond Power, and Linda Holden Givens.

During these years I, too, added to the body of knowledge about Jackson Street, collaborating with guitarist Greg Ruby on *Frank D. Waldron: Seattle's Syncopated Classic* and with a committee of community stakeholders who launched the Jackson Street Jazz Trail, a self-guided online tour (JacksonStreetJazzTrail.org) of the old jazz district. I also delved into the background of the murals Tanya Woo discovered under the Louisa Hotel, which turned out to be the old speakeasy the Club Royale.

Thanks to the internet, these more recent research projects were a lot less arduous than those for *Jackson Street After Hours* in the late 1980s and early 1990s. Back then my assistant Ted (Theo) Dzielak pored over microfilm of Seattle's old Black newspapers. Today, all those newspapers are digitized and searchable online. What a treat it has been to go back to them to find new gems about Oscar Holden, Gene Coy, the Whang Doodle Orchestra, the Black Elks Club, and the Black and Tan and to finally settle, once and for all, that old Bruce Rowell wasn't lying to me forty years ago when he said blues singer Mamie Smith played Seattle. Because there she is, big as life, in the May 7, 1923, edition of the *Seattle Post-Intelligencer*. Digital technology—and the passage of time—has also unearthed many recordings that were unavailable thirty-five years ago.

But as much new material as I found for this new edition of *Jackson Street After Hours*—and there's a lot—the core of the book remains the same: the sound of the voices that tell the story. Going over the manuscript these past few months, I found myself delighted all over again by the kaleidoscopic language and syncopated cadence these musicians used to tell their tales or, as the eminent ethnomusicologist Chris Waterman put it in his review of the first edition, the "polyphonic" quality of their story. That was always exactly the point. Not to recite a litany of facts, but to offer a chorus of overlapping community voices. They are all still here, maybe with a few more facts tucked in around them, but still jamming into the night, sometimes until the next morning. I invite you, once again, to listen.

PAUL DE BARROS
Seattle, 2026

Introduction

FOR SUCH AN OUT-OF-THE-WAY PLACE SEATTLE HAS HAD A REMARKABLE jazz history. The action began as early as 1912, when the Whang Doodle Orchestra played the Dumas Club. It kept going strong all through Prohibition, as an authentic Black jazz scene developed around the hub of South Jackson Street and Twelfth Avenue. Even Jelly Roll Morton stopped off to play in the district, in 1920; he later wrote a rag, "Seattle Hunch," to commemorate the visit.

The scene peaked between 1937 and 1951, years during which Seattle came of age as a nerve center of the defense industry. A plentiful supply of soldiers and civilians, out looking for a good time, made Seattle a boomtown for musicians. In 1948 there were more than two dozen nightclubs along Jackson Street, clubs where jazz and bootleg liquor flowed as freely as money from a soldier's pocket. Pianist Gerald Wiggins, stationed at Fort Lewis during World War II, put it best: "They did everything but go home." This same lively scene nurtured the early careers of Quincy Jones, Ray Charles, and Ernestine Anderson.

Other musicians who played in the Jackson Street clubs went on to national jazz careers. Bassists Buddy Catlett and Wyatt Ruther worked with Count Basie. Pianists Wiggins, Phil Moore, and Jimmy Rowles went to Los Angeles, where they became exceptional accompanists and soloists. Patti Bown forged a career in New York. Still others, such as Floyd Standifer and Roscoe Weathers, never became well-known outside the region, but when touring musicians came to town, they treated these Seattle players as peers. The "locals" may not have taken to the road, but they kept an authentic tradition alive at home.

Seattle has never been as musically isolated as most people might imagine. In 1910 the town was the center of the largest vaudeville circuit in the country, a network of theaters owned by Alexander Pantages. Seattle audiences heard W. C. Handy and Freddie Keppard in Pantages theaters. And at every successive stage of jazz history, most major exponents of each new style found their way to the Northwest. The So Different Orchestra, one of the most important early jazz groups on the West Coast, played the Black and Tan in 1920. Duke Ellington played Seattle as early as 1934. Charlie Parker and Lester Young came through several times. Seattle may have been an outpost, but it certainly never lacked for jazz.

And yet, while Seattle has produced its share of great players, as a jazz town it made no stylistic contributions to the development of the music. Why, then, one might reasonably ask, write the history of jazz here? For those of us who live in Seattle, the answer is easy. To learn more about who we are, we look back at who we *were*, hoping to find clues to our identity. We know, for example, that Quincy Jones and Ray Charles rose from among our ranks. Does this tell us anything about who we are or who we might become? Is there something about the music these people have made that reflects us or our city?

For Northwesterners there is also the issue of cultural hegemony. Western American history, and certainly West Coast jazz history, seems always to have been written by people for whom the West was at best exotic and at worst an inconsequential footnote. Even "West Coast jazz," acknowledged as a bona fide aesthetic movement, has been largely interpreted as a kind of aberration, a diluted form of the "real stuff" happening back East—even though Eric Dolphy and Charles Mingus were every bit as much West Coast figures as Gerry Mulligan, Shorty Rogers, or Chet Baker. This provides an important rationale for writing a book about Seattle jazz: to know it and to name it accurately.

But what about people outside the Northwest? Why should they be interested in this sort of local chronicle? Jazz history typically has been written as the story of a main stem, growing through certain locales and styles—New Orleans, Chicago, Kansas City, and so on. Such a model is useful for getting a handle on the subject, but American culture—literature, visual art, music, or whatever—has always been a product of our whole land, not just a handful of urban areas. As important as New York is to the culture of jazz, the music's pulse has made itself felt all across the country. Jazz scholar Gunther Schuller treats this idea in his book *The Swing Era*:

> It is fascinating to contemplate the role that geography and chance encounters have played in the history of jazz. Although often the impression is that "it all happens in New York"—even Basie and his Kansas City cohorts had to go there to really "make it"—it is useful to remind ourselves that . . . the crisscrossing of bands over the length and breadth of this nation over the decades, with the chance encounters between musicians, has been a factor of virtually incalculable importance in the development of jazz. The long hard tours, the endless one-nighters, though at times

painful in actuality, have also played a crucial fertilizing role in the growth of this music.

Lionel Hampton, for example, who is associated with Benny Goodman and who grew up in Chicago, clearly formed his musical aesthetic in Los Angeles and, for reasons that seem to be mostly coincidence, drew upon Seattle for an inordinate share of his sidemen. Andy Kirk's swinging, blues-inflected style is associated with the Midwest, yet one of his most illustrious soloists, Dick Wilson, learned to play jazz from Joe Darensbourg, a New Orleans Creole clarinetist who worked in Seattle, and from a San Francisco–bred saxophone teacher named Frank Waldron. In the complexities of such relationships between the national and the local, in the crisscrossing of lines all over the American map by the great and the mundane, the sung and the unsung, lie the secrets of the real history of jazz. The point here is not to make an exaggerated artistic claim for Seattle per se, but to illustrate the cross-pollination and interplay that make up the fabric of jazz's rich history.

There is another, related, and perhaps even more compelling reason for chronicling this local history, and that is to honor the people who made the music. If, living in the West, one feels from time to time a sense of having been written out of history, it is nothing compared with the invisibility that African Americans have experienced in general. Anyone who has done research of this kind is well acquainted with the scarcity of public documentation about Black people, but I was frankly unprepared for the sweeping neglect I encountered when doing research for the first edition of this book. As I scoured old newspapers and magazines for information about Black jazz musicians, it became increasingly clear that a whole era had gone by unnamed, unhailed, and unrecorded by the mainstream press. Musicians famous and not so famous came and went, put down roots, influenced other musicians, started bands, ended them, had heydays and down days, but barely anyone bothered to take notice or keep track.

It's astonishing that brilliant musicians like Quincy Jones, Ray Charles, and Ernestine Anderson—the very ones who would go on to be claimed by Seattle as illustrious native sons and daughters—could have been "coming up" in the late 1940s on Seattle's Jackson Street without any consistent observer publicly documenting their progress. It is doubly ironic to sift through old newspapers and find review after review of mediocre chamber music concerts during the same period. This amounts to a systematic veiling, albeit unwitting, of one of the richest aspects of Seattle's cultural history.

Looking back, we can see that constructs of race and class permitted this veil to be hung. Jazz often thrived in Seattle, as elsewhere, in what were perceived then as "dives," in a Black ghetto where gambling, prostitution, and illegal drinking were as central to the action as the music itself. The notion that something of cultural importance might be brewing outside the law, on the outskirts of respectability, was virtually inconceivable to the white reporters, editors, and cultural pundits of the time who might have documented what was going on. Even when such people did take friends down to, say, the Black and Tan at Twelfth and Jackson for a drink and some hot jazz, as often as not they saw only a "colorful" diversion from their routines, not the unfolding drama of an American music culture in the making.

There were exceptions. Thank goodness for Black newspapers such as the *Northwest Enterprise* and *Cayton's Weekly*, with their listings of local Black entertainers and occasional articles about them. Without this information there would be virtually no historical record of early Seattle jazz. Thanks, too, for Washington's Black historian Esther Mumford, who began this difficult investigative work long ago, documenting the contributions of Black people in Washington in the nineteenth century. Breaking out of the mainstream press mold were Johnny Reddin, the intrepid *Seattle Times* reporter who kept track of night people, and Doug Welch, another reporter who clearly loved jazz and advocated it in the *Seattle Post-Intelligencer*. For the most part, though, Seattle's newspapers and magazines ignored the music and the musicians who created it. (About the only time the clubs ever got any notice was when they were raided; today these sensational reports are often the only reliable source of club addresses.) One needn't look very far to find a parallel in the media coverage of Black neighborhoods that persisted for many decades: the same kinds of cultural constructs were still very much at work and, in some cases, still are.

Jazz was not only ignored by local pundits; it was often actively suppressed. Though Seattle briefly turned into a "city of sin" during and after the Yukon Gold Rush, the predominant Northwest mood has always been a sober, pragmatic, and antiexpressive one in which the business of life is business. Though jazz was tolerated, even during the notoriously liberated Jazz Age of the 1920s bluenoses consistently pushed the music underground. As if national Prohibition itself were not enough, the city passed additional ordinances against dancing, imposed taxes on cabarets, and tried to enforce irrational regulation of entertainment of all kinds. Confusing prudence with intolerance, vice with artistic expression, these measures slowed the cultural progress of the region and continued, with the despised Teen Dance Ordinance, finally repealed in 2002.

Curiously, the culture of official corruption that arose in response to this repression kept Seattle jazz alive during the first half of the century. The city's notorious "tolerance policy," the 1947 formalization of a practice that had existed for decades, ensured that bold entrepreneurs could continue to open nightclubs where jazz musicians thrived. Under this policy police officers were paid under the table for winking at illegal practices such as gambling, prostitution, and bootlegging. When the tolerance policy finally collapsed in 1970, an odd disjunction occurred. Jazz, already on the downswing with the onslaught of rock, went into a decade of near-hibernation. By the time it reappeared with force locally, almost all the major players of the old era had died, moved away, or given up music. As a result, a generation of musicians and fans knew very little about Jackson Street's heyday. The few remaining older Black musicians who had been part of the lively Jackson Street era felt passed over when the jazz scene revived, somehow robbed of their own legacy.

This book is an attempt to restore that legacy. For despite being forced underground, harassed by the authorities, and ignored by the press, Seattle jazz musicians have fared remarkably well. It is good for Seattleites to know that behind the bland veil of the official story, there is also this rich and expressive history. This book is a tribute—in many cases a memorial—to the musicians who lived that history, the locals who have kept the jazz fire alive in the Northwest for more than a century.

PAUL DE BARROS
Seattle, 1998, 2026

Prologue

A Fantasy

NOON. SEATTLE, MAY 1, 1864. A lone Black man walks along the muddy street that will become First Avenue. Over his shoulder is slung a military snare drum, the kind whose tattoo can still be heard east of here as armies collide in the brutal War Between the States. The man's hair is thick and curly and well-groomed—he is a barber, after all—and his face open and proud. He is pleased to be here, in this new Northwest, where a man seems able to get a fresh start, away from enslavement, abolitionism, and the caste-bound traditions of the East Coast.

The man's drumbeat sprays out over the stumps, half-built clapboard houses, and offices that have sprouted along the steep hill that rises from the edge of Puget Sound. The water sparkles below. A half-dozen sailing ships idle in the wind. One, from San Francisco, is taking up a load of fresh-cut timber. Smoke rises from a brickyard and mill. The man looks up. The sun is high. Time for a break, says the beat of the drum. Time for the noonday meal . . .

Below, on First and Main at the new Plummer's Hall (which everyone has taken to calling Snoqualmie Hall), excited preparations are underway. Mr. Charles Plummer, proud procurer of the county's first liquor license (in 1854) and owner of Seattle's first saloon (complete with tinkling piano), has engaged the first traveling theatrical company ever to play the hopeful little pioneer town. Tonight the Excelsior Minstrels, with the Taylor Brothers and whistling Tom LaFont, known as "the American Mocking Bird," will introduce Seattle to an entertainment craze that will sweep the nation when the war is over.

The performance is to be upstairs, in the meeting hall. The troupe raised its sets and rehearsed the show this morning, hanging a curtain to create a makeshift backstage area. All the accoutrements of the trade—cork, charcoal, tap shoes, makeup—are laid out on a table behind the sheet. LaFont himself, a tall actor in a top hat who has seen much of the States and all of Europe, descends the steep stairs to the barroom, where he discovers Plummer.

"Everything is at the ready, sir," says LaFont. "I wonder where I might find a dining establishment?" Before Plummer can answer, the noise of the snare drum comes within earshot. "Sir, what on earth is that noise? Has the war come this far west without my knowledge?"

"Why no, my good friend, that's only Lopes, the heartbeat of Africa itself, my dear sir. Every day at midday he strikes up that rhythm, to spread the news of his barbershop and the midday meal. Manuel Lopes, the barber. From Africa, he says, though I have it on good authority he comes from somewhere in the Caribbean Isles. I don't know how he knows when it's noon, since the sun never shines on this wretched bay."

"Why Mr. Plummer, I do not mean to be disagreeable, sir, but it appears the sun is out today." They step outside.

"Why, so it is, so it is."

"An African, you say?" LaFont's stomach is rumbling. "I once had some hot peppered stew in Antigua that nearly singed off my eyelashes."

"You don't say, don't say. Damn fine barber. Trimmed my whiskers just last week. Brought that chair around the Horn, he did. Finest damn barber's chair north of San Francisco."

Lopes's beat begins to fade. He has turned his march back toward the shop.

"I do believe I'll stroll over and have a look. Seven sharp, then, is it?"

"Seven it is!"

LaFont strikes out toward the drumbeat. It is a fine day. As he enters Lopes's modest shop, a step down from the street, he finds the African hanging his snare drum on a hook. His topcoat, much the worse for wear, looks like British military, with tassels and pleats. Beside the drum hangs a large fragment of whalebone; on the floor, two glass floats that have followed the current from Japan. The place smells of cologne and gumbo. LaFont spies a bubbling pot on the sawdust-burning stove behind the elegant barber's chair.

Lopes's back is to the actor. When he hears LaFont's footfall, he suddenly turns on one heel in a smooth, almost mechanical motion, smiles, and gives a mock salute. The poise of it catches the actor's eye. LaFont makes a mental note. He can use it.

"At your service, sir," says Lopes, taking in the fine cut of the thespian's frock and his friendly eyes, which promise sympathy. "And what may I do for you?"

"I have found the emerald isle, yet am I sore confused," says LaFont, adopting a mock Shakespearean manner. "Shall I answer the call of my lowly stomach and sup on spicy gumbo, or succumb to vanity and fatigue and have you shape my face and sprinkle sweet waters on my hair, while I lay in the embrace of that soft and sloping couch?"

Lopes laughs. "Gumbo first, since you are a man of such good taste. Then we cut the sauce out of your beard!"

"Done!"

1 "Seattle Hunch"

1864–1920

ONE NIGHT IN AUGUST 1920 the great Ferdinand "Jelly Roll" Morton, who claimed to have "invented" jazz, sat down at the piano at Seattle's Entertainer's Cabaret on South Main Street near Twelfth Avenue South, put his big, Creole hands on the keys, and shook the house until the sun came up. Morton was fresh off a gig in Vancouver, British Columbia, with clarinetist and pianist Oscar Holden, who would later become the number-one piano man in Seattle. Morton wasn't famous yet. He was just another "sport" in the district, with a diamond front tooth and a cool hand for pool, trying to raise a dime. The pianist had been kicking around the West Coast since leaving New Orleans in 1917, playing piano, hustling pool, shooting craps, and—when he could—running a string of girls. After a stint in San Francisco, Morton and his wife, Anita, had opened a "rooming house" at Ponder's Corner, outside Tacoma. He spent around ten months in the Northwest. The Entertainer's Cabaret, which opened in 1919, was advertised in *Cayton's Weekly*, a Black-owned newspaper, its coy language reflecting that Prohibition was in full force:

The club was in the heart of a thriving nightclub district, where music rang out day and night, crap games sometimes ran for a week, and a man on the prowl could find any kind of pleasure he was seeking, as long as he had the cash to pay for it. The hub of the district was the corner of Twelfth Avenue South and South Jackson Street. This is where Seattle jazz was born and where it flowered, from the late 1910s until the 1960s.

At first glance, early Seattle doesn't seem the sort of place where Jelly Roll Morton—or jazz of any kind—would be found. A sleepy, remote village in the Northwest corner of the country, it was settled largely by Scandinavian immigrants who worked in the primary industries of fishing and logging and by earnest businessmen intent on building a modest, bourgeois life. Yet several peculiarities made Seattle a fertile spot for jazz. Early on, the town had developed a culture of legalized corruption that tolerated vice in exchange for official payoffs, which in turn supported venues for music. In the 1890s a honky-tonk atmosphere evolved in Maynard Town (today's Pioneer Square), where a logger or sailor could liven up his weekend. Jazz was also encouraged by the city's passion for theater, which continually exposed the populace to new forms of entertainment. Some of the earliest jazz acts to leave New Orleans—as well as minstrel shows, which preceded jazz and made important contributions to its development—toured the Northwest on a theater circuit that was well established by the 1890s. A migration of African Americans that began before the turn of the century made Seattle a likely spot for jazz as well.

From the late nineteenth century the district south of Yesler Way—"across the deadline," as they said in the early days—had been a tenderloin full of whores and touts, gamblers and pimps, where brass bands and saloon pianists competed nightly for customers' attention and loot. Originally the district lay in a rectangle bounded by Fifth Avenue, Yesler, the waterfront, and King Street. This was "Skid Road," the raw neighborhood where Seattle pioneer Henry Yesler "skidded" logs down the hill to his mill. After World War I, as the city became more settled, the action moved up the hill to Fifteenth Avenue South, taking in what is now called the Chinatown–International District (Chinatown, Nihonmachi [Japantown], a Filipino strip along South King Street, and the Vietnamese neighborhood Little Saigon) and merging east of Twelfth with the Central District, where in the 1920s a Black population began to settle. In the 1910s and 1920s this was Seattle's version of New Orleans's fabled Storyville, where "sports" and hustlers provided entertainment and rooming houses for casual laborers, drifters, and railroad porters. Yesler Hill, where the Yesler Terrace housing project stood until its 2013 redevelopment, became an area of concentrated prostitution; the junction of Twelfth Avenue South and South Jackson Street was an entertainment hub for gamblers, bootleggers, railroad men, and sailors.

"The most highly regarded people of the area were the pimps and the whores and the madams," recalled pianist Phil Moore, whose father, George Moore, was a notorious gambler. "I remember one time I was honored to play at this yearly party with a little band at the Entertainer's Club. . . . I think it was a Sunday afternoon. It was pimps and whores and madams. Sport people they used to call them. Gamblers." Imagine South Jackson Street during its heyday: at 2 a.m., pedestrians roamed the sidewalks, ducking in and out of nightclubs and bars.

There was no I-5 freeway and a trolley ran up the hill. Beyond Twelfth Avenue South, to the north, where Bailey Gatzert School and its playfield are today, a four-block grid of now demolished buildings hosted the Entertainer's Cabaret, the Blue Rose, Finnish Hall, and, a little later, Al's Lucky Hour and Ayers Café. Above Fifteenth the neighborhood became essentially like the rest of the city—quiet and residential. But from First Avenue South to Fifteenth Avenue South, Seattle rocked with wine, women, whoopee—and jazz.

Seattle's founders encouraged this underworld of vice while maintaining an image of respectability. This contradiction in the city's psychology, a kind of dual personality that flip-flopped between sobriety and naughtiness, would endure for many decades. Running a "wide open" town was a profitable tradition that involved everyone from the cop on the beat to the mayor and chief of police. By the early part of the twentieth century, corruption was so deeply imbedded in local politics that candidates often ran for office on the "wide open" platform, arguing that Seattle's vice industry generated income and a healthy economy for its more prudent citizenry. Figures such as Police Chief Charles Wappenstein and Mayor Hiram Gill reaped fortunes from the payoffs they received from whorehouses, opium dens, casinos, and later—when liquor was outlawed too—speakeasies. Seattle's flamboyant Wild West attitudes attracted the attention of the national magazine *McClure's*, which recorded breathlessly, "No American city has ever seen anything comparable with it. The most hardened sports would telegraph to their pals to come to Seattle and inspect it, if only as a curiosity. . . . The city seems to have been transformed almost magically into one great gambling hell."

Into this colorful fray of organized sin, where a man could run any kind of operation as long as he paid off the right fellow, came new arrivals from America's Black population. As chance would have it, the first Black citizen of Seattle was a sometime musician, an African sailor and barber named Manuel Lopes, who in 1852 signaled mealtimes in the little village by marching down the main street beating a snare drum. More African Americans trickled into the Northwest once the transcontinental railroads were opened in 1889. The Northern Pacific Railroad imported groups of Black workers from the Midwest to break a strike (unbeknownst to the recruits) at its coal mine in Roslyn, east of the Cascades. In 1889 Black domestic help was brought from Chicago to staff Seattle's new Rainier Grand Hotel, and two years later the Oregon Improvement Company recruited six hundred Black strikebreakers to the mines at Franklin and

Newcastle on the western side of the mountains. In Yakima, William Jackson, a barber and violinist, put together one of Washington's first Black bands in 1910. His daughter, LeEtta Sanders King, was sixteen at the time; she would later become an important piano teacher in Seattle. In the early twentieth century hundreds of thousands of Black migrants left the rural South for the industrialized North, forming the great Black enclaves of Harlem and Chicago's South Side. By 1910 six thousand Black individuals lived in the state of Washington, eight hundred in Seattle.

"Noodles" Smith.

One of the earliest and most colorful Black entrepreneurs to reach Jackson Street was Earl Russell "Noodles" Smith, in some sense the father—or perhaps the midwife—of Seattle jazz. Smith was a gambler and a businessman who was nicknamed "Noodles" because no matter how much he risked in a crap game, he always set aside enough cash to buy a bowl of noodles before he went to bed. Smith came from Denver to Seattle during the Alaska-Yukon-Pacific (AYP) Exposition in 1909 with $17,000 in his wallet, a stake he claimed to have won gambling for two days and three nights in Tonopah, Nevada. Others say he earned it pimping in a mining camp. Smith was a hard-nosed, miserly man who amassed a fortune from nightclubs, bootlegging, gambling, and real estate. Noodles's nephew Robert Wright, whose father Floyd Wright sometimes partnered with Smith, described his uncle as a "self-made man" with "a lot of mother wit. He knew people, he studied people . . . he knew what made them tick, and he exploited that." One musician recalled Smith as a perennially exhausted boss who was "so busy making money" that if he asked you a question, he would fall asleep before you could answer.

On February 22, 1912, Smith and Burr "Blackie" Williams—who had the letter "B" studded in diamonds on his belt buckle—opened the Dumas Club, at 209 Fifth Avenue South, which at the time still had wooden sidewalks. A social club for Black people, the Dumas stayed open at least five years. On opening night, it presented the Whang Doodle Orchestra, a band that had appeared in quartet form two years earlier, according to a grocery ad in the *Seattle Star*. The Whang Doodle Orchestra was led by mandolinist and pianist Ace Brooks, who first showed up in Seattle playing a "cakewalk" at the AYP in 1909. Though its precise 1912 personnel is unknown, a 1925 band photo includes Brooks, mandolinist (first name unknown) Hughes, pianist Coty Jones, and the profoundly influential

The Whang Doodle Orchestra, ca. 1925. *Left to right:* (first name unknown) Hughes, Ace Brooks, unknown, Frank Waldron, Coty Jones.

trumpeter, saxophonist, and teacher Frank Waldron. The Whang Doodle Orchestra was a popular group and one of a select few Black bands tolerated downtown, performing at the Bon Marché in 1914, at Seattle's Woodmen of the World Lodge and Levy's Orpheum in 1918, and for what appears to have been a regular engagement for waterborne excursions on Hood Canal between 1919 and 1921.

Though many think of early jazz as an outdoor music played by brass bands with tailgate trombone and a "second line" of kids following the parade, it was played indoors too, often on stringed instruments, including mandolin and violin. One fascinating detail about Brooks's band is that its mandolins were manufactured in Port Townsend, Washington, by the well-known luthier Chris Knutsen. Two of Knutsen's creations, a harp guitar and harp mandolin, appear in the 1925 band photo. It's fascinating to imagine the sound of their strings and a lilting trumpet melody, wafting over the water.

From the Dumas Club forward, Noodles Smith was the most important figure in Seattle's jazz nightlife, having a hand at one time or another in the Entertainer's Club, the New Harlem, the Ubangi, the Hill Top Tavern, the Coast Hotel

The Black and Tan nightclub (originally called the Alhambra), corner of Twelfth Avenue South and South Jackson Street, 1937. The marquee, washed out in the photo, says "Black and Tan."

(demolished to make way for I-5), and the most illustrious and longest-lived jazz club in Seattle, the Black and Tan.

Every kid who grew up in Seattle in the 1950s and 1960s knew the Black and Tan as the hub of Seattle soul music. What they probably didn't know was that the club had been running since February 10, 1920. That's when prominent businessman Harry Legg opened a social club in the basement of his successful Alhambra Cash Grocery, at the southeast corner of Twelfth Avenue South and South Jackson Street. Dubbed the Alhambra Cabaret, in its first year the club hosted one of the most important early jazz bands in the West, Reb Spikes and the So Different Orchestra. The venue also hosted a debate between prominent white Republican candidates running for office in King County. Like the Dumas Club before it, and many that came after, the Alhambra served the Black community as a gathering place for activism as well as entertainment. Legg died just three years after the Alhambra opened, and the club passed through several owners, including nightlife figure and pimp Felix Crane.

Noodles Smith bought the venue in 1931 and changed its name to the Black and Tan, which he opened on Christmas Eve. A "black and tan" was a generic name for a nightclub that admitted both Black and white patrons. In the spirit of Legg's original Alhambra Cabaret, the Black and Tan soon became known as a place where all races were welcome. In 1934 ragtime pianist Eubie Blake played the Black and Tan; in later years, so did the entire Duke Ellington Orchestra, Lucky Millinder, Louis Jordan, Fletcher Henderson, Jay McShann, Ray Charles, Ernestine Anderson, George Benson, and Etta James, among many others. In 1941 the name of the venue changed again, reopening as the Colored Waiters, Porters and Cooks Club, operated by an association of that name. For a while, the venue names were used interchangeably, but by the 1950s most people still knew the place as the Black and Tan. The club remained open until 1969.

Across the street from the Black and Tan, on the northeast corner, Noodles opened the Hill Top Tavern, where one could down a beer watching short jazz movies called "soundies" on a jukebox, a sort of precursor to MTV. Down the street, in the same two-story wooden building, toward Fourteenth Avenue South, were the Two Pals and the Main Event. Nearby, another operator started the Monarch Pool Hall. Up the street Bill Bowman owned a place called simply Bowman's Joint. Noodles also opened the Golden West Hotel, with Burr Williams, and the Coast Hotel, both in Chinatown. Touring celebrities such as Louis Armstrong, Duke Ellington, and Erskine Hawkins would come to know the rooms of the Coast and Golden West well, as they were prohibited from staying in whites-only hotels downtown. "Twelfth and Jackson *belonged* to Noodles Smith," recalled Marshal Royal, the great Count Basie alto saxophonist who married Noodles's sister-in-law. "He was the ward boss. He was the biggest dude in that part of town. You see, in those days you couldn't open up a nightclub unless you passed by Noodles Smith. The man downtown would call him up and say, 'Such and such a guy wants to open up a club over at such and such a place.' And he'd ask Noodles if it was all right for him to open up or not. If you didn't pass his observations, you just didn't exist."

The heavy action on the corner attracted big-time gamblers, including Lena Horne's father, Teddy Horne, who lived in Seattle for a while and gambled with "Big George" Stevens. Bruce Rowell, a sometime saxophonist who was Noodles's righthand man, remembered Stevens well. "He'd go way back up here into his suit coat—he had a pocket between his shoulder blades—and he'd pull out a thousand dollars. That's right! Right there in the Main Event, on Jackson Street. Then he said, 'Okay, let's keep gambling. Let the good times roll.'" Smith apparently had boundless entrepreneurial energy. Several months before he opened the Black and Tan in the basement premises of the Alhambra, he and a partner named Jimmy Woodland advertised a joint called the Entertainer's Club (not to be confused with Entertainer's Cabaret, the venue where Jelly Roll Morton had played) at the same address. Rowell said this was a separate venture. "It was the upstairs of a four-plex," he recalled. "On one side of the upstairs, there was a front room that wasn't used, then there was a room where the poker game was. Then there was the barroom. And then you go across the hall and the next two rooms was the dance floor and the musicians."

In 1934, Smith made an even more audacious move. Looking to cash in on the post-Prohibition boom in legalized beer and wine, he opened a nightclub in downtown Seattle, the New Harlem, on Fourth Avenue, between Stewart and Virginia Streets. An upstairs room large enough to accommodate elaborate floor shows, the New Harlem was billed as *the* venue for "Seattle's only all-colored nightclub entertainment." For a while, Noodles delivered, presenting Seattle singer Evelyn Williamson as well as other local and touring acts. He even scored a fifteen-minute remote radio broadcast. (The club's theme song was the jaunty Duke Ellington tune "Drop Me Off in Harlem.") But the venture was short-lived. Black musicians were generally not welcome downtown. The club was raided almost immediately for liquor violations. Charles Lewis, an observer familiar with the sporting life, speculated that the eccentric white bandleader Vic Meyers got together with "the city fathers" and told Smith "to go back to Jackson Street." It's certainly plausible. Meyers was by this time serving as lieutenant governor and also ran a competing venue nearby, Club Victor. For whatever reason, Noodles took their advice. A month after ads for the New Harlem ceased to appear, notices for the Little Harlem Beer Tavern showed up, noting that it had moved from the Coast Hotel to Noodles's old stomping grounds, the Golden West Hotel. It's a good bet Smith had a stake in the action.

In the 1920s Noodles and Burr "Blackie" Williams lived the lives of flamboyant gangsters, driving fancy cars—Noodles owned a Stutz Bearcat and a Packard Twin 6—and showering food and drink on their friends and relatives. The late Emma Gayton, wife of drummer Leonard Gayton, was a child when Blackie took a room in her mother's house. "He used to drive me to school sometimes. I'd feel so important. He bought me earrings for my birthday. He always drank a brandy when he got up in the morning. All the policemen used to come to wish him a happy Christmas! We had great big bowls of eggnog, great big turkeys on the table. We entertained all the celebrities in Seattle. I was just a little thing sitting on people's laps. They'd send me to bed when the party got good."

Williams died in 1922, but Smith lived the high life for several decades. He amassed a good deal of real estate over the years, buying up buildings along

South Jackson Street and South Main Street, though he preferred to live on a houseboat moored in Portage Bay, just off Boyer Avenue. Smith often staked other operators, taking a cut off the top. If the fellows he staked couldn't make a go of it, he'd collect their property. According to Rowell, Noodles kept a safe in the basement of a house he owned on Twelfth, just north of Jackson. The safe housed brown bags full of cash. "It was laying right there waiting for an opportunity. There's open-up money, for a joint. Under that open-up money, there is the poker game money. Here is the crap-table money. Here is the Chuck-a-Luck [a dice game] money. Here is working money. All in bags. Cash. These four or five bags are together. Here's another four or five. He would open a joint, right tonight. Just grab one of those bags. . . . It never went to the bank."

Smith, who was married to Elbe Williamson, also kept a flamboyant mistress, whom he eventually married—a nightclub singer named Zelma Winslow. Noodles and Zelma carried on so brazenly that Elbe eventually filed for divorce, receiving as part of the settlement the Coast Hotel, where she became a popular host. Smith himself retired from the nightclub business in 1940. In his later years Noodles became a beneficent community elder who helped rehabilitate ex-convicts, paid the jail fines of losers and underdogs at Christmas, and bankrolled amateur sports teams. However, he remained a miser. When a relative told him, "You can't take it with you," he answered, "I don't intend to leave it to no one else." When Noodles Smith died in 1952, he left no will, and no one ever found his fabled sacks of cash.

Though jazz historians traditionally have focused on colorful "sporting" districts such as Smith's Jackson Street empire, middle-class neighborhoods also have exercised a tremendous, if usually unheralded, influence on the art form's development. Far from the raucous nightlife of the Black and Tan was Seattle's respectable East Madison neighborhood, where Black pioneer George Grose had sold off a tract of land in parcels to churchgoing, middle-class families. Life there was pleasant, secure, and hopeful, especially compared with the horrors that beset Black people in other American cities. LeEtta Sanders King, born in 1894, painted a pastoral picture of Seattle during and just after World War I:

> There weren't too many colored people in Seattle then. There was all kinds of things we did, though, just as if there were a lot of people here. We had activities, dinner parties, and outings. Oh, we had a great time. . . . Before the war there was just lots of pleasure: boat rides, dances, and just a great deal of pleasant, happy life.

> . . . Dances were given at the Renton Hill Club House, which was at 18th and Madison. We wore pretty party dresses and the men wore tux[es]. . . . There was no segregation in the theaters as I recall it. We sat where we wanted to sit. So in a sense, Seattle was quite an open city. We went to the parks and we'd go to any of them and enjoy them. Sunday-afternoon band concerts were greatly enjoyed in those days.

Though King's recollections are generally accurate, the Strand and Palomar movie houses seated Black patrons in the balcony, and some lunch counters were known to turn away Black customers.

Church picnics provided the occasion for some of Seattle's early Black music-making. In 1891 the Seattle Comet Band performed at the African Methodist Episcopal church's first picnic. These affairs continued well into the twentieth century. One of bassist Buddy Catlett's earliest musical memories was of hearing the great Creole clarinetist Joe Darensbourg at a picnic near Enumclaw, a small town outside Seattle, in the 1930s. Darensbourg likely played for another picnic on July 7, 1930, at Kenmore Park, which advertised a $100 prize for the best jazz band, along with an afternoon of baseball, swimming, racing, and a "jumping contest." Musical contestants included the Jungle Temple Band No. 2 (which often featured Darensbourg) as well as outfits from the Nanking Café and the Chinese Garden, which means Frank Waldron and Oscar Holden were there as well—an early Seattle jazz all-star show!

Residents of East Madison were not always sanguine about their less inhibited brethren on Jackson Street. Horace Cayton, son of the editor of the Black Seattle newspaper *Cayton's Weekly*, vividly captured the division between the two neighborhoods—the one staid, quiet, and religious and the other noisy, illegal, and profane—in his autobiography *Long Old Road*. "There were parts of the city, the sporting area," writes Cayton, who was raised in a Capitol Hill mansion, "where we were not even allowed to ride through in our carriage, for those people were morally corrupt and of great discredit to the race." Despite such class tensions, the two neighborhoods enjoyed a symbiotic relationship. For while young Black musicians may have learned to jam all night in "hot" swing bands on Jackson Street, it was within the secure and hopeful boundaries of East Madison, with its church socials and concert band picnics, that many of them acquired the technical skills—not to say aspirations—that it took to become quality players.

No individual better demonstrates the importance of this kind of environment than alto saxophonist and music teacher Frank Waldron, one of the most important figures in early Washington jazz and a man whose influence would be felt on the scene for half a century. Born in San Franscico in 1890, Frank Dordan Waldron learned to play music from his white mother, Marguerite "Maggie" Elizabeth Waldron, who taught piano lessons to support herself and her son after Frank's father deserted the family. The Waldrons lived in the Duboce Triangle, south of Market Street just west of Van Ness Avenue, an area entirely decimated by the 1906 San Francisco earthquake and fire. While Marguerite later resumed her career as a teacher in San Francisco, the earthquake was likely the catalyst that led Frank to strike out on his own at the age of sixteen. In 1907 he was listed in a Seattle city directory as a "porter" living downtown on Seventh Avenue. In 1911 he appears as a musician living at Bessie Young's Boarding House, 1242 South Jackson Street, in the very heart of the jazz district. "Any acts that came to Seattle, they came to Bessie Young's Theatrical Boarding House," recalled Rowell. "Bessie Smith, Mamie Smith, Williams and Walker. That's where Frank Waldron had the big room upstairs. He'd teach up there." By all accounts, Waldron was a master of both saxophone and trumpet. He had a classic tone, perfect articulation, and immaculate phrasing. Rowell said Waldron was the best saxophonist in Seattle, "as far as technique is concerned."

Frank Waldron.

The run-up to World War I found Waldron in the Tacoma area, where musicians found work entertaining soldiers. A student of Waldron's, Lawrence Smith, recalled seeing his teacher playing for soldiers at a pavilion near Camp Lewis (now part of Joint Base Lewis-McChord), south of Tacoma. In 1914, Waldron was listed by the *Chicago Defender* as playing a popular cornet piece, "Goodbye," by Paolo Tosti, at a September 27 memorial for Afro-British composer Samuel Coleridge-Taylor (a somewhat tardy salute, as Taylor died in 1912). Waldron's students later described him as having a military bearing, and indeed he registered for the draft in 1917 but never served. In 1918 he did, however, copyright and publish a patriotic song, "The Kaiser's Got the Blues (Since Uncle Sam Stepped In)." Aficionados will recognize the title as also having been used by W. C. Handy for a tune he copyrighted later that year, "The Kaiser's Got the Blues (Those Weary Blues)." Whether Handy knew about Waldron's tune is unknown.

In November 1918, Waldron apparently came back to Seattle, where he played regularly with the Whang Doodle Orchestra. In 1919 he formally opened the Waldron School of Saxophone and Trumpet at Bessie Young's Boarding House. He played a Christmas gig in Vancouver, British Columbia, in 1920 with a band that included trombonist Baron Morehead, who later played with Fats Waller, and several musicians who would wind up in Seattle: drummer William Hoy and singers Esmeralda Edwards and Lillian Goode. Waldron stands out during this period for publishing a book of his own compositions for saxophone, an instrument that enjoyed a faddish popularity in the 1920s akin to the guitar craze of the 1960s. Though the saxophone had been invented by a Belgian, for use in military parade bands, it was popularized in America by African American jazz musicians. Saxophone studios, how-to books, and saxophone quartets sprang up all over the country. Seattle even had a saxophone orchestra.

In 1924, Waldron published a saxophone method book, *Syncopated Classic*, in which he used nine of his compositions, including "Climb Them Walls," "Pretty Doll," and "With Pep," to demonstrate the new jazz techniques of slap-tonguing and flutter-tonguing. The tunes are difficult, requiring complex fingering and advanced ability. Seattle's first generation of jazz musicians—which included Jimmy (sometimes spelled Jimmie) Adams (trumpet), his brother Wayne Adams (saxophone), Creon Thomas (piano, violin, banjo, drums), and Evelyn Bundy (piano)—were all probably familiar with this book, as they all studied with Waldron.

But Waldron was more than a teacher. Throughout the 1920s he performed with a five-piece group called the Odean Jazz Orchestra at the Nanking Café, a high-class Chinese restaurant with a dance floor, on Fourth Avenue between Pine and Olive Streets. Waldron must have been very highly respected, since, as a rule, Black groups were not allowed to play downtown, and integrated jazz groups were virtually unknown at the time throughout the United States. "Frank used to sit up there with his sun visor on and play alto," remembers white drummer and trumpeter Chet Ramage, whose Musical Knights later played in the same establishment. "He was a hell of a musician." Pianist Palmer Johnson, who came to Seattle from Los Angeles in 1928 and later roomed with Waldron, said, "Frank was bald-headed, big, and loved to drink whiskey. He played both [trumpet and saxophone], but he lost his 'lip' for trumpet. He was a hell of a good teacher." Waldron also reportedly worked at some point with the prominent Central District piano teacher Gertrude Harvey Wright on a job in Gold Bar, Washington. Though Wright's name does not turn up as a member of jazz bands, she was a respected player and teacher who took an active role in Black union affairs.

By 1931, though the Depression was in full swing, Waldron had saved enough money to buy a one-story house around the corner from his studio, on Fifteenth Avenue, where he lived for the rest of his life. He continued to compose, registering copyrights for "Waltz Queen Ann" in 1932, named after Seattle's Queen Anne Hill, and "Valse Celeste" in 1935. The following year, Waldron led a band at the Apex Club featuring his pals from his Vancouver days, drummer Bill Hoy and entertainer Lillian Goode, and he also formed a saxophone quartet.

In 1942, after the United States had entered World War II, Waldron registered for the draft again, at age fifty-two. The next year, he married for the first and only time. Waldron's wife, Eva Redmond, filed for divorce in 1944, alleging that he caroused with his friends until all hours of the night, forced her to work days, and often became violent, at one point knocking out one of her front teeth. After the war, alone again, working from his home, Waldron began to train the next generation of Seattle jazzers, including trumpeter Quincy Jones and alto saxophonist (later bassist) Buddy Catlett. Catlett remembered Waldron as a superb technician, if also a rogue, who scolded his students fiercely if they didn't practice.

> If you came to your lesson and you hadn't been doing anything but playing football all week, you'd be sitting there sweating bullets. He'd say, "You'll never play with Duke Ellington if you keep going this way." You'd play your lesson, and he'd light up a cigarette—he smoked so much he had safety matches laid out on his Victrola so he could light up one after the other—and he'd pour himself a glass of gin, and he'd stand up over you and say, "Now, boy, that's the worst batch of shit I ever heard!" Oh, and another thing. He'd say, "Listen here, I want to tell you something. I want you to leave them bitches alone. And leave that booze alone. And leave those cigarettes alone!" Him with a cigarette in one hand and a glass of gin in the other. Then you'd hear this voice from the back room: [*falsetto*] "Fra-a-nk? Are you through in there yet?"

Waldron taught the same basics that white classical teachers did—sight-reading, tonguing, embouchure, phrasing—but to his more advanced students, he also taught theory and ear training, using jazz improvisers as models. White clarinetist Ron Pierce, who took lessons from Waldron in the 1940s, recalled: "With my [white] teachers, it was all 'Play time, play section, play in tune.' [Waldron would] say, 'Play me a seventh chord.' Now the thing was, I had never

Infantry Band, 1926. *Left to right:* Powell Newington Barnett (son of Powell Samuel Barnett), unknown, Albert Buford (father of Vernon "Pops" Buford), Floyd Turnham Jr., unknown, Powell Samuel Barnett (tuba). *Directly below Barnett:* Charles Adams (cornet); (*third from right*) Tim Waldron; (*second from right*) (first name unknown) Young; (*extreme right*) Tom Jones.

experienced this kind of thing before. He was a memorizer guy. Then he'd lean over and play a record on the Victrola and show you how Louis Armstrong did it. This guy really turned on my ear."

The list of Northwest musicians who reflected Waldron's legacy is long and deep. Not only Catlett, Jones, and Pierce, but Dick Wilson, Barney Hilliard, and Jabo Ward also came for weekly lessons. Waldron died in 1955, leaving no heirs or relations in the area. In 2017, Seattle guitarist Greg Ruby arranged and recorded tunes from Waldron's *Syncopated Classic*, releasing them in a package that includes complete transcriptions of Waldron's compositions, a recording, and a chapbook about Waldron's life and work (coauthored with Paul de Barros).

Another early Black immigrant who had a profound impact on Seattle's musical history was Powell Samuel "Shorty" Barnett, whose family had come from Indiana to Roslyn, Washington, in 1906 to work in the mines. The son of a former enslaved person, Barnett stood a few inches over five feet, had biceps as thick as tree trunks, and boasted that his hands were so rough he could scrape an inch of skin off before it hurt. Barnett started out on tuba in a brass band formed by Roslyn's Black miners, then performed in Seattle concert and military bands at the gingerbread pavilions at the foot of East Madison Street and at Leschi Park. Barnett also played for a time with the early Washington jazz

The Edythe Turnham family minstrel show, Spokane, ca. 1910, including Spokane bandleader Edythe Turnham (*third from left*) and her sister, Maggie (*second from left*).

band Edythe Turnham and Her Knights of Syncopation, as did one of his Seattle brass-band mates, trumpeter Charles Adams.

In 1909, when Seattle's city fathers were gearing up for the AYP Exposition, Barnett approached the fair organizers to ask if they wanted to hire his brass band. His request started a controversy that led to the foundation of a separate musicians' union for Black players. At that time Seattle musicians were organized under the American Federation of Musicians (AFM), Local No. 76. There were no Black members. "I went to the man in charge of music for the Fair Association," recalled Barnett. "He told me that if I got the Negro band in the union they could play all year at the fair. But the Negro musicians wouldn't do anything about it. . . . I encouraged them to join the union, but they were determined to create their own. So I decided that half a loaf would be better than none. If they organized their own union, perhaps they could join the other musicians' union later." Later, indeed—it would be forty-seven years before Black musicians would get another invitation to join Local 76.

Barnett, for his part, joined Local 76 in 1913 as a prerequisite for playing in the mostly white, fourteen-piece Volunteers of America Marching Band. He was the only African American to ever join the white union, as the majority of Seattle's Black musicians thought it would be more advantageous to have their own local. In 1918, along with a group of musicians whose names are unknown, Barnett reluctantly agreed, cofounding Local 458 (Colored), which in 1924 was succeeded by Local 493. Barnett retained membership in both Local 76 and Local 493 until 1956, when the two locals voted to amalgamate.

Seattle's segregated musicians' unions were not an anomaly. Rather than admit Black musicians to white unions, where they could compete for high-paying jobs, white locals across the country encouraged Black musicians to form their own unions. Territories were marked off. In Seattle the dividing line between Black and white was Yesler Way, which separated downtown from the honky-tonk neighborhood where Seattle had first sprung up from the mud. Though segregation was morally abhorrent, it had a bright side. Local 493, with its Black membership, quite naturally became the focal point for Seattle's thriving jazz scene. Every major player, from Frank Waldron in the 1920s to Quincy Jones in the 1940s, would at some point become a member of the Black local, jamming on 493 sessions, studying with 493 teachers, and forming groups with 493 musicians. In the 1950s the Local 493 "clubhouse," the Blue Note, on Jefferson Street between Thirteenth Avenue and Fourteenth Avenue, hosted the hippest jam sessions in town.

Powell Barnett, who later became one of Seattle's most important civic leaders and had a city park on Martin Luther King Jr. Way named after him, spent much of his life trying to convince Black and white musicians alike that segregation in any institution was a bad idea. He mounted several attempts to amalgamate the unions but did not succeed until 1956. That he met resistance from the Black community as well as the white is not surprising in light of the Black experience in early Washington. At the time most unions didn't admit Black people at all. When they did allow them to work, anti-Black violence often occurred. The fact that Barnett held a brief for unions in the early part of the century made him the exception in the Black community, not the rule. As it turned out, an all-Black band did play at the AYP Exposition, but it was not from Seattle. Lacy's Dixieland Band, a forty-five-piece group from the South, represented Southern culture at the fair. Had Powell Barnett and his brass band played at the AYP Exposition, however, they would have encountered the sophisticated scrutiny of a Seattle public already exposed to much of the best that show business had to offer.

Pioneer boomtowns traditionally have erected opera houses as a badge of culture, but Seattle had a mania for theater that surpassed by many degrees even the most ambitious settlement. In 1859, eight years after the city was founded, Plummer's Hall, one of the town's first buildings, was being used as a theater. Pioneer Charles Plummer had also obtained the county's first liquor license and operated Seattle's first saloon, thus establishing two precedents—boozing and theater—that would have a huge impact on local jazz. From Plummer's Hall forward, Seattle built one theater after another. The Great Fire of 1889 burned everything except a building called Turnverein Hall, at Fourth and Jefferson, but by the 1890s a golden era had dawned, helped by hard cash from the Yukon Gold Rush of 1898. An impresario named John Cort, who had broken into show business in New York as a blackface song-and-dance man, refurbished Turnverein Hall, renaming it the Seattle Opera House. Cort also opened the Standard Theater, at Occidental Avenue South and South Washington Street, followed by the Moore Theatre, in 1907.

Across the street from the Seattle Opera House, John Considine operated the People's Theatre. Considine is credited with putting in place the world's first popular-priced vaudeville chain, eventually hooking up with a New York booking agent and building the $100,000 Grand Theater in Tacoma. Considine monopolized a curious early Seattle institution called the "box house," a rowdy basement theater with "entertainment rooms" upstairs. He was soon eclipsed by Alexander Pantages, who would create the largest network of theaters outside New York City—the Pantages Circuit—with the entire business centered in Seattle. In 1904, Pantages built an eponymous theater on Second Avenue, relocating it to Third Avenue and University Street in 1915. This theater, later known as the Rex and the Palomar, hosted big jazz shows from the 1930s through the 1950s. Thanks to its many entertainment venues, stars of classical music made stops in Seattle as well. In 1925 alone, Anna Pavlova, Sergei Rachmaninoff, the Hungarian musician/composer Ernö Dohnányi, American tenor Roland Hayes, violinist/composer Fritz Kreisler, and the Russian basso Feodor Chaliapin all performed on Seattle stages.

Seattle's wealth of theaters attracted a flood of vaudeville and minstrel shows, including the city's first visiting theater company—Tom LaFont's Excelsior Minstrels. Between 1864 and 1912 no fewer than 156 touring minstrel troupes passed through Seattle. In minstrel shows actors—both Black and white—smeared their faces with burnt cork and did outrageous parodies of

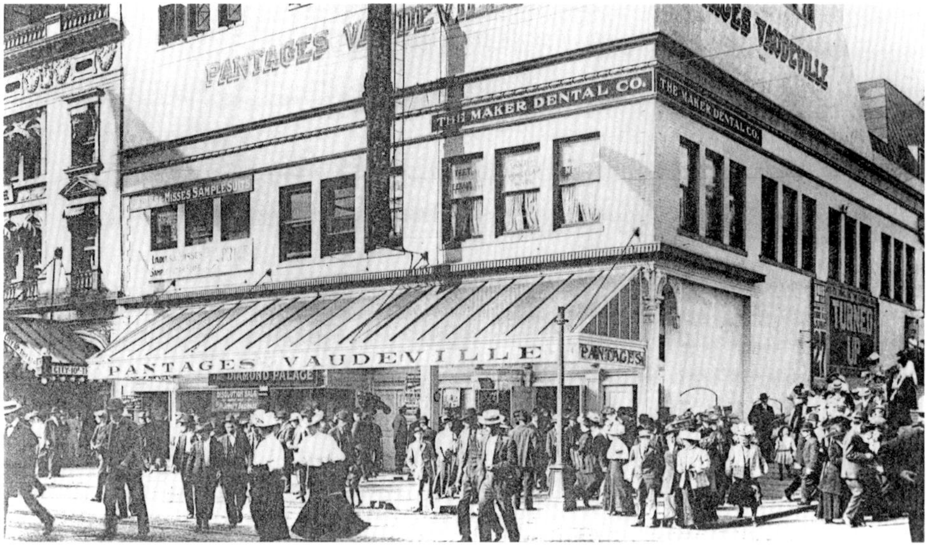

The first Pantages Theater, on the corner of Second Avenue and Seneca Street.

Black behavior (antics that were originally a parody of the pretentious behavior of white plantation owners). In spite of the genre's racist and demeaning content, one of the ways early Black jazz musicians such as Jelly Roll Morton, Eubie Blake, and Fats Waller made a living was by performing in minstrel shows. (Some of San Francisco's early Black jazz musicians came from the Georgia Minstrels.) Vaudeville provided opportunities too, sometimes with serendipitous consequences. In 1911 a Black vaudeville troupe broke up in Seattle, stranding Nora and Ross Hendrix. Their grandson, Jimi, would change the face of popular music. Ironically, as Black entertainers such as Ross Hendrix trickled into town and began to establish the roots of a jazz tradition, the white population was more likely to attend a blackface show like Tom LaFont's than a jazz performance by Black musicians. This pattern—of white performers reaping rewards for imitating Black artists while Black artists went unrecognized—was rooted in minstrelsy and would permeate the history of jazz. Unreported in the newspapers and masked by socioeconomic custom, Seattle jazz developed with few whites ever knowing it existed.

W. C. Handy was one Black musical figure whites probably were aware of in the early twentieth century. Handy, who wrote "St. Louis Blues," among other hit songs, was musical director for W. H. Mahara's Minstrels, which played three times at the Seattle Theatre, at Third Avenue and Cherry Street, where the Arctic Building now stands. For his 1898 performance Mahara brought twenty-six performers and offered a daily parade to drum up business before the show. It must have worked. There were no vacant seats at the opening. A review from the *Seattle Times* of March 21, 1898, reflects the combination of exuberant approval and blatant racism the white press reserved for Black entertainers:

Nora and Ross Hendrix, Jimi Hendrix's grandparents, Seattle, 1911.

> In such a performance as that last night the attention of the musical ear is fascinated by the negro melodies, arranged for solos, quartettes or choruses, as the case may be, but all rendered in that vibrant, sympathetic passionate tone quality characteristic of the negro race. In all the range of musical art there is nothing quite like a negro melody rendered by a son or daughter of the African race. . . . An air quite foreign to the plantation tunes usually associated with colored minstrels, rendered by a quartette of well-trained negro singers, assumes a quality quite its own. Take the popular melody, "All Coons Look Alike to Me."

Early jazz acts followed minstrel shows in Northwest theaters. In 1914 the Pantages played host to the first jazz band ever to tour outside New Orleans—Freddie Keppard's Creole Orchestra. Keppard, an important early stylist on the New Orleans scene, was admired by Louis Armstrong—and even by Jelly Roll Morton, who usually had nothing good to say about any other musician. Keppard appeared in Seattle, Tacoma, and Vancouver, British Columbia, after spending six years in Los Angeles. His music was one of the hottest, most modern things going at the time, and Northwesterners were hearing it three years before the first jazz record was released. This, along with the visits of W. C. Handy, dispels somewhat the myth that audiences in the Northwest were isolated from national trends.

The presence of touring jazz artists in the Northwest in 1914 is a good reminder that the well-known theory of the dissemination of jazz from the South, "up the river from New Orleans," has largely been discredited. Though jazz probably originated in New Orleans around the turn of the century, jazz scholarship has shown fairly conclusively that musicians were playing various styles of pre-jazz or jazzlike music in Black communities in Texas, New York, Los Angeles, and San Francisco before jazz musicians found their way from New Orleans to Chicago in the 1910s. Tom Stoddard, in his groundbreaking book *Jazz on the Barbary Coast*, has shown that Black musicians in San Francisco were improvising as early as 1907 and that early jazz-associated dances such as the

Texas Tommy, the turkey trot, and the bunny hug originated before World War I in San Francisco—not in the South. Several of the musicians mentioned in Stoddard's book, including Buck Campbell, Albert Paddio, and Gerald Wells, also spent significant portions of their careers in the Northwest. (Campbell was from Spokane.) Since small numbers of Black people began to trickle into Washington in the 1880s, it is quite possible that young African Americans in Seattle, Tacoma, and even Spokane—including the members of Seattle's Whang Doodle Orchestra—were playing syncopated, pre-jazz music before 1920, though no recorded evidence exists to support this theory.

The Original Creole Orchestra, 1912. *Front row, left to right:* Dink Johnson, James Palao, Leon William. *Back row:* Eddie Vinson, Freddie Keppard, George Baquet, Bill Johnson.

One bit of evidence that does exist suggests that jazz may have traveled to the Northwest via the armed forces. The November 25, 1917, issue of the service newspaper *Trench and Camp* features this intriguing notice:

> ORIGINATOR OF "JAZZ" IN 347TH ORCHESTRA
>
> Bobby Hayes—drummer and slide whistle player from San Francisco—is now stationed at Camp Lewis. He is famous in San Francisco and all of California. Hayes plays at Camp Lewis dances. He has, moreover, so many different kinds of technic [*sic*] that there seems to be no limits to the things he can do with the weird outfit which comprises that stock of a trap man.

Research has turned up nothing about Hayes. But it's worth noting that when the above article came out, jazz had become a full-blown fad, thanks to the raging success of the first jazz record, "Livery Stable Blues," released by the Original Dixieland Jazz Band in March 1917. From that moment on, musicians and promoters started attaching "jazz" to their names, whether or not they knew anything about this new syncopated music.

In Seattle the first group to do so was an all-white orchestra at the Coliseum Theater, which advertised itself as the Coliseum Jazz Band in the *Seat-*

tle Post-Intelligencer on July 15, 1917. Others followed the trend. The Tavern Café, at Second Avenue and Union Street, advertised a "New Jazz Band" in 1918, and the following year, the Breakers, at First Avenue and Cherry Street, touted its own "Jazz Orchestra." In June 1919 a white Queen Anne High School grad named Harold Weeks, who would go on to compose the million-selling jazz standard "Hindustan," performed at the Masonic Temple on Capitol Hill with his own jazz orchestra.

Though these bands may have played a species of lively syncopated music, a show in the Central District probably holds a more authentic claim as the first documented jazz performance in Seattle. On June 10, 1918, Lillian Smith's Jazz Band played at Seattle's Washington Hall, which still stands at Fourteenth Avenue and Fir Street. The show was billed as a "Grand Benefit Ball" to raise money for the NAACP. Smith, who was born in Fulton, Missouri, won a "syncopated piano" competition as a teenager at the Saint Louis World's Fair in 1904 and moved to Seattle in 1909, where she formed the Syncopated Knights. On July 14, 1919, Smith was out playing on a "Moonlight Excursion" sponsored by the Efficiency Club, and the following month she had engagements at the Renton Hill Club House at Eighteenth Avenue and East Madison Street and at the Odd Fellows' fifteenth annual picnic at Wildwood Park. In November she was back at Washington Hall, leading the Grand Ball for the Elks Club. "Plenty of Jazz Music by the Best Jazz Band in Town," said the ad.

It's likely that Smith played syncopated dance music with a ragtime-to-jazz feeling, though it's hard to say just how "hot" Miss Lillian's band really was. Donald Gatewood, whose mother directed the choir at Mount Zion Baptist Church, remembers Black society bands such as Smith's playing mostly ballroom dance music. Hot jazz numbers with solos were thrown in for spice. Whatever her jazz quotient, Smith was the first in a long and honorable line of Seattle jazz bandleaders to come.

After he left the Northwest, Jelly Roll Morton recorded a rag called "Seattle Hunch," perhaps in honor of one of the many nights he spent throwing dice, or perhaps it was the name of a horse. It is a cheerful, lilting composition laced with stop-time sections and quick little glissandos that zip up to melody notes. Did Morton have a hunch Seattle was becoming a West Coast hub of jazz? If he had, he could have doubled his money. With the Jackson Street

Jelly Roll Morton (*right*) in Los Angeles, in 1917.

scene heating up and a stable Black middle class in the East Madison district, forces were starting to line up that would create a fertile environment for jazz. The theater and vaudeville scene was in place, ready to bring in national acts. The port and military bases were bringing in individuals of curiosity and abandon who would patronize the clubs. And a corrupt political infrastructure was firmly in place to support the vices that supported the music. The style of Frank Waldron and Lillian Smith may have been somewhat old-fashioned, with the watch fob and frock coat trappings of the turn of the twentieth century, but the next generation would have all the flamboyance of the Jazz Age to come.

2 The Jazz Age

1920–1933

> The orchestra was clashing out a "red hot" melody, flashily dressed women and escorts were laughing in the spacious dance hall and supper room—and upstairs, the agents declared, half a dozen couples were standing at the bar, drinking real bonded liquor while numerous others were shooting craps. . . . After more than a year of untrammeled operation Seattle's liveliest "night club" was closed and the rattle of its dice, the tinkle of its highball glasses, and the clashing cymbals of its jazz band were silent.
>
> —*Seattle Times*, March 23, 1931

IN THE ROARING TWENTIES, Seattle, like the rest of the country, went wild. There were speakeasies, roadhouses, raccoon coats, bobbed hair, the Charleston, bootleggers, and federal agents. There was also jazz—not a lot of it, but certainly enough to qualify the town as more than a whistle-stop on the Jazz Age express. Because of a strong, rurally based antisaloon movement east of the Cascade mountains, Prohibition started in Washington in 1916, three years earlier than in the rest of the nation. As a result, the hermetic arts of bathtub gin, "Joe sent me" speakeasies, and Canadian rum-running, which rose in reaction against Prohibition, got a head start in the Northwest.

In some ways Prohibition fit right in with the Northwest ethos. Seattle and Tacoma already had an institutionalized underground firmly in place to deal with the distribution of vice. Bootleg liquor became simply another profit center—albeit a broader-based one—for the mayor and police chief to add to the casinos, whorehouses, and opium dens they already tolerated. On the other hand, the reaction against Prohibition broadened the clientele for such illegal activities, stimulating the nightclub business enormously. Whereas only single men—sailors, loggers, miners, and the like—had patronized Skid Road, everyone wanted a drink. And everyone, it would appear, had one. Clarinetist Joe Darensbourg, who had seen a lot of action before arriving in Seattle from Los Angeles in 1928, found Seattle's speakeasy scene one of the wildest in the country. "There's never been a town like Seattle, to my idea," wrote Darensbourg in his hilarious as-told-to autobiography, *Jazz Odyssey*. "Seattle and New Orleans is the two distinct towns in the U.S.A., so different from any others." Bootleg liquor was to be found practically anywhere. "The illegal stuff was ferried in by ship, dinghies, dories, speedboats, and even by canoe," according to a 1970 article in the *Seattle Times*. "Booze arrived in Washington in the gas tanks of cars, by horse and wagon and airplanes."

Roadhouses, freestanding nightclubs serving illegal booze on the outskirts of town, provided a popular form of entertainment during Prohibition. Beyond the reach of local police jurisdiction, and sometimes protected from the feds by lookouts, roadhouses were made possible by the sudden accessibility of the automobile and the expansion of drivable highways. Because of Seattle's proximity to Canada, where liquor was still legal (with the exception of a brief period in British Columbia, from 1917 to 1921), dining and dancing clubs sprang up along the Everett and Bothell highways going north (now Highway 99 and Lake City Way, respectively). The new Everett Highway, which opened in October 1927, attracted a spectacular cluster of clubs along a three-mile stretch from the Snohomish County line to Lynnwood (then called Seattle Heights). Along this notorious strip, drivers could fill their flasks at the Jungle Temple No. 2, Doc Hamilton's Barbecue Ranch, the Maryland Tavern, McKenzie's Bungalow Inn, the Blakewood Inn, Merry Mak's Dine and Dance, the Olympic Tavern, and the Golden Slipper. In 1930, south of the Snohomish County line, Dick Parker opened Parker's Dance Pavilion, which eventually became the storied R & B and rock club called, simply, Parker's.

Dick Parker started out in the roadhouse business with Parker's Highway Pavilion, in 1923, along the other great artery north, Bothell Way. This highway was home to the Jungle Temple No. 1, McKenzie's Bungalow Inn (No. 1), and a second outlet of Doc Hamilton's Barbecue Ranch, before the more remote Highway 99 location lured both the Ranch and the Jungle Temple away. Sometimes punningly called "the Bottle Highway," the Bothell road also hosted Marino's, Willard's, and the Green Mill (named after the famous Al Capone speakeasy), where in February 1927 the Sid Saunders band performed. In addition to musical delights, Bothell Way attracted a slew of Southern fried chicken and waffle joints. Johnny Maxon's Orchestra played for college students at the Coon Chicken Inn. (Part of a chain of Southern fried chicken establishments that closed in the 1950s, the Coon Chicken Inn was a grotesque monument to racism whose front entrance was the mouth of a grinning railroad porter.) In 1934 the China Castle opened on Bothell Way, later becoming a blues mecca, the Jolly Roger, which burned down in 1989. The Jolly Roger boasted a tower

Doc Hamilton's Ranch on Highway 99.

suggesting a Prohibition "lookout," but it was built after Prohibition, so this was likely a nostalgic architectural touch.

Willard's, a roadhouse on Bothell Way that featured a fan dancer, was a good restaurant with a large dance floor that brought in "name" white musicians from San Francisco, such as Art Hickman and Paul Ash, as well as Johnny Robinson's Varsity Vagabonds, from Portland, considered by some observers to be the hottest jazz band in the Northwest. To the south, down East Marginal Way, were the China Pheasant and in 1930, near the old Meadows racetrack, the Cotton Club, run by Lewis (sometimes spelled Louis) Todd, who later ran the Little Harlem Night Club for Noodles Smith, off South Jackson Street. Near Enumclaw, the Snake Ranch, also known as Red Neck Kelly's, flourished. Even Police Chief Louis Forbes acknowledged with dismay in a 1931 interview that "everybody, nearly, carries a bottle on his hip when he goes to a roadhouse."

Along South Jackson Street, from First Avenue to Fourteenth, with detours through the International District, a thirsty, fun-seeking citizen could find not only bonded Scotch but jazz, dancing, and just about any other kind of entertainment, including opium dens, brothels for men and for women, elaborate casinos with roulette wheels and dice felts, and a daily Chinese lottery that sometimes paid big bucks. One establishment featured female mud wrestlers. Downtown, huge beer parlors, such as Lyons' Music Hall, on First Avenue, and the Virginian, on Stewart, featured music, dancing, terrible sandwiches, and all the beer you could drink, courtesy of beat cops who were paid off in an orderly fashion. Johnny Reddin, a columnist who remembered putting phony labels on bathtub gin as a kid to sell out the back door of a Queen Anne drugstore, liked to put it this way: "A Seattle visitor asks a policeman where he can get a drink—'See that building on the corner?' says the man in blue. 'That's the Methodist church. It's probably one of the few places in town that you *can't* get a drink.'"

Not that the feds didn't try to squelch all this. As soon as Prohibition was enacted nationally, agents began making war on the clubs. In 1923 alone, 1,306 persons were arrested in Seattle for liquor-law violations. As fast as the feds busted them, the proprietors of the speakeasies devised new ways of evading the law. One clever bartender, known as "Doorbelly" because of the size of his gut, stored vats of liquor in the loft of his house and installed pipes down to the bar faucets, through which the gin ran like water. The local cops, many of whom were on the take, were almost as frustrating to the feds as the operators. The night the Chinese Garden speakeasy was busted in 1931, Seattle's sergeant of detectives was found working in the hatcheck room. The most celebrated tale of police corruption during Washington's Prohibition era involved police lieutenant Roy Olmstead, who was caught red-handed unloading Canadian liquor from a motorboat north of Edmonds. Convicted and expelled from the force, Olmstead was later caught again, in his Mount Baker home, with a house full of liquor. When federal officers burst in, Olmstead's wife was broadcasting her "Aunt Vivian" bedtime stories over the radio, later thought to have disguised messages to smugglers, though this is probably an urban legend. Olmstead served four years at the McNeil Island federal penitentiary.

The most important musician to walk into this wide-open scene was Oscar Holden, the patriarch of early Seattle jazz. Born in 1887 in Nashville, Tennessee, Holden had played on Fate Marable's famous Mississippi riverboat excursions, where he met Louis Armstrong and other young New Orleans musicians. (Armstrong would later visit Holden at his home when he played Seattle.) According to Joe Darensbourg, Holden also worked with "Keppard and those guys" in the early days of New Orleans jazz. Anxious to get away from the South, Holden had settled in Chicago, where he taught and performed at South Side venues. According to one family member, Holden moved to Vancouver, British Columbia, in 1917, stopping first in Seattle. In his autobiography Jelly Roll Morton says he brought Holden to Seattle from Vancouver, where Holden played clar-

Oscar Holden, the patriarch of Seattle jazz.

inet in Morton's band, but Morton was fibbing, and in more ways than one. It was Holden who hired Morton, and the gig was in Vancouver, though Morton may also have played with Holden in Seattle later. From 1919 to 1920, Holden led a jazz band at Vancouver's Patricia Hotel that for a few weeks featured Morton and, for much longer, the great New Orleans trombonist Albert Paddio, who lived in Seattle off and on between 1910 and 1917. The Patricia was one of several nightclubs where Seattle musicians played from time to time in Vancouver, a city where Morton appeared again, in 1920, at the Regent Hotel.

The jazz scene north of the border was driven by British Columbia's dubious decision to follow the state of Washington down the path of prohibition, from 1917 to 1921. As in the United States, outlawing liquor gave rise to a culture of speakeasies and bootleg liquor there. William Bowman, who had an interest in many Seattle jazz ventures, came out to Vancouver from Chicago, where it's possible he had first heard Holden, and hired him to play at the Patricia. A night watchman left behind a recollection of Holden's band, noting with admiration that the pianist's "notes come pattering from that music box just like hailstones falling on a corrugated roof." The Patricia outfit featured not only Morton but

Chicago entertainer Ada "Bricktop" Smith, who would later become a famous club owner in Paris; Seattle entertainer Leo Bailey, recently on tour with the vaudeville team Austin and Bailey; drummer William Hoy, who also performed on the Seattle scene; and New Orleans trombonist Albert Paddio, who had come through Seattle with Keppard in 1914.

Holden's granddaughter Linda Holden Givens reckoned Oscar moved to Seattle in 1925, though the first notice of him playing locally appears in an ad for a Thanksgiving engagement at the Jungle Temple, in November 1927. Oscar's daughter Grace Holden said: "Our mother, Leala, played piano. The two met while playing different gigs in the North End of Seattle. Oscar was playing at the Jungle Temple, in 1928. A little further up the road was another nightspot I don't remember the name of. One of them had a flat tire and my mother was asked if she wouldn't mind bringing Oscar back to town." Holden was a powerhouse player with a deep classical background and a stride style similar to Fats Waller's. According to Grace, also a pianist, her father played piano, saxophone, clarinet, trumpet, and bass and could transpose tunes into all twelve keys, accompany singers sensitively, and work with a band or play solo all night long and keep it interesting. Recalled Palmer Johnson: "Oscar was my idol, man, because he could read so good! Anything you set before him, he's gone! He had a wonderful musical education. He was one of the first ones up here. Oscar was real black and had a soft voice. He was a great, great performer. I always asked him to play some Chopin, and he did. [And] he'd play 'Rhapsody in Blue' right off from the beginning to end."

Holden had seven children, five of whom pursued musical careers. Probably the best-known was Ron, a vocalist whose calypso-tinged rock 'n' roll "Love You So" hit the *Billboard* charts. Seattle rhythm-and-blues fans knew Jimmy Holden as the soulful electric keyboardist of the archetypal bar band the Reputations, while fans of an earlier generation knew Grace as the original keyboardist and vocalist with the Charlie Taylor band, where Quincy Jones got his start, and Oscar Jr. as that group's original alto saxophonist. Dave Holden worked in Seattle in an organ trio for years before moving in 1966 to Los Angeles, where he worked several decades both as a solo act and with singers.

Like many musicians in the area at the time, Oscar Holden also held a day job, working as a pipe fitter at Todd Shipyards. Grace vividly recalled her father racing off to catch the ferry after work to play a graduation in Kirkland or switching from his pipe-fitter's clothes to his tux for a job at the Clover Club downtown. "He'd come home from swing shift," she recounted, "then go right straight upstairs, take his bath, change his clothes, and be right back out the door at twelve-thirty so he could be on the job at one o'clock. He'd play from one until four-thirty or five o'clock in the morning." Holden had tremendous stamina. As a regular constitutional, he swam two miles across Lake Washington. His family would drive around the lake—there was no bridge at the time—and pick him up on the other side. Holden also fixed old pianos in his spare time.

Ron Holden recounted: "One of the fondest memories was Friday and Saturday nights. . . . I can remember lying in bed with butterflies in my stomach because I knew any minute my mom would come in and kiss me good night. She would come in all dressed up for the gig and Dad would be in his tux. I would go to sleep with that in my mind. Two glamorous people kissing me good night." According to Ron, "Every Sunday, the family would get together and play the same music that they played for the dances." Grace recalled: "There was a piano in the basement, and a parlor grand upstairs. We ate music, we lived music."

Unfortunately for posterity, Holden so despised life in the South that he never talked to his family about his past with New Orleans musicians. He did not mention, for example, that he had been cited in Jelly Roll Morton's autobiography. (This may have been out of pride, as Jelly Roll wrote, "[Holden] was no hot man, but he played plenty straight clarinet.") He told his children he purposely did not marry until he had fled Dixie, so his children would not have to be born there. "He hated that music," remembered Grace. "He associated that with the South and the bad old days. He could play that type of jazz, with the banjo in there doing its thing, but the Al Jolson kind of thing was against his nature. That was what he left behind."

Oscar Holden performed until 1966, when he had a stroke. He died three years later. The musical traditions Holden carried to Seattle from the South and the Midwest have lived on through his children, but only rarely has his contribution been acknowledged. Jimmy Holden fondly remembered an exception. "I was playing at the Scarlet Tree one night, and this guy, a local saxophonist, passed me a note that said, 'Your father was one of the greatest piano players in Seattle.' That did a lot for me, to know that somebody remembered him the way we do."

One of the places Oscar Holden played as a regular was Doc Hamilton's Barbecue Pit, which opened in 1924 on Twelfth Avenue, across from where Seattle University stands today. Of all the illustrious Prohibition hangouts, none was more famous—nor its owner more widely heralded—than Doc Hamilton's; it was Seattle's Prohibition equivalent of Harlem's Cotton Club. John H. "Doc" Hamilton was a tall, dapper man with a devastatingly deferential, gold-toothed smile that masked an angry pride. A man of sophisticated airs—the *Northwest Enterprise* dubbed him Seattle's "Black Prince"—he held a lifelong passion for dice and barbecued meats. (According to Darensbourg, Hamilton registered a patent for his "secret" barbecue sauce.) Born in West Point, Mississippi, Hamilton first arrived in Seattle in 1916. He served in France in World War I in the Ninety-Second Infantry Division (nicknamed the "Buffalo Soldiers"). When he returned to Seattle after the war, he opened his first speakeasy in his home at 1017½ East Union Street. Charles Lewis, who grew up a block away, remembered Doc as a classy, tall, handsome man who drove a National (a fancy car) and wore a "big overcoat that had money coming out of all the pockets." When the cops axed their way into the place on Union in July 1924, hacking through three barred doors, they found a cozy nightclub with four pianos, silver cocktail shakers, and high-class glassware.

Hamilton obtained his booze from Roy Olmstead, the cop turned bootlegger, but survived the 1926 trial that put Olmstead out of business. The following year, however, Doc got nailed and spent a couple of months in jail, all the while proclaiming his innocence. Upon release, he relocated to the outskirts of town, first to Bothell Way, then to the even more remote Highway 99, north of the county line. "When the running boats would dock," recalled Bruce Rowell, "they would come right up on the beach where the Ranch was, on 99."

In 1931, Doc was back at his old stomping grounds on Twelfth Avenue, operating his most famous establishment, the Pit. Doc Hamilton's Barbecue Pit was elegant. Limousines lined the curb out front, while Seattle's social elect, including the mayor, ducked in and out of the club. At the door, Jim Baker, a short fellow in an admiral's uniform, variously called "Buttons" or "Napoleon," welcomed the guests. Inside was the restaurant and bar, where "liquor was to be had with no more effort than asking for a glass of water." Here, Doc worked at his huge barbecue pit, turning the spit and slicing Southern-cured ham. Downstairs was the action—roulette and an all-night dice game. Should there be a raid, the Barbecue Pit was prepared. A complete alarm system, with a complicated apparatus of bells, bars, and pulleys, snaked through the building. A button convenient to the foot of the cashier at the lunch counter was wired to a buzzer at the triple-barred doors of the cabaret in the basement.

Usually Doc had singers working in his place. Oscar Holden accompanied them or played solo (sometimes falling asleep at the keyboard, according to one account). The place was a hangout for the best musicians. Recalled Joe Darensbourg: "Doc's was a good job. We made good money and tips, got all our food. . . . I met Jimmie Lunceford for the first time at [Doc's] place. We went to breakfast. The next night, after the band got through playing, Willie Smith and Trummy Young came in and sat in with us. Willie brought his saxophone and his clarinet down there."

Like the rest of the speakeasies, Hamilton's club was protected by payoffs. Nevertheless, it was raided so often one begins to suspect someone downtown had a grudge against this elegant Black man who was raking in the dough. Terry Pettus, an old Seattle radical, went to his grave convinced that Hamilton had offended public sensibilities by building a house in Mount Baker, at the time an all-white neighborhood. Whatever the reason, Hamilton eventually was hounded out of town by the police, who raided the club again and again. What had started as a joking cat-and-mouse game, played out in the press between the cagey Hamilton and Sheriff Harry Lewis, eventually turned ugly. "If some dice accidentally fell out of someone's pocket," Doc told a reporter after one of his periodic busts, "I was too busy roasting chickens to notice."

When Hamilton was hauled off to jail after an undercover raid by Lewis on May 25, 1931—"This place is pinched!" Lewis had shouted—he was smiling. "I guess the sheriff wanted some extra good cooking in his jail kitchen," he quipped. But when the judge padlocked the club and sentenced Hamilton to federal prison instead of the usual overnight stay in jail and a light fine, Hamilton angrily appealed the case. "I ask you," he pleaded, "is this right? Can they do this to a man? Can Prohibition agents come into a man's restaurant with liquor, mix their drinks behind his back, and then padlock his place because drinking has been done in it?" When Doc lost the appeal, he was devastated. The judge sentenced him to five years. Hamilton gave an eloquent courtroom farewell, charging Judge Howard Findley with racism. After all, Doc argued, no white speakeasy operators were going to prison: "Your Honor, sir, you know that the laws are unjust, and that because I am a colored man I can shine shoes or scrub floors or cook for somebody, but that if I try to rise above that position, the public is against me. If I go to the penitentiary, sir, there will be twenty-five people who will starve to death. They are my father, mother, my children, and my employees. If you send me to the penitentiary, sir, God Himself will curse you for it." Hamilton was pardoned two days before Christmas, in 1933, after serving ten months. Despite his early release, he was a broken man. He had lost his Seattle house. He farmed for a while in Auburn and made several unsuccessful attempts to reopen his club. He died in 1942, alone in a Chinatown hotel.

When running his famous Barbecue Pit, Hamilton had catered to white patrons, as the Cotton Club in New York did. The white population caught on quickly to the mania for jazz through the media and phonograph records, despite the fact that most early jazz stars (Louis Armstrong, Duke Ellington, Fletcher Henderson, Bessie Smith) did not visit Seattle during the 1920s. White vaudeville acts soon began to flaunt jazz as part of the show. In September 1917 longtime veterans Kolb and Dill played the Metropolitan Theatre with "their own jazz orchestra" and returned annually for several years. A few days later, Tom Brown's Princeton Five billed itself as a jazz act at the Palace Hip, at Second Avenue and Spring Street, and returned there in 1920 with a routine dubbed the "Rube Jay Jazzers."

In November 1917 white superstar Sophie Tucker played the Moore Theatre with her Five Kings of Syncopation, described by the *Seattle Post-Intelligencer* as a "jazz band," and the great white alto saxophonist Rudy Wiedoeft, whose astounding technique inspired countless early jazz players, followed her at the Moore in December with the Frisco Jazz Band. In June 1920, Fanchon and Marco returned with "A Jazz Opera," featuring "a jazz orchestra and 30 of the most beautiful girls in the world." Modeled on the Ziegfeld Follies, the show had an all–West Coast cast and made a successful East Coast tour. The first group touted in Seattle as a "big name" jazz act from out of town was the Sid Hall Orchestra, a hotel band from New York, which played the Palace Hip on May 12, 1925. Earlier that year, in March, a group with the intriguing name the Chinese Stringed Band, billed as "six syncopated players of modern jazz," played the Columbia Theater "on their way East." Also on the bill was local bandleader Francesco Longo's "Evolution of Dixie."

According to Bruce Rowell and Emma Gayton—whose mother had rented a room to Blackie Williams—the great blues singers Bessie Smith and Mamie Smith also performed in Seattle, though no record of Bessie Smith's appearance can be found. Mamie Smith, however, who released the first blues hit record ("Crazy Blues," 1920), received massive coverage in the *Seattle Post-Intelligencer* in advance of her appearance in "Struttin' Along," the first Black musical revue to play Seattle. Mamie Smith and her Jazz Hounds performed May 6–19, 1923, in a cast of seventy-five that included Eddie "Rochester" Anderson at the Metropolitan Theatre. Mamie Smith shared her view with reporters that there were two kinds of jazz—the raw stuff (which she played) from the Black South, with blues feeling, and a sweeter version popularized by commercial—she didn't say "white" but clearly meant that—musicians. The *P-I* reviewer noted that her eagerly received renditions of "Don't Mess with Me" and "You've Got to See Mama Every Night" won "the kind (of) applause that can only be answered with an encore."

By 1928 jazz had taken over the popular music scene to the extent that theater orchestra leader Jules Buffano would warn the musicians' union that "legitimate players who refuse to deviate into the jazz realm are finding it increasingly difficult to find and hold good jobs." His use of the verb "deviate" is revealing. Like rock 'n' roll in the 1950s, jazz was greeted by many as a cacophonous symptom of a society run amok. When local newspapers and magazine editors wrote about it, they were often less interested in the music than in the social behavior that accompanied it. "Jazz is a return to the primitive, to the savage who used music as a physical stimulant," wrote the comically dubbed "Jazz Investigator" for the *Seattle Times* on June 14, 1921. "Jazz is a cross rhythm that carried far enough could so irritate the nervous system as to derange it entirely. . . . Jazz is one of the greatest contributing factors to the recklessness of young people today."

The Musical Arts Society agreed with the *Times*. The same year, it passed a resolution denouncing jazz as something that "tears down the moral fiber." Four years later, a Spokane music professor went them one better, bringing a $4,000 suit against the leader of a local orchestra for syncopating the old masters. One of the most intriguing responses to the new music came from *Cayton's Weekly*, which, though a Black newspaper, was beside itself with bourgeois embarrassment over jazz. Owner Horace Cayton's daughter, Madge, wrote: "One must be careful that the alluring god of jazz, Mumbo Jumbo, does not lead us so far from the true god of music, Pan. . . . Is there not a chance of jazz becoming the key to open our souls to the passions our forefathers once spent generations in trying to overcome?"

All of this publicity for jazz was a great boon to local Black entertainers, who could now command not only an audience of sailors looking for action at one of Noodles Smith's joints but a more middle-class crowd in a speakeasy as well. The pianist who became more popular in this vein than anyone else over the years was Palmer Johnson, whom Oscar Holden took under his wing after Johnson's arrival in Seattle from Los Angeles. A big-framed, straight-backed man with enormous hands, childlike eyes, and the booming intonation of a country preacher, Johnson was born in Houston, in 1907, and grew up from the age of three in Los Angeles. His childhood along Central Avenue near Thirty-Third Street, where his mother ran a soul-food restaurant, was rich with musical memories. Johnson was nurtured in an era when pianists Henry Prince and Harvey Brooks were at their peak, Paul Howard and his Serenaders had just hired Lionel Hampton to play drums, and Louis Armstrong had come out to play at Frank Sebastian's Cotton Club. Johnson remembered his mother and aunt talking about Jelly Roll Morton playing at Normandy Hall.

> In those days they gave parties every Friday or Saturday night, or a stomp, as they called it. We weren't allowed to play jazz, or rags as they called it in them days, in the house, so all the neighbors from around who knew that we kids could play would say, "Come on over. Friday night, so and so's going to have a ball." You walk down the street, you could hear the player pianos, playing "Down at the Savannah lives a fellow named Hosanna." . . . "Bluein' the Blues," that was called, on a pump piano. Hear that all over town, man.
>
> In 1923, my cousin took me to Doctor Gordon's Hummingbird, on Twelfth and Central, where Harvey Brooks was playing piano. . . . Harvey Brooks, Leon Hereford played alto, and Paul Howard, tenor. Jazz player, but he played in church, too, on Sunday. I used to follow them around getting pointers how to play. . . . Every time I had an opportunity to see Henry Prince play, who lived in Pasadena, I'd stand outside the Parish Hall. I didn't want to go inside, just stand outside and listen to Henry.

Johnson started on violin, at age seven, but soon turned to piano. His first professional job was in 1924, playing Friday and Saturday nights at the Chicken Inn, across the street from Frank Sebastian's Cotton Club, with an entertainer named Gutfoot. A year or two later, Johnson and a friend hitchhiked to the San Francisco Bay Area, where they heard one of the region's early Black jazz piano men, Wesley "Fess" Fields. In 1927, Johnson returned to San Francisco and began working at a lesbian bar, where he remembered playing "Two Cigarettes in the Dark" and "Valencia," new tunes at the time. The following year, he traveled by boat from Los Angeles to Seattle to play a gig at the Maryland

Tavern on Highway 99 with guitarist Freddy Vaughn. Vaughn had been working one night a week in Los Angeles with Curtis Mosby's Blue Blowers when he heard of steadier work in Seattle. He invited Johnson, saxophonist Elmer Fain, drummer Ellis Walsh, and (male) vocalist Sally Harper to come with him. Recalled Johnson:

> We caught a boat. We landed here in about November 1928, and we were scheduled to go to the Maryland Tavern, which is out Old Bothell Highway [*sic*]. It was almost to Everett. It was the farthest one, and just before you got to it, there was another one called Rubenac's Tavern and then across the street was the Ranch, where they used to do a lot of gambling. Didn't do any gambling at the Maryland Tavern. It's a roadhouse. We had an old Victrola, with one of those horns on it, and we fixed it to a box and [you could] throw silver dollars in it. That was the kitty. All silver dollars in those days. The songs we played were "My Blue Heaven" and "When Evening Is Nigh." The music at the Maryland Tavern was loud. The louder you played, the better. Because there was so much noise going on, the music had to drown out that noise. There wasn't no microphones then—we took a megaphone and sang. Until we got to the sweet stuff, like "My Blue Heaven."
>
> The Charleston was still in vogue, but we were tired of the Charleston. It's monotonous. And here's some guy just learning it. And we said, "Oh nuts. We saw that stuff down in Los Angeles." Every person that you looked at could do the Charleston. . . . We had to educate them.
>
> Sometimes, there was nobody in the joint. We'd be sitting around the table playing a game called mellow, something on the order of whist. We'd see some lights from a car coming and the band would jump on the stand and play like mad, like there was something going on, you understand! And pretty soon, they'd come in. It was a funny thing how that happened. As soon as that bunch came in, here was another bunch that came in. Pretty soon, the joint would be rolling. Jumping, man. And we playing all their requests. . . .
>
> The madams would close down their whorehouses about, say, two o'clock, and go out nightclubbing. They bring the whores down there. The gals, gee whiz, man, when you had those girls come in, they'd be coming out to spend some money. Probably a thousand dollars, which was nothing to them then. All five or six of her girls, and they had a chance to dress up in their new rhinestone slippers and their new dresses and their new capes or whatever they got. Some of them had mink, or imitation mink, and they came out to show it off.

Johnson was considerably advanced as a player when he got to town, a master of stride, boogie-woogie, chromatic modulations, and a deftly sliding left-hand chordal style that used tenth intervals. He also had picked up the flowery, classically influenced pianisms of the Los Angeles players. "Palmer Johnson used to always laugh to himself as he played—'Ha-ha-ha-ha-ha!'—looking at the keys," recalled Julian Henson, a Portland pianist who moved to Seattle in 1932. "He'd be playing and laughing. He was just marvelous!" Joe Darensbourg remembered: "Palmer was very good. Played with the class of Billy Kyle and could work with anybody's band."

Johnson was good, but he considered Oscar Holden his superior. "In those days, Oscar was very, very much better than I was. He was kind and considerate and he wanted to see me learn. I loved him. He helped me so much. He helped me on my reading. He gave me inspiration." The band that accompanied Johnson to Seattle had some intriguing players, not the least of whom was vocalist Sally Harper. Johnson and Harper were already well-known partners in Los Angeles, as evidenced by a collegial item that ran on July 13, 1930, in that city's Black newspaper, the *California Eagle*: "Palmer Johnson and Sally King are doing too fine in Seattle. We hope Pal pays L.A. a visit soon. Don't we." Harper has been described by trumpeter Buck Clayton, who knew him in Los Angeles, as a "beautiful lyric tenor singer." Harper popularized an old gambling tune from the Klondike, "Ace in the Hole," and made it a permanent part of the Seattle repertoire, much to the chagrin of singers who were still fielding requests for it thirty years later.

Elmer Fain, who could not read music but was a good improviser, later returned to Los Angeles, where he worked with Clayton at the Paradise Club and became the business agent for the Black Los Angeles Musicians Union, Local No. 767. Drummer Ellis Walsh went on to a career that included playing on the Louis Jordan record "Is You Is, or Is You Ain't." When the Maryland Tavern was shut down by federal agents—hacked to pieces with double-bitted axes—the band broke up. Johnson moved on to Marino's, on Bothell Highway, known for its excellent food. He played there with trumpeter Charles Adams, then worked briefly at the Main Event, the gambling joint Bruce Rowell remembered for its high-stakes games. During World War II owner Charlie Beale ran an ad every week in the *Northwest Enterprise*, encouraging folks to come down to the Two Pals to buy a war bond and "have a chat," which might include making a bet on a prizefight. Later, Johnson also worked next door at the Two Pals, with singer Dee Dee Hackett, but after the Main Event he moved to Herman Myers's Taxi Dance Hall, on the corner of First Avenue and Yesler Way, this time with Darensbourg, Freddy Vaughn, Seattle trumpeter Lee Philips, a drummer whose name no one remembers, and Gerald Wells. The job lasted two years. The taxi dance was a curious institution in which young women were paid by a hall to dance with customers. Myers's establishment catered to soldiers and sailors. Johnson explained:

> It was ten cents a dance. The band just played continually, never stopped. Just round and round and round. A guy buys tickets and all these girls are sitting around and he chooses his partner, and he dances and dances and gives her so many tickets. Then when he runs out of tickets, he goes to the counter and gets some more. A man would hold up his finger. Like, [if] he wanted a waltz and then he wanted a two-step or a fox-trot, he held it up, or if he wanted a real fast one he held up his fingers and the band knew how to answer him with these numbers. That was a good job. I think we made thirty-five dollars a week then.

Darensbourg recalled that he and Johnson worked at a roadhouse on Everett Highway called the Jungle Temple, with a group named the Jungle Temple Syncopators, "around the back end of 1929." The Jungle Temple had two incarnations, numbered accordingly, but it's often unclear which one musicians are referring to. Johnson didn't remember the band. Darensbourg's recollections of his time in Seattle were not always reliable—even he admitted he was drunk most of the time—but they are undeniably colorful and entertaining. An olive-skinned Creole clarinetist from Louisiana who would later play a major role in the New Orleans revival, Joseph Wilmer Darensbourg was an immensely likable, open-hearted man who loved to spin tall tales, cook jambalaya, drink tremendous quantities of alcohol, and play practical jokes on his bandmates. Born in Baton Rouge, Louisiana, he was a student of the great Alphonse Picou (noted for his clarinet solo on "High Society") and toured as a young man with minstrel and medicine shows.

In 1925, Darensbourg played briefly in Saint Louis with Jelly Roll Morton and, like Oscar Holden, on Fate Marable's riverboat excursions, before being recruited into Hill and Vesthon's Original Dixieland Jazz Band. The band broke up in California, and Darensbourg settled in Los Angeles, where he continued to work as a musician and an instrument repairman. He got his first glimpse of Seattle in 1928, while traveling up and down the West Coast with the Freda Shaw band aboard the SS *H. F. Alexander*. In 1929, attracted by the easy money and wild lifestyle, Darensbourg decided to move there.

> When I was in Los Angeles a lot of musicians would come back from Seattle and tell you how great it was, how much money you could make. When I was offered the job on the boat I had that in mind. . . . We'd get in, just for two nights, and meet some broads, and when we got through we'd go down to 12th and Jackson. [Seattle] was a money town. You went to work in a joint there and you always had forty-five dollars a week guaranteed. They had legitimate red-light districts, which consisted of Jackson Street, King Street, and Yesler Way. At these after-hours clubs we had a lot of the sporting class of people used to come in, like pimps and prostitutes. They'd come to show off . . . and see who could outspend each other putting money in the kitty. The house usually had a kitty cast out of plaster of paris and painted; it would have a big mouth and they put a light in it. You had a lot of silver dollars in those days, and people would throw a dollar into the kitty and hit a little lever inside and its eyes would light up. People got a kick out of that, seeing the goddamn cat blink his eyes. . . . In a place like the Black and Tan we'd have several entertainers that would go to the tables and sing songs. We would wind up sometimes making 200 or 300 dollars apiece.

Darensbourg had worked briefly with Palmer Johnson in Los Angeles, so it was only natural that his first Seattle engagement would be with the big pianist. In addition to their gigs at the Jungle Temple and Herman Myers's Taxi Dance Hall, they worked at the Blue Rose, a "pretty elaborate after-hours joint" on Fourteenth Avenue South near Yesler Way, later called the Rocking Chair, where Darensbourg stayed for about six or eight months. The band included "Banjoski" Adams (on banjo, of course, plus vocals) and drummer Bill Hoy. Darensbourg also worked with Oscar Holden often, first at the Jungle Temple, later at the Blue Rose and the Black and Tan. In 1932 he formed a quartet with white pianist Vic Sewell. Sewell and his brother, Monty (a trumpet player), were the sons of Slim Sewell, a trombonist who played at the Pantages Theater for thirty years and also played with the Seattle Symphony. Because Vic lived on Genesee Street, Darensbourg, who had a name for everything, dubbed the band the Genessee Street Shufflers.

The Freda Shaw band aboard the SS *H. F. Alexander*, 1928. Shaw (*center*); Joe Darensbourg (*far right*).

The Shufflers were a popular band and featured, in addition to Darensbourg and Sewell, drummer Jack Foy and bassist/guitarist Bill Rinaldi, both white. Darensbourg, an unremitting practical joker, played one of his best tricks on Foy while performing with the Shufflers. As Foy remembered: "I kept smelling this terrible smell around my drums every night, you know? I figured a cat died under the riser or something. Finally, I kept smelling it on my hands. Joe had put Limburger cheese under all of the cymbals. I'd touch them with my hand and I'd get it on me. As the days went by, it got riper and riper, of course. Oh, my God, it smelled!" Rinaldi, one of Seattle's most enduring sidemen, whose career bridges the "hot jazz" period and the swing era, was a roughneck, a husky ex-prizefighter remembered as much for his solid sense of time as for his continual scraps.

"Bill was a jealous guy," according to Darensbourg. "If he'd see Lorna [a chorus girl he married] getting too close to a guy or the guy holding her too close, he would jump off the bandstand and hit the guy in the mouth. He'd start a big fight like that. It was a lot of fun." Foy agreed: "He was the toughest guy I ever met in my life. Joe called Bill Rinaldi 'Tiger.' If he went down the street and somebody beat him to a parking place, he'd jump out and beat the hell out of the guy, just for kicks. Loved to fight. If there was a fight in the joint where we worked, he'd go and throw the guy out, like a bouncer. He was the unofficial bouncer of every place we'd work."

Darensbourg and Palmer Johnson both worked at various times with another important early Seattle musician, Gerald Wells. Though Wells was a better reader than improviser, he is an extremely important figure in the story of early West Coast jazz, and his influence ranged from Los Angeles to Honolulu. Wells was born in Saint George's, Grenada; locals identified his accent as "Jamaican." As early as 1914, Wells was playing flute in Sid LeProtti's jazz band in San Francisco. He first came to Seattle in 1913 but spent most of the late 1910s traveling with one of the most influential groups in the West, Reb Spikes's So Different Orchestra. In 1917 the So Different Orchestra shipped out to Honolulu for a six-month engagement at the Alexander Young Hotel. When the United States entered World War I, the whole band was absorbed into the service, becoming the first jazz band to play in Army uniform. When an offer to tour the East Coast developed, Wells wanted to go and the others did not, so he left the band and returned to Seattle. It's not clear whether he rejoined the So Different Orchestra when it subsequently came north to play the Alhambra in

July 1920, but it makes sense that he would have, even if he had already left the band. As Darensbourg remembered of Wells:

> [Gerald] played saxophone and piccolo. Gerald was a prominent bandleader in Seattle and always had a pretty good little band. It was a mixed band: We had about seven pieces and some good arrangements, and we considered ourselves the top band in Seattle. . . . Originally he had been in San Diego working at Jack Johnson's club.
>
> . . . Gerald was a fine musician, a good legitimate man, but he wasn't a jazzman by any stretch of the imagination. . . . Most of our stuff was for dances and we had singing entertainers in there with us, like Lillian Goode. We'd play for the vocalists and sometimes for shows, where you had to do a lot of reading.

Wells later became president of Local 493, which initially began at the 2024 Fourth Avenue headquarters of Local 76, but Wells ran it out of his home during the 1930s and 1940s. He had a real estate as well as music career, from which he retired in 1963. He died in 1966. Regarding the development of early Seattle jazz, Wells, Holden, Johnson, and Darensbourg were the most influential migrants in the city in the 1920s. They brought with them sophisticated new styles and a higher technical standard than had existed in town before. Without recordings from the period, however, it is difficult to know what they sounded like. From talking to them and other sources, and listening to their more recent recordings and to other music from the period, it is clear that these musicians were not playing traditional New Orleans jazz, or "Dixieland" as it is sometimes called. Oscar Holden's children made a point of saying that the pianist had "left all that Southern music" behind him. "We didn't play no Dixieland," said Darensbourg. "In the first place, Gerald [Wells] never knew anybody in that style or anything about the music. Our group was a jazz band; we didn't call it Dixieland."

Johnson was even more emphatic:

> We never used any Dixieland. Only on a few, certain numbers. We played "Tiger Rag" on request, but we weren't crazy about "Tiger Rag." Even in those days that was what we called old-time stuff. We were all the time getting something new. For instance, when we heard Duke Ellington's record, we'd study that record. And you never heard no tuba in it. These guys tried to make their playing sound as near to

> the Duke [Ellington] as they could. Not only the Duke had a good band, at those times McKinney's Cotton Pickers was a hell of a band.
>
> We played pops. What I call pops is, when you can get a tune and fix it up the way that we wanted to fix it. We learned how to take one of them tunes apart, man, and put it back together again. We learned it by ear, then we'd tear it to pieces. No Dixieland and no two-beat. The drummer made four beats. One-two-three-four. Four beats. No two-beat stuff. That's old-time stuff. It was jazz, man.

What Johnson and Darensbourg seemed to be saying is that their little combos were playing classic jazz, danceable rearrangements in four-four time of popular tunes, played in small ensembles, with some improvised solos and a looser, less "ricky-ticky" feeling than the ragtime bands of an earlier era. Swing, or simply jazz, is a more accurate description of what they were playing than Dixieland.

Another distinction between Seattle jazz and Dixieland is that many early New Orleans musicians played by ear. Johnson, however, came from a generation of Los Angeles musicians who put a premium on the ability to read sheet music and play European classics. This was the milieu that produced Lionel Hampton, Curtis Mosby, Les Hite, and Charlie Echols. The fact that Gerald Wells had been playing on the West Coast since the early 1910s, but, according to Darensbourg, knew nothing of the New Orleans style, goes a long way toward making a case for the existence of an independent West Coast jazz style that had developed very early in the music's history, in which Seattle participated at the outer edge, picking up influences as musicians moved in and out of town. Like West Coast jazz of the 1950s, this music emphasized melody, intricate arrangements, an accommodation of popular taste, a somewhat pretentious intimation of "classical" overtones, and a light-footed sense of swing.

Seattle jazz was also, at least at this early stage, not very bluesy. Johnson even expressed a distaste for this basic building block of jazz, preferring technically complex music to the simple folk lines of blues: "I never did like blues anyway, from having it for breakfast, dinner, and supper when I was a little kid coming up. That's all you could hear around the neighborhood is blues, blues, blues. I wanted to hear something fantastic. I used to like to go and hear Yehudi Menuhin." Not until the 1940s, when a wave of African Americans came to Seattle from Louisiana, Texas, Arkansas, and other points south, would the blues, gospel, and the gutsier side of Black music arrive in the Northwest.

When Johnson and Darensbourg got to town, there were two organized bands working on a regular basis. One was led by pianist Evelyn Bundy and drummer Leonard Gayton and the other by Edythe and Floyd Turnham. Bundy and Gayton's band was called the Garfield Ramblers. Formed in 1926 and named after Garfield High School, the Ramblers played for high school and tennis-club dances and various Black society affairs. In addition to Bundy and Gayton, the band included Wayne Adams on saxophones, his brother Jimmy Adams on trumpet, and Creon Thomas on piano, drums, violin, and banjo. When Evelyn Bundy graduated from high school, the Garfield Ramblers became the Evelyn Bundy band. Born in Seattle, Bundy played piano, banjo, drums, and saxophone, and sometimes sang. Her father, who had sung in a local quartet that sometimes performed at the Rainier Club, encouraged her to study classical piano. She studied with Frank Waldron and began performing professionally at age thirteen. Emma Gayton, Leonard's widow, remembered Bundy's mother traveling with the band to "make sure Evelyn was in good company. She would dress her out of this world."

According to Emma, Leonard "would walk from table to table, singing through a megaphone, with high hat and brushes in tow. Money was collected in a kitty." This is the earliest known reference to "table singing" in Seattle, a custom that became even more popular during the 1940s. Singers would roam the floor of a club or dance hall, sometimes accompanied by a horn player (but not usually a drummer), and collect tips from customers for playing their favorite tunes. This not only pleased the customers, it also provided the musicians a living wage. In the early days of jazz, salaries were low; the only way to really make money on a gig was through tips.

In 1929, Evelyn Bundy married Charles Taylor, a plasterer who promoted the band on the side. The Garfield Ramblers was usually a four- or five-piece group, with alto man Kenny Pernell sometimes replacing Wayne Adams. "They used to go to their gigs in a hearse," recalled Bundy and Taylor's son, Charles Jr. "That's right, one of the guys that was playing worked at the undertaker's. And so that was a joke of theirs." Horn chores in the Bundy band were covered by the Adams brothers, Wayne and Jimmy, two of the strongest sidemen in town. Both were students of Waldron and played music well into the 1930s. They enjoyed success with their own band, variously called the Collegiate 4, Collegiate 5, or Collegiate 6, depending on who was available. In 1925 the band was playing a fifteen-minute set before the movie at the Gala Theatre, another instance of a

Black band playing downtown; in 1926 their band was advertised at the Shanghai Restaurant on Second Avenue, near Yesler Way; on New Year's Eve, in 1927, the band played Renton Hill Hall, at East Madison Street and Eighteenth Avenue. Jimmy also led his own band in 1931 at Faurot's Hall, worked with Joe Darensbourg at the Jungle Temple, and was billed as the "trumpet king" at a 1932 summer ball at Washington Hall. Tragically, in 1937, he died by suicide over a failed romance. Wayne left Seattle with Palmer Johnson in Earl Whaley's band in 1934.

Evelyn Bundy with her son, Charles Taylor, ca. 1935.

Multi-instrumentalist Creon Thomas had perfect pitch. "A streetcar would go by and he'd say, 'A-flat!'" recalled Julian Henson. "Guys used to play a note on the piano and take bets if he could guess what it was. Creon was always going along humming or playing drums. Music was in his mind twenty-four hours a day." Thomas later moved to San Diego, where he played music through the 1940s and 1950s.

When Leonard Gayton graduated from Garfield in 1927, he too struck out on his own, playing the 908 Club (formerly Doc Hamilton's), the Plantation, and the New Harlem. In 1930 he was the inaugural act at a club that would have a venerable local history, the Chinese Garden, on Seventh Avenue South between South King Street and South Weller Street. Gayton also performed on pleasure cruises that ran to Alaska and California.

In the 1930s the Bundy-Taylor household became a hub of the Seattle jazz world. When touring musicians came to town, they would congregate in the basement music room and bar of the Bundy-Taylor home, which was adorned with jazz photos and memorabilia, to socialize and jam after the gig. Charles Taylor Jr., who later formed an important band of his own, recalled: "In those days, Black people didn't have any place to stay or to go. There was a lot of singing. Everybody would play. Everybody would take turns singing songs and telling stories and laughing. Lionel Hampton, Erskine Hawkins—they all came to our house." Taylor remembered his mother as a sophisticated, two-handed pianist, rather than a strictly stride, "boom-chunk"-type player. Taylor's high school pal Quincy Jones went Charlie one better, dubbing Evelyn the "mother of Seattle jazz," so widespread was her influence. Bundy stopped performing regularly in 1937.

———

On April 30, 1926, Seattle's *Northwest Enterprise* quaintly noted, "Mr. and Mrs. Floyd Turnham, 'popular musicians,' bought a house at 707 22nd and will be moving in shortly." The Edythe Turnham Orchestra (also called the Knights of Syncopation) was already a going concern when it arrived from Spokane and became the other important jazz group in Seattle in the mid-1920s. Turnham was born Edythe Pane, in Topeka, Kansas, around 1890 and started playing piano when she was three years old. She came to Spokane in 1900; about eight years later she married Floyd Turnham, a carpenter from Texas. In 1922, with her sister, Maggie, Edythe put together a vaudeville act featuring two blackface comedians and toured throughout eastern Washington and Idaho. Four years later, the band featured Powell Barnett on tuba. Edythe also worked solo in Spokane. Sometime in the early 1920s, she formed a five-piece family band, the Knights of Syncopation, later called the Black Hawks Orchestra. Edythe played piano; Floyd was on drums; Floyd Jr. played saxophone; Maggie was a dancer and entertainer.

Floyd Jr. recalled his mother taking him to Twelfth Avenue South and South Jackson Street in Seattle as early as 1922, where as a twelve-year-old he sang "The End of a Perfect Day" for tips. He also remembered playing in a five-piece band at the Black and Tan for Noodles Smith. Once the Turnhams were in Seattle, they played at the Kopper Kettle (later known as Todd's Dixieland Café), the Alhambra, the Tennis Club, the Coon Chicken Inn, Willard's, the Black Elks Club, and the Bungalow Dance Hall. The Kopper Kettle, owned by "Six Fingers" Taylor, was on East Madison Street, near Twenty-First Avenue; the Elks Club, down the street at Eighteenth. The Bungalow was located on Third Avenue, just north of the Bon Marché department store. Gigs downtown were normally reserved for white musicians, but, according to Bruce Rowell, who briefly played saxophone with the band, engagements for fashion shows at the Bon Marché and Frederick & Nelson got Turnham past the color bar. When the Bungalow moved to Eighth Avenue, however, Local 76 protested, said Rowell, and Turnham's orchestra was not permitted to play.

Edythe Turnham and Her Knights of Syncopation, 1925. *Left to right*: Floyd Turnham Sr., unknown, Edythe Turnham, Floyd Turnham Jr., Charles Adams.

Edythe Turnham's style of music was "right on the edge between Dixieland and ragtime we classify as jazz," explained saxophonist Marshal Royal, who heard her later in Los Angeles. "The only one that survived out of that into the new era was the son, Floyd. He turned out to be a good saxophone player." Floyd Jr. remembered that the band played tunes in sets of three—"waltz, fox-trot, and standard little jump tunes. We'd always start a slow one, medium one, and a little fast one . . . three tunes. When we played [Fats Waller's] 'What Did I Do to Be So Black and Blue?' the whole audience stopped." Floyd Jr. and his sister, Frances, attended Garfield High School, where they came to know Wayne and Jimmy Adams and Creon Thomas of the Garfield Ramblers, bass and tuba player Joe Bailey, and the rest of the Garfield jazz crowd. Floyd said he remembered Oscar Bradley, a drummer with whom he later worked in Los Angeles, peeking through the window of the Tennis Club to listen to Edythe's band.

The Turnham group played the Garfield Funfest using all the kids in the family; Floyd Jr. became the leader of the pep band. He studied saxophone with Frank Waldron and pursued his goal of being a complete entertainer—singing, dancing, and performing on violin, saxophone, and piano. Edythe, for her part, played rehearsal piano for a dance school and occasionally took bands out

The Edythe Turnham Orchestra, 1927–28. *Left to right:* H. A. Jones, Charles Adams, Floyd Turnham Sr., (first name unknown) Boone, Edythe Turnham, Fats Wilson, Floyd Turnham Jr., Bruce Rowell.

on Alaska cruises, while Floyd Sr. worked part-time as a tailor and drove the band around in a huge Hudson. According to Floyd Jr., his father "had a hell of a rhythm on the bass drum, and snares and socks in them and stuff. He was solid. Never missed a beat. Right on the beam. He was a card." Al Hilbert, Floyd Turnham Sr.'s nephew, recalled hauling the band to a gig in the back of a truck, in 1928, with the piano strapped down and the band playing as he drove for fifteen or twenty blocks.

In 1928 the Knights of Syncopation got their big break—an audition for the Orpheum Theater circuit. The band was booked in theaters from Winnipeg to Long Beach. A few months later, however, they found themselves stranded in Los Angeles. The Turnhams eventually flourished in Southern California, where the band became known as the Dixie Aces, featuring, in addition to the three Turnhams, many of Los Angeles's finest sidemen, including Frank Pasley and Teddy Buckner. In 1934, Duke Ellington heard Edythe at the Jazzland Cafe. "Girl," Duke reportedly said, "you sure can play. You sure are heavy." Floyd Sr. died in 1936, but Edythe continued to work until 1945, at one point playing at Los Angeles's Cotton Club with a band led by Charlie Echols that included Bumps Myers, Paul Howard, and Lee Young. Floyd Jr., meanwhile, became a prominent fixture on the Los Angeles scene.

A lanky fellow given to naughty winks and stories, Turnham was an amiable, slow-talking man, proud of the way he played yet completely unpretentious.

After leaving the Dixie Aces in 1933, Floyd Jr. worked in both jazz and rhythm-and-blues groups, as a regular for Les Hite, Gerald Wilson, Joe Liggins, and Bardu Ali, and subbing or working short stints with Count Basie, Benny Carter, Teddy Wilson, and others. From 1938 to 1941, Turnham led his own orchestra, which had a moment of glory in Los Angeles when he won a much celebrated "cutting contest" in 1939 against tenor saxophonist Vido Musso. In late 1939 or early 1940, Les Hite took over Floyd's men, adding some of his own, including Oscar Bradley and the great trombonist Britt Woodman. Hite, one of the best early bandleaders in Los Angeles, used several sidemen with Seattle connections over the years, including Joe Bailey and pianists Phil Moore and Gerald Wiggins. In 1942, when Dizzy Gillespie came into the Hite organization and made the first recording of a bebop solo (on "Jersey Bounce"), Turnham, Bradley, and Wiggins were all in the group. Turnham and Woodman continued to be close associates after their tour with Hite. When Johnny Hodges and Lawrence Brown made their famous defection from Duke Ellington's band to form a group of their own, Turnham and Woodman were recruited as replacements.

Floyd played dates in Los Angeles with Ellington but never left town with the band. Curiously, he never seemed to regret this, despite the fame and wealth the Ellington chair might have yielded. He turned down Coleman Hawkins once too. "I guess I was just so in love with my wife," said Turnham, "that I wanted to stay home." Duke and Hawk were no doubt attracted to Turnham's firm, elegant, solidly projected alto sound—in the old-fashioned tradition of Hodges, Benny Carter, and Willie Smith—a perfect fit with Duke's conception, which, like Turnham's, was formed in the 1920s. Count Basie also admired that sound. He dubbed Turnham "Iron Jaw" because he played so loud. Albert McCarthy, in his book *Big Band Jazz*, mentions being impressed by "several of [Hite's] soloists, notably an alto player who was almost certainly Floyd Turnham."

In the late 1950s, Turnham started playing rhythm-and-blues tenor saxophone with Joe Liggins and His Honeydrippers. His shift from jazz to R & B was not surprising, since Los Angeles was a hotbed of the new dance music after World War II, and one of the Turnhams' first important contacts in Los Angeles had been the father of Jack McVea, whose song "Open the Door, Richard" was one of the first big R & B hits. Turnham was a featured soloist with Liggins on "Red Top" and "Flyin' Home." He retired in 1974, but an offer in 1979 to tour internationally with a revivalist show called "1000 Years of Jazz," led by British jazz aficionado and drummer Barry Martyn, rekindled his career. Turnham toured all over the world in the 1980s with Martyn's group—an unusual one in revivalist circles, since the band featured older Black musicians. Revivalist, or Dixieland, groups were usually white.

Turnham is represented well on several recordings. He had a good alto solo on Les Hite's "The Lick" and also played on "T-Bone Blues," recorded when T-Bone Walker was with the Hite band, "T.B. Blues," and "Board Meeting Time," with Joe Wilder and Dizzy Gillespie. In 1946, Turnham waxed Melba Liston's tune "Mores," with Los Angeles bandleader Gerald Wilson. Turnham died in Los Angeles in 1991 in comfortable circumstances, cared for by his wife, Georgia, a jazz fan who loved nothing better than to hear him play.

The 1920s in Seattle were represented by vocalists as well as top instrumentalists. Easily the most important was Mildred Bailey, who, like Edythe Turnham, came west from Spokane, Washington. Bailey was the first white jazz singer of any significance. Born Mildred Rinker in 1907, she grew up in the small farming community of Tekoa, sixty miles southeast of Spokane, then moved to Spokane in 1912. Her mother, Josie, was one-quarter Coeur d'Alene and taught Mildred Native American songs, which she later performed. Following Josie's death, Mildred's father married a second time, and Mildred was sent to Seattle to live with an aunt. She had a rough time of it. Before the age of eighteen, Mildred had been married twice. As a teenager in Seattle, Bailey played piano in silent-movie houses, plugged songs in downtown department stores, and demonstrated sheet music, first at Woolworth's, then at Bush and Lane's music store. Her first, and very brief, marriage was to a man named Bailey, from whom she adopted her stage name. Probably around 1925 she moved to Los Angeles, where she married her second husband, a bootlegger named Benny Stafford.

Bailey's brother, Al Rinker, had a duo with another famous Spokanite—Bing Crosby. Al and Bing followed Mildred to Los Angeles in 1926, stopping off in Seattle long enough to sing at the Butler Hotel for two weeks with bandleader Jackie Souders. In Los Angeles, Mildred helped Al and Bing get an audition with the "king of jazz" himself, Paul Whiteman. Three years later, when Crosby and Rinker were gaining fame as the Rhythm Boys, Rinker convinced Whiteman to hire his sister. Bailey sang her way to fame on a recording led by the innovative Whiteman sideman guitarist Eddie Lang, on Hoagy Carmichael's "Rockin' Chair." It became her signature song. "Rockin' Chair" marked the first recording by a "girl singer" with a big band, an innovation that would set the pattern for the swing era. Bailey's successors could scarcely have had a better model.

She sang impeccably in tune, in a hauntingly pure, tiny voice that seemed to float in thin air. Her phrasing incorporated the blue notes, sudden swoops, dives, and surprise leaps of the great Black blues singers, but she never sounded like a white singer mimicking Black vocal effects.

Mildred Bailey, on the cover of *DownBeat* magazine, 1944.

Bailey was popular with improvisers, a jazz singer's singer. Her small group sides over the years with Johnny Hodges, Benny Goodman, Teddy Wilson, and others hold up well against similar, better-known recordings by Billie Holiday. After working with her third husband—bandleader Red Norvo—through much of the 1930s, Bailey went into decline. In 1944 she made a comeback at Manhattan's Café Society and secured a national radio program, "The Mildred Bailey Radio Show." The producer was ex-Seattle pianist Phil Moore. *Time* magazine described her in a feature article as "just about the greatest popular songbird in the U.S.," and the jazz journal *DownBeat* put her picture on the cover. Bailey's comeback didn't last long, however. She died in 1951, broke, alone, and unhappy.

While Bailey was in Seattle learning the ropes and listening to records by Bessie Smith, there were Black vocalists in her own backyard whom she likely never heard. One of the best was Evelyn Williamson, who was raised by Noodles Smith (he had married Evelyn's older sister, Elbe). The wealthy entrepreneur made sure that Evelyn wanted for nothing. Born in 1910, she graduated from Garfield, where she and Frances Turnham had won first place for their cabaret act at the Garfield Funfest. Afterward she went to finishing school in Washington, DC, where she studied voice and piano. Williamson lived in Los Angeles with her husband of over fifty years, saxophonist Marshal Royal. "In those days, to be a cabaret singer meant you were classified with a lower element," she said. "But I always wanted to be a singer. I went to Doc Hamilton, who had a little after-hour club. Just select people could go down there. I went there as a waitress, then in between customers I would go downstairs and sing. That's where I met Oscar Holden."

Williamson was soon making her living as an entertainer, singing mostly with piano accompanists in small clubs and occasionally at dances. The *Northwest Enterprise* lists her playing dances at Broadway Hall in 1931 and 1933 and singing at the Black and Tan in 1933. Palmer Johnson recalled working with Williamson at the Chinese Garden in 1930 or 1931. She did some "rhythm tunes" but admitted she "wasn't too good" on blues. Her real specialty was ballads. Johnson recalled her as having a "sweet" voice and doing "more than justice" to "Rockin' Chair." She must have been a good sport too. At Doc's a rich lumberman who always brought his own Champagne perennially asked her to sing "Street of Dreams"—all night long. "He would stay there for hours. And that's a very short song! I'd sing it and he'd say, 'Sing it again.' When I first met him was at Doc Hamilton's. He would give me twenty to thirty dollars every chorus. I'd never seen so much money in my life."

Though Williamson and pianist Evelyn Bundy were Garfield schoolmates and the best of friends, Williamson preferred working with Oscar Holden, by far the better musician. Oscar was always tied up at Doc's though, so she usually worked with pianist Marion Fulmighter, who according to Julian Henson had a "cute style," or with "Princess" Belle, who had come to Seattle from New Zealand. For a while, Williamson worked at the Jungle Temple with the great Seattle-bred tenor saxophonist Dick Wilson, who later played with Andy Kirk. In 1935 an amusing mishap befell the demure, polished Williamson when she and Fulmighter got their first break to sing on Seattle radio. "I was going to sing 'Smoke Gets in Your Eyes.' I don't know whether Marion was drunk or nervous, but she started in the wrong key. I had a pretty good range, but that was just a little too high. I had never sung on radio and the first lick I took, I said, 'Shit! That's too high!' That was our first opportunity and our last." Evelyn and her friends were quite naive about the rough-and-tumble life going on around them in the clubs. Once, when they were rehearsing with Joe Darensbourg, he got drunk and became unruly with a policeman. They tried to bail him out by going down to the jailhouse and "entertaining" the officers. "We were lucky to get to our rehearsal," laughed Williamson.

In 1936, Evelyn Williamson married Los Angeles tenor saxophonist Bumps Myers, who had worked with Darensbourg at the Jungle Temple and come back to town with Les Hite. Her destined love, however, was another sax player in the Hite band, Marshal Royal, whom she married two years later. This took her away to Los Angeles for good, where she pursued a career as a big-band singer with Hite and Lionel Hampton. She would later return to Seattle for a triumphant visit with Hamp at the Trianon, riding high with her popular number "I Nearly Lost My Mind," which she recorded with the band. After the war she sang in exclusive supper clubs in Hollywood and retired in the early 1950s.

Williamson sang in Seattle for ten years, from 1928 to 1938, working six or seven nights a week, usually until the late hours of the next morning. There was lots of work, and a pleasant spirit of cooperation, she recalled, between her and other singers. "There was never any jealousy or competitiveness. If I was working and somebody called me for a job and I couldn't take it, I would immediately call up one of the others and tell them it was open." Some of the jobs Williamson referred her friends to were likely at various small resorts, outside of town. Seattle is surrounded by little lakes. Before the days of suburban sprawl, nearly every one of these puddles had a "resort," sometimes just a little dance hall. The Grove, at Angle Lake, near the present site of Sea-Tac International Airport, was one. Another was the Bungalow Inn, at Silver Lake, east of Interstate 5 and north of Lynnwood (not to be confused with the Bungalow in Seattle, where Edythe Turnham's group played). The Bungalow Inn burned down in 1929.

The steamship lines that ran pleasure cruises to Alaska, California, and East Asia were another venue for work-hungry musicians. Joe Darensbourg, Leonard Gayton, Palmer Johnson, Oscar Holden, and Edythe Turnham all played on the President Line steamship cruises, making good wages and often bringing back booty from Asia to sell stateside at inflated prices. Lillian Goode, who had been an entertainer at Frank Sebastian's Cotton Club in Los Angeles, may have come north to Seattle on just such a steamship. "Goody," as she was known to her friends, influenced Evelyn Williamson with her interpretations of ballads and impressed Palmer Johnson a lot. "She had a voice like a canary," he recalled, "way up high. She could sing stuff like 'Indian Love Call,' which was very prominent at that time." Not a great deal is known about Goode. She sang for a while with Gerald Wells and the Hi-Hatters and performed at a benefit dance with Williamson and Zelma Winslow (Noodles Smith's mistress and another fine singer on the scene at the time) at Broadway Hall. Leon Vaughn, a trumpet player who came to town somewhat later and remembers Goode singing at the Black and Tan, said, "She could really sell a teary-type ballad."

Zelma Winslow.

Winslow was so hot-tempered and had so much trouble with Noodles that apparently she didn't have a lot of time to concentrate on her career. Once during an early Sunday morning raid on the Black and Tan by the county constables, she got so mad at a cop who swore at her that she socked him in the jaw. It was quite a melee. At her trial the officer dared her to hit him again, which she did. Winslow did a little time for that. In his unpublished memoir "Things I Forgot to Tell You," pianist and vocalist Phil Moore confirmed that Winslow slugged an officer but said it was in retaliation for pistol-whipping Noodles. "Zelma was an awesome, statuesque, imposing personality and could cut you down with a devastating glance," remembered Moore. Winslow worked at the Jungle Temple with Oscar Holden and later at a private room upstairs at the Chinese Garden. Noodles Smith kept Winslow highly visible but strictly off-limits. She "could sing her butt off," according to Bruce Rowell. "She had dimples you could put your whole finger in," remembered pianist Julian Henson. "She was so beautiful! She did torch songs and blues."

The zaniest entertainer in this period by far was a fellow from Los Angeles named Eddie Rucker, who had performed there with the early jazz group the Black and Tan Orchestra. (The term "entertainer," as used by Joe Darensbourg and Palmer Johnson, refers to a table singer with an "act," not necessarily a dancer or comedian, as it might today.) Said Darensbourg: "People came from all over the Pacific Northwest to hear Eddie. He used to do a lot of X-rated, off-color tunes. He made so much money. The Jungle Temple had little individual booths with a drawn curtain so you could have private entertainment. You had to pay Eddie a lot of money to come in and sing for you. He might keep the curtain open a little, push in a little roll-away piano which had four octaves, and we'd stand around outside and play. We would average seventy-five or a hundred dollars a night in that kitty!" Rucker worked most of the time at Noodles Smith's Entertainer's Club, an intimate speakeasy, like a little apartment where a few customers would go up for a drink, laugh, and make requests. "Eddie liked that room all for himself," said Evelyn Williamson. "He didn't like when I worked with him up there. Whenever my brother-in-law [Noodles] would get mad at me, he'd send me up there."

Rucker was a jive artist. He often told customers he could sing in French, which he would promptly do, making up a lot of nonsense, to their delight. One night, however, he got caught. As Darensbourg remembered it:

> One night at the Black and Tan, Harold Weeks, the Seattle composer who wrote the swing hit "Hindustan," came into the club. Eddie prided himself he could sing any song you could name. For songs he didn't know, he would make up the words. So he said, "Why, sure I know that song." He started singing "Hindustan" and told the band to make an introduction, although we had never played it or heard it before. Then Eddie sang some funny words and Harold let him finish. Eddie asked Harold how did he like his version of the song and Harold said, "I like it fine, but it ain't the one I wrote!"

Palmer Johnson worked several times with Rucker, in both Seattle and Portland. "Great? He sure was!" Johnson said. "When he first walked into the joint and we were ready to play, he'd tap that cane on the floor, singing, 'She's my weakness now!' The only thing, Eddie had to get full of his cocaine. He used to booze it down with whiskey. He liked them straight shots of Scotch. I sure remember that."

Working with Rucker at the Jungle Temple or on society dances at Finnish Hall was drummer "Baby" Borders, called "Baby" because of his high voice. Little is known about Borders, but since Johnson described him as being from the South, Borders may have been the Samuel Borders who played drums in the Black Birds of Paradise, a Montgomery, Alabama, band formed in 1925. In any case Baby Borders came to Seattle via Los Angeles and in 1931 was playing a dance every Monday night for the Elite Social Club; in 1933 he worked with the ten-piece Harlem Knights at the Black and Tan. Borders was in Seattle until at least 1938; he later moved to Detroit. He lived with Marion Fulmighter, Evelyn Williamson's accompanist, who later left town in a show with Mae West.

Williamson, Fulmighter, and Zelma Winslow were all arrested one night in a police sweep of the Chinese Garden, a club that experienced its fair share of raids but was spared the relentless harassment endured by the basement boîte across the street, the Club Royale. Run by a ring of petty bootleggers and ensconced under what is now the Louisa Hotel, at 511½ Seventh Avenue, the Club Royale operated behind a front called the Hong Kong Chinese Society Club (though no Asians were involved). It was also known colloquially as the "Bucket of Blood," though it does not appear to have been particularly violent and was in fact the most elaborately and glamorously decorated nightclub in the district. The walls of the stairwell leading down to the double doors that protected the club from casual visitors (and the police) boasted beautiful, stylized murals depicting a racial mix of men in tuxedos and women in furs. In red, above the lintel, art deco lettering above a radiating design declared "CLUB ROYALE." Downstairs, more murals with an Asian floral and flamingo theme graced the walls.

Opened in 1930, the Club Royale had a full kitchen, hard liquor, and plenty of room for dancing. Joe Darensbourg recalled playing there with Gerald Wells and a pianist named Anson "Polly" Butler, who was unlucky enough to get arrested in 1931 during one of the many raids. The Club Royale was rowdy, but musicians liked to go there because it was a good place to jam. "You could play anything you wanted there," recalled Darensbourg's drummer Jack Foy. "They'd have an organized band, about four pieces, and they'd always have at least eight or ten on the stand, jamming." The club was shuttered by the authorities on New Year's Eve 1932, but by 1935 another bootleg joint, the Sky-High, was operating in its place. Three years later, Palmer Johnson recalled working at the Blue Heaven, another club on the alley side. Upstairs, a gambling club on the alley called the Wah Mee later opened and was the site of a horrific 1983 massacre and robbery that resulted in thirteen deaths. The Wah Mee massacre is well-known, but the jazz history of the Louisa was not discovered until 2018, when former Seattle City Council member Tanya Woo, whose family owns the Louisa Hotel, discovered the murals while renovating the building. The murals in the stairwell have been carefully preserved. The basement is now a parking lot for the workforce housing tenants who live upstairs.

Three blocks away from the Club Royale, at 410 Seventh Avenue South, was the Golden West Club, on the fourth floor of the hotel of the same name. The faded red lettering can still be made out on the side of the building.

After finishing up at Herman Myers's Taxi Dance Hall, Palmer Johnson often worked at the Golden West after hours, as a single. Thanks to the action in Seattle, many musicians drifted in from Los Angeles or elsewhere, and stayed a while before moving on. The most outstanding was pianist Phil Moore. Born in Portland in 1917, Moore moved to Seattle in the early 1930s, after the Great Depression bankrupted his father, a professional gambler named George Moore who was a close associate of Noodles Smith. Phil Moore had enjoyed a comfortable middle-class life in Portland, taking music lessons and playing golf on the weekends. In an unpublished memoir, he described how shocked he was, walking up Jackson Street from King Street Station, to discover he would now be living with his parents in a one-room flat in the Governor Apartments. Wrote Moore:

> I unloaded my things and then went about trying to find someplace to get something to eat. You must remember I was twelve, going on thirteen or something like that, and this was a rather rough neighborhood. . . . I noticed that on the other side of the street there was a restaurant with swinging doors. . . . Just as I started to enter, the doors swung violently and a woman came flying out and landed on the sidewalk right in front of me. And she was a white lady, and after her came a Black man and he kicked her ass all down the street. . . . I went in and ordered my first meal in Seattle. This was a place called the Tokiwa Restaurant. And upstairs was the Tokiwa Hotel.

Life did improve for the young musician. When Moore graduated from Garfield High School in June 1935, he was living on Twentieth Avenue and helping support the family with his income from paying gigs. His father had introduced him to Charlie Louie, owner of the Chinese Garden, who hired Moore to play with Frank Waldron. Moore's colorful description of the band is worth repeating and may include a reference to drummer Baby Borders. Moore's memoir continued:

> The band there consisted of a drum and a piano and a saxophone. There was a huge Black man, he looked like Buddha kind of, playing the saxophone. He was so large that the alto saxophone looked like a toy in his hands. . . . The drummer, whose name I can't recollect, (was) a very dark Black man who had a very lecherous laugh and one or two gold teeth, and he loved to beat his tom-toms. I

> remember that Frank Waldron, the leader, would get orchestrations. And I would have to fill in all of the parts that were cued for trombone or for trumpet and everything else.

Moore worked seven nights a week at the Black and Tan, sometimes till the early hours of the morning, when only the table singers were on duty. In his memoir he says he dabbled in pimping, until his "girls" got arrested and he had to turn to a veteran in the neighborhood for help. Moore's attitude toward women was unfortunately endemic to the Jackson Street milieu of that time. A raunchy "soundie" he released later with his snappy, popular combo the Phil Moore Four, called "The Chair Song," says it all. For all that, Moore was a highly literate, educated man. While he was in Seattle, he wrote an arts column, "Phil's Bits," for the *Northwest Enterprise* and also broadcast a two-hour Friday-night program, *Phil Moore Rhythm*, on radio station KXA. By 1935 he went on the road with Eli Rice, then settled in Los Angeles, where he became one of the first Black musicians to break into the Hollywood studios, eventually working as a staff arranger and conductor for Metro-Goldwyn-Mayer, scoring the films *Broadway Melody* and *A Song Is Born*. Moore also worked as an accompanist and vocal coach for Lena Horne, wrote the popular wartime hit "Shoo Shoo Baby," and played on Fifty-Second Street, in New York, with the Phil Moore Four.

Another outstanding musician in Seattle at the time was Los Angeles–born banjoist and guitarist Ceele (pronounced "C. L.," short for Cecil Louis) Burke. Burke and Palmer Johnson had been schoolmates in Los Angeles, and they worked together in Portland in 1931. After leaving the Northwest, Burke picked up Hawaiian steel guitar and moved to Honolulu. His Hawaiian bent earned him a small niche in jazz history: it is his wonderfully slinky steel guitar introduction on Louis Armstrong's classic version of "I'm Confessing."

A Seattle player whom Palmer Johnson much admired was Beverly Harrison, an alto saxophonist who led a band Johnson worked with around 1931. Harrison made a smart arrangement of Duke Ellington's "It Don't Mean a Thing If It Ain't Got That Swing" that was quite popular locally. The Hoy family had the respect of Seattle musicians as well. Bill Hoy worked with Oscar Holden at the Jungle Temple, and his sister-in-law, Sue Hoy, was a well-known entertainer on the LA scene whom Buck Clayton described as "one great singer." Joe Darensbourg, for his part, admired guitarists Rudy Goldberg and Bill Page:

I remember one time we was playing some place with Page and a guy came in with the score of "Rhapsody in Blue" in a special arrangement. On the part which old [Mike] Pingatore did on banjo with Paul Whiteman, he had it written out for guitar. Now, Bill had fooled us all that he could read, he had such a good ear. But when he got to the guitar solo he didn't know what to do. Finally, Gerald Wells says, "That's a guitar solo. I thought you could read. Why don't you play it?" Bill admitted he couldn't read at all, but he says, "One of you guys play that thing and let me listen to it once!" Old Gerald took his piccolo and played it for Bill. After that Bill just played it like nothing happened, the whole thing.

Johnson credited Ivan Ditmar, a white staff pianist at one of the radio stations, with being one of the swingingest players on the scene. Wilbert Barranco was another pianist who commanded both Johnson's and Darensbourg's respect. Darensbourg had known Barranco in Baton Rouge, Louisiana; Barranco later had his own group in Oakland, California, in 1933 through 1934, and played with LA bandleader Curtis Mosby's group, fronting the traveling show "Change Your Luck," which came to Seattle in 1933. Other names from the late 1920s and early 1930s crop up again and again, about whom there is little information: Jack Brackman (saxophone, also mentioned by Buck Clayton), Slim Taft (trombone), Bill Trent (vocals), Glover Compton (a pianist who appears in a 1920s promotional photo of a quartet that includes Frank Waldron), P. G. Lowery, Oscar Low, Jack Henshaw, Frank Bufaro, Arnie Sewell, Eddie Swanson, "Big Foot" Smitty, "Shelby," Moses Johnson, Tommy Thomas, Lee Caldwell, and Jim Juicy.

Since it was illegal, the roadhouse and after-hours scene where most of these musicians played was largely an underground affair, where only bold pleasure-seekers ventured. It was also where one was likely to find the hottest music, since that was where the progressive Black musicians played. As jazz became more popular locally, however, the music caught on with white musicians as well, and scores of more visible but usually less authentic bands cropped up. Throughout the 1920s white bands with pasted-down hair, wire-rimmed glasses, and starched collars, holding saxophones, banjos, and violins and often calling themselves "syncopators" or "serenaders," were continually described as "jazz" groups on the entertainment pages of the *Seattle Times*. Jackie Souders, who would become one of Seattle's leading "sweet" bandleaders, was billing himself in 1921 at the Pantages as "Offering Jazz Music in the College Style." The white orchestra conductor Jules Buffano, playing at the Seattle Theatre (which later became the Paramount), described himself as the "Crown Jewel of Jazz." The Del Monte Blue Dogs, the J & V Syncopators, the Highway Pavilion Dance Orchestra, the Goodrich Silvertown Cord Orchestra, Warren Anderson's Symphonic Dance Orchestra, the Rainier Serenaders, the Charmed Land Serenaders, the Stevens Dance Orchestra, the Honeymoon Serenaders, Gene Paul and his Seattle Sax Band, and Shorty Clough's Melody Boys are some of the other bands that gave themselves "jazz" billing.

How much jazz these bands played is open to question. Hot, improvised jazz, said white drummer Chet Ramage, was mainly confined to the speakeasies where Black musicians performed, in the clubs along Jackson Street and the roadhouses. "Local 493 had most of the jazz players," he said. There has been perennial controversy among jazz enthusiasts over the authenticity of this or that band. In the 1920s and early 1930s the terms of the argument were expressed as the opposition between "sweet" bands and "hot" bands, though such a distinction was often more a matter of taste than musical detail. Among early jazz fans, a "sweet" band was one that played satiny, lilting rhythms for ballroom dancing, with an eye to variety. A "hot" band, however, would play a good portion of jump rhythms, with lots of surprising solos and blues feeling. The new rhythms of jazz and ragtime were originally incorporated into popular dances for the masses by Irene and Vernon Castle, just before World War I. The Castles took the hot rhythms of the "animal dances"—the Texas Tommy, turkey trot, and fox-trot—and domesticated them for the middle class. In the 1910s ballroom and taxi-dance establishments sprang up all over the United States and Europe to accommodate this new "social dancing" craze. By the 1920s, though, the excitement of these rhythms had worn off or been watered down. That's why when bandleaders like Fletcher Henderson came along in the 1920s with a harder-hitting, hotter style, jazz fanatics turned up their noses at the "ricky-ticky" two-step feeling of the hotel bands.

Some of the "syncopating" hotel groups probably played pretty hot jazz. Of all of them, the Del Monte Blue Dogs had the most success as a touring item. The members were from Seattle, except pianist John Murphy. The other players were John Ashton, violin, banjo, sax, and leader; Frosty Hedden, trumpet; Joe Adams, saxophone; and Mike Mallia, drums. In 1928 the Dogs hit the road on the Keith Orpheum circuit; an Ohio reviewer described them as "red hot." The year 1929 found the Blue Dogs playing in New York and Chicago. The next year, under the name the Ashton-Hedden Blue Dogs, they were home, minus Murphy but with pianist Wally Anderson and bassist Clyde Willison. Anderson later led a "tenor band" (a sweet band with three tenor saxophones) at the Olympic Hotel and worked at the Magic Inn behind the Will Mastin Trio, with Sammy Davis Jr.

The song list for the Goodrich Silvertown Cord Orchestra suggests that this band, like the Blue Dogs, was genuinely inspired by the jazz hits of the day. Listed under "Jazz" on the *Seattle Times*'s weekly "radio page," they played "There'll Be Some Changes Made" and "Popular Street Blues." The J & V Syncopators listed "Copenhagen" and "Arkansas Blues" in their repertory and advertised, "You'll love these Harmony Hounds." Groups who promoted themselves as "dogs" or "hounds" and played blues generally had some connection to jazz. Chet Ramage, who played with white drummer Shorty Clough, said Clough's Melody Boys were jazz-oriented and that Clough was a "very fine drummer" who taught at Hopper Kelly's music store. In 1929, Shorty and his boys played Seattle's Bungalow, with "Tia Juana Slim" Pratt, Jim Murphy, and Perry Ridder. *Musicland*, the official newsletter of the white musicians' union, referred nostalgically to the Bungalow as a place where "the boys played their hearts out." This language, as well as the self-consciously jazzy nicknames of Shorty's outfit, suggests that Shorty's group played some authentic jazz. A couple of other white sidemen have been singled out by observers as having jazz chops. One was trumpeter Paul Clifford, who played at the State Theatre (later the Rivoli); another was guitarist Virgil Ireland, who came to Seattle from Kansas City to work on the pleasure cruises. Ireland was described by one musician as an advanced guitarist in the style of Eddie Lang, who played single-string solos and some "chord jazz."

One important white group that certainly played bona fide "hot" music in the Dixieland vein during the 1920s was Barney's Jazz Band, led by drummer Clarence Barney. Barney was born with a distortion of the upper spine and grew up in the 1910s in Sedro-Woolley, a rural town in the upper Skagit Valley, about fifty miles south of the US-Canada border. In 1924 he brought an enthusiastic bunch of guys from the northern counties into Dick Parker's Highway Pavilion, on Bothell Way, just outside the Seattle city limits. Chet Ramage recalled Barney's Jazz Band as an extremely popular five-piece that commanded high prices. Barney's sidemen included the hot Sedro-Woolley clarinetist Clarence Thue; Lou Lillpop on piano; a trumpet man from Anacortes named Charlie; Clarence Smith, from Mount Vernon, on banjo; Bellingham violinist Art Thal, later replaced by Dave Burnham, from Anacortes; and Bill Stendal, also from Sedro-Woolley, on vocals.

Clarinetist Doug Finch, who grew up with Barney and Stendal in Sedro-Woolley and subbed in the band, played saxophone and clarinet with another jazz group, the Washington Ramblers, throughout the 1920s.

Another white bandleader who had a great deal of influence on local acceptance and understanding of jazz was the stately Jules Buffano, the orchestra conductor at the Paramount Theater. Buffano was another musician who had worked with Fate Marable's Mississippi riverboat bands and was a successful leader in Chicago before moving to Seattle in 1928 to open the newly constructed Seattle Theatre at Ninth Avenue and Pine Street. On opening night Buffano conducted a show called "The Mikado of Jazz," written by Paul Ash. According to Palmer Johnson, Buffano was not only an impressive conductor but also a "fine jazz pianist" with a strong left hand. He spent the years 1937 through 1939 in Hollywood, then returned to Seattle, where he worked at the Town Ranch and the Senator Ballroom.

During Buffano's heyday theater orchestras were a popular form of entertainment. They played everything from light classics to jazz, similar to the fare one might hear at an outdoor band shell. In that era, as opposed to today, live music was a primary and prevalent source. There were musicians playing everywhere. Jackie Souders was at the Olympic Hotel, Sam Wineland at the Coliseum, Hermie King at the Palace Hip, Otto Crowhurst at the Pantages, Leonard Hagen at the Blue Mouse, William Winder at the Egyptian, George Lipschultz at the Fifth Avenue, Francesco Longo or Liborious Hauptmann at the Columbia, Charles Burnett at the Orpheum, and Henri Damski at the Camlin. Many of the theaters employed organists. Bands also played at the burlesque theaters, roadhouses, and nightclubs as well as in radio orchestras.

"We had 680 members and 610 of them were working steady," said Chet Ramage, who joined the white musicians' local in 1926 and served as president for many years. "We had theaters. We had music in the lobby of the Olympic Hotel. We had ballrooms. The guys could make a living." It was from this vast pool of musicians that the budding white jazz players on the underground scene arose. Many of them worked for Vic Meyers at one time or another, the most famous of the pops bandleaders and one of the most eccentric figures in Washington history. Meyers and his notorious venue, the Rose Room of the Butler Hotel at Second Avenue and James Street, with its chandeliers and bootleg whiskey, would go down in the memories of white Seattleites as the very life of the Jazz Age. Technically Vic was a drummer, but he was known primarily

The Vic Meyers Orchestra.

as a front man. His orchestra featured elaborate saxophone and brass sections as well as tuba, banjo, violin, piano, and drums. Joe Darensbourg played with Meyers for a short time (on saxophone), as did Ramage.

Vic Meyers was a charismatic figure who was leading his own dance orchestras in the Seattle area by 1922. He recorded several sides for Columbia and Brunswick, the latter of which included "Shake It and Break It" in 1923, the earliest commercial record produced in Seattle. Meyers also had a hand in composing "Ada," with Seattle songwriters Harold Weeks and Danny Cann. In the early 1920s the dapper bandleader toured his men down the West Coast to Monterey and San Diego, California, then crossed the country to New York's Arcadia Ballroom and several venues around Chicago. When Meyers returned to Seattle in 1926, he found himself a genuine celebrity. His band was regularly aired live on Seattle station KFOA, and in 1932 his orchestra became the first in Seattle to be broadcast over national radio, on Walter Winchell's NBC show.

The Butler Hotel was a college hangout where couples danced and drank and, on the night of the Apple Cup (the University of Washington versus Washington State University football game), occasionally shacked up in one of the dollar-a-night rooms upstairs. Meyers and the proprietor of the hotel, John Savage, flaunted the new flapper culture of the 1920s in the face of Seattle's authorities. They did not go unnoticed. One of the curious anomalies of Seattle's Roaring Twenties—and even later decades as well—is that while the city was, on the one hand, excitedly embracing each new trend of the Jazz Age in a vast underground of nightclubs and hot spots, on the other hand, it was continually passing laws and regulations that spoiled the party. With almost predictable regularity, one administration would encourage what came to be known as a "tolerance policy," under which nightclubs flourished, and the next would emphasize reform, passing increasingly convoluted laws against drinking, gambling, dancing, music, and cabarets.

This was an ambivalence deeply rooted in the city's psyche and sometimes exemplified in a single person. The notorious opportunist Hiram Gill, for example, was first elected mayor on a "wide open" ticket, then reelected as a reform candidate. During the 1920s council member and then mayor (1926–28) Bertha Landes waged a continuous war against not only alcohol but dancing, which she apparently found disgusting, much to the financial chagrin of ballroom and hotel operators. In Seattle the celebrated Jazz Age of hedonism and permissiveness was a kind of post-pioneer hysteria that delighted in sophistication at the same time as it rejected it. The same forces would appear to have been in play in 1943, when the city enacted a punishing 20 percent admissions tax on entertainment establishments (later reduced to 5 percent), and again in 1985, with the repressive Teen Dance Ordinance, which was not repealed until 2002.

The first raid on the Butler Hotel was in 1918. Over the next eleven years the Seattle Police Department and federal authorities waged war on the hotel, citing the establishment on average once every two months, for everything from illegal sales of alcohol to dancing on Sunday. Though other music venues were harassed during this period, the Butler's size and visibility made it a favorite target, particularly for the redoubtable council member Landes. In 1921 she began a campaign to give the city more control over the taxi-dance establishments, citing that such places attracted the "wrong kind of girl." Judge J. T. Ronald, who backed Landes, agreed. "There is a potential evil to society in all dance halls," he argued. The 1923 Landes Ordinance, as it came to be known, outlawed taxi dances and required regular dance halls to hire a police-department matron as a chaperone. It also specified a lengthy inspection process, a nightly closing time of twelve-thirty, and draconian control to the city in regard to licensing. The effects of this ordinance would be felt as late as the 1950s, when matrons were still legally required at certain kinds of dance halls.

In June 1922 the Alhambra, the Butler Hotel, the Bungalow (the one in town), and the Lodge all came under attack for not conforming to Landes's idea of what a dance hall should be. The following year, the Butler was hit again for allowing dancing on Sunday, about which there was yet another, older city ordinance. In 1929, Mayor Frank Edwards, following Landes's lead, closed the ten-cent dance halls in the South End, calling them a "moral menace," although they were permitted to reopen, thanks to pressure from the musicians' union. John Savage, operator of the Butler, was a survivor. He charmed the press into treating his various transgressions as harmless fun. Vic Meyers, ever the prankster, fell into the scofflaw mood. When the feds filtered into the Butler to make arrests, the bandleader would strike up a jaunty version of "How Dry I Am." The Butler was finally padlocked as a "nuisance" on May 7, 1929. Its demise, however, had no dramatic effect on the career of either Savage or Meyers. Savage moved over to the Trianon Ballroom, and Meyers opened his own club (named after himself, of course) upstairs at 2221 Fourth Avenue. For a year Club Victor kept alive the spirit of the Rose Room, which the newspapers described as the culture of "jazz and whoopee," until the feds closed it in late June 1930.

Undaunted, Meyers moved to a new location on Sixth Avenue. But by this time other forces were at work in the bandleader's life. In 1932, on a whim, he ran for mayor of Seattle, poking fun at the political process in a way that has ever been appealing to Northwesterners. When all the candidates were invited to speak at a luncheon, Vic arrived dressed as Mahatma Gandhi, leading a goat. He lost the mayoral race, but to the horror of his sponsors he was shortly elected lieutenant governor. Meyers hung on to his post for four consecutive terms, retired from music (though he kept Club Victor until it closed in 1936), and became a noted authority on parliamentary procedure. He also fathered Sun Lakes State Park and, more relevant to the story of Washington jazz, led the fight in the 1937 state legislature against a bill that would have made interracial marriage illegal in Washington, as it was in Oregon. Ironically, in the 1960s Meyers took a political dive in a scandal over an antigambling petition, just the sort of issue he had spent a lifetime laughing at. He died in 1992.

As a bandleader, Meyers was cut out of the mold of the famous Paul Whiteman. Both men understood that the white public liked jazz but perceived it as music from the gutter, so they cloaked its hot rhythms and raucous self-expression in phony orchestral sophistication. Most of the public liked its jazz thus disguised, just as it had preferred minstrel shows by white actors in blackface. Although Whiteman could sound pompous and stilted, he hired some of the greatest jazz musicians who ever lived—Bix Beiderbecke, Joe Venuti, Jack Teagarden, and Jimmy Dorsey—and won over a white middle-class world which at that time would not have dreamed of setting foot in a speakeasy. He also commissioned George Gershwin to write *Rhapsody in Blue*.

Whiteman was a huge celebrity, one of the few jazz bandleaders to cross over to the "middle of the road." The Seattle papers gossiped over his impending arrival. The day before his six-day appearance at the Civic Auditorium (where McCaw Hall now stands), a dinner-dance was arranged at the Spanish Ballroom of the Olympic Hotel (now the Four Seasons). The governor, the mayor, and their wives attended, along with the rest of Puget Sound high society. Whiteman's every move was noted, as he drove through the winding, mountainous roads from Los Angeles behind the wheel of his V-16 Cadillac. The *Seattle Times* noted that the Rhythm Boys, with Spokanites Bing Crosby and Al Rinker, were in the show. Mildred Bailey was almost certainly in this performance as well, although she is not mentioned. Three thousand people attended Whiteman's first show. Wrote the reviewer for Local 76's *Musicland*:

> Jazz so presented that it tore down the prejudices of even the most cynical was offered Seattle. . . . Outstanding among the numbers was the interpretation of George Gershwin's "Rhapsody in Blue." This piece, which has been heralded as one of the most significant works of American composers, was presented with such masterly finesse and expert attention to coloring and cadence as would have been worthy of a symphonic ensemble. Swinging from the sublime to the ridicule were the antics of an amazing trick fiddler, Wilbur Hall. Cutting ludicrous capers, and deftly juggling his bow while playing, he indulged in clowning acrobatics and danced a measure or two without missing a note. . . . Clever stuff.

The Meyers/Whiteman model of the jazzman belongs decidedly to the 1920s—carefree, showy, pleased with its own naughtiness, a little stiff, and still tied to the grandiosity of early-twentieth-century ringmasters. In the next jazz period, the swing era, the music would be looser, bluesier, immensely more popular, and quite a bit less concerned with concocting links to classical music. In Seattle some of the foundations for the new era had already been laid. Musicians were moving in, the state was welcoming African Americans, and a jazz tradition had been established in after-hours joints and major theaters.

In 1928 the city went on a building spree that would be important to the future of local jazz. All in one year, the Civic Auditorium, the Trianon Ballroom, McElroy's Spanish Ballroom, and the Seattle Theatre rose on the skyline. These venues would become the focus of the swing craze, providing thousands of dancers with the strains of Gene Krupa, Tommy Dorsey, Harry James, Jimmie Lunceford, and the rest. Even more significant than the construction boom, Prohibition was on its way out. On November 7, 1933, the liquor ban was finally repealed. Bashes were held all over town. At the Marine Club, the Mardi Gras (the new name for Doc Hamilton's), Ciro's, the New Yorker, the Little Silver Slipper, Bill Hengely's Argonaut, Don's Alaska Bar, and the Alhambra crowds merrily lifted their glasses, hailing the end of the days of federal agents, bootleggers, and bathtub gin. In the same year Washington passed the Steele Act, legalizing the sale of beer and wine—but not hard liquor—by the glass and creating the Washington State Liquor Control Board.

Still, the swing era would be slow to take root in Seattle. The Great Depression cut deeply into the number and scope of venues, and the state's Calvinist reluctance to legalize whiskey prolonged the speakeasy culture of the 1920s. The 1930s would be a scuffling era for jazz musicians.

3 Combos and Dives

The Depression Years

THE GREAT DEPRESSION HIT Seattle with full force in 1933. For jazz musicians things were slow, if sweet. Most of the action was in small clubs, played by combos struggling to get by on tips. Marion Fulmighter and "Baby" Borders were the top act in town, working at the Black and Tan. The most intriguing musician on the scene was pianist Julian Henson, who would later have a tremendous influence on pianist Jimmy Rowles. An almost completely unknown player who transmitted a great deal of jazz tradition during his two decades in Seattle but never received any recognition for it, Henson was emblematic of the "unsung local" whose career thrived out of the limelight. A self-taught player who never learned to read music, Henson was born in 1914 in Omaha, Nebraska, spent his early childhood in Minneapolis, Minnesota, and started to play piano by ear after moving to Portland, Oregon, when he was fourteen. In the 1930s he came under the spell of Art Tatum and began to copy the master's intricate, filigreed improvisations and complicated harmonic developments. Henson had perfect pitch, which helped him find on the keyboard the melodies he heard in his head.

When he was eighteen, Henson struck out for Seattle and, except for some time in Minneapolis in the late 1930s, remained there until 1948, when he returned to Portland. In Seattle he connected immediately with the city's early generation of Black performers—Joe Darensbourg, Wayne and Jimmy Adams, Baby Borders, Marion Fulmighter, Creon Thomas, Frank Waldron, and others. Henson himself worked the Blue Rose, an intimate, two-room club in a house on Fourteenth Avenue South, just south of Yesler Way. The Blue Rose was owned by "Big Lewis" Richardson, who poured liquor in the kitchen and brought it out to his customers, who were seated on the club's three davenports. During Henson's break Big Lewis cranked up the jukebox.

When he arrived in Seattle, Henson was probably the most advanced pianist in town. He played in a flowery, ornamental style that showcased intricate runs and arpeggios, modulations from key to key within one tune, and complicated chord extensions. Henson credited Archie Jackson, the Saint Louis–born pianist who worked with Frank Waldron at the Nanking, as one of his early mentors:

> Archie was a power piano player, a big guy with great big hands. He played those big tenths [an interval spanning ten white keys]. Anything I'd ask him, he'd show me. Because my hands were small, I learned to play tenths between this [ring] finger and my thumb. I used to push my hands against the piano keys until I got my hand stretched out.
>
> There were so many marvelous piano players and they were all very open and generous. There was a guy named Ralph Richardson. He was fantastic. He was from some small town in Washington—Yakima, I think. He was better than most.

Henson also named Palmer Johnson, Oscar Holden, and Princess Belle as among the finest pianists in town. Princess, whom Evelyn Williamson and most other singers in the area counted as their favorite accompanist, was reputed to be a Maori, from New Zealand. She dressed "like a schoolteacher" and played exclusive places downtown—a "real elegant lady," in Henson's words. Joe Darensbourg, who remembered working at a roadhouse with her, said Princess was the girlfriend of Los Angeles bandleader Curtis Mosby. Drummer Duke Turner said he played in San Francisco with Princess Belle in a band led by Elmer Fain.

But for Henson there was more to life on Jackson Street than piano players. The district was also home, providing a world of rich street life in a safe, relaxed, multiracial atmosphere that is hard to imagine today. The neighborhood was a great cultural stew of immigrant groups, dominated by Jewish and Japanese populations. Black residents were the next-largest group, with Italians and Chinese close behind. Japanese businesses flourished (although most were later destroyed, when Japanese and Japanese Americans in the Pacific Northwest were forcibly removed to concentration camps during World War II). Those many businesses included beer parlors, hardware stores, movie theaters, and restaurants.

A block-long Filipino business district evolved along South King Street between Sixth Avenue South and South Maynard Avenue to serve what in 1930 was the largest Filipino population in the United States. A journalist visiting from the Philippines described it as Seattle's "Filipino barrio." The Manila Serenaders were active at the Manila Dance Hall, a taxi-dance establishment. Filipino saxophonist Frank Osias often played with the Moonlight Serenaders at Rizal Hall, named for Filipino patriot José Rizal. A taxi-dance establishment located in 1933 at the corner of South King Street and Sixth Avenue South, the Rizal closed in 1937 when owner Demetrio Ente moved the club to Stockton, California. Thanks to Charlie Beale, in 1943 the club reopened. In 1945 saxophonist Tootie Boyd led a group there called Tootie Boyd's Rizal Club Band, which suggests that the club was open at least through the end of the war.

The Tokiwa Hotel, at the corner of Maynard Avenue and South Jackson Street, was home to many jazz musicians, some of whom were stragglers from vaudeville shows that had crashed in Seattle. Rooms at the Tokiwa were only a dollar or two a week, which made survival fairly easy for a young musician. Despite hard times, and in decided contrast to the impressions of the teen-aged Phil Moore (related in chapter 2), Henson remembered life along Jackson Street as fairly idyllic:

> Most of the musicians who lived at the Tokiwa owed them money, but they wouldn't put you out. You could go to these Japanese restaurants and get twenty-cent meals. You could have four or five different kinds of bread in there. Then down on Skid Road, they had some places where for ten cents you could get some great beef stew. Good meals. Most of the entertainers, they'd get off and they'd go down there. Then there was Bob and Freda's. They sold beans for ten cents a bowl up there on 12th Avenue, right off Jackson. Everybody went to Bob and Freda's to get some beans. They sure were good, too. Out on the street, there was a guy they called "Whistling Jim." He was always whistling and he sold hot tamales out of a cart. They'd cost ten cents apiece.
>
> My dad was a bartender at the 411 Club, so he had a lot of friends. I was on my own, but every once in a while, I'd go in there and he'd say, "Kid, you doin' all right?" And he'd hand me a ten. Hell, that'd pay my room rent for a month. It was a town-and-a-half, man. It had so much going for it. You could get drunk and lay down in the middle of the street all night long and nobody'd bother you! Nothing happening 'til after twelve o'clock, then it came alive! All night, people running from club to club. It was an after-hours circus.

Alto saxophone man Marshal Royal also fondly recalled the family atmosphere Seattle provided musicians in those days:

The Tokiwa Hotel, South Jackson Street and Maynard Avenue South, 1937.

> They were a different type of people up in Seattle. You had a lot of fun. They were nice, they were cordial. I'm not just speaking of Black people. I'm talking about the Chinese guys that owned the cab companies and things. They were our buddies. Everybody was just in it for a family. Like the Mar boys, big-time tong [gang] people out of Fresno, we had a ball. After we finished our job, they would have a midnight picture at the Atlas Theatre, open all night long. You could go in there and tell the owner what picture you wanted and he'd have it for you two or three days later.

But out on the road, making it as a jazz musician during the Depression was still a scuffle. Joe Darensbourg's peripatetic career during those years is fairly suggestive of the unpredictable and often dangerous enterprises a journeyman musician had to undertake to survive hard times. Darensbourg had a run of hard luck that reads like a Woody Guthrie talking blues. In 1931 the clarinetist took a trio to Green River, Wyoming, where he was stranded. In Billings, Montana, he was hit by a truck, which put him in a cast for almost a year with a broken back and punctured lung. When he developed tuberculosis, he spent the winter taking the cure in Phoenix. Feeling better, he played with dance bands and with a Mexican band. In Prescott, Arizona, he pumped a player piano while playing clarinet. But the job dried up and he was stranded again.

In 1932, Darensbourg was back in Seattle, first with the Genessee Street Shufflers, then with Oscar Holden at the Blue Rose, and later at the Black Elks

Club, then on Eighteenth Avenue and East Madison Street, with Zelma Winslow, Bill Hoy on drums, Bill Page on guitar, and Bill Trent and Oscar Low on vocals. A multiplicity of jobs, both musical and nonmusical, followed: he did a stint in a food distribution warehouse, cooked in the galley of a crab boat, taught kids through a Works Progress Administration (WPA) "make work" program, ran his own Italian restaurant in Seattle, and made several trips to the Far East and Portland, Oregon, on cruise ships. In Asia, Darensbourg confessed, the band bought cymbals and smuggled them back inside the bass drum, selling them back home for an exorbitant profit. In 1935 things picked up for Joe. He landed a regular gig on Kitsap Lake (near Bremerton, Washington) at a place called Houghton's (later the Shellback Inn), sometimes working with a barrelhouse pianist known to posterity only as "Big Foot Smitty." It was on the Bremerton ferry that Darensbourg met his future employer, Louis Armstrong, who was delighted to discover "another home boy" way up in the Pacific Northwest.

> He [Armstrong] was going over there with his band to play a one-nighter. . . . It just happened all of us was on the ferry boat together. I ran into "Fireman" George—old "Pops" Foster—who was there drinking beer, so I says, "What the hell you doin' on this boat?" and he says, "Well I'm here with Pops, with Louis." He seemed surprised to see me. He said, "Would you like to meet Pops?" I hadn't seen Fireman George since '28 and the days with Papa Mutt. He took me over to where Louis was eating and, right off from there, Louis started calling me "another home boy."

Back in Seattle, Darensbourg went to work at Doc Hamilton's, where he played with saxophonist and vocalist Tootie Boyd, another struggling musician. Originally from Ellensburg, Washington, Boyd settled in Seattle in 1935 and worked with Phil Moore and Herman Whaley in the early 1930s. Boyd modeled his tenor saxophone playing on the great Illinois Jacquet and worked with Palmer Johnson and the early Seattle swing bandleader Al Pierre. "Tootie sang beautifully," asserted Palmer Johnson. "He used to sing 'I'm going to move way out on the outskirts of town. . . .' What a voice he had!" Boyd often took groups east of the mountains for work, or into California, Oregon, or Vancouver, British Columbia. One of the steadiest gigs the saxophonist secured was at the Shantytown, a country roadhouse near Bellingham, Washington. He held a regular job there for over a year, working with drummer Junie Bradford, "Banjoski" Adams, and bassist Buddy Groves. Working conditions were less than ideal. "They had

Combo at the Shantytown, 1937, near Bellingham, Washington. *Left to right:* Junie Bradford, "Banjoski" Adams, (Lee?) Philips, Buddy "Moose" Groves.

pianos in there that you'd come home bloody from playing," remembered Julian Henson. "The keys'd be all jagged. I remember I was playing there one time, playing 'Willow Weep for Me,' and I used to do a gliss on that and I did like that right along the edge of the keys and I sliced my finger right to the bone. The only piano in town with red keys!"

Darensbourg left Seattle in 1936. After a brief reunion of the Genessee Street Shufflers in 1938, he took bassist-guitarist Bill Rinaldi, pianist Jack Henshaw, and guitarist Virgil Ireland out to Grand Coulee, in eastern Washington, where construction forces were completing the great dam on the Columbia River. They found work at a rough-and-ready saloon called the Silver Dollar and played after hours at another joint.

Far away from the Shantytown and the Columbia River, in Kansas City and New York, jazz style was changing dramatically during the Great Depression. On the models of Fletcher Henderson and Bennie Moten the big-band format developed, with brass and reed sections trading riffs in a dynamic call-and-response pattern. Rhythm took on a loping, lighter four-four feel. Written arrangements became more important, as bands got bigger and each searched for a signature style. Individual soloing became more complex. This new big-band style of swing music didn't enter the public imagination at large until 1935, when on-location radio broadcasts by Benny Goodman lit a musical brushfire that wasn't put out until the middle of World War II. But "swing" had been taking shape in Black communities since the late 1920s. In Seattle, swing caught on, but for a variety of reasons it was played in small combos rather than big bands through most of the 1930s. Earl Whaley, an alto saxophonist and bandleader from the Bay Area, led an early West Coast swing band, the Red Hot Syncopators, at Seattle's Broadway and Finnish Halls in 1932. He also worked in a variety of combos with Palmer Johnson, Joe Darensbourg, and Evelyn Williamson. In 1934, Whaley took a bona fide swing band that included Palmer Johnson to Shanghai, China.

But the first real harbinger of modern swing to reach the Northwest was Gene Coy, an Amarillo, Texas, bandleader and drummer who, according to Darensbourg, may have been living in Seattle as early as 1929, working at the Butler Hotel (normally reserved for white musicians). Coy also appeared at Washington Hall in 1932, but his name begins to appear regularly in the Black press in 1933. His hot, nine-piece unit came from the heart of the Kansas City/Houston belt, where the foundations for the loping, blues-drenched new music were being laid. Coy had been associated with some of the most illustrious names developing in swing. The great saxophonist Ben Webster had worked with him in Amarillo in 1929 and 1930. Bassist Walter Page (with Count Basie) remembered Gene Coy and his Happy Black Aces from this period as "really jumping." John Lewis, the influential pianist who would later found the Modern Jazz Quartet, recalled being impressed by the band and the playing of Coy's wife, Marge, whose piano, he said, sounded like that of the great Mary Lou Williams. The Coy band found its way to San Diego, Los Angeles, and Tijuana in 1932, and on January 5, 1933, the *Northwest Enterprise* announced breathlessly: "Coming to Seattle! Gene Coy and His Eleven Black Aces, famous broadcasting and recording band. . . . At Washington Hall. 'You'll Rock. You'll Roar, You'll Holler for More. They're Hotter Than Fire!'"

Al Turay, a white guitarist and bass player born in Seattle, remembered Coy and the Black Aces as "the closest thing we had around here to jazz—along the lines of Jimmie Lunceford and Bennie Moten, Kansas City–style." Palmer Johnson concurred, singling out the Coy band as the one superior, up-to-date group in the area at a time when Seattle was decidedly behind the times stylistically.

The Coy band, which changed its name to the "Nine Rhythm Racketeers" while in Seattle, booked a string of engagements at Finnish Hall and Broadway Hall from January through March 1933, then took its "entrancing, enthralling syncopating" music to Portland, Oregon. Coy later returned to Seattle for an extended period, from 1937 through 1941, working often at Finnish Hall—once on a show featuring the Duke Ellington Orchestra—as well the Black and Tan, where Coy led the house band for several months.

During this first Seattle period, Coy picked up his most important soloist—the great and almost completely forgotten tenor saxophonist Dick Wilson. Originally from Illinois, Wilson had lived in Seattle since he was five years old and attended Broadway High School, though he dropped out in 1929 to pursue music. He was a handsome young man with reddish curly hair, a light complexion, and a thin mustache—"a great lady-killer," according to bandleader Andy Kirk. Wilson started out as a pianist and vocalist, but in Seattle took saxophone lessons from Frank Waldron and Joe Darensbourg. Darensbourg told the story like this:

> Around this time I got to know a kid who would probably have been the greatest of all tenor men if he'd lived. This was Dick Wilson. His father died when he was real young and he was raised by his mother, a nice iron-willed woman. . . . When Dick was about seventeen years old his mother asked me if I would teach him saxophone. I didn't really want to be bothered with pupils, but I said if he came over to the house I'd give him some pointers, just as a favor. I started giving him lessons on alto sax. When he started playing he kinda copied my style a little, but he had an individual sound even then. He was just a natural. A year after I taught him he was a better saxophone player than me.

Wilson played with Darensbourg's band briefly, then with Dick's mother's permission, Joe sent the young sax man off to Portland to apprentice with pianist Don Anderson's big band, using Joe's tenor sax. Anderson was not unknown to Seattle jazz fans. Back in 1928, Jimmy Adams had flown to Portland to pick him up as a last-minute substitute for a Seattle gig. Wilson returned to Seattle a mature player, rejoining Darensbourg at the Jungle Temple No. 1 in a combo with Jimmy Adams (trumpet), Babe Hackley (piano), and Baby Borders (drums). The band reportedly played a style that later would be identified with John Kirby—understated, small-group combo swing—and broadcast on the radio

A combo at the Jungle Temple No. 2, ca. 1931. *Left to right:* Dick Wilson (playing clarinet), Baby Borders, Oscar Hurst, Freddy Vaughn, unknown.

twice a week. In January 1933, Wilson was directing a band at the Black and Tan called Bill Roberts Rhythm Racketeers. Later that year, Wilson left town with the Gene Coy band. A year later, he joined Zack Whyte, followed by Andy Kirk's Clouds of Joy in 1936.

Andy Kirk had one of the best of the Kansas City bands. His biggest hit was a ballad that featured vocalist Pha Terrell on "Until the Real Thing Comes Along," but Kirk swung like mad on other recordings. It was during Wilson's tenure with Kirk that the saxophonist recorded the dozen or so solos on which his reputation rests. "Lotta Sax Appeal" (1936), "Christopher Columbus" (1936), "Moten Swing" (1936), "Wednesday Night Hop" (1936), "All the Jive Is Gone" (1936), "In the Groove" (1937), and "Little Miss" (1940), among others, show Wilson as a soloist with a light but substantial and highly personal sound, advanced harmonic concept, a genius for melody, and a faultless execution that put him in a class with Chu Berry, Don Byas, and Herschel Evans. Wilson also recorded four sides to good advantage with a small group spin-off of Kirk's band led by Mary Lou Williams called Six Men and a Girl. Like his Kirk bandmate Byas, Wilson occupied that interesting transitional style between the gruff, vertical, diatonic approach of Coleman Hawkins and the more loping, chromatic, "modern" style of Lester Young. Darensbourg claimed that Byas confessed in a conversation in Paris that he had been influenced by Dick Wilson. Albert McCarthy, the prominent swing-era historian, casts Wilson as "one of the five or six best tenor saxophone soloists of the swing era." Dizzy Gillespie, in a 1989 interview, emphatically agreed: "Dick Wilson was a bitch. . . . Stylist, too, creator of a style of sax. You know, not very many musicians followed in his footsteps, or learned his style, but he was right up there with Lester Young and Herschel Evans. He was considered one of the best. The head guys then were Coleman Hawkins and then Chu Berry. Coleman Hawkins was the king, but Dick Wilson and Chu Berry, they were the crown princes."

Wilson returned to Seattle at least once, in 1941, billed as "Seattle's own Dick Wilson," when the Kirk band performed at the Senator Ballroom. Photographer

Al Smith caught Wilson standing up in the saxophone section, wearing sunglasses and playing one of his memorable solos. It would be one of Wilson's last choruses. A few months later he died at age thirty of a lingering disease that some report was tuberculosis; Darensbourg says it was syphilis contracted from a prostitute in Canada. Wilson was the most important swing figure to come out of Washington State, and his early death was understandably a blow to his friends. Darensbourg described him as "one of the guys I sincerely liked in this business." Palmer Johnson remembered Wilson as "a soft and easygoing guy. . . . He was very nice, always happy and smiling."

Wilson was not the only member of Gene Coy's band with Seattle connections to achieve notoriety. Alvin "Junior" Raglin, who later joined the Duke Ellington Orchestra, also played with Coy's Eleven Black Aces. Raglin and trombonist Andy Duryea apparently left the band during one of its Seattle gigs, because both their names begin to appear on Seattle combo announcements in 1938. Marshal Royal says the Coy band was falling apart at this point: "They came to town raggedy as a nickel mop. They weren't making too much money, so they broke up and went all different kind of ways. Junior Raglin was the guitar player. After they got stranded, that's when Junior took up bass playing." For a time, Raglin and Duryea both worked for Palmer Johnson at the Congo Club in a sextet with local tenor saxophonist Aaron Davis and drummer Gilbert "Punkin" Austin. Raglin, an exceptional talent, was born in 1917 in Omaha, Nebraska, where he started on guitar. Twenty years later, he was working with Coy at Seattle's Ubangi Club, one of the Jackson Street district's most glamorous Black-owned nightclubs. In the words of Palmer Johnson, who played with Raglin in Coy's band for that engagement, "Junior could play guitar and walk the dog on a bass." Al Turay concurred: "Junior Raglin was a real great bass player. He was playing bass when I would come into the 411 Club with my guitar. He was also just one bitch of a guitar player. God, he was just an amazing guitar player. So he'd play guitar, a Gibson L6, which he loved to play, and I'd play bass. We'd switch off like that."

Raglin at this time was said to have been playing a two-necked guitar with bass strings on one neck and guitar strings on the other. Today this is not such an unusual instrument, but it was a rarity in the 1930s, perhaps the first one ever made. Raglin worked in Seattle for a couple of years with Palmer Johnson's sextet, in a duo with Seattle guitarist Milt Green, and in at least one gala jazz concert at the Metropolitan Theatre. Sometime after 1940, he went to Los Angeles and joined the Duke Ellington Orchestra, replacing Jimmy Blanton.

The Andy Kirk Band, with tenor saxophonist Dick Wilson (wearing sunglasses), Senator Ballroom, February 17, 1941.

Duke was based in Los Angeles from 1939 to 1941, recording and writing film scores and producing an original musical. In these years Jimmy Blanton was rewriting the book on jazz bass, extending the range of the instrument from its undifferentiated *thump! thump! thump! thump!* into a precise, single-note style, the signature for which became his melodic bass introduction to "Jack the Bear"—an announcement to the world that the bass fiddle would no longer be just a rhythm instrument. But the young Blanton was cursed with tuberculosis. He was hospitalized in late 1941 and died the following June. Raglin reportedly played beside Blanton for a few nights before joining the band. Soon he went into the recording studio with a close approximation of Blanton's sound. On December 2, 1941, Raglin recorded, with Duke, Billy Strayhorn's great new tunes "Raincheck" and "Chelsea Bridge," issued on Victor. Two weeks later he was back in Seattle playing with Ellington at the Palomar Theater. The *Seattle Times* noticed the performance: "Seattle's Alvin Raglin won great applause with his work on the fiddle in 'Jack the Bear.'"

Raglin spent the next four years with Ellington, appearing on more than thirty sides with the master. It is Raglin who plays on "Come Sunday," "The Blues," "Worksong," and other sections of Ellington's masterful suite *Black, Brown and Beige*, which debuted in Carnegie Hall. That's also Raglin on the 1945 recordings of "Black and Tan Fantasy" and "Caravan." During and after his stint with the Duke, Raglin went out with two of the small groups that spun off from the Ellington band—with Ray Nance in 1944 and Johnny Hodges in 1948. Raglin left the Ellington organization in 1945 and enjoyed some success. His picture appeared in *Life* magazine in 1944; *Esquire* gave him the New Star award in its 1946 jazz poll; and *DownBeat* pictured him leading his own trio at the Three Deuces, on New York's Fifty-Second Street, the same year. However, Raglin's career went downhill after this brief blast in the limelight. By the early 1950s he had moved to Boston and stopped performing. He died in 1956, reportedly from the effects of alcohol abuse.

Long after the departure of Dick Wilson and Junior Raglin from his band, Gene Coy remained a popular figure in Seattle, playing between 1938 and 1940 at Lyons' Music Hall, Finnish Hall, the Ubangi, and other venues. Coy's prolonged tenure in Seattle is important not only for the sidemen who flowed in and out of the band but because of the stylistic authenticity he offered young musicians. It is surprising, considering the availability of authentic stylists and the popularity of swing, that a Black swing band along the lines of Coy's did not emerge from Seattle. But one didn't. Why? It could be argued that Gerald Wells's ten-piece group, which played the Hi-Hatters club in 1931, took a step toward orchestrated, large-group jazz, but no one who heard this band is prepared to confirm that it played in a modern swing-era style. And Earl Whaley's group, although it evolved closer to the swing model, never grew beyond combo ambitions.

The most obvious reason Seattle remained a combo town without big bands in the 1930s was the small number of Black people in the region—just over four thousand in the entire state of Washington, with a total population of three million at the time. "You didn't have forty [Black] musicians in Seattle," commented Marshal Royal dryly. "Probably didn't have twenty. It was a very, very small scene." Add to the small population the fact that big-band leaders had to keep fifteen or twenty men on the payroll, week in and week out, and it becomes clearer why no large local band evolved. Besides, downtown venues were closed to Black musicians. Even if an enterprising Black bandleader had tried to start

Veteran Seattle jazz musician and Local 493 president Gerald Wells (*center*) plays tenor saxophone in a swing band with Joe Gauff (alto saxophone) and Len Brooks (piano), 1940s.

a big band, the lucrative jobs in the hotels and theaters would have been off-limits. Big bands would not develop in Seattle until the 1940s, when the Black population grew by thousands. In the meantime, Seattle's combo scene heated up, as the Great Depression passed into the more prosperous war years. From Fifth Avenue in the Chinatown–International District to Fourteenth Avenue in the Central Area, nightclubs and speakeasies such as the Ubangi, the 411 Club, Basin Street, Two Pals, the Green Dot, the Congo Club, the Little Harlem, the Black and Tan, and the Black Elks Club opened, reopened, or rebounded with the economic impetus of President Roosevelt's war-readiness plan.

According to Robert Wright, who worked as a bellhop for his uncle Noodles Smith at the Golden West Hotel, people flocked to these clubs from all over the city. "You could see as many white people on 12th and Jackson—at midnight—as you'd see on Third and Union in midday," he recalled. "They'd be wandering up and down Jackson Street, from Maynard Street to 14th." Though America didn't join the war until 1941, the president's strategy to make the United States the "arsenal for Europe" had boosted the shipping industry and secondary jobs related to it around Puget Sound. Young single men had begun to arrive in Seattle and Tacoma, a migration that would continue through 1945. Many of these men were looking not only for work but for a new home in the West. Some of them, like the Black railroad porters and waiters who had made Noodles Smith's ventures a success, were looking for a good time on the town and for the recreational music that was familiar to them—jazz and blues. They had money in their pockets.

Talented musicians came and went, dropping out of "name" bands, staying long enough to sow the seeds of new styles developing around the country, then packing up again. Local musicians in turn were picked up by well-known bands. This constant interchange between local and national scenes was the underground interstate highway system on which the jazz tradition traveled. One of the brightest travelers was Jimmy Rowles, a young musician from Spokane who would later become famous as a band pianist with Benny Goodman and Woody Herman, as a superb accompanist for Ella Fitzgerald, and finally as a trio artist of the first order. Born in 1918, Rowles was a gruff, gravel-voiced customer whose exterior belied the extreme sensitivity and subtlety of his music. An unabashed disciple of Lester Young and Art Tatum with a love for reworking harmonies, Rowles could find more beauty and intricacy in one simple popular tune than most musicians can find in a night. As a teenager in Spokane, Rowles was taken on as a protégé by a Blackfoot musician from Montana named Tom Brown who played tenor saxophone. Rowles remembered the day they met:

> I was fiddling around with the piano in the gym one afternoon, and this guy came around. He was a genius, I found out later. He was arranging for the pep band. He said, "That's not it." Then he left. One day he came [and played me] a Benny Goodman Trio record. It was "Someday Sweetheart." He put that on the windup and said, "Listen to this." And I heard Teddy Wilson playing. He says, "That's the way you're supposed to play, and I can help you." That quick, my whole life changed. I had a purpose. I didn't know what I was going to be, but I knew I wasn't going to be a lawyer.

For the rest of that year in Spokane, Rowles studied informally with Brown, listening to every note of Teddy Wilson, Art Tatum, and Fats Waller, and working with Brown in clubs. One night, when Les Hite's band came through town, Jimmy went backstage and played for Marshal Royal, who at that time was Hite's alto saxophonist. Royal counseled, "I think you could do well, but you've gotta get out of here. Go to Seattle first. You can learn in Seattle. Then come to L.A."

Rowles happily took Royal's advice, telling his stepfather he wanted to study pre-law at the University of Washington. That fall, with his portable record player in tow, Rowles found a room in a Seattle boardinghouse and enrolled at the university. He attended one lecture—"It was in anthropology, I remember"—and promptly hitched a ride from a roommate to Jackson Street. "It was like the beginning of a new, whole life," Rowles recalled. "In Spokane there was nothing like this. This was a city. And it was right at Seattle's almost peak period." For a young pianist like Rowles, the Jackson Street combo scene actually was preferable to a big-band milieu, since in small groups he could learn to improvise and develop his own style. That first night in 1937, he heard Gene Coy at the Black and Tan—but he was much more interested in the solo style of a twenty-three-year-old Kansas City tenor saxophonist named Aaron Davis, who came on for a jam session after Coy had finished. Rowles described their first meeting: "This guy sounded like Lester Young, like all the records I'd been listening to. I had memorized those solos. So I'm sitting over there itching for the keys and I finally went over and told Aaron I was from Spokane and told him I'd been listening to Lester Young, and asked him if I could play 'Lady Be Good' with him. He laughed. So I sat down and whipped off Count Basie's first chorus on 'Lady Be Good.' He came in and played Lester's solo. I was laughing, and he was laughing."

When the evening drew to a close, Davis told Rowles that if he wanted to find more action, he should go down to the 411 Club and introduce himself to Palmer Johnson. Johnson remembered the night Rowles walked in. "Jimmy Rowles! He had kind of short, cropped hair, rosy cheeks, and he never had a nickel. Tall, skinny kid. Going to school. He used to come in and I'd want to get off for a little while. Let Jimmy up and play, while I took a little walk." The club Palmer occasionally turned over to Rowles was one of Seattle's better—and newer—ones. The 411, on Sixth Avenue between South Jackson Street and South King Street, in a long, wood-sheathed building that is no longer there, was a modest establishment that opened in 1938. The front room was vacant, reported Tacoma-bred tenor sax man Bob Dugan, a "front" to fool the police. In the back room, Dugan said, "Palmer and his gang held sway Sunday night. Things would start going around 10 or 11 o'clock."

The 411 was known for its excellent barbecue and Sunday jam sessions. On weekends, students from the University of Washington packed the place. "If

Louis [Armstrong] was in town, or Duke, they'd come down to the 411 Club and jam," remembered Johnson. "Ben Webster came down one night. This is where we met this kid Corky Corcoran. He was fifteen years old and we let him in the back door. I'll never forget that night. Little baby-faced kid, but he could play saxophone." As Rowles recounted, "The sun was up when I'd get on the streetcar to go back to the University District. The streetcar guy never even used to charge me. He says, 'You! For Christ's sake, are you ever going to sleep?' 'I'm going to sleep today, I promise ya.' Next morning I'd see him again, he'd say, 'Jesus Christ, you're really after it, aren't ya?' 'Yup, I gotta learn.'" Jam sessions at the 411 gave Rowles his first experience on the firing line, with eager musicians calling tunes he might or might not know, in keys he might or might not have rehearsed. It was priceless training, and it was the time-honored method for learning to play jazz among musicians of the old school. But if Johnson gave Rowles the simple gift of turning over the piano bench to him, it was Julian Henson who initiated him into the mysteries of modern harmony.

"Julian Henson played crazy chords," Rowles recalled. "Palmer was sort of Fats Wallerish; he played nice, full piano, but he wasn't too modern. Julian Henson showed me things. I'd hear something and I'd ask, 'What the heck you doing there?' and he'd show me. He had some good stuff. I used to love the way he played." Rowles soaked up as much as he could, subbing in sweet bands led by Center Case and Jimmy Crane and jamming at the Blue Rose—once, when Jimmie Lunceford's vocalist, Dan Grissom, was there. Gene Sargent, the Seattle arranger, composer, and accordionist who would later record with Woody Herman, hipped Rowles to Duke Ellington's harmonies, and Ike Young, a dapper alto saxophonist playing with Gene Coy, befriended and encouraged him.

Rowles grew weary of maintaining the ruse on his family, however, who still thought he was attending the University of Washington. He returned to Spokane, briefly attending Gonzaga University and working for his father. But Spokane was not where he belonged either. Rowles declared to his parents that he was going to be a musician, not a lawyer, and, like Bing Crosby, Al Rinker, and Mildred Bailey before him, he left Spokane for Los Angeles. It was the right move. By the fall of 1940, he was playing every night with his idol, Lester Young, and sitting at Art Tatum's feet after hours. A call from Benny Goodman in 1941 set fire to Rowles's career. He eventually was honored at jazz festivals around the world and recognized as a distinctive, mature stylist who respected the tradition of the popular song (often rarely played ones) without descending into cocktail sentimentality. He encouraged Canadian pianist Diana Krall, who studied with him in Los Angeles, to sing—advice that turned out pretty well. Rowles died in 1996.

It had been Marshal Royal who encouraged Jimmy Rowles to come to Seattle in the first place. No one was in a better position to know just how hot the Jackson Street scene was cooking in those days than Royal and his colleagues in the Les Hite band. In 1936, Hite had been the opening attraction at the Ubangi. This was one of Seattle's first floor-show nightclubs and was opened by Noodles Smith as a response to the booming swing-band business from out of town. The Ubangi was located in the Golden West Hotel, at 410 Seventh Avenue South, which Smith had owned and operated from 1920 through 1927. The hotel hosted a variety of clubs over the years, including "a joint up on the fourth or fifth floor" managed by vocalist Lillian Goode's husband, in 1929, where Palmer Johnson recalled playing, and, in 1934, the Little Harlem Beer Tavern, which featured an eponymous group and presented the fledging Lionel Hampton band on the Leschi ferry in 1935.

A large, beautiful upstairs cabaret with potted palms, the Ubangi was Smith's last hurrah. Hite worked there as well as soon-to-be-famous bandleader Erskine Hawkins, who would go on to have the hits "Tuxedo Junction" and "Tippin' In." The club became a sparkling social center for the Black community, a place to celebrate grad night or just be seen. The chorus line was a regular item in the *Northwest Enterprise*, which on July 19, 1937, reported: "Our scout tells us the floor show is veddy veddy good this week. Marking an all-time high in a string of good shows." According to Bruce Rowell, who managed the Ubangi with Smith's nephew Harold, the club catered mainly to a white clientele. To kick off the place, Bruce and Noodles took a trek to the Cotton Club in Los Angeles to find talent for the club's debut. They recruited Hite, plus a line of chorus girls. According to Rowell, "We had 'em for twelve weeks. We had the chorus line from Frank Sebastian's Cotton Club and got all of our costumes from Madame Ouida in Los Angeles. They'd change the show every two weeks. After Hite left, we got an offer from a guy by the name of Basie, out of Kansas City. Noodles said, 'I never heard of this Basie guy.' So we booked some band from the East Coast that wasn't any good, got rid of them after two weeks, and then brought in Wyatt Howard." Howard was a major local white bandleader who later led the house band at the Town and Country Club, downtown on Sixth Avenue. Local musicians who followed

Howard into the Ubangi included Palmer Johnson, who remembered working as a single on the "mezzanine level" of the club ("Gee," he recalled, "how the people used to flock to that joint!"); Marion Fulmighter (billed as Marion Fullove); and Noodles's consort, Zelma Winslow.

The Ubangi was occasionally nabbed by the state liquor board, and Rowell claimed he had a unique way of dealing with raids that hearkened back to Prohibition:

> There were secret doors and slides and you could get down below the street. 'Til this day, there's still old gambling setups, places to one side where there's cribs to smoke opium. You could go down there and come up in the alley by the Wah Mee Club [the Blue Heaven in those days, the site of a notorious mass murder in 1983]. That's how I got away from the Washington State liquor board, three times. Heh-heh-heh-heh! When they came in, I'd go to the office, see, and say, "Let me get my overcoat." Then I'd zip down that little deal, you know, near the floor, and *shee-oop!* I'm downstairs in the basement. Next thing I know, I'm coming out, go down to the Mar Hotel, get a room, take a bath, and go to bed! They're all up there lookin' for me and I'm in the shower!

Rowell's story is seductively detailed and tempting to believe. But no evidence has ever surfaced that underground tunnels existed in the Chinatown–International District. Such often repeated tales, as Ron Chew suggested in his autobiography, *My Unforgotten Seattle*, are more likely Orientalist fantasies projecting "mystery" onto Asians. Rowell's corollary assertion, however, that even when there were raids, the "fix was in," is probably true. The routine, he said, was to send a designated man to the courthouse to be arrested who would be back to work in half an hour. At one time, said Rowell, Noodles had as many as seventy "cases" pending against him.

The Ubangi only lasted a couple of years. When the building was sold in February 1938, the *Northwest Enterprise* bid the club a sad farewell, touting it proudly as the "largest race-owned enterprise . . . north of Los Angeles." For a while, Rowell and Harold ran a place on Maynard Avenue South, the 416, next to the Atlas Theatre. Noodles bankrolled Louis Todd for another club, the Big Apple, located on South King Street between Fifth Avenue South and Sixth Avenue South. Neither lasted very long.

Around 1940 a lavish place owned by Sherman Spates took up the slack. On the north side of Jackson between Maynard and Sixth, the Congo was located on the ground floor of one of two beautiful buildings with ornamental white-stucco exteriors, buildings that still exist, erected by the Rainier Heat & Power Company. The other structure is the Governor Apartments, where Phil Moore lived. The Congo Club was the classic Prohibition-style "blind," a circular bar and ballroom hidden behind a swinging door at the back of a spacious, well-lit restaurant called the Congo Grill. Johnny Reddin, a *Seattle Times* columnist who liked to hang out in after-hours clubs, wrote that the Congo was his favorite place to eat in the district, especially for the steaks that arrived hanging over the edge of the plate.

In 1940, Palmer Johnson took a band into the Congo with Herman Grimes, one of the best musicians ever to linger in Seattle. Grimes grew up in Birmingham, Alabama, in a family band that included his older brother Johnny, a well-known swing trumpet player in New York. In 1923, Herman led Roger's Sunshine Minstrels (out of Florence, Alabama), and during the Depression he worked with several Kansas City bands, including Tommy Douglas's. "He was one of your top trumpet players, one of your real powerhouse men," recalled Darensbourg, who heard Grimes in Alabama before meeting him again in Seattle. According to Marshal Royal, who later played with Grimes in a Bay Area Navy band during World War II, Noodles Smith "sent for" Grimes from Kansas City. "He thought Herman Grimes was just the greatest," said Royal. "He thought he was better than Louis Armstrong."

Palmer Johnson was a fan as well: "I call Grimes the greatest trumpet player out of this Northwest. He could play as much trumpet as anybody in the country. And he could sing and he was a comic. Watching him walk up and down that floor, with his trumpet under his arm and singing. And his big eyes! Oooh! Those high notes, when we'd play 'Chinatown.' He went way up, to the trumpet's high F, man! He had a lip of iron!" According to Bruce Rowell, "Every band that came to Seattle—the Dorsey brothers, any band—they came down to try to steal Herman Grimes. But Herman Grimes would not go on the road! 'I want to stay right here in Seattle,' he'd say. 'I got a lady I'm living with, she's doing all my laundry, cooking all my meals. We split the kitty every morning. When I was nine years old, I was third trumpet on the Barnum & Bailey's Circus, riding on the bandwagon and the parades. I've *been* on the road.'"

In 1933 Sherman Spates and Ray Chavis opened the Green Dot, a tonsorial establishment with a secret nightclub in back, on this block of Jackson Street. Though the club's marquee isn't visible, the barber pole that marked it is.

During the day Grimes wrote horse-race tickets at the Green Dot, a barbershop also opened by Sherman Spates in 1933, across the street from the Congo, which sometimes featured piano players in back. Later on, Johnson worked with Grimes at the Green Dot and at Coe's Tavern, on Roosevelt, and Grimes himself led a trio at the Dutchman Tavern with Beulah Bradford (Junie Bradford's sister) on piano and Art Bradford (no relation) on drums. In 1947, after his stint in the Navy, Grimes briefly replaced Shorty Baker in the trumpet section of the Duke Ellington Orchestra. In November 1947 he recorded "Do Nothin' till You Hear from Me" with Duke. Royal said Grimes subsequently joined the merchant marine and died aboard one of the boats sometime in the 1950s. He does not appear to have come back to Seattle.

The Congo Club, the Ubangi, the Blue Rose, and the 411 were bootlegging establishments devoted to entertainment, alcohol, and sometimes gambling. But Chinatown (now part of the Chinatown–International District) also sported legitimate Chinese restaurants friendly to jazz. One of the most venerable was the Chinese Garden, which opened on December 21, 1929, at 516 Seventh Ave-

Herman Grimes (trumpet) gives the boys in the Gay Jones Orchestra a few pointers, ca. 1940. *Left to right:* Grimes, Carle Rising, Floyd Tebelman, Sven Sandstrom, Ernie Sears, Freddie Thompson, Dick Krafft, Glenn Martin, Aaron Shearer.

nue South, near South King Street. This reportedly excellent restaurant, jazz club, and gambling den was owned by Charlie Louie, who was well-liked by musicians, even though they joked about his habit of requesting "The Stein Song," a chug-a-lug collegiate anthem recast as a smash hit in 1930 by vocalist Rudy Vallee. Louie came to the United States from Guangzhou, China, first living in Portland, Oregon, in 1904. His original intention was to open a Chinese grand opera theater, for which he commissioned the building on Seventh Avenue South in 1923. But Seattle had little appetite for classical music, and Louie soon found himself promoting prizefights to keep the place open. Closing in 1928, he retooled for jazz and dancing and the club took off.

The Chinese Garden was more formal than the clubs. Women wore evening gowns and men wore ties. Louie featured the best musicians in town, including drummer Leonard Gayton; pianists Oscar Holden, Palmer Johnson, and Phil Moore; vocalists Zelma Winslow and Evelyn Williamson; clarinetist Joe Darensbourg; and saxophonists Frank Waldron and Dick Wilson. That an opera-loving Chinese immigrant like Louie wound up providing an outlet for an African American jazz musician like Holden, who had fled the South, epitomizes

The Chinese Garden, Charlie Louie's restaurant, jazz club, and gambling den at 516 Seventh Avenue South.

the best of what Jackson Street had to offer. Or, as the *Northwest Enterprise* put it in 1933, Jackson Street was a "poor man's playground," where "all races meet on common ground and rub elbows as equals." The Chinese Garden survived until after World War II, hosting a variety of bands and jam sessions until it was sold, in 1959.

Outside of town, one of the most illustrious Chinese-run establishments was the China Pheasant, a roadhouse casino between Boeing Field and the Duwamish River opened in 1940 by Danny Woo and Kai Eng. Woo, who would later run the very successful New Chinatown, was succeeded at the China Pheasant by Harry Lew.

Seattle also had a few downtown venues for jazz-oriented white musicians during this period. The State Theatre, just up the hill from First Avenue on Madison Street, hired players for burlesque shows. The Virginian, a large, plain beer garden at Virginia Street and Fourth Avenue, used three dance bands, alternating sets from one o'clock in the morning until dawn. On First, near Union Street, was Lyons' Music Hall, owned by Al Lyons, who would later build the Showbox Theater, where many of the greatest swing-era bands performed; and at Eleventh Avenue and Pine Street was the Cocoanut Grove, a vast basement establishment that seated a thousand.

But the music downtown was mostly commercial. If musicians wanted to play jazz, they had to go to Jackson Street. Jack Foy, the drummer who played with Joe Darensbourg's Genessee Street Shufflers, would go down to jam at the Hong Kong Chinese Society, aka the "Bucket of Blood": "A bass player named Ben Johnson showed me more things. He knew enough about the drums that he could show me how to play with a bass, or with a rhythm section, you know? [He] really taught me how to play with a band, which was most important. How to play behind a guy taking a solo. Be a little different between clarinet and saxophone and trumpet, trombone, piano." Foy recalled an unusual place named the Jailhouse, where one night he met Lionel Hampton, Marshal Royal, Walter Page, and Les Hite: "It was quite a joint. The tables were all cells, with bars. The keeper—the 'jailer'—would show you to your cell like a maître d', you know, like a guard, and put you in the table and lock you up. Then the waiter'd come and unlock the cell and take your order. Kind of a crazy place. The band was dressed in convict uniforms."

Despite such colorful distractions, the Depression era was tough on jazz musicians and drove some of them out of Seattle altogether. Though Palmer Johnson managed to snag a steady Seattle gig with Herman Grimes at the Dutchman Tavern, on Spokane Street and First Avenue South, he spent two years in Portland (from 1931 through 1932) working in speakeasies and brothels. In 1934 he took the most exotic flyer of all—a three-year trip to the elegant ballrooms of Shanghai. During the 1930s a wealthy international elite lived in Shanghai, enjoying greyhound racing, jai alai, gambling, and jazz. Scores of elegant bands—both Black and white musicians—were ferried over to play in the ballrooms owned by wealthy Chinese promoters, including groups led by trumpeters Buck Clayton and Tommy Foy (Jack's brother).

By all accounts, Shanghai was a good deal for the musicians, particularly those who were Black, who said they were treated with respect for the first time in their lives. Players were given excellent quarters in the international settlement, with maids and personal tailors who made them uniforms on request. There were American cooks to provide familiar meals. The pay ranged from $100 to $200 a week, and the city was full of exotic attractions, including rickshaw rides and a newly popularized drink from Russia called vodka. Everything about the place, from the palm-lined streets to the elegantly turned ballrooms—the Canidrome, Saint Anna's Dance Hall, the Casa Nova—was like a Hollywood movie, complete with international spies and mysterious women dropping handkerchiefs on the ballroom floor.

The Earl Whaley Band at Saint Anna's Dance Hall, Shanghai, China, 1934. *Left to right:* Fate Williams, Oscar Hurst, Gilbert "Punkin" Austin, Earl West, Wayne Adams, Earl Whaley, Palmer Johnson.

Palmer Johnson went to Shanghai reluctantly. The pianist was making good money in Portland speakeasies, but bandleader Earl Whaley finally convinced him to go. Whaley's original band had three horns and three men on rhythm: Wayne Adams (saxophones and clarinet), Oscar Hurst (trumpet), "Fate" Williams (trombone), Earl West (guitar), Johnson (piano), and Gilbert "Punkin" Austin (drums). Later, Whaley picked up bassist Reginald Jones from Buck Clayton's band. Jones, known as "Jonesy," was another Gene Coy veteran who had moved to the Northwest. His brother, Reunald, played trumpet for Count Basie. The band was given its quarters and immediately went to work at Saint Anna's Ballroom. As Johnson remembered:

> It was the most beautiful ballroom you ever looked upon. They had revolving chandeliers, man, that go around and around this way. Three of them. It was a vast place. And all these Chinese girls and some Russian girls, sitting around there, and prospective customers came along and choose a girl to dance with. Music never stopped. Just one after the other. The Chinese were crazy about "This Evening About a Quarter to Nine." Fred Astaire and Ginger Rogers had made this movie,

> *Flying Down to Rio*, so we played "Carioca" and "Cheek to Cheek," "Accent on Youth" and "Stay as Sweet as You Are." Buck's band played afternoon tea dances. Ours never started 'til around seven o'clock, so sometimes I went over and heard his band. After he left, they brought up another band from Los Angeles.

Before long, bad weather blew over Johnson's Asian retreat. The way he told it, he had befriended a tap dancer, Buster Dunston, who was gay.

> We were working in the open-air pavilion one night, at the outskirts of the city. This was in 1935. It was raining cats and dogs. Buster and I had just gone out to eat one of the delicacies over there, frogs' legs. They were delicious, man. Tastes better than chicken. About two o'clock, in walks Buster, and he had two fellows with him. And Earl Whaley says, "Here comes Palmer's boy."
>
> I just waited. Just waited until after the band played the last number. And I says, "I didn't like that crack you made about Buster when Buster walked in here." And he said, "What you going to do about it?" and I let this left go, and it hit the piano and broke this finger and busted his nose. So they bandaged my finger up and I quit.

After leaving Whaley, Johnson took a job with a Filipino band in Penang, in what is now Malaysia, led by a trombone player, then worked six weeks at Singapore's famous Raffles Hotel.

In January 1937, after an apology and a raise, Johnson rejoined Whaley in a Hong Kong dance hall. The following month, the band was back in Shanghai's Ambassador Ballroom, across the street from the racecourse. But the atmosphere in the colorful cosmopolitan city had gone sour. Japanese soldiers were doing maneuvers in the streets, a foreshadowing of the invasion and occupation to come. Musicians began to think seriously about getting back to America. Some ballrooms had deducted a small amount from each player's paycheck for the passage, but many musicians were stranded. Being that far away from home with no way to get back was frightening, according to Johnson:

> I had been watching [the Japanese Army], riding around up the main road in these little tanks. They were gathering troops to go to war. I says, I don't want none of this. I started going to the jai alai games to try to win my fare back. I want to get the hell out of there. So I read this paper, it said, "'*President Grant*'

> [the ship] arriving." Beautiful Shanghai day. I put on my whites and I go down to the Wussong River and hire a water taxi and go out in the middle of the stream and get on board the *President Grant*. It just so happened that one of the waiters had took a dose of clap in Manila and they had him quarantined on the ship. I played piano and waited tables all the way back, man. When I got back, they used to call me "China Seas."

Not all the musicians in Shanghai were as lucky as China Seas. Earl Whaley, Earl West, and Wayne Adams, who continued playing in China, were interned in 1943, at a camp in what is now Weifang, Shandong Province. Whaley worked as an interpreter for American troops, and Adams was employed in the bakery, though they were also allowed to continue to play music. Despite later rumors of ill treatment, a 1944 Department of State letter to Adams's mother reported that Adams was in excellent health and that conditions at the camp were fine. All three musicians were released in 1945. Whaley reportedly worked for the post office, took up real estate in Los Angeles, and died in 1959. Adams returned to Seattle but does not appear to have continued in music. Two years after his return, he died of complications from a disease he had reportedly contracted overseas.

Palmer Johnson's return in 1937, the year the young Jimmy Rowles came to town and subbed for him, marked the beginning of a high point in the senior pianist's career. His engagements at the 411, the 908 Club, and the Congo Club set the pace for the district and for Seattle jazz. But in 1942 wanderlust seized the chuckling pianist again, and he made for Alaska, where fortunes were to be won entertaining servicemen and the rough pioneers who were guiding the snow-blown territory toward statehood. Johnson would not return to Seattle until 1977. His contribution to the Seattle scene, spanning fourteen years over three different decades, is enormous. Along with Elmer Fain, Bumps Myers, Frank Pasley, and others, Johnson brought to the Northwest the new, sophisticated sense of jazz that had developed in Los Angeles as well as a high level of reading, transposing, and improvising that would become the standard for all jazz players who followed him. He was generous to younger musicians, accessible to audiences, and conveyed a contagious sense of joy. In 1994, Johnson was recognized as an example of the living tradition of jazz when he received the Governor's Heritage Award. He died in 1996.

The Palmer Johnson Quartet at the 908 Club, 1940. *Left to right:* Gilbert "Punkin" Austin, Milt Green, Tootie Boyd, Palmer Johnson.

Palmer Johnson's departure from Seattle marked the end of an era. His colorful style of solo piano and combo swing belonged to the early phases of jazz that had been forged in the 1910s and 1920s, a style that was fast being replaced by the new style of big-band swing. But the combo scene during the Depression, with its colorful characters and speakeasy flair, had been a great school for young players such as Dick Wilson, Junior Raglin, and Jimmy Rowles. Rowles in particular would not forget his debt to the town. "To have been able to participate in that experience in Seattle," he recalled, "and learn at the same time from all these musicians—not be standing around watching, like it is today—I was very lucky."

Meanwhile, though it had been a long time coming, Seattle's next generation of jazzers was developing a top-notch swing culture of its own. Ironically, the first big band to become well-known in Seattle would come not out of the Black community but from two white college kids. Their energy would bring Seattle into the big-band era and leave the scuffling Depression behind.

4 Swingmania

The Big Bands Roll

SWING WAS A YOUTH CRAZE, much like Beatlemania in the 1960s, and very popular on college campuses across the country. Part of the reason for this popularity was that the music was more danceable than early jazz, even at fast tempos, and therefore fit nicely into the adolescent ritual of growing up and falling in love. This was the era of the jitterbug and dance marathons, when the Lindy Hop replaced the fox-trot and the Charleston.

Swing was also big business. Bands led by Benny Goodman, the Dorseys, Duke Ellington, Jimmie Lunceford, and Woody Herman made enormous sums of money touring the country, playing one-nighters in ballrooms. Bandleaders became stars both on radio and in the movies. When Artie Shaw married Betty Grable, it was front-page stuff. When Gene Krupa was busted for smoking pot, the roof came off. Local copy bands sprang up in every city, imitating the name bands. Even the underground slang of jazzmen seeped into the mainstream. Swing fanatics called themselves "jitterbugs" and "alligators" and picked up expressions like "groovy" and "cool" from Black musicians. Cab Calloway published a tongue-in-cheek *Dictionary of Jive* that became an underground favorite. A cult of enthusiasm and experience, which would have its apogee in the bebop 1940s, spread through America's teen culture, which had been created by the automobile and affluence. White drummer Don Manning, who later became an important jazz collector and historian, recounted: "In 1941, I remember going down to interview Duke Ellington in his dressing room for the school newspaper. They did five shows a day, which a kid could get into, and they had a special matinee, down at the Showbox on First Avenue. When I met Duke, I talked to him in 'jive.' Duke was so tickled, he brought the band out. 'Say that again to these guys!' he said."

Though Black swing bands such as Ellington's started coming to Seattle in the mid-1930s, and Black swing combos such as Palmer Johnson's had been playing in the clubs for years, the first local swing big band was formed and popularized by white college students. Norm Bobrow, who was raised in New York's Westchester County, had been to more Broadway shows by the time he was a teenager than most Seattleites would see in a lifetime. More important, he had been taken up to Harlem, where he'd fallen in love with Black music and style at the Apollo Theater. When the Bobrows moved to Seattle in 1936, the town seemed strictly from squaresville to the young New York–bred university freshman. The most popular orchestra on the University of Washington campus was an "ickie band" (swing slang for a corny group) led by Jimmy Crane, who was also a yell leader. While the rest of the country was stomping at the Savoy, Seattleites had yet to hear Lunceford live.

"One morning," explained Bobrow, who in his seventies still exuded a boyishly disarming Broadway enthusiasm, "I decided that with all these bands around here, there must be one that is playing good Benny Goodman, good Artie Shaw, good Duke Ellington, good Jimmie Lunceford. I called Gay Jones off a blind list in *The Daily*. When he answered the phone I said, 'I'd like to present a good, listenable band that has a jazz flavor.' Gay said, 'We're having a rehearsal right now, come on over!'"

Gaylord Jones and his young wife, Marilyn, had been living hand-to-mouth ever since graduating from West Seattle High in 1936. Gay was a student at the University of Washington, but he spent most of his time rehearsing the band, listening to hot new records, and writing his own arrangements—that is, when he and the guys weren't down at the Black and Tan or the Dutchman Tavern. Music was their life. Gay's best friend since childhood, Leslie "Tiny" Martin, lived down the street and played bass. Their new takeoff on the Bob Crosby hit "Big Noise from Winnetka" had become one of the highlights of their act. Sven Sandstrom, the band's jazz trumpet player, lived in Gay and Marilyn's basement; he had the annoying habit of getting up early and practicing Bunny Berigan's solo on "I Can't Get Started."

Gay had grown up with music. His father had played solo jazz piano at Lundeen's. In their early teens, Gay and Tiny had started a "kid band," the Cosmopolitans, which played dances, assemblies, and sock hops. Some of the players from the Cosmopolitans—Floyd Tebelman (sax), Dick Krafft (sax), and Carle Rising (trumpet)—were now with the Gaylord Jones Orchestra. Marilyn, who used the stage name Mars Mercer, was a fan of the Boswell Sisters, the hip harmonizers with the Benny Goodman band. She had a vocal trio that sang at the Spanish Castle, in Midway, south of Seattle. When they all graduated, they expanded the band to five saxes, four trumpets, three trombones, and four rhythm players, and started looking for jobs. They had no idea that the happy-go-lucky student who

Glenn Martin, Norm Bobrow, and Gaylord Jones (*left to right*) discuss a new arrangement, ca. 1940.

came around that morning to give them a listen was going to help them so much. "When I got there," recalled Bobrow, "they were doing 'One O'Clock Jump,' 'Begin the Beguine,' and 'Back Bay Shuffle,' and all the Artie Shaw and Benny Goodman charts. Man, I just flipped out! I never expected to hear a band which was so organized and tight. Gay was a goddamned perfectionist."

This was the beginning of Bobrow's fifty-year career as Seattle's most important jazz impresario and the much-belated starting gun for the city's swing era. On March 2, 1939, in a sensational style that would become his trademark, Bobrow announced a concert by Gaylord Jones and the formation of the Husky Hot Club, a new campus organization dedicated to swing. The show attracted a turn-away crowd of 250 to Clark Hall, not to mention the unwanted attention of the university president, who told Bobrow he objected to having a campus organization with the word "hot" in its name. There it was, the puritanical face of Bertha Landes looming over Seattle again. "I believe that some people believe that 'hot' has licentious connotations," said the president. Bobrow played it cool. "I reminded him," Bobrow recounted, "that there was a very famous, legendary Hot Club of France, which had nothing whatsoever licentious about it at all." The president thought for a moment. “Well—could you at least change the name?”

Overnight, Bobrow had discovered the causes he would ride for the next five decades—the cultural superiority of jazz, the rights of Black people, and local neglect of local talent. He moved the show off-campus to the basement of the nearby Meany Hotel. The mob scene there soon rippled through town, and the Gay Jones Orchestra became the most popular swing band in Washington. Bobrow got the band booked into the Trianon Ballroom. Because of the publicity generated from the Hot Club incident, people lined up around the corner. The jitterbuggers turned out in full force.

Advertisement for the Husky Hot Club.

“Some of them were really spectacular,” remembered Jones, “throwing the gal around and under their leg and up in the air. There were some of those tunes we’d play where the whole doggone place would—I’d be worried about the floor giving way. Everybody was really jumping.” From 1939 to 1942 the Gay Jones Orchestra was the house band at the Trianon. The ballroom, which was becoming the nerve center of Seattle’s swing era, was already a venerable institution when he started playing there. Built for $175,000 in 1927 by John Savage—the notorious crony of Vic Meyers at the Butler Hotel—and bankrolled by bandleader Herb Wiedoeft, the Trianon covered half a block at Third Avenue and Wall Street. It was the biggest ballroom in the Northwest. The dance floor, made of springy white maple, spanned 80 feet by 185 feet, accommodated more than five thousand dancers, and was fitted all around with ducts that sucked away stale air. Around the dance floor were 150 three-person settees; upstairs, the loges seated three hundred to four hundred people, and there were sixteen arched, open-air balconies where lovers could retreat. In later years, Ted Harris, who managed the ballroom for Savage from 1930 until it closed in 1956, would say, “More people met their future wives and husbands at the Trianon than anywhere else in Seattle.” The ceiling was draped with cloth and had a huge glitter ball, and the walls were decorated with tropical scenes. At the far end of the room was the prize of the establishment: a silver clamshell hood over the bandstand that projected sound beautifully over the dancers. Out front, or backstage managing the autograph hounds, was a six-foot, four-inch deputy sheriff named Elmo Hudgins who loved swing enough to have requested the ballroom for his beat.

Jitterbugs, 1940s.

Posters from the 1940s for concerts by Duke Ellington and Jimmie Lunceford at the Trianon Ballroom.

Wiedoeft was the brother of saxophonist Rudy Wiedoeft, whose Frisco Jazz Band had played one of the first jazz shows in Seattle, in 1917. Herb logged another milestone in May 1927, when his orchestra, a syncopated regular on KFOA radio broadcasts, opened the Trianon Ballroom. According to local legend, the bandleader subsequently lost the venue to John Savage in a card game. At first, Savage booked sweet dance bands from the West Coast, such as those led by Vic Meyers, Owen Sweeten, and Anson Weeks. But in 1933, Savage started experimenting with national acts, bringing in Ted Fio Rito (who came in with an unknown sixteen-year-old singer named Betty Grable). Popular sweet-band leaders Guy Lombardo and Ted Lewis followed.

At about the same time, Black revues featuring swing bands started to come to town as well. Los Angeles bandleader Curtis Mosby brought his Dixieland Blue Blowers to the Rex Theatre in August 1933, in an "all-Negro revue" titled "Change Your Luck." The next year, blues queen Ida Cox visited with the show "Darktown Scandals." In 1935 three similar acts followed: "Harlem Follies," with dancer "Jazzlips" Richardson; "Harlem on Parade," with the Lennox Avenue Boys and dancer Tommy Harris (in blackface); and "Brown Skin Models," featuring what it advertised. Today the ads for these shows featuring half-naked "brownskin beauties" and parodies of African features strike us as racist caricatures, but they were also the sincere legacy of the Harlem Renaissance, which, in great Black musicals of the 1920s such as *Shuffle Along*, had affirmed Africanness in African American culture.

In 1934, Les Hite brought his twelve-piece unit to the Paramount. That same year, Duke Ellington played the Music Hall Theater. Major Pigford, a budding trombone player who would later work with Quincy Jones, was eight years old when he attended the concert: "When the band came on, as each instrument played, there was a spotlight on him and it went through this blue gauze which sparkled. I thought it was pure magic. I vividly remember [clarinetist] Barney Bigard was playing a solo, and then a trumpet, and then Tricky Sam [Nanton] on the trombone. He was making some of the most unbelievable sounds I'd ever heard in my life. Then this magnificent figure came out in this white tuxedo. And that was Duke Ellington. I was completely awestruck." Ellington's visit to Seattle was followed by Lionel Hampton's first band, on its inaugural road trip from Los Angeles. The group played the Rex Theatre but dissolved when work dried up. "Most of the musicians decided to sign on with a ship that was taking a pleasure cruise somewhere," according to Hampton. Hamp wasn't the only

A marquee advertising the Duke Ellington Band at the Showbox, ca. 1940.

bandleader to have trouble making ends meet in the Northwest. Even Guy Lombardo lost money at the Trianon.

In 1936, Duke returned, playing five shows a day at the Palomar (the old Rex), and Glen Gray, the great white bandleader whose Casa Loma Orchestra was one of the seminal big bands, played the Trianon. Fletcher Henderson hit the bandstand the following year. By the early 1940s nearly every jazz name of note, Black and white, had passed through Tacoma and Seattle, and sometimes Spokane: Earl Hines, Andy Kirk, Gene Krupa, Ella Fitzgerald, Benny Goodman, Eli Rice, Harry James, Charlie Barnet, Sammy Kaye, Kay Kyser, Phil Harris, the International Sweethearts of Rhythm, Roy Eldridge, Bob Crosby, Jack Teagarden, Lawrence Welk, Teddy Hill, Cab Calloway, Count Basie, Artie Shaw, Jimmie Lunceford, Woody Herman . . . they all came through. Oddly, Glenn Miller was the exception; he never got any closer than Jantzen Beach, outside Portland.

The stately (now demolished) Finnish Hall also presented touring swing bands. Nestled behind the Entertainer's Cabaret (called the Cotton Club in the

International Sweethearts of Rhythm at the Black and Tan, September 1944.

1930s) and facing a block of South Washington Street that no longer exists, Finnish Hall opened in 1924 with a community mission to host all manner of events, from theater and political rallies to music and dance. Swing fans jitterbugged on the grand hall's maple dance floor to the strains of Black big bands led by Louis Armstrong, Earl Whaley, Cecil Finley, Gene Coy, Eli Rice, Erskine Hawkins, Fletcher Henderson, Noble Sissle, Jimmie Lunceford, Red Allen, and Lucky Millinder. Local leaders Evelyn Bundy, Al Pierre, Joe Darensbourg, and Palmer Johnson played there too. When Ellington played the Music Hall in May 1934, Noodles Smith took out an ad in the *Northwest Enterprise* to let people know he had booked his New Harlem Band into Finnish "in honor of Duke and (boxer) Gorilla Jones." Noodles invited Duke and the members of his band to come on down, which many of them probably did.

As swing caught on, more ballrooms sprouted up, including McElroy's, Parker's, the Senator, the Showbox, Faurot's, the Everstate, and the Palladium. In Fife, outside Tacoma, there was the Century Ballroom; outside Olympia was the Evergreen, a roadhouse/ballroom; south of Seattle were the Spanish Castle, the Cinderella, the Crescent, and the Aragon. The crowds outside the ballrooms became news items in themselves. Particularly after the war had started, witnesses reported that lines of thousands streamed along Third Avenue, by the Trianon. Swing-shift dances lasted until five in the morning. One Tommy Dorsey show was moved from the Trianon to the larger Civic Auditorium, where it drew a crowd of sixty-five hundred. There were lines five blocks long in both directions.

Though Seattle teenagers no doubt would have discovered swing music on their own through recordings, they were assisted immeasurably by the promotional zeal of Norm Bobrow. The enthusiastic presenter, described by the *Seattle Post-Intelligencer* as "a young visionary who believes that swing is fraught with significance," came to jazz with a liberal, civilizing mission as well as a genuine love for the music. One way of expressing this sense of mission was to present jazz in a concert hall, with the notion of "dignifying" the art for a mass audience, an idea that had gained currency with the legendary 1938 "Spirituals to Swing" concert at Carnegie Hall. Like Bobrow, many fans felt that American racism kept jazz buried in the underworld of nightclubs. Putting the music in a concert hall would take a much-needed swipe at Jim Crow.

Flyer for Norm Bobrow concert at the Metropolitan Theatre, with photographs of Palmer Johnson (*left*) and Gaylord Jones (*right*).

On February 4, 1940, Bobrow produced the first bona fide jazz concert on the West Coast, at Seattle's Metropolitan Theatre, predating by four years Norman Granz shows in Los Angeles normally credited with that accomplishment. In part, Seattle was fertile ground for such a show precisely because the town had erected so many theaters earlier in the century. The bill included Gay Jones and the Palmer Johnson Sextet, with Aaron Davis, Andy Duryea, Gilbert "Punkin" Austin, Herman Grimes, and guitarist Milt Green. Bobrow was quite aware of the historical importance of what he was doing. "I would like to see swing music attain in Seattle the same respect with which it is regarded throughout most of the country," he wrote in what amounted to a manifesto in the *Seattle Star*. "After all, swing is an American music and Seattle

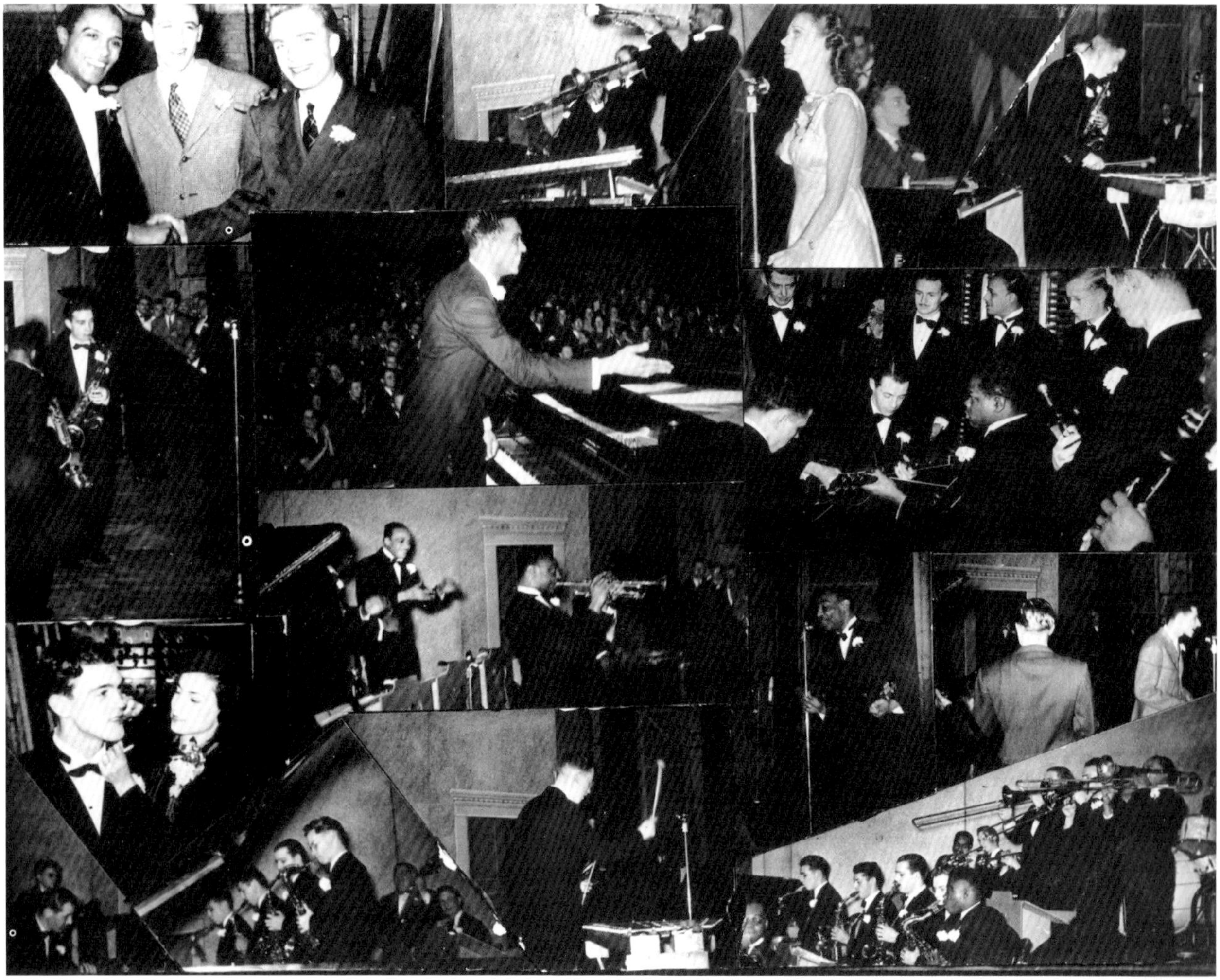

Seattle's first swing concerts, 1940. *Top row of photos, left to right:* Palmer Johnson, Norm Bobrow, Gordy Challstedt; Andy Duryea (trombone), Herman Grimes (trumpet); Mars Mercer; Gordy Challstedt. *Second row, left to right:* Joe Darensbourg, Aaron Davis, tenor saxophones; Palmer Johnson, piano; Frank Spencer and Irv Ashby play guitar as band watches. *Third row, left to right:* boy and girl, unknown; Andy Duryea, Herman Grimes; Herman Grimes, at microphone facing left; Norm Bobrow, at microphone facing right. *Bottom row:* unknown; Gay Jones Orchestra saxophone section; Gordy Challstedt; Gay Jones Orchestra, with Illinois Jacquet, tenor saxophone, at right end of sax section.

an American city. Why shouldn't we accept the music of our own country—or at least try to understand it?"

The concert was a resounding success, with a full house of "alligators" attending the three-hour bash. Emboldened, Bobrow planned an even more ambitious night later in the year. Lionel Hampton, at the height of his popularity after leaving Benny Goodman, was debuting a new band at the Trianon. Bobrow rented the nearby Moore Theatre and booked Johnson, Grimes, Jones, and an all-star Hampton combo, with guitarist Irv Ashby and the great tenor saxophonist Illinois Jacquet. The house went bananas.

Seven months later, Bobrow got a call from Gerald Wells, who had become president of Local 493. The members wanted to book Fats Waller for a dance at the Senator Ballroom, but they didn't think they could raise the money. Could Bobrow possibly book a concert around the same time? Fats was in the twilight of his career but was still hot on the charts. "Jitterbug Waltz" had just come out, a novelty Fats played on the Hammond organ. The two dates would probably make it worth his while to come out. The night Fats played the Moore Theatre—July 13, 1941—Ozzie Nelson's big band was at the Trianon Ballroom and *Citizen Kane* had just opened at the Metropolitan. The show was a critical, musical, and financial success, and would remain a calling card for Bobrow for years to come as he booked dozens of national acts, including Charlie Parker and Dave Brubeck.

Meanwhile, in Los Angeles, Norman Granz was advancing the cause of jazz in the concert hall as well, with shows that featured a Northwest swing musician—Corky Corcoran. Tenor saxophonist Corcoran was the region's most important contributor to the swing era. Born Gene Patrick Corcoran in 1924 in Tacoma, at fifteen this sawed-off Irish kid was catching rides to Seattle to sit in at the 411 Club. Guitarist Al Turay was there the night Corky came in and blew the famed tenor saxophonist Ben Webster off the stand. "Webster was mad," recalled Turay, "because he'd been drinking. He slammed his horn down." The following year, Jimmie Lunceford heard Corcoran in Tacoma and invited him to join the band. "I'll have to ask my mother," had been his reply. Corcoran played briefly with Lunceford, then joined the Sonny Dunham orchestra in 1940 and Harry James in 1941. James and Betty Grable legally adopted the underage saxophonist so he could tour with the band. James, an avid baseball fan who habitually organized games among various big bands, is rumored to have asked Corky if he could play second base before hiring him. It was the right question. Corcoran had Babe Ruth's jersey number 3 etched on his saxophone. Corcoran became a star while he was with James. In 1944, *DownBeat* readers voted him No. 8 in the Best Tenor Saxophonist category. Corky's name was featured in ads for the band, and he played on all of James's Columbia recordings.

Corky Corcoran, Los Angeles.

Corky played with a swaggering, virile tone on swing tunes and—like his idol, Ben Webster—with full-bodied tenderness on ballads. He had a natural melodic imagination. His normal tone was woody and piping, with a burry edge and broad vibrato, but he wasn't afraid to abruptly alter his timbre with salty exclamations, honks, and wails. Corcoran performs on one of the most famous jazz albums of all time, *Just Jazz*, a live recording produced by LA promoter Gene Norman of a 1947 concert at the Los Angeles Civic Auditorium, with Lionel Hampton's All Stars. Corcoran's solo on "Stardust" is a tour de force in which he spits out jawbusting explosions, chuffing descending figures, and dazzling harmonic substitutions.

As is the case with so many prodigies, Corcoran's story did not turn out well. Belligerent, spoiled, and eventually alcoholic, the young tenor saxophonist habitually got into fights. He was married and divorced several times. One drunken night in Tacoma, a bus pulled up and he jumped on, thinking he was still on a road trip. Corcoran quit drinking in 1955 and eventually regained his musical stature, if not his marquee value. He appeared at the Newport Jazz Festival in New York in 1974 and presented his own group at the New York Jazz Museum. "He was such a sensitive player," recalled Fred Radke, a Seattle trumpet player who later led the Harry James ghost band. "All he ever wanted to talk about was baseball and golf, but when he put his horn into his mouth, he was so deep." Corcoran died in 1979, and Radke established a scholarship in Corcoran's name at North Seattle Community College.

Along with Dick Wilson and Junior Raglin, Corky Corcoran was one of the few Northwest musicians who achieved notoriety during the swing era. None of the big bands that came out of Seattle became well-known. In a way this is not surprising. Because the economic machinery of the music business—agents, advance men, critics—was far away from the Northwest in the 1930s and 1940s, even when local bands were good, they had trouble moving into the limelight. However, quality music was being made in the region. Many musicians feel some groups deserved to be better known. As Gay Jones's trumpeter Pete Barrington put it:

> You know, I traveled a great deal after that—L.A. especially—I went to a lot of jazz concerts and I didn't hear anything, especially at the local level, that was a hell of a lot better, and a lot of it was definitely inferior to what I used to hear around Seattle. I always felt that if Tommy Dorsey or Jimmie Lunceford had heard the Gay Jones band of '38, '39, '40, he might have said, "Wait a minute here, let's get some financing, put this thing together, and get some records and some air dates." Because it was a good band. I always kind of resented that.

Of the dozens of local musicians who had the talent to make the big time, Jones is at the top of the list. When his band broke up in 1942, as the draft claimed its members, the bandleader struck out for Los Angeles. He got on as staff arranger for Freddie Slack, the ex-Dorsey pianist who started the boogie-woogie craze. Bassist Tiny Martin went on to a career with the Boston Symphony. Jones had sold several charts to Lionel Hampton, including his own theme, "I Nearly Lost My Mind," "Standing Room Only," and a riff called "Boogie Woogie." The whiz from West Seattle High also penned Slack a winner, "Riffette," which shot up to the top ten on *Billboard* magazine's "Harlem Hit Parade," and did some arranging for Dave Hargrave. Several months later, Jones was drafted. He returned home to Seattle to play club dates downtown and in Chinatown until the early 1950s.

"I Nearly Lost My Mind" (Lionel Hampton–Gay Jones), Victor record label.

Occasionally Jones toured with Curt Sykes, who succeeded him as house bandleader at the Trianon. As the swing craze died, Jones and his wife, Mars, were drawn more and more to their second love, sport fishing. They ran a successful charter fishing boat out of Port Angeles for decades, while Jones played fine piano in a local trio, for fun. Interviewed in 1989, he had no regrets. "I never had the push," confessed the mild-mannered pianist, adding that if it hadn't been for Norm Bobrow, the band never would have gotten as far as it did. In 2000 the Charlie May All Star Big Band recorded a live album of Jones's arrangements at bassist Red Kelly's jazz club in Tacoma.

The punchy swing numbers and intricately arranged ballads on *Opus 2000* offer a sweet glimpse of what the swing fanatics danced to so enthusiastically back in the day. Jones died in 2004; his wife, Marilyn, in 2002.

Woody Herman once pointed out that "few of the swing-era bands . . . ever played jazz," a distinction swing nostalgists often fail to make. What made Gay Jones stand out from other, less jazz-oriented white dance-band leaders in Seattle, such as Putt Anderson, Wyatt Howard, and Archie Loveland, was his unmitigated commitment to swing—in particular, to the hot, two-beat feeling of the Lunceford band and a "fat" jazz arranging style with extra notes added to the chords for color, a style Stan Kenton and Woody Herman would make famous.

There were a few other white bandleaders who also played jazz. Chuck Reisdorf's organization featured drummer and vocalist Charlie Blackwell, who sang the nonsense bebop lyrics of the Glenn Miller hit "Wham!" in a Cab Calloway style. Blackwell left Seattle in 1942 and later worked with Benny Carter, Stan Kenton, Count Basie, Art Tatum, Nat "King" Cole, and Dave Brubeck. Vern Mallory, who came to Seattle during the Depression, led a hot dance band that was highly influenced by Jimmie Lunceford and Erskine Hawkins. Mallory's band was so hip that it was booked to play for Black audiences at the Savoy Ballroom, on Madison. Trianon bandleader Curt Sykes toured the Northwest and provided steady work for many jazz musicians, including Gay Jones, Pete Barrington, Dave Stetler, Fred Greenwell, Red Kelly, Don Manning, and the incredible drummer Buzz Bridgeford, Seattle's version of Dave Tough, Woody Herman's rhythm ace. In 1948, Sykes's band placed No. 34 in the *DownBeat* poll's Best Swing Band category, largely on the strength of Bridgeford's reputation.

Sykes, Mallory, and Jones often drew sidemen straight out of high school, particularly once the war had siphoned off most of the professional talent. These high schoolers usually were already playing in kid bands, which were a breeding ground for a generation of new players. "You could buy arrangements for seventy-five cents," recalled Manning. "We could buy those Count Basie charts, Duke Ellington charts. Glenn Miller. We had a kid band first and then bands in high school. The Men About Town were the best. And then came the Chevaliers." The Chevaliers were a college-age dance band led by Stanton Patty. (Patty later became a reviewer and travel editor for the *Seattle Times*.) Playing saxophone in the band was a zany fourteen-year-old named Ronnie Pierce, whose entrepreneurial exploits later became a part of local music legend. Pierce

The Men About Town, ca. 1942. *Left to right:* Dick Woodhouse, Alf Lauritsen, George Hartwell, Stan Ball, Bob Bateman, Pete Barrington; drummer (*hidden*), Dave Stetler.

joined the Noteworthies at Seattle's Roosevelt High School, a kid band that included pianist Kenny Kimball, trombonist Bob McDermid, and drummer Keith Purvis, all of whom would play significant roles in jazz after the war. The Men About Town was started before the Noteworthies, by fourteen-year-old trumpet prodigy Pete Barrington, who, like Gay Jones, was a big Lunceford fan. Barrington remembered: "Art Doll, a saxophone player from Tacoma who didn't play in the band, would sit down and laboriously transcribe these Lunceford arrangements for us, those double-timing saxophone things. Lunceford came out to an assembly at Roosevelt and we played that stuff for him. Well, he went nuts. He had us down to the Trianon that night, as his guests, and offered us any charts we wanted."

Many of the youngsters in Men About Town became professional musicians, including bassists Red Kelly and Hal "Champ" Champeness, who later worked with comedian/musician Stan Boreson, and drummer Dave Stetler. When Stetler came home after a Men About Town gig and told his mother he had decided to become a professional musician, she was horrified. "I thought she was going to cut my throat," said Stetler, who lived and worked in Seattle all his life, playing with both jazz and commercial groups. He became a professional musician right out of high school, in the International District, where he paid some dues, particularly at Club Maynard, a dining and dancing dive at the corner of Maynard Avenue South and South Weller Street that presented white entertainers from 1937 through World War II:

> [Combos] generally didn't have a bass because the Chinese figured if you had a piano and a drummer you had two rhythm. They'd hire another horn, but they wouldn't hire a bass, which is pretty grim, from a drummer's point of view, when the bass drum is your bass note. . . .
>
> At the Club Maynard, [there were] no civilians except on the bandstand. They had a little two-by-four around the bandstand. [One night], two great big girls got into a big, screaming fight right next to me, over a sailor, and one of them caught the other one by the throat and leaned her over the two-by-four and *bam!* her head is right on my snare drum, and she's gouging her eyes. About a half-hour later, some sailors and soldiers got into it. And now, it's like a John Wayne movie, smashing tables and bodies are flying around the floor and the guys are clubbing each other. The SPs and MPs come in and the whistles are blowing and the clubs flying and they're knocking guys on the head. They dragged out about twelve guys. Down the stairs they go. And we're playing through all of this.

After failing an audition with the Bob Chester band because of sight-reading problems, Stetler took lessons from Shorty Clough, whose syncopated salad days with the Melody Boys had given way to teaching in a drum studio downtown. Stetler worked with Bob Harvey's band at the China Pheasant, the Marginal Way roadhouse operated by Harry Lew. Bass player Tiny Martin and trumpeter Carle Rising from the old Gay Jones Orchestra also were in the band. Stetler took a brief look at the Fifty-Second Street scene in New York in 1945. He was dazzled by the music but decided to come home, where he joined Wyatt Howard at the Town and Country Club. As a young white musician, Stetler had the option of taking a steady commercial job at a place like the Town and Country when hot jazz work was scarce. Because of segregation, however, his counterparts in the Black community did not. Stetler remembered his ingenuous horror at coming up against Seattle's segregated musicians' unions as a young man: "At the time I joined the union, I wasn't even aware that there was a Black union. I'd been playing at dances with [Black] kids like Sonny Booker and Billy

Tolles. Then I got in the union and it was suddenly, 'Wait a minute, you can't have any Black guys in your band.' The rules were very strict."

Though Black name bands often played under the Trianon Ballroom band shell, local Black bands rarely did, and Black audiences were forbidden to attend, except under special circumstances. The Trianon did not admit Filipino or Hawaiian musicians either. As a consequence, the memories of Black swing-era musicians in Seattle, though nostalgic to be sure, have a somewhat more complex flavor. Black fans were not allowed in the Trianon because owner John Savage did not want them there. He felt that it was "bad for business." During the 1920s, when he ran the Butler Hotel, he hadn't allowed Black people, and he wasn't about to change his ways for swing. On the contrary, as the Black population of Washington mushroomed during the war years, many white business owners, like Savage, dug in their heels even more resolutely against Black audiences. This dogged resistance to integrated spaces was emblematic of a social upheaval taking place all over the West, where an unprepared white population, with little experience of African Americans, particularly from the South, suddenly found itself dealing with a large group of people whose accents were different, whose food seemed peculiar, and whose manners struck them as "rustic."

Things came to a head at the Trianon in 1940, when Lionel Hampton's new band was booked. Hampton was well-known in both white and Black communities, and, because he and Teddy Wilson had been the first Black musicians to play regularly with Benny Goodman, he was also something of a hero. Naturally, Black audiences wanted to see the band, as did the white swing alligators, who had kept their ears pressed to their radios listening to live broadcasts of the band since 1936. There were local Hampton connections too. Hamp's new vocalist was Evelyn Williamson, who had been raised in Seattle by Noodles Smith. Her first husband, tenor saxophonist Bumps Myers, was also in the band. Evelyn's featured number was the Gay Jones tune "I Nearly Lost My Mind." Hamp's drummer Oscar Bradley and his alto saxophonist Floyd Turnham had also spent time playing in Seattle. The Black community swung into action. They approached the Trianon's manager, Ted Harris, and pressured him to open the ballroom to Black swing fans.

Harris responded by asking the *Northwest Enterprise* to sponsor a special "Jim Crow" night, for Black patrons only. The editors were appalled. Why should they agree to Jim Crow in the ballroom when they were fighting it everywhere else? They refused. Gerald Wells, however, already inured to segregation

Evelyn Williamson sings with the Lionel Hampton Orchestra at the Trianon Ballroom, December 1940.

as president of Local 493, agreed to the sponsorship, no doubt hoping for more cooperation down the line. The result, as with Powell Barnett's hopeful acquiescence in the original formation of Local 493 three decades earlier, was less happy. After the Hamp dance the Trianon instituted a regular policy of hosting "Colored Folks" Monday-night dances (known pejoratively in the Black community as "spook nights"), while continuing to bar Black fans and rarely book Black bands during the rest of the week, thereby tightening racism's hold over the Seattle music business.

Ted Harris and John Savage justified this segregation policy by disingenuously citing a Seattle city ordinance against "mixed dancing" that prevented them from admitting Black patrons, even if they had wanted to. For more than five decades this schoolboy's tale of a segregationist city ordinance was repeated in dozens of newspapers and journals, but in fact it was nothing more than a cynical ruse on the part of ballroom operators to keep Black people out. No such law ever existed. That locals actually believed there was a law in Seattle against Black and white people dancing together—and could accept its existence—says as much about Seattleites' ignorance of their own special history as it does about the general American acceptance of racism as a fact of life. For despite frequent de facto segregation, in most areas Seattle had always rejected segregation as retrograde. The state of Washington has a remarkably progressive civil-rights record, in comparison not only to the South but to other Western states.

The reason most Black people gave for moving to Washington in the early 1900s, for example, was that "Black Laws" in Oregon prohibited African Americans from owning land or marrying white people. Washington embraced civil-rights legislation before many other states did. As early as 1890, the year the state constitution was adopted, the legislature approved a Public Accommodations Act, which provided for "equal enjoyment" of inns, public conveyances, restaurants, theaters, and other public places. Historian Esther Mumford wrote:

> Some of the most prominent black members of the Seattle community came here in quest of "free air." Almost without exception, they came to Seattle with expectations of a better life. They found few legal barriers erected against them, although race prejudice was often as effective as proscriptive laws. . . . Despite numerous obstacles to the realization of their full capacities as useful human beings here, Seattle and Washington State offered considerable improvements over the places most Blacks had left.

This is not to say that racism and segregation did not exist. Pianist Patti Bown remembered that well into the 1950s, a Black entertainer as famous as Marian Anderson would stay with Bown's parents rather than undergo the humiliation of staying in one of the hotels in the International District open to Black people—the Coast, the Tokiwa, the Golden West, or the Mar. Restrictive real-estate covenants against Black, Jewish, and Asian people and the insurance company practice called redlining, which made it almost impossible for people who were not white to get mortgages, were also common. These created the segregated residential patterns that exist today in Seattle, Tacoma, and Spokane. But such policies were milder and less predictable (not to mention, illegal) in Washington than elsewhere. Theater facilities, for example, were sometimes segregated and sometimes integrated. The balcony of the Palomar Theater, known as "Peanut Heaven," was reserved for Black patrons. At the Liberty Theater, however, seating was open.

During the 1940s the Seattle tradition of tolerance between the races was put to the test. Prior to the war, fewer Black people than Japanese Americans lived in Seattle. Between 1940 and 1950, Seattle's African American population in the city grew from 3,789 to 15,667. It was the promise of war work—in the aluminum plants, shipyards, and airplane and electrical power industries, plus the armed services—that drew these new migrants. What they found, unfortunately, wasn't always as hospitable as the "free air" they had hoped for. Boeing, for example, had a policy of hiring only white people, which it blamed on the charter of the Aero-Mechanics Union. As we have seen, the musicians' union was also segregated.

White migrants from the South attempted to impose their "separate but equal" customs on the Northwest; some Northwesterners, panicking at the sudden multiculturalization of their home turf, found themselves chiming in. The Black press bristled with angry stories. Signs saying "WE CATER TO WHITES ONLY" sprang up in all but three restaurants in the city of Bremerton, Washington. The town's Housing Authority built separate facilities for Black and white citizens. The Navy base spent hundreds of thousands of dollars constructing duplicate facilities for Black families; Quincy Jones grew up in one of them, called Sinclair Heights. The commander at the Bremerton Navy Yard recommended Black workers be rerouted "somewhere else." An advertisement for Christmas help placed by the Frederick & Nelson department store in the November 12, 1941, *Seattle Post-Intelligencer* requested white applicants only. Five Black soldiers were told by the owner of Tacoma's Grill Cafe, "I won't feed you in here—you'll have to go back to the Chicken Coop." The Madrona Theatre, at Twenty-Eighth and East Cherry Street, attempted to eject a Black family for sitting "on the wrong side of the house," and a downtown roller rink refused admission to a group of Black children on a birthday outing. The Pacific Foundry Company in Renton, Washington, segregated its bathrooms; the Black workers went on strike.

A race riot broke out at Fort Lawton, in Seattle, and a white soldier was lynched. When episodes of violence threatened to erupt into full-scale riots, such as the one that occurred in Detroit, Black leaders, in concert with the NAACP, appealed to the mayor, the City Council, the governor, and the courts. The membership of the Seattle chapter of the NAACP increased from 85 to 1,550 during the war years. A Committee for the Defense of Negro Labor's Right to Work at Boeing Airplane Company was formed. Eventually jobs began to open up to Black workers. By the summer of 1944, Boeing had sixteen hundred Black employees.

It was against such a background of racial struggle that the swing era unfolded for Black musicians and fans. For white audiences the Trianon Ballroom was a gala, glittering dreamland, one that would provide nostalgic memories for decades. For Black fans it was an off-limits place where one could attend dances only on "spook night." For white music lovers, after-hours clubs were an optional, "colorful" recreation. For Black artists they were the only places where a musician could make real money and where Black fans were allowed to enjoy the music. For many white folks the swing era offered a great job at the Boeing Company or Kaiser Aluminum, with plenty of money to spend to see Tommy Dorsey. For Black folks it meant joining the NAACP to see if the Renton Foundry would stop trying to shove them into a "colored" bathroom. For Black musicians the main issue was finding a place to work. Though apparently there was no written policy at Local 76 prohibiting them from working in downtown venues, they didn't, and every musician, white or Black, who played during this era speaks with certainty of "turf," "jurisdictions," and "color lines." Downtown—the area north of Yesler and west of Eighth Avenue, which included all the theaters—was for white players only; "cross-town," from the First Avenue dives up through Chinatown and the hub of Twelfth and Jackson, was for Black musicians, as were the all-night roadhouses outside of town. Exceptions were few.

Ken Boas, a young white player who worked mainly with Black musicians, became so furious at the segregation policy that he resigned from Local 76 and joined Local 493. Other white musicians, including Bill Rinaldi and Traff Hubert, followed suit. The Black union, for its part, was pretty loosely run. Gerald Wells presided over the union out of his house, though much of its business was conducted after 1950 from the Blue Note "clubhouse" at Fourteenth and Jefferson, where musicians congregated to jam after their gigs and take advantage of the twenty-five-cent drinks. At its peak the Black union probably had no more than 160 members. Emmett Lewis took over the presidency in 1954, tightened it up, and eventually presided over its merger with Local 76.

For white musicians the benefit of maintaining two unions was that it reserved the best-paying, "legit" gigs—in the pit for touring theatrical shows, at radio stations, and in ballrooms and downtown hotels—for them. The after-hours dives were left to Black musicians. Members of the white union sometimes defended this exclusionary practice by charging that Black musicians had crude musical skills, couldn't read music as well as white musicians, played out of tune, and were not dependable. This was a racist and self-reinforcing argument for perpetuating segregation and obviously not accurate as a generalization. But for some white musicians there was enough truth to it to keep the stereotype alive.

Part of the conflict was cultural. Jazz has a different set of standards than European music. To play it effectively, a musician must develop an inner metronomic time sense, the ability to improvise, a personal sound with varying timbres, and a rhythmic attitude usually called "swing." The white European tradition, on the other hand, stresses rigid intonation, strong sight-reading, section playing, and conformity. As long as the unions were segregated, white musicians had the advantage of being able to freely mine the skills of Black musicians in after-hours clubs—sitting in, collecting ideas, and honing their improvising jazz skills—while Black musicians did not have the reciprocal privilege. How could a Black musician learn to sight-read effectively or play in section with standard European intonation when he was denied the right to play in the very situations where he might learn to do so? This one-way street guaranteed that while white musicians could learn to play jazz, Black musicians would continue to be barred from the "legit" jobs. Understandably, when white musicians in turn went on to make a great deal of money playing and recording jazz, Black musicians were bitter.

Leaving the dive jobs to Black musicians did have an ironic effect, however. Many of the gigs in the Black clubs paid fivefold in tips what the downtown jobs could yield. "All those others, you go down there and make a little piddling salary, maybe twenty-five dollars a week," recalled trumpet man Bob Russell. "And we were doing better than that. At least a hundred to a hundred and a half, anywhere in there. So that's one reason why we stayed with those after-hours clubs." The band that epitomized this situation—and indeed the Black swing era in Seattle—was led by a Northwest musician who paid his dues on the Depression scene up and down the coast. Though Al Pierre did not start a bona fide swing band in Seattle until the early 1940s, his Portland group, the Royal Knights, must count as the first homegrown Black swing band in the Northwest. Pierre, who learned to play piano from his mother, was born in Tacoma in 1902. According to Pierre's sister, Johnie Spearman, she and her brother and four other siblings grew up in Midland, a rural suburb of Tacoma, in a big house, formerly a hunting lodge, with a stone fireplace and a winding staircase. In the fall the boys would hunt pheasant with their father in the nearby woods. Musicians often came out for rehearsals and fried-chicken feasts.

Pierre moved to Seattle in 1922, where he organized his first band, Al Pierre's Royal Knights. In the late 1920s he relocated to Portland, where his group played

The Little Harlem Rondivoo, in Tacoma, 1935. Pianist is unknown.

a steady gig for twelve years with Seattle trumpeter Jimmy Adams in the lineup. During this period Pierre also appeared in Seattle at Washington Hall and Finnish Hall, as well as in Los Angeles with Charlie Echols in 1926 and Joe Darensbourg in 1927. Duke Turner, an Oakland drummer, remembered playing with Pierre in Palo Alto, California: "Al was a very good pianist. . . . You put a piece of sheet music in front of [him] and [he] could play. [He] played in a dance style and improvised quite a bit." At this time vocalist Russell Jones and drummer Chester Wells worked with Al. Leonard Gayton left Seattle for Portland to do the same. In 1939, Pierre's band broke up and he moved back to Seattle, where he organized a group that played on cruises up the Inside Passage to Alaska.

Pierre was well-liked, an amiable, professional leader who could easily get the best from his musicians. As a player, he was a competent stride man who knew his scales in all twelve keys, but his style seems to have been somewhat ornamental. "Al was a 'butterfly' piano player," said trumpeter Leon Vaughn, who worked for him. "*Phur-ur-ur-ur*—you know. He wasn't the real jazzy piano player with a steady beat, like Mary Lou Williams." Joe Darensbourg's main recollection of the pianist was that he owned a tuxedo, which other musicians habitually borrowed: "We used it so much the knees was stretched out of shape; look like they had a couple of footballs in there. It was all frayed to hell. Anybody would see us, they'd say, 'I see you got Al's tuxedo!'"

After the Alaska foray and during World War II, Pierre probably settled in Seattle. In 1943 his band had a steady gig every Tuesday at the Savoy Community Center, on Twenty-First Avenue and East Madison Street. In 1944 he played regularly at the New Chinatown. In the same era he put together his own book of arrangements for a little big band and started working after hours at the Union Club (also called the Marine Club) at First Avenue and Cherry Street. The Union Club was a large speakeasy with a long bar, a dance floor, and a casino where you could often find prizefighter Eddie Cotton's manager rolling dice. The waitresses wore drape trousers and gabardine shirts.

Pierre used mostly stock arrangements of commercial and jump tunes and relied on table singers—usually Palmer Johnson's old cohort, Russell Jones and torch singer Dee Dee Hackett—to please the crowd. The band was impeccably rehearsed. A 1944 acetate recording of the tune "Jammin'" reveals the Pierre band as fiery and vivid, with nattily executed lines crisscrossing each other in an excited, Lunceford-like manner. The lineup included Pierre on piano, Bill Rinaldi on bass, Vernon Brown on drums, William Joseph on alto saxophone (later replaced by Terry Cruise), Jabo Ward on tenor saxophone, Bob Russell or Leon Vaughn on trumpet, and Major Pigford on trombone. "It was primarily a dance band," remembered Al Turay, who sometimes sat in after his own gigs. "But it was a Black dance band, and their type of dance music was jazz." According to saxophonist Jabo Ward, who worked with Pierre from 1943 to 1949:

> The band played tunes by Ellington, Basie, and blues things. We played at the Union Club from 1 a.m. 'til 5 a.m. Sometimes Harry Fox sang bawdy songs. He'd get to singing [at one table] and everybody would want to know, "What is he singing over there?" So they'd be wanting to go over there and listen, too. We'd tell 'em, "I'll be over to your table in a few minutes."
>
> The place used to be packed. They had two bands. We were the late band. People were ready to hear music by the time we got there. They were ready to dance and drink. After a while, it'd be just like a little floor show. The band would play a number, then we'd have the singer come on and do two or three numbers, then the band would play, then they'd feature one instrument, then we'd go back to the

The Al Pierre Band at the Yukon Club, 1944–48. *Left to right:* Vernon Brown, Al Pierre, Bob Russell, Terry Cruise, Jabo Ward.

dancing. In other words, one musician would be in the spotlight. Floor show, table singing, band.

Pierre's central role in Northwest jazz was highlighted in 1945, when his group christened the bandstand at the Dude Ranch, soon to be the most popular spot on Williams Avenue (Portland's answer to Jackson Street), and in the same year he opened his own bar, Al's Lucky Hour, at 1315 Yesler Way in Seattle. Pierre remained a celebrated figure in the Black community throughout the 1940s.

Pierre himself played in the flowery, California manner, but his band was steeped in modern, Kansas City swing. Vernon Brown, Bob Russell, Leon Vaughn, Jabo Ward, and William Joseph all came to Seattle from the Midwest. The importation of these five players marks a stylistic turning point in Seattle music, the

The Vernon Brown band at the Marine Club (aka the Union Club), 1945. *Left to right:* Bob Russell, Roscoe Weathers, Vernon Brown, Jabo Ward, Bill Rinaldi, Lucky Cook, unknown conga player.

birth of a blend between California and Midwestern influences. Brown may have been Pierre's greatest gift to Seattle. Brown grew up around the great nascent swing bands in Kansas City and performed intermittently with several minor ones, including those of Grant Moore and Eli Rice. In 1943, through a mutual friend, Pierre got word to Brown that he would pay him $100 a week if Vernon would come to the Northwest. "Vernon Brown was the Jo Jones–type drummer, Kansas City–style," remembered Leon Vaughn. "He would catch up real quick on your riffs and back you with the drums. Vernon accentuated what you were doing. He was one of the best big-band drummers that I played with."

Brown became one of the city's legends, a steady timekeeper who sat behind his cymbals and played all night, sipping from a bottle of Thunderbird. Bob Russell remembered that unlike many other musicians who were led to ruin by liquor, Brown seemed to thrive on it: "Vern would drink just as much as you'd pass him and it never bothered him. He'd sit there with his big self, just sittin' there, never strain. He got so that he would get tired of straining and he'd get comfortable. When he'd get tired, he'd work on the sock cymbal. When he'd get to working on that there wasn't no need to bother him, 'cause he was going to do nothing but keep a steady rhythm all night. I don't think I know of anybody around here that was any stronger than he was." "They'd say that once that he set a time, you could not shake him from it," remembered his wife, Wanda, a white vocalist whose career paralleled Vernon's. "He would never go away from that. He was steady. He wasn't a flamboyant-type drummer. He didn't throw his sticks up in the air and all that sort of stuff. He just kept good time."

Bob Russell, trumpet "screamer" supreme, brought a KC résumé to the Pierre wind section paralleled by no one else in Seattle. An opinionated but gentle fellow whose health was failing badly when he was interviewed in 1989, Russell was born in Zion, Wyoming, and raised in Kansas City and Denver. Russell said that despite the legends about Bennie Moten, Harlan Leonard, Count Basie, and others who were reshaping jazz in the 1920s, there wasn't a lot of steady work in Kansas City. "Moten organized a band and talked to me about joining, but I decided, no, I'd stay right where I was at, playing in theaters and nightclubs. Right across the street [from the club where he was working] was the Lincoln Theater. We'd finish there around 11:05 or 11:10 at night and I'd go right across the street, go upstairs and play until four or five o'clock in the morning." Russell worked for Harry Dillard in a small pit band. Everyone in the outfit could read: "There wasn't no goofin' there. Wasn't *no* sliding over and saying 'Let's play this.' You played what was on that sheet." At intermission the band played jazz.

Sometime around 1928, Russell went out with Bennie Moten's chief rival in Kansas City, George E. Lee, who billed himself as the "Cab Calloway of the West" and later hired the young Charlie Parker. One of Lee's calling cards was his gold-plated instruments. Even his tuba was gold. Russell didn't care for Lee's ostentatiousness ("All that gold just didn't look right to me"), but indirectly the shiny array of instruments led to a chance meeting that jazz fans are still grateful for. One day, when the Lee band was playing Parsons, Kansas, a young man named Wilbur Clayton happened to come to the dance. Recalled Clayton:

> We all went to the dance and as soon as I entered the hall I saw all of those beautiful instruments standing on the bandstand and I flipped. . . . I stood in front of this band and watched them as they began to tune up. I became rooted right to the spot. During the dance, I talked with one of the trumpet players in the band, Bob Russell. He was one cool cat and so sharp. He had four or five different kinds of horns in front of him. He took me under his wing a little bit and told me how much money they made, what nice times they had, and how he enjoyed playing. He had just joined George's band and was a well-known trumpeter among the "territory

The Terry Cruise Orchestra at Dick Parker's Ballroom, ca. 1957. *Left to right:* Johnny Moton, Terry Cruise, Bob Moffat, Kenny Pernell, Junie Bradford, Carlos Ward, Dick Thorlakson, Bob Russell, Ish Dotson, Don Glenn, Leon Vaughn, William Joseph, unknown conga player.

> bands," as they were called. . . . After talking to Bob I said to myself, "This is it! I'm going to get a trumpet."

Of course, Wilbur was none other than "Buck" Clayton, who became not only a seminal stylist in the Basie band but a leader in his own right.

While Bob Russell was in Texas with the Lee band, Grant Moore and His Original New Orleans Black Devils sent for him. With Moore, Russell toured a circuit of ballrooms in Iowa, Nebraska, Oklahoma, the Dakotas, and Minnesota. He soloed on two sides Moore recorded, the driving "Original Dixieland One-Step" and "Mama Don't Allow," a novelty number. Russell left Grant's band and joined Tommy Fox, a nightclub bandleader in Milwaukee, then played with Burt Bailey, in whose band he worked with Vernon Brown. Brown referred Russell to Al Pierre.

"He was experimenting with mouthpieces," recalled Major Pigford, a trombone player familiar with such practices. "He would take a mouthpiece and shave it down crossways so with that very little cup he would play high notes." Leon

Vaughn remembered Russell as "one of those guys who could stand up and take ten choruses above high C." Russell worked with Al Pierre until the band broke up in 1951, then worked in a big band with saxophonist Terry Cruise throughout the 1950s and 1960s while holding down a day job at Seattle City Light.

Leon Vaughn was the other trumpet player who worked a lot with Pierre. Like Bob Russell, Vaughn, who was born in Topeka, Kansas, had a deep background in Kansas City music, though jazz took a back seat to college before he came to Seattle. Vaughn's story reads like a textbook illustration of the way racism forced many African Americans into the music business. He was a compact, straight-talking fellow with a head for statistics, a knack for telling a good yarn, and a great impatience with anything he called "bull." Retiring after twenty-five years as a site engineer for Boeing, Vaughn became an avid gardener (he grew herbs for a local restaurant) and a proud grandfather. The walls of his spacious home above Madison Park were covered with plaques and certificates marking his many ventures into community service.

Born in Topeka, Kansas, in 1916, Vaughn graduated from Washburn University with the intention of becoming a civil attorney. When he finished college, he won a statewide legal contest, the Corpus Juris. "The winner was supposed to join one of the big white firms, in Topeka," he said. "When I went in there I had an appointment with the top partner. He looked up and saw me and said, 'We don't need the janitor up here at this time.' I knew then that it was a dead issue. At that time the only thing a Black lawyer could do was criminal law and I didn't want to do that." The idea of becoming a musician grew on him slowly. When he was four, his mother started him on piano; at seven, he started trumpet, playing in the school concert band and marching band.

> When I was twelve years old, Jo Jones came to town. He was playing what they call "Ten Cents a Dance" at the Kansas State Fair. His trumpet player got appendicitis and had to be operated on, and they wanted somebody that could read music, so they recommended me. I can remember the first tune I ever played as a jazz musician was "When Kansas City Kitty Smiles at Me."
>
> Jo Jones took me down to Kansas City, but before he took me away my mother made me promise I would play music in the summer, but in the fall I had to come back and finish school. So I faithfully went back and finished all of my school. Jo Jones paid us twenty-eight dollars a week. When I brought that home, my dad

> went through the ceiling. He was making seventeen dollars with four kids. From then on, I found out I could put my brother and sister through school with my money from playing music.

Vaughn formed a small band. He played around Kansas City clubs and on jaunts outside of town, sometimes working with luminaries such as Mary Lou Williams, Ben Thigpen, or bassist Adolphus Alsbrook, who later moved to Seattle. Vaughn greedily drank in the new sounds, hanging out at the Sunset Club and the Reno Club, listening to Jay McShann, Big Joe Turner, George E. Lee, Bennie Moten, Count Basie, and the rest. "We would grab up anybody we could—Wynton Graham, Ben Webster, Cliff McTier, Jay McShann. Take off on a little gig in the surrounding towns. None of the bands had steady employment. It was all one-night stands."

After a couple of brief stints in Omaha with Cluss Webb and his Spiders, and the Nat Towles band, Vaughn worked in Minneapolis for a while, then got a telegram from Colorado, where Alsbrook was playing with Eli Rice. A Midwest tour with the Rice band landed Vaughn in North Carolina, where he remembered finding the Pettiford family band stranded (including the great bassist Oscar Pettiford) and helping take up a collection to send them back to Minneapolis, where Vaughn returned as well. As the nation moved toward war, musicians were subject to conscription unless they took on vital work in factories or in the transportation industry, so in 1940, following his friend Alsbrook's lead, Vaughn got a job with the railroad.

> I gave away all my old band uniforms—I must have had eight or ten of them—but I kept my Bach trumpet. We were running on the Great Northern Empire Builder from Chicago to Tacoma. We'd catch the train in Minneapolis, go to Chicago, then come back and "walk across the country." We were waiters. We would stop in Seattle for the day. Then the next morning we had to put new groceries in the train for the ride back across the country. We came out here a couple of times in December. The grass was green, the roses were blooming. It had been thirty-six degrees below zero for thirty-six days in Minneapolis. So I decided I had enough of that!

One night in Seattle in 1942, at the Porters and Waiters Club (aka the Black and Tan), Leon met a white bandleader named Bud Storm who needed a singer/entertainer to spice up his group. Vaughn, who had done some ballad singing with the Rice band, agreed to play the part. His railroading days were over. With Storm, Vaughn played trumpet and sang, doing the popular Bunny Berigan feature "I Can't Get Started." Vaughn stayed with Bud Storm for ten months before joining the Al Pierre band in 1943 or 1944. He remembered Pierre's group as having a raw and bluesy Jay McShann sound and featuring novelty songs favored by gamblers, such as "Ace in the Hole" and "Big Fat Butterfly"—the latter a silly blues takeoff on "Poor Butterfly" that crowds went crazy for.

> I had never heard this song. But it got so famous around here. They had a lot of songs that people in this section, especially from Alaska, the gamblers, liked. I can remember one night when one of the landladies from Alaska who ran one of the big whorehouses up there came in. She started off giving us twenty dollars for a song. Well, there's a guy in there that's a gold miner and a fisherman. He says, "Don't play that bitch's song, play mine! Here's a hundred dollars." So they started a little bidding war. We ended up making something like eight thousand dollars in that one night. We stayed 'til about ten o'clock in the morning. It was real wild, something that I'd never seen before.

When he left the Pierre ensemble, Vaughn formed his own band at a basement club on Maynard, the Basin Street, using Adolphus Alsbrook and ex-Pierre alto man William Joseph, among others. Vaughn also occasionally used Clarence Williams, an ex–Al Pierre sideman and blues singer/guitarist who reportedly played in the style of T-Bone Walker. At one point Williams led a band in Los Angeles featuring the great R & B tenor man "Big Jay" McNeely. He also proved himself a solid blues vocalist on three jazz-oriented R & B recordings in 1947 led by alto saxophonist Luke Jones for the Atlas label. In the late 1940s, Williams moved to Portland, where he was known as "the Prince of the Blues" but could also be found working in Seattle as late as the 1990s. Even after Vaughn went to work for Boeing in 1948, he continued to play music with Pierre, Terry Cruise, and Joe Gauff, and in his own big band composed of other Boeing employees during the 1950s. Vaughn died in 2015.

Terry Cruise, the lead saxophone player for Al Pierre (and later, the emcee and front man for the band), was originally from Los Angeles. "He had a tone big as a house," according to Bob Russell, who contributed arrangements to Cruise's band in the 1950s. "He wasn't too fast as far as getting it down the horn. But he had such a beautiful tone. And he could swing it for you. And

Clarence Williams sings with the Leon Vaughn band at Basin Street, 1948. *Standing,* Williams. *Seated, left to right:* Ralph Stephens, Vaughn, Aaron Davis, Milton Walton.

when he would swing it, he still kept it beautiful." Cruise, who also played excellent clarinet, later became a board member of Local 493 and managed the Blue Note. He also worked with saxophonist Jabo Ward at the New Chinatown, an after-hours place on Sixth Avenue and Main Street, and he played for many of Norm Bobrow's shows. In the 1950s Cruise went to work days for the state liquor board and led a big band that included many of the sidemen who had worked with Al Pierre. He died in 1988.

The other reed man in the Pierre organization was Ulysses "Jabo" Ward, a remarkable musician who turned a late start into an asset, studying music so intensely he pushed past his swing-era counterparts into the world of bebop. Ward, like Vernon Brown, was from the Midwest, born in Kansas City in 1918. Although Ward did not play music as a teenager, he was exposed to the best of the swinging Southwest sounds. A tall, thin man who spoke in nervous fragments that were a bit like the bebop phrases he played, Ward sang in the school glee club and in a quartet. He remembered his father playing blues piano in the living room and his mother singing in the church choir. He heard Kansas City locals Count Basie and Thaymon Hayes, and he recalled that "Harlan Leonard and the Kansas City Rockets was a local group that we used to go and hear all the time and dance to."

Ward's father was a Pullman porter. In 1937 he gave Jabo a ticket to Seattle to visit a couple of schoolmates and look for a job. Ward wound up staying for three years, working in a lumber mill near Onalaska before joining the merchant marine. He returned to Kansas City briefly in 1940. Once back in Seattle, he boarded out. Ward had started teaching himself the trumpet, but on one of his trips to Alaska he decided he really wanted to play the saxophone. "As soon we docked in Seattle," he recalled, "I went right downtown and bought a Buescher sax. I went to a teacher, Frank Waldron, and paid for lessons in advance. I'd take a couple of lessons ashore and then be on a ship for eleven days. Because we were moving troops to Alaska, and not cargo, the ship would be empty on the return trip. I'd go up into my stateroom and play and play. That's how I learned."

From Waldron, Ward learned the "countermelodic" method of improvising: "You learn the melody and then you play your own melody behind that note. [Waldron] was technical, very technical. He liked finger independence. He loved execution. He loved tone quality and, above all, he wanted you to practice. He didn't have any time for students that didn't practice. And he could tell when you practiced. I've heard him tell his students, 'Have your parents come over with you next time, that's right. Because you're wasting your parents' money.'" Other models of technique and style for Ward at the time included saxophonist Aaron Davis and trumpet man Frank Walton. "These were my idols," he said. Ward was studying both tenor and alto saxophone—he would later take up flute as well—but for Al Pierre, Ward generally played the baritone sax. He played at first with a white band led by Vern Mallory, then joined the Pierre band, with whom he stayed for six years, from 1943 to 1950, playing six nights a week at the Union Club. During this period Ward also played in nearly every other after-hours venue. "When we got off from work, we'd usually tend to look for the jazz places. So there's where 14th and Jefferson [the Blue Note] came in. That's the place to unwind. Or we'd go to the Basin Street, where we could have sessions and everything. There's where we let our hair down and played the things that we wanted to play. 'How High the Moon,' 'All the Things You Are,' 'Indiana'—you could take those tunes and increase the tempo and make them jazz."

Ward told of one late-night jam when Vido Musso, Kai Winding, and Ray Wetzel, in town with the Stan Kenton band, came down. It was those after-hours sessions, oddly enough, that led Ward into an obsession with golf: the top of the piano in his Central District home was covered with golf trophies. "The guys who played at the Union Club would go out in the mornings after playing all night and play a round of golf," he said. "I thought it was pretty stupid, 'til one day they got me out there as a kind of joke, and I got hooked. When you play golf you have to relax and concentrate at the same time; you have to overcome obstacles like sandtraps; you have to challenge yourself to get better every day. It's just like music."

The Vern Mallory Orchestra, USO Club, Second Avenue, Seattle, 1943–44. *Left to right:* Don Lindley, Bob Mullaly, Jabo Ward, Marv Thomas, Chet Pietruszewski.

Swinging instrumentalists such as Ward and Vernon Brown were the musical backbone of Pierre's band, but what kept the customers coming back night after night were the vocalists—Russell Jones and Gertrude "Dee Dee" Hackett. The vocalists were also the key to making tips. A good night could net several hundred dollars in requests in the kitty—a lard can, in the case of the Union Club. Saxophonist Billy Tolles remembered watching the Al Pierre band work the tables:

> They had two singers, a man and a woman. They always had a saxophone between the band and the singer to play a little phrase to let the band know what the singer wanted to sing, what key it was in. Maybe this big pimp would have ten girls here and he'd be supporting the party, and this girl would want "How Deep Is the Ocean" and this one would want "Poor Butterfly," or "Stardust," or "Body and Soul." They'd be there at that table twenty or thirty minutes, just singing for them and getting three-, four-, and five-dollar tips. They could never go to their pocket, they had to keep it in between their fingers. When they'd get their fingers all full of money, they'd come back and drop it in the big, galvanized tub, sitting right here by the side of the piano player. And boy, in the middle of the night, man, Al Pierre would be taking his foot, stuffing that money down in that tub. They'd take home

eighty, ninety, one hundred dollars a night [apiece].

Dee Dee Hackett at Club Rizal, 1944.

Dee Dee Hackett, who came to Seattle from the San Francisco Bay Area, was by some recollections not only a crowd-pleaser but a stylist of national caliber. In Palmer Johnson's words: "When Ella first came out with 'A Tisket . . .' Dee Dee was around here singing up a storm, and the band was way up in tempo and she was out there scatting. She had a sense of timing, man. Dee Dee was the best I ever seen. Absotively! She learned her singing as a child in church, like spirituals and stuff. She was a singer, man. A SINGER. She loved to swing with the band. You could see her bouncing, and never, you could never lose her, no matter what riffs you made." One of Hackett's specialties was blues with truly "blue" lyrics, no doubt a favorite with gold miners and Yukon types. "She could sing all them nasty songs," remembered Russell. "Good, bad, nasty. When we had Dee Dee singing with us, why, it was just buy, buy, buy, buy, buy, man. Give her five, ten . . . and guys think nothing of it."

Originally from Alameda, California, Hackett was the daughter of a San Francisco preacher. She first performed in Seattle in 1933 at the Mardi Gras, at 908 Twelfth Avenue, with a "Colored Revue" that also featured Eddie "Rochester" Anderson, later famous on *The Jack Benny Program*. That same year, she toured nationally with a show called *Change Your Luck*, with musical director Curtis Mosby and pianist Wilbert Barranco. After several years touring the country with various revues, in 1935 Hackett found a comfortable niche working Black clubs in Stockton and Sacramento, California, taking time out for a Northwest tour in 1936 with bandleader Les Hite, a jaunt that very likely brought her back to Jackson Street, as that's the year Hite opened the Ubangi. Two years later, Hackett began to divide her time between Seattle and San Francisco. In 1938, per Johnson's recollection (Fitzgerald's "A-Tisket, A-Tasket" was a hit that year), Hackett worked regularly in Seattle, often at the Two Pals and the Club Rizal. San Francisco claimed her again, from 1940 through 1942, when she played a very popular engagement at the Club Alabam. The band was led by Hackett's old road mate, Wilbert Barranco, with ex-Seattleite Junior Raglin on bass. Hackett appears to have returned to Seattle after World War II, where she could be found singing at the Black and Tan and Finnish Hall. She left Seattle around 1951 and was last heard of in 1954, singing in a Roseburg, Oregon, lounge.

Pierre's other vocalist, Russell Jones, kept the rounders happy too. Jones specialized in songs that celebrated the gambling and hustling life, including the perennial "Ace in the Hole," plus "True Blue Lou" and "Carry the Torch." Born a year before Palmer Johnson, Jones had grown up in the same Los Angeles neighborhood, serving his apprenticeship in the Charlie Echols band in 1931, along with Bumps Myers and Kid Ory. The following year, Jones was in Seattle playing the African American Mid-Summer Ball but appears to have returned to LA during the 1930s. Jones worked with Palmer Johnson as well as Al Pierre. In 1943 a *Seattle Times* review of a Paramount Theater show with Johnson noted Jones's "rich baritone voice" and his "ability to use [it] well, as he demonstrated in his second number, often sung by Paul Robeson, 'Without a Song.'" With Jones's voice and Johnson's boogie-woogie piano, the hour-long act brought the house down every night. They took it to the Cave, in Vancouver, British Columbia, and to Portland's Cloud Room, then returned the following year to the Palomar Theater in Seattle. When Johnson left town for Alaska, Jones continued to sing with Al Pierre, at the Union Club, Charlie Beale's Rizal Club, and Basin Street. In February 1946 the singer performed with a ten-piece group called the Basin Street Band for a big dance at Finnish Hall.

Al Pierre kept working till the end. In early 1949 his little swing band moved from the Union Club to the Showbox Theater, on First Avenue. But the swing era was over; business started to wane. When the band's bookings were cut from five to four to three nights a week, Pierre, like Johnson, began to look north to Alaska. He found the band a regular job in Fairbanks, at the Green Lantern, but his musicians didn't care for the cold climate and remoteness of the Far North. The band gradually fell apart. "We went up there with six pieces," remembered Russell. "Dee Dee was with us. Everything but the bass player—Vern, Al, Jabo, Terry, myself, and Dee Dee. Dee Dee came back first, then Jabo. Then I come down."

Al Pierre became ill in Alaska and died in Seattle of emphysema on October 13, 1949. Stylistically his group represented the pinnacle of Black swing in Seattle—danceable music with hot solos, table singing, and, due to the small market it catered to, some accommodation to the popular taste for romantic and novelty songs. Though Pierre and his arrangers did not generate an original style, the group afforded an authentic opportunity for young players to learn what real jazz music was. The band also had a genuinely local flavor, with its emphasis on the Alaskan rounder tunes.

Pierre spent much of his working life in Seattle along First Avenue, in the white honky-tonk area dominated by sailors and transients. There was a reason for this. The Central District boasted dozens of small after-hours clubs, but there was no major ballroom or social center for African Americans, comparable to the Trianon Ballroom, in their own neighborhood. This glaring lack of recreational facilities was a major civic issue for Seattle's Black community. "There wasn't too much for us to do, as a group, unless you were a musician, or some sort of hustler," recalled Buster Clayborn, an African American whose father had been a friend of Noodles Smith and who worked with a citizens' committee to integrate Seattle's Jefferson Park golf course in the 1940s. "That's the thing that bothered me more than anything else when I come out here. There wasn't nothin' for us to do."

As early as the 1920s, Black leaders had approached the City of Seattle to complain about statutes and encumbrances that barred the way of Black entrepreneurs attempting to create social venues in African American neighborhoods. One city ordinance prohibited dance halls east of Eighth Avenue or south of Dearborn Street. In 1920, Powell Barnett, who had railed against segregated unions a decade before, chaired the Committee to Establish the East Madison YMCA, arguing that the Central District needed a neighborhood place to keep Black youth from getting into mischief. In the mid-1930s, "Doc" Hamilton had made the same argument, though admittedly from a rather different perspective. Ironically, Barnett's opponents argued this was a "Jim Crow" idea, because the new Y would be all Black! Barnett's success on the YMCA issue—the branch opened in 1936—would later mean that kids like Quincy Jones and Gerald Brashear had a neighborhood place to try out some of their first music.

In 1939 members of the Black community took a petition with 118 signatures to the City Council and hired an attorney, requesting a dance-hall license be given to Ira F. Norris, who owned a tavern at Twenty-First Avenue and

East Madison Street. He was turned down. Two years later, a neighborhood entrepreneur named Lemuel Honeysuckle succeeded where Norris had failed. Though the City Council didn't officially grant him a dance-hall license until February 1946 (by which time it was under new ownership), Honeysuckle went ahead and remodeled the Gala Theatre at Twenty-First and Madison (originally a roundhouse for streetcars), named it the Savoy Ballroom, and started throwing Saturday-afternoon dances there. For the next two decades, in its numerous incarnations as the Savoy, the House of Joy, and Birdland, this establishment, along with the East Madison YMCA, would ring with the sounds of Black swing, blues, jazz, and rock 'n' roll. The Trianon might have Curt Sykes and Gaylord Jones, but the Savoy would host Al Pierre, Billy Tolles, the Jive Bombers, Bumps and Charlie Blackwell, Vern Mallory, Al Hickey, Tootie Boyd, Banjoski Adams, Ernestine Anderson, and Dave Lewis, among others.

The first Black swing band to debut at the Savoy Ballroom, in December 1941, consisted of a bunch of high school kids led by tenor saxophonist Billy Tolles. Called the Savoy Boys, it would be the spawning ground for a new generation of hot swing-to-bebop players who took the music to the next stop beyond Al Pierre. Tolles was one of the more colorful characters in Seattle jazz. Arrogant, natty, vain, and restless, he combined a college education with a streetwise wit, a pairing that led him into all kinds of social and musical situations. Tolles seemed more like the kind of saxophone player you'd meet on the road with James Brown than with Duke Ellington, but he was a complete master of the instrument. Born in Waukegan, Illinois, in 1924, Tolles came to Seattle when he was five. His father was a cousin of the Midwestern territory bandleader Nat Towles, though their names were spelled differently. Tolles grew up in Seattle's East Madison neighborhood, with all its attendant cultural aspirations. He remembered: "My grandmother was an advocate of Josephine Baker. She wanted me to be artsy and have the 'right kind of background' so that I could do something else besides wait tables or be a domestic, which is what most Black people were doing in those days. I started on piano at about the age of nine or ten, then I studied dance with Syvilla Fort, a disciple of Katherine Dunham. But the real music came from Mount Zion Baptist Church, where I sang in the junior choir. That's where I got my foundation."

Tolles learned to play trumpet from a friend of his mother, and in high school he played in the marching band. He also played in a swing quartet, the Four Sharps, formed by Charlie Blackwell, with classmates Gerald Brashear and Sonny Booker. A couple of years later, Tolles lost his front teeth playing

"Eastside Hall," known in the 1930s as the Gala Theatre, later as the Savoy Ballroom, and finally as Birdland, at 2201 East Madison Street.

football and switched to sousaphone. He was a popular dancer, and he and his jitterbug partner, pianist Betty Marshall, won prizes for their performances. But up to this point, Tolles had had no desire to be a professional musician, nor had he considered playing the saxophone. Then he saw Illinois Jacquet at a Norm Bobrow concert at the Moore Theatre.

> That Illinois Jacquet almost made me jump out of the balcony, man. I've never been so roused up in all my life. From that day on, I started listening to the saxophone. One afternoon, I was in Bill Washington's basement, lagging tax tokens to the wall, and I beat him out of some money. I accidentally kicked open this old saxophone case. We opened it up, and here's this moldy, C melody saxophone. I said, "I'm going to take this saxophone for security 'til you pay me." I took it home and rubbed it all up and put rubber bands on it and made all the notes work and put some kind of reed on it and played "I Love You Truly," right off the bat. *Bam!* It scared me. That was the end of my piano career. I was thirteen years old.
>
> I went over to Gerald's to show him what I was doing and, lo and behold, here's Gerald sitting on his back porch, playing a C melody saxophone that he had got from someplace, so we set out there and played duets. Gerald was probably about a year or so older than me. We decided that we should have a swing band. We all met down at Gerald and Buddy [Brashear]'s house.

At first the group copied Count Basie records. The saxophones would go into the kitchen and the rest of the band would stay in the living room. Then Tolles began to write simple arrangements of his own. "I wrote out parts

(*left*) Billy Tolles as a teenager, when he started with the Savoy Boys, ca. 1941.

(*right*) Betty Marshall and Billy Tolles competing as a jitterbug team, 1940s.

for Charlie Barnet's 'Redskin Rumba' and Erskine Hawkins's 'Uncle Bud,'" he recalled, "and I came back and taught each one how to play his part at a rehearsal. Boy, that neighborhood jumped! People came from miles around. The police came. That was the beginning of the Savoy Boys orchestra." This was in 1941. The personnel of the Savoy Boys was Billy Tolles, Gerald Brashear, Floyd Franklin, and George Francis (the son of vocalist Lillian Goode), saxophone; Don Alexander, Carl Valley, and Sonny Booker, trumpet; George Turner, Major Pigford, and Billy Anderson, trombone; Bobby Catlett (Buddy Catlett's brother), guitar; Delbert Brown, drums; and Kenny Boas, the only white member of the group, piano.

Don Manning, who was playing over at Roosevelt High in the white counterpart to the Savoy Boys, remembered the Savoy Boys playing Charlie Barnet's version of "Cherokee." "Boy, did they swing," he said. "They just swung like maniacs." According to Major Pigford, "It was a good band. We played a lot of things from written music, from orchestrations I guess that Billy bought. Then a lot of things we just put together by head. We featured Bobby Catlett on 'Floyd's Guitar Blues.' Sonny Booker could play the heck out of 'Stardust.' Buddy Brashear played 'After Hours.' We also did 'Tuxedo Junction,' 'Stompin' at the

The Savoy Boys at the Savoy Ballroom, ca. 1941. Buddy Brashear, piano; Sonny Booker, trumpet; Billy Tolles, tenor saxophone; Gerald Brashear, alto saxophone.

Savoy,' and 'Blues in the Night.'" The Savoy Boys got their name, their first gig, and early guidance in the ways of the street from Lemuel Honeysuckle, who had owned a pool hall on East Madison Street. "Honeysuckle and his brother owned a lot of property on Mercer Island," remembered Sonny Booker. "Honeysuckle always had a nightclub or a bootleg joint. He was like a pillar of the community. He'd put jobs up on the board if you wanted to work a certain place downtown. He had good connections with City Hall."

Sonny Booker, Savoy Boys trumpeter, became pretty well-connected himself. Booker was a slight, slow-talking man with delicate features, a sweet smile, and bedroom eyes. He is remembered by fans from the 1960s as the proprietor of the Checkmate nightclub, at Twenty-Third Avenue and Union Street (at one time the informal clubhouse of the Black Panthers), and as the co-owner of the Silver Fox limousine company. A generation of Hollywood stars also knew him as a fencing coach, a sport at which he was a master teacher until his death in 2003. But in his youth Booker was a star quarterback at Garfield High School who discovered that his charm and wit could win him as good a living on the street as his trumpet. His sense of the district, its characters and milieu, had a special, knowing quality.

Born in Canada in 1923, Booker was raised on a farm by one of the only Black families on Mercer Island, in the middle of Lake Washington, east of Seattle. He started music as a bugler for the Boy Scouts. At Garfield High School he was given a trumpet by guitarist Al Mitchell; lessons from Frank Waldron and a chair in the high school band followed. While at Garfield, Booker and Gerald Brashear took a quartet into the New Chinatown, a legitimate Chinese restaurant at Sixth Avenue South and South Main Street with a thriving bootleg business. Booker was astonished at how much money he could earn, and how much respect he suddenly commanded on the scene as a musician: "Musicians, they were the glamorous part of life, in those days. The peak of the jobs for the Black community were like mailmen and porters and skycaps. So if you weren't a musician or a pimp, you were riding on the boats or a shoe shine or a skycap, or on the railroad."

Booker's observation illuminates the important point that before the civil rights movement, playing jazz was one of the few economic opportunities available to African Americans. Booker's easy parallel between playing music and selling sex—"if you weren't a musician or a pimp"—highlights that the various "hustling" professions of gambling, pimping, and bootlegging, viewed as lowlife criminal activity by mainstream society, were entrepreneurial choices open to Black people. These were often the professions chosen by the most intelligent, ambitious, and magnanimous people in the community, who became highly respected regardless of their dealings. Booker continued:

> Prostitution was always a part of the Black community, in a sense, because that's what we ended up doing to make money. But the Black pimps that you had in those days were different than what you have today. They were like gentlemen. They dressed up. It was a way of life. A lot of the pimps were musicians—musician/pimps. Most of the pimps and hustlers were the pillars of the society, because they had the money to donate to the church. The pimps were respected and everybody knew they were pimps, and the whores, everybody knew they were whores. They were dressed up and they had money and everybody talked about them "going to work." It was just an understood deal, a way of life.

Booker freelanced throughout the late 1940s, playing with Al Pierre, Jabo Ward, and bandleader/promoter Bumps Blackwell, then left music in the early 1950s, when he and fellow Savoy Boy George Francis became the first Black bartenders to work in a downtown restaurant, the Barbecue Pit. In 1952, Booker moved to Pasadena, California, where he studied bass at the Westlake School of Music, played with Gerald Wilson's big band and saxophonist Teddy Edwards, and worked as a fencing coach for movie stars. In 1965 he returned to Seattle to open the Checkmate. In the early 1990s, Booker was a silver-haired gentleman with a bit of Jackson Street mischief in his eyes, who occasionally showed up at Lofurno's restaurant to blow a few tunes of sweetly crafted music. In the late 1990s and early 2000s, Booker presented a local jazz concert series at the Interbay Golf Center, Jazz on the Green.

Sitting behind Sonny Booker in the Savoy Boys was Major Pigford, a huge, imposing trombone player. Pigford's career was notable in that it extended through the three major 1940s Black bands—the Savoy Boys, the Al Pierre Orchestra, and the Bumps Blackwell Junior Band. Born in 1925, Pigford started out on clarinet but switched to trombone at age eleven. He asked Frank Waldron to teach him, but Waldron didn't feel qualified to teach trombone. Through studying the standard method books and by playing in the Washington Middle School band, Pigford learned the instrument. At Garfield High School music teacher Parker Cook was his mentor. According to Pigford, the Savoy Boys got together for the express purpose of playing the Garfield Funfest, which had a nightclub theme in 1941. Then the group started working at the Black and Tan. There, Major and his mates discovered the same high-rolling world that had opened Sonny Booker's eyes. "Those clubs," Pigford said, "some nights you'd sit around and make nothing but scale—eighty-four dollars a week. Other nights, here comes a big spender and every time he wants to hear a tune, he throws ten or twenty bucks in the kitty. Sometimes I'd go to school with five or six hundred dollars in my pocket!" Like many other young musicians, Pigford learned to play his instrument through jam sessions, sometimes taking it on the chin but always returning for more:

> You ran your scales at home, but the only place you could really learn to play was at a jam session. I mean sessions of the Jazz at the Philharmonic type, where you start a blues number, then anybody could come in and play two or three choruses. If you played halfway decently, they let you play. If you didn't, they'd tell you to get off the stand. You see, they'd make you feel so bad if you messed up, you had to go home and learn it if you wanted to keep on playing. Say, "Hey man, look past your foot so you can come in on time," or "Listen to yourself, you're playing flat," you know, whatever.
>
> One night, an all-girl band called the Darlings of Rhythm were playing at the Black and Tan. Quincy [Jones] and us, we all went down to hear them. I was drinking a lot. I got to feeling real good, and somebody said, "Hey, man, go up there and blow against that trombone player!" I didn't want to have no woman playing no trombone, you know. I hauled out my little horn and went up on the bandstand. They were playing some blues. I played one chorus, then she'd do the same thing I blew. I looked at her and then I blew what I thought was something a little more difficult. And she played what I played and also played something even a little more difficult. Pretty soon . . . "The hell with this!" I put my horn up. Well, the trombone player was Melba Liston!

Major Pigford went straight from the Savoy Boys to Al Pierre's band, later playing with a group Pierre put together for a locally mounted Black revue, "Blackbirds." He then joined the Bumps Blackwell Junior Band, which nurtured the next generation of Garfield kids—Quincy Jones, Buddy Catlett, and others. When the Blackwell band broke up, Pigford shipped out to sea, playing in a band in Yokohama, Japan. In 1953 he gave up music and moved to Detroit, where he earned a degree in biology. He returned to Seattle in 1974 and began working as a bookkeeper for Pacific Northwest Theatre Associates and playing private parties and dances with an eight-piece band, the Mixed Bag. Pigford died in 1992.

The Savoy Boys stayed together until the fall of 1943, when Billy Tolles left town to attend A & T (Agricultural and Technical) College, in Greensboro, North Carolina. Some of the other sidemen in Tolles's extraordinary "kid band" who went on to pursue music careers included Floyd Franklin, who played rhythm-and-blues gigs in Seattle in the early 1950s; Gerald Brashear, who became, at least briefly, the most successful and certainly the best bebop saxophonist in the city; Ken Boas, also a top early bebopper and an intimate of Ray Charles; and, of course, Tolles himself.

The world of music these young men faced after the war was much changed. Once the boys came home, the vogue shifted from swing to vocalists. Peggy Lee and Frank Sinatra replaced Tommy Dorsey and Benny Goodman as the public's idols. Soldiers came home, married, and stopped dancing. Ballrooms began to close. Money did not flow so freely. In addition to the new sweet vocals, three principal genres emerged to replace swing—bebop (or "progressive" jazz), lounge trios, and rock 'n' roll.

Bebop quintets inherited and expanded upon the tradition of the featured swing combo, which had stepped out in front of the bandstand during the swing era to play a hot tune or two. Rock 'n' roll was a commercial distillation of the blues-charged shuffles and jumps played by the postwar "little big bands" of Louis Jordan, T-Bone Walker, and Jack McVea. While bebop and rock 'n' roll were worlds apart—the former became difficult "art music" that demanded attentive listening, while the latter was simple and direct music for dancing—they both shared the common root of the swing band, which had for a while combined the two functions of art and dance. The piano or guitar lounge trio, developed by Nat Cole, was an extension of the big-band rhythm section, combining a modern approach to the keyboard with the once-over-lightly style of the Kansas City Six. The development of these postwar styles was influenced, at least in part, by an economic pinch that forced bandleaders to cut down from large groups to small.

The new styles also expressed the freedoms won by the Black community after the war. Bebop asserted the intention of African American musicians to present themselves as artists and intellectuals, not grinning entertainers. Rock 'n' roll signaled that Black musicians would express in public the raucous blues culture they had previously kept to themselves. Nat Cole's sophisticated piano and smooth crooning let the world know there was an upwardly mobile, Black middle class as suave and cool as—or cooler than—the white elite. The intimacy of the new musical styles reflected a change that crossed racial boundaries—namely, a shift in mood that occurred after the war. Gay Jones's trumpet player Pete Barrington captured it nicely: "You know, when the war ended, a great deal of sentimentality went out the door. There were songs during the war about the soldiers and their girlfriends and the loneliness. That kind of disappeared when the guys came back. And I've always thought this contributed to the demise of the big-band thing. Guys wanted to go to a small place, with an intimate little group, three or four guys. They weren't interested in competing at the ballroom level. They wanted to sit down and have a few drinks and talk to their lady."

All of the postwar styles emerged along Jackson Street between 1946 and 1951—sometimes in the same band—even as swing bands themselves continued to hang on. A great, cacophonous swell came over the town as bebop, Southern blues, swing, rhythm and blues, piano trios, and even Dixieland revivalist groups played all night up and down Jackson, from First to Fourteenth Avenues, and along the East Madison Street hub between Twenty-First and Twenty-Third Avenues. Musicians moved to town from Chicago, Florida, Louisiana, Texas, and West Virginia, bringing new sounds and ideas with them. When Billy Tolles came back to Seattle after the war and heard the Al Pierre band again, it sounded old-fashioned. "I said, 'Boy, that style is going out, man. That's that old-time "comp" playing the bass note and the chord [stride piano].' I had been in New York and heard piano players like I was trying to play. Quincy played piano like I wanted to play. And Ray Charles. People like that. I knew I wanted to be more modern than that."

The after-hours scene was headed for its zenith.

5 Ernestine Anderson and the First Beboppers

IMAGINE A TIME WHEN SEATTLE, which now rolls up its streets by midnight, was full of people walking up and down the sidewalk at two o'clock in the morning. When you could buy a newspaper at the corner of Fourteenth Avenue and Yesler Way from a man called Neversleep—at three a.m. When limousines pulled up to the 908 Club all night, disgorging celebrities and wealthy women wearing diamonds and furs. When "Cabdaddy" stood in front of the Rocking Chair, ready to hail you a cab—that is, if he knew who you were. Since the war had begun in earnest, the district had gone plain wild. Whatever a young sailor or soldier wanted—liquor, drugs, gambling, women—he could pretty much get on demand. There were clubs with full casinos upstairs—roulette wheels, blackjack, craps—and poker games that ran night and day. There wasn't a brand of liquor you couldn't buy. Women? There were gentlemen pimps behind and in front of the bar; sometimes they doubled on the bandstand too. Even heroin and cocaine were for sale. According to pianist Gerald Wiggins, who was stationed at Fort Lewis during the war, "Seattle was a hot town then. Believe me. You could get anything you wanted. It didn't make any difference. They had a guy, he'd come by your home and take your order. You want Johnnie Walker or Seagram's? You tell him. Half-pint, fifth, quart. He'd bring it to you. The music was good and money was like dirt. It was everywhere. Talk about high rollers. You couldn't believe it. You know, boom time. Shipyards and all this. Guys didn't know what to do with their paychecks. They did everything but go home."

Trumpet player Leon Vaughn said that in 1948, if he started walking up Jackson from First Avenue, by the time he reached Fourteenth, he had passed thirty-four nightclubs. Veteran establishments such as the 908, Two Pals, Congo, Showbox, Black and Tan, Yukon, and Union clubs were still going. In addition, new venues had opened, including the Washington Social Club, the Black Elks

Club (relocated from East Madison Street to Jackson Street, near Sixth Avenue South), the Savoy Ballroom, Club Maynard, and Basin Street, Rocking Chair, Blue Note, New Chinatown, Spinning Wheel, and Mardi Gras. There were bars where jazz came and went as well, like the Forty and Eight Club, the Submarine Room, the Aero-Marine Club, the Tuxedo, the Athens Club, and the Green Dot. The military bases too—Fort Lawton, Fort Lewis, Sand Point Naval Air Station, and McChord Air Force Base—hired musicians for both enlisted men's clubs and NCO clubs.

Many of these spots were full-fledged cabarets, with a floor show, fancy decor, doormen, and waiters. Others were simply joints set up as an excuse to sell bootleg booze. As white bassist Chuck Metcalf remembered: "There was this tremendous pressure during the war to have liquor on Sunday and liquor after hours. So what you had then was a lot of little clubs. A lot of them were like a little hole in the wall . . . really a small place with just a bar in the corner of the room that would be set up as a bandstand with round, plastic-covered tables and some chairs and a space cleared away for a dance floor. It would be kind of crowded and there'd be a jukebox and there would be a band." Large or small, the clubs brought out the customers. "Along Jackson Street, it was almost like Mardi Gras," said Al Turay. "Musicians would be traipsing up and down the street with their instrument cases, going in one club, sitting in, and going from one place to another." According to Wanda Brown, then a "dice girl" and singer who later married drummer Vernon Brown, "You could practically walk out of one door and walk right into another one."

"It was a very serious, New Orleans–kind of feeling," said white saxophonist Freddie Greenwell. "Just gala whoopee-time, all night long." Since liquor was still an illegal business, to flourish it had to be subsidized by either organized crime or City Hall. In Seattle there was no "mob." The boys in blue had been on the take since the Yukon Gold Rush. In 1947, Seattle mayor William Devin formalized the city's historic embrace of corruption with what he called the "tolerance policy," a citywide licensing system for low-stakes gambling, even though it was still prohibited by state law. Though the tolerance policy aimed specifically at gambling, not other forms of vice, in the mind of the general public it came to stand for the idea that the police would "tolerate" anything you paid them to ignore, because they always had. And while Devin idealistically thought the tolerance policy might curb police corruption by substituting city licenses for surreptitious payoffs, the old culture of handing off bags of cash to cops continued. It would be two more decades before the city finally cleaned up its act.

Gambling thrived, citywide. Al Hilbert, a Spokane native and nephew of bandleader Edythe Turnham, started working as a card dealer at the Basin Street Club after it opened in 1939. His boss, Dave Lee, paid a professional gambler to teach Hilbert how other gamblers cheated. "He made me go to a man who showed me how to run up a hand in poker and deal seconds and to read the cards that were marked," recalled Hilbert. "Then he gave me the game. I got forty percent of all the take in this game for two years. Completely run for two years, twenty-four hours! I got ten percent of the other shifts, because I was the head of it. The game was mine. So I made a lot of money." While surreptitious gambling went on behind closed doors, anyone could play the "Chinese lottery" out in the open. A form of keno in which customers bet on daily numbers, the Chinatown lottery was a popular form of entertainment that yielded hefty jackpots. Lottery headquarters was on Maynard, across from Basin Street. "The Chinese lottery was funny, because you could look right in the window. There was a storefront," Sonny Booker remembered. "They'd turn this thing up and the dice would fall down, and the numbers would come down. You could watch. *Bloom, bloom, bloom,* these little dice would fall down. They'd be marking the numbers all in Chinese."

As a dealer, bartender, and later assistant club manager, Al Hilbert became a savvy fellow, familiar with all aspects of the tolerance policy and how its system of payoffs worked. "Someone got six hundred [a month] for gambling and they got six hundred for the liquor," explained Hilbert. "The policemen on the beat were supposed to get twenty-five dollars a week." Every once in a while, to keep up a good front for the public, the police staged a raid. It was all quite routine. They would call in advance, and an employee—usually the bartender—would be chosen as the designated arrestee for the evening. As a precaution, Hilbert had all of his bartenders fingerprinted in advance at the police station, so they wouldn't have to waste time downtown when they were arrested. "When the bartenders got busted," said Al, "we'd give him an hour, so he could stop someplace and get him a hamburger on the way back to the club. The jail was not that far from Maynard and Jackson. And all you had to do when you went down there was sign your name."

"It's an old, old story for many of the prisoners," reported the *Seattle Times* in a 1940 exposé of the system. "They stand around for a few minutes in the booking office until their regular bondsmen post necessary bail. Then they are freed. . . . Almost without exception—it is always the same group of men who are defendants. They trot in and out of the jail and in and out of Judge Knott's court with surprising regularity. . . . The addresses at which they operate are usually typed on the complaints."

Though Seattle had no organized crime in the 1940s, many of the clubs were controlled by small-time hoods. The most notorious was a dapper but menacing fellow named "Russian John" Lasso, who specialized in the clip joints along First Avenue, including the Yukon Club, where Al Pierre played for a while. Lasso had come to Seattle from Russia by way of Alaska, and he spoke with an accent as thick as his cigars. He liked women with furs and large diamonds, sported a fifty-dollar hat and expensive suits, and always wore a gold four-leaf clover on his lapel. Lasso made sure he was well-connected downtown. When a rival tried to compete for the peep-show business on the strip, he got the cops and a crooked judge to set up the interloper on a drug rap. He was also rumored to have a homemade collection of "dum-dum" bullets. "He owned a club I worked in called the Cabin, in Tacoma," recalled drummer Jack Foy. "He was married to a white Russian girl, a singer, the whitest blonde you ever saw in your life. She kind of took a liking to me, which he didn't like, so one of the guys in the band told me I better find another gig. I did."

Though fellows like Russian John were occasionally arrested, essentially they operated with impunity. Periodic public outcries against the speakeasies led to police crackdowns, but soon enough, everyone would be back in business. A month after a particularly gruesome triple murder at the 410-B Tavern (which had been "raided" twenty-two times), a *Seattle Times* columnist spent a whole evening in illegal establishments and even received directions to the clubs from policemen. The military was not unaware of the recreational habits of its recruits. In May 1943 the district was declared "out of bounds" for soldiers stationed at Paine Field. But as Gerald Wiggins observed, such interdictions did little to stop the steady flow of soldiers to the area. The party lasted throughout the war and even a few years after it ended.

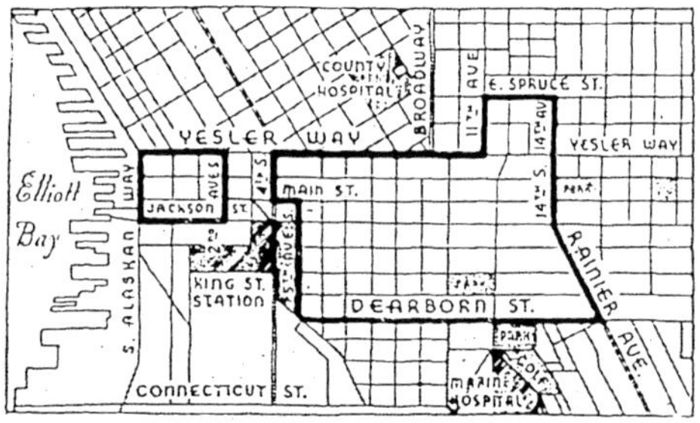

Areas in Seattle's "South End" were declared "out of bounds" for soldiers from Paine Field Army Air Base near Everett.

Despite what sounds like a dangerous underworld atmosphere, almost everyone who spent any time on Jackson Street in the 1940s reported that it was surprisingly safe. Wanda Brown described the scene this way:

Pete Peterson entertains soldiers out for a night on the town, 1940s.

You could walk up and down Jackson Street and you didn't have any fear. . . . I used to carry my whole bankroll up Jackson Street, used to go in the alley away from Jackson over to Maynard to catch a cab to come home. By myself. Nobody ever bothered me. I'd just be swinging this bankroll in my hand. And everybody knew I was a dice girl. They knew I had money in there. I used to go up to the Black Elks Club and I'd sit there with the bankroll and open it up, and pay for my drinks out of it.

Jackson Street was not only safe, it was racially relaxed to a degree that would be startling to a contemporary observer. "For people who came of age in the 1960s," said Chuck Metcalf, "it's really hard to imagine what race relations were like in those days. As someone who was totally naive, going into this club where practically everybody was Black, I can't think of any time when I didn't feel totally safe." Jim Gilles, a white pianist who played the Black Elks Club in the early 1950s, echoed the sentiment in 1989: "In those days, it was actually easier to mix racially than it is now. Even though there was strict segregation, it was like the back-door thing that everybody understood and nobody paid any attention to. On that particular scene, it was very harmonious."

Seattle's racial tolerance was not lost on mixed couples, for whom Seattle became—and remains—a beacon. Drummer Leonard Gayton recalled friends coming to Seattle from Portland because interracial marriage was illegal in Oregon. On the Jackson Street scene mixed couples were common: Wanda and Vernon Brown, Leon and Lorraine Vaughn, and Al and Dorothy Hilbert were three examples. This easy give-and-take between the races in Seattle's nightlife district had a profound influence on music. Barriers between Black and white traditions were never as clear-cut as they were in other Western cities, such as Los Angeles, where a "cool" white school evolved in contradistinction to the "hard bop" played by Black musicians. In Seattle the music of both Black and white folks tended to merge toward an agreeable middle, resulting in a melding of traditions that later was felt worldwide in the work of Jackson Street denizens such as Quincy Jones, Ray Charles, and Bumps Blackwell.

While Seattle's reputation as a harmonious place for racially mixed couples sizzled on the underground wire, few people outside the city knew it was also a hot spot for nightlife. This turned into a lucky break for fifteen-year-old vocalist Ernestine Anderson, whose father, ironically, was in part trying to get her away from the nightclub scene in Houston, Texas, when he moved to Seattle in 1944. Like thousands of Americans, Joseph Anderson was searching for a big paycheck in the shipping industry when he came to the Northwest; and like thousands of African Americans, he was seeking a better life—away from the South—for his wife, twin daughters, and two sons. Joseph was a fanatical blues fan who often spent his evenings listening to records by Bessie Smith and Lightnin' Hopkins. He sang bass in a male gospel quartet. Music was part of his life.

But ever since Ernestine had won a talent contest at the Eldorado Ballroom, at the age of twelve, she had thought about nothing but singing and jazz. Her grades were slipping. Anderson recalled:

> I got my first professional job when I was twelve. My godmother entered me in a talent contest. At the time, I only knew two pop songs. They were "Sunny Side of the Street" and "So Long," a song that was very popular at that time, written for servicemen going off to war. I won the contest and got to sing at this ballroom in Houston, one night a week—with a chaperon, of course. I would go every Thursday night and do my two songs and they would give me all the pop I could drink. People would throw big silver dollars on the stage. I can remember trying to stay out of the way. . . . This Eldorado Ballroom where I won the contest used to have dances for the kids on Sunday. Big, big huge ballroom, upstairs. Russell Jacquet [Illinois's brother] had a seventeen-piece band there, and it was bad. I l-o-o-oved to dance. I used to go every Sunday and dance and dance and dance until I just dropped.

Concerned that his daughter was slipping onto the wrong path, Joseph wrote a letter to his old quartet partner Joe Denman, who had moved to Seattle, and asked what the situation was. A few weeks later, Denman wrote back. "Anderson—Come on up. There's plenty of work, the weather's mild and there's no nightclubs for a hundred miles around!" Denman was right on two counts, anyway, but he obviously hadn't taken a walk down Jackson Street lately. The action there would be the undoing of Joseph's plans, and the making of one of the great vocal careers in jazz.

Ernestine Anderson was a petite woman who maintained a stunning, youthful complexion and a cheerleader grin that belied her age for most of her life. She stared out from a firm presence with strength and candor, though one got the feeling she would rather laugh, which she did often and fetchingly. Her conversation was punctuated with responsive "Yeah's" and evenly accented "You know's." Her voice was deep and soft. Sometimes her sentences trailed down to a close, like dying phrases of music. Overall she gave a feeling of warmth, vulnerability, and a perhaps sorely won sense of self-preservation. Seattle was a big shock to her, after Texas. Since Houston was segregated, Anderson had never been around white people. The local kids found her accent a curiosity. She soon made friends, however, and before long was teaching everyone in school the Texas Hop.

The word spread that Ernestine could sing. Two weeks after she arrived, the son of the very man who had assured Ernestine's father Seattle was a dead town took her to the YMCA on Twenty-Third Avenue and Olive Way and introduced her to Sonny Booker and Gerald Brashear. When the two young hipsters saw this cute Texan gal wearing penny loafers and bobby socks, pleated skirt and sweater, they enthusiastically invited her to sing. "I don't remember what I sang," said Ernestine, "but they asked me to join the band. I told them my father would never allow me to sing on dance jobs. But somehow, they talked him into letting me do a few gigs, on a trial basis. My father said, 'You must keep your grades up. If your grades start to suffer, no more working.'"

Soon, Sonny and Gerald had Ernestine working weekends with their band, playing parties, weddings, and bar mitzvahs. Bumps Blackwell, the local promoter and bandleader, noticed her, and started placing Anderson with the bands he booked at the Washington Social Club, Finnish Hall, the 908, and, occasionally, the Trianon Ballroom, to open for a national act. Blackwell took Anderson under his wing, making sure she wasn't hassled at the clubs. "I remember they had this security lady on the door at the Washington Social Club," said Ernestine. "When I'd come to work, she would turn her head and look the other way. This place got raided several times and we had routes that we would take to get out of the clubs. Many times, I would be outside the club,

The Ernie Lewis Band, Oakland, California, 1944. *Left to right:* Vernon "Pops" Buford, Walter Oakes, Pony Poindexter, Warren Thompson, Earl Boatley (aka Earl Thompson), Lewis.

sitting in a car watching them load up the paddy wagon. I'd be the first one they got out of these places."

One night in 1946, without waiting for Blackwell's cue, Anderson ventured into Basin Street, a huge basement speakeasy full of smoke with a floor show and a crowd full of rounders ("Adults went there," she said, with mock awe), and introduced herself to the bandleader, Ernie Lewis. Lewis was a pianist and union honcho from Oakland, California, who was making waves on the West Coast with a nimble new sextet. The group included the remarkable alto saxophonist Pony Poindexter and tenor man Vernon "Pops" Buford, plus Walter Oakes (bass), Warren Thompson (drums), and Earl Boatley (guitar). Pianist Gerald Wiggins played when Lewis was away on business. (Boatley also played trumpet with Andy Kirk, under the name Earl Thompson.) Lewis was an excellent pianist with an ear for the new, once-over-lightly Kansas City Six style that had caught on with modern players. The band smoked. He was also a powerful, well-connected figure who would become involved in strengthening Black locals and helping them amalgamate with the white unions. Hooking up with Lewis set the stage for Anderson to make the jump from sometime kid singer to full-time professional.

"Bumps was trying to hold her," said bassist Wyatt Ruther, who had come to Seattle by way of Fort Lewis. "But he couldn't hold her very long after Ernie

A couple seated at the Basin Street Club, 1945, and a sign with the house slogan on the wall behind them.

Lewis got up there. Ernie started exposing her to some of the other people that were coming to town. And then she took off."

Basin Street had opened in 1939, when Davey Lee, a local businessman, won a stake playing the Chinese lottery. The club was at 413 Maynard Avenue South, between South Jackson Street and South King Street, in a long and lean storefront and basement inside the Olympus Hotel, which in those days stood beside the Bush Hotel. (The Olympus was demolished; Hing Hay Park occupies most of that block today.) Al Hilbert ran the card game at street level; below was the nightclub. Although it was an after-hours club, Basin Street was a tightly run ship with strictly enforced rules. As you entered down the stairs, the first person you saw was the bouncer, Gorilla Jones, a former middleweight champion and an old beau of Mae West's, who still sent him a fresh white carnation every day. On the wall behind Jones hung a sign: STAY WITH YOUR PARTY AND OUR SERVICE IS YOURS, a rule aimed at keeping people seated, which was required by the 1934 law that had legalized liquor but also discouraged quarrels.

The club held about two hundred patrons and, unlike the 908 Club, welcomed people of all races. At the height of its popularity twenty waiters and five bartenders worked there full-time. The music began at noon with a single pianist, graduated to trios at three, and a four-piece band at nine, followed by the main attraction—the Ernie Lewis band—at one in the morning. The after-hours set lasted all night, six nights a week. Every once in a while, out-of-town acts came in, including the Ink Spots, Dexter Gordon, the great tap dancer Teddy Hale, and Sammy Davis Jr., who at that time was working with his uncle's vaudeville group, the Will Mastin Trio. Jabo Ward considered Basin Street one of the two or three places where, musically, players felt they could let their hair down. Floor shows with chorus girls and exotic dancing were a specialty, including a drag act in which one dancer flung another around by the hair. The club's habitués included an eccentric fellow named Harold

Curry, who came in nightly with a pet turtle on a leash, and another guy who routinely brought a bucketful of silver dollars. "He had two bodyguards bringing them in," according to Leon Vaughn. "When we'd play, he'd throw a whole handful at you. You had to tell him to 'Watch it! Don't hit me with that stuff!'" Vaughn also recalled that some of the women at Basin Street also had a colorful idiosyncrasy: "On the last number of the evening, everybody played a solo and then got off the bandstand. The last solo was taken by the drummer. I don't know why, but he seemed to instill in these chicks the idea to come out, pull up their dresses, and dance. That used to be one of the things that people came down there to look at. I used to say, 'Show your linen, baby! Show your linen!' And they would!"

This was the after-hours atmosphere in which the seventeen-year-old Anderson was learning the art, and the business, of singing jazz. One of the biggest things she learned there was how to "work the room": "From the stage, I could see people coming down the stairs. In those days, there were lots of pimps and prostitutes, people from the sporting life. They would be out with their number one girl for a good time. What you would do was learn everybody's favorite song, so when these hustlers would come down the stairs, their song started playing. This made them feel good. That was a big tip for you. I learned a lot of songs that way." Even though Davey Lee paid the beat cop weekly to keep his poker game and bootleg business afloat, occasionally there were raids. The young singer found the atmosphere intriguing. "They had a light in the dressing room that would flash when there was a raid," Anderson recalled. "One night, I was dressing with these two dancers and the light flashed. They grabbed me and shoved me under the table and pulled the drapes. I heard this running and romping and people trying to get away, but I couldn't see anything that was going on. It was exciting."

Anderson made a strong first impression on anyone who heard her during this period, both for the purity of her voice and her surprising versatility. "Ernestine sounded like honey at dusk," recalled Quincy Jones. "Yes, Lord. She could kill 'Lover Man' and 'Body and Soul.' And she didn't do too bad on 'Big Fat Butterfly,' either. 'All of Me.' She was a killer." Anderson had been raised on home-fried Texas blues, but the melodies of popular songs such as "How Are Things in Glocca Morra?"—and a yen to improvise on the melody—came naturally to her. She recalled:

My family was blues people. They loved the Bobby Blue Blands and B. B. Kings and Muddy Waters. They had stacks and stacks of old blues records. We had an old Victrola that you had to wind up. Whenever bands would come—Jimmie Lunceford, Andy Kirk, Cab Calloway, Basie—they would go. I would hear them talking about them the night before, about how crowded it was. When I was a little kid in Texas, they had this one record by Bessie Smith [actually, it was Memphis Minnie] that my mom and dad said I used to sing all the time—"Bumblebee, bumblebee. . . ."

When I went to audition at the Eldorado Ballroom, the piano player asked me what key did I do these two songs that I knew in. I automatically said C. It turned out to be the wrong key. So I improvised around the melody, because my grandmother had told me that if I wanted to be a professional singer, once you start singing, you don't stop. When I finished, one of the musicians told me I was a jazz singer.

By 1946, Ernestine had become a thoroughly modern devotee of bebop and of the beboppers' favorite singer, Sarah Vaughan, whose polished technique, huge range, and improvising ability paralleled the advances in instrumental jazz. Anderson became known later in her career for her raspy, dark sound, but in the 1940s her voice was lighter and clearer and her style more "ingenue" than "wise woman of song." Norm Bobrow was still waxing eloquent in the 1980s over the teenage Ernestine, whom he preferred even to Vaughan. "Ernestine had that vulnerability," he said. "I didn't hear that vulnerability in Sarah. The people that had heard the story of Ella [Fitzgerald]'s discovery, you know, when she was fifteen, sixteen at the Apollo, playing with Chick Webb, it's almost like this was what it was like. Ernestine was just a spellbinder."

Bobrow did everything he could to promote Anderson, calling her the "new Ella," praise that at one point drew fire from a local critic. Reviving his concept of all-star, all-local jazz shows, in November 1946 Bobrow put Ernestine in front of the Ernie Lewis band at the Metropolitan Theatre on a blockbuster show with Gerald Wiggins, doing a solo piano set; the Gay Jones combo; a trio fronted by Ernestine's only serious rival, Juanita Cruse; and a virtual catalog of Seattle sidemen, among them Fred Greenwell, Rollie Morehouse, and Dave Tuttle. Ernestine sang "Rich Man's Blues" and "Can't Help Loving That Man." Over the next two years she enjoyed star status on Bobrow's shows, singing the tunes each week from the *Lucky Strike Hit Parade*.

After this taste of stardom at home, Anderson became smitten with ambition. "I was determined to make it," she said. "I told my folks that when I was eighteen, I was going to go on the road with a band." As it happened, she was right. In early 1947, Ernestine Anderson became the first of the Garfield High School crowd to be picked up by a name band.

> Shortly after my eighteenth birthday, the big band of Johnny Otis came to town. Paul Quinichette heard me at a jam session and he asked me to come down to the theater where Johnny was working. When I got there, Johnny said, "They tell me you sound like Sarah Vaughan." I auditioned and got the job.
>
> Johnny at that time had a seventeen-piece swing band. That was a really rocking band. Paul Quinichette. Preston Love. Some "bad" players. He was on tour with the Ink Spots, Honi Coles and Cholly Atkins, and Slappy White and his partner Lewis [stage name for Clarence Schelle]. Comedy team. And a woman singer named June Richmond. I talked them into letting me come on the band earlier than I was supposed to, so that I could watch June Richmond, learn from her. This woman was one of my idols. She had a great voice and great control. She used to sing, "Figaro, Figaro, Figaro. . . ." She was something else. Every performance, she would have people just laughing. She could do to an audience whatever she wanted. She just had 'em. I watched her and tried to figure out how she did this. She was a big lady. I did my apprenticeship, ironing her gowns in the dressing room and wondering if I'm ever going to get around the whole length and breadth of this gown!

After three months of ironing, Anderson finally got to sing. She toured with Otis for six months, winding up with an extended engagement at the Club Alabam in Los Angeles. When Otis disbanded there, Ernestine decided to try her luck in California. She had a rough time of it.

"When I left home, my folks bought me some alligator luggage. I'll never forget it, because I'd sit there [in Los Angeles] and think, 'Who needs luggage if you don't have no clothes?' I was just so poor. I was there for over a year. In all that time, I never got out of that area." It wasn't such a bad place to be. Central Avenue in Los Angeles was popping, much like Jackson Street. After-hours clubs flourished. Dexter Gordon was coming on strong; so were Howard McGhee and Wardell Gray. There were jam sessions every Monday night, sponsored by Gene Norman. Cedric Henry, a mild-mannered junkie affectionately known as "Shifty Henry," kept an eye out for Ernestine:

Shifty was like a big brother to me. He was always trying to help me. He was a great jazz bass player. Somehow, he always managed to work and he always managed to be on top of it, even though he was a junkie. I knew when he was high, but he always took care of business and he was always very protective of me. He got me my first recording [an R & B number, "Good Lovin' Babe"]. He had to find me. That's how bad things were. I was moving from place to place and nobody could keep a finger on me. A few jukeboxes had [my record] in L.A. I knew where each one was. I'd go there and put my nickel in!

An unusual—some would say psychic—experience led to Anderson's return home from her first shot at the road. Her twin sister, Josephine, was developmentally disabled. All their lives the two had been extremely close. When things hit bottom for Ernestine, her sister seemed, somehow, to be tuned in to her misfortune.

I finally got a job working weekends at Jack's Basket Room on Central for meals and room and board. He had some houses in back of the club. Little rows of houses. Units. He let me stay back there. And fed me. Then I got sick. I had strep throat. I hadn't been to work in days, which turned into weeks. Nobody came back to see me or anything. I was just so sick, I couldn't eat, couldn't do anything.

My family was living out in the projects [in Seattle], above Sicks' Stadium. [They] were up this hill. My sister sat in a window, looking down the hill. She sat in the window for a week and they couldn't get her to eat. They couldn't get her to go to sleep. She just kept looking down the hill, calling my name. My mother finally thought, "Well, there must be something wrong with Ernestine, because she just keeps calling her name." So my dad got the Seattle police to get in touch with the L.A. police. When they found me, I was so sick I couldn't move. They got me to a doctor who gave me penicillin. I don't remember how long it took me to recuperate, but I came home. Josephine saved my life.

While she was on tour with Johnny Otis, Paul Quinichette had taken Ernestine aside and advised her to stop trying to sound like Sarah Vaughan and start sounding like herself. It was a revelation. "That sort of sunk in," she recalled. "I started thinking about it. 'How do I change? Where do I start?' So I stopped listening to singers. And I started listening to Diz and Bird."

During the war Dizzy Gillespie and Charlie "Bird" Parker were in the vanguard of the bebop movement. Coupling the harmonic evolutions of Art Tatum and Lester Young with fierce new rhythms and angular melodic lines, the beboppers created a fast and furious, sometimes shrill music that well reflected the anxiety of the postwar period. The music also reflected new attitudes on the part of young Black people, who, after fighting a war for the United States, were reluctant to remain disenfranchised or, worse, to be hoisted onstage as entertainer buffoons. Quincy Jones explained: "Charlie Parker was saying that inside, we have some musical ideas that go just a little bit beyond entertainment. We do not feel like shakin' our heads and grinnin' and stuff when we play. That, to me, was a social comment—that we have minds, too. And that was much more important than being 'natural rhythm machines.' To me, it was a prelude to Martin Luther King, to that social awareness."

The first bebop records had reached Seattle by 1946, before Anderson left town with Johnny Otis. A tiny group of young musicians had begun to listen to, and try to play, the new music. Ernestine was one of the first:

> We used to go to each other's houses. In those days money was really tight, so whoever was fat enough to buy a record, or an EP, we'd gather at their house. Usually nobody had any furniture. They had pillows and we'd sit on the floor. That was the days of the red and blue lights. There had to be colored lights in the room. Mood lights. They'd put a red light on the ceiling and put the records on and everybody would sit around and groove on these records and we'd learn all the licks. . . . You had to be able to sing all of Bird's solos, and all of Dizzy's solos. And if you couldn't do that, then you weren't happening.

As her style matured, Anderson continued to sing locally, on Bobrow's shows and elsewhere, but Seattle couldn't keep her. After a couple more false starts, Anderson was swept into the maelstrom of the modern-jazz era, first with Lionel Hampton, then as a star in her own right.

———

While Ernestine and her friends were soaking up the new sounds of bop, another future Hamptonite and acolyte of Sarah Vaughan's was working behind the counter of a downtown Seattle record store, making plans of her own to make it big in bebop. White vocalist Janet Thurlow is a special figure in the

Janet Thurlow.

Jackson Street story. Today she probably would be called a groupie (though that is too crass a term for such a gentle soul), because she made a virtual profession of tracking the action in the Central District and of putting musicians in touch with one another. It's amazing how often her name comes up in interviews as the key that unlocked the scene for this or that player. But Thurlow was also a quality vocalist, the second Seattle musician (after Evelyn Williamson) to get in the Lionel Hampton group, and the first white singer to work with a Black big band. Once she was in, she encouraged Hampton to bring up the troops left behind in Seattle.

A Seattle native, Thurlow started her musical career on violin at age five, then studied classical voice. Her youth was marked by sadness. First her parents got divorced, then her mother died. At age twenty she was left with four younger siblings. Thurlow recalled:

> After she died, it just didn't seem like there was anything left. She and I were very close and I didn't have anything, I didn't have anybody. So I started going around and listening to jazz. The Black musicians, I grew very close to. They seemed to fill a kind of void that I was lacking. Prior to that, I hadn't heard any jazz. It was a growth period for me. I had never been out on my own at all. It was a little scary at times. I didn't have any idea what I was going to do or what was going to happen to me.

When Jimmie Lunceford died in Seaside, Oregon (in 1947), Thurlow became friends with his band while they waited in Seattle for passage home. Soon thereafter, she moved into the Central District with her younger sister, Diane, just a few blocks from where Ray Charles had moved, in 1948. Living in the Central District was an extraordinary thing for two young white girls to do during this era. "Ray Charles used to call me quite a few times to come down and fix his lunch for him, or his dinner," Thurlow said. "He'd play piano and I'd sing with him. I started going out to the after-hours places. I had a really good record collection—Sarah [Vaughan]'s old things on Musicraft—'Lover Man,' 'Black Coffee,' 'Summertime.' I knew I liked jazz and I wanted to sing."

Thurlow took a job—as well as voice lessons—at the Sherman and Clay music store but soon moved over to Al Siedel's record shop on Third Avenue, which carried more jazz. Whenever musicians came in, she gave them a free listen to the latest sides: "When Floyd [Standifer] or Freddie Greenwell would come in, I'd tell them, 'Oh, man! I got this great record and you gotta come in and hear it. 'Course, a lot of the time they didn't buy anything. My boss didn't like it too much." As Standifer remembered it: "We'd listen to things like [Dexter Gordon's] 'The Chase.' I wrote all this stuff down and took it off the record right there in the booth."

Thurlow, who sometimes sported a fashionable spit curl and a blue jacket with shiny buttons, worked in a combo with pianist Cecil Young, drummer Eddie Cole (Nat's brother), and Gerald Brashear at the Officers' Club at Fort Lewis. Once Sammy Davis Jr., working in town with his uncle's group, the Will Mastin Trio, came along. Thurlow recalled that "Sammy went with me for nothing—would you believe it? He used to come over to my house and I'd give him ice cream and Coca-Cola."

When Anna Mae Winburn came through town with the Sweethearts of Rhythm, Thurlow auditioned; she didn't get a callback. When Ivory Joe Hunter passed through, the tables were turned: He liked her singing so much, he not only asked her to join the band, he asked her to marry him. She declined both offers. In the late 1940s, Thurlow received her first public notice, for a performance with Curt Sykes at the Trianon, which described her as "the home-town girl who starts in where Mildred Bailey left off as a soulful interpreter of modern songs." The comparison was apt. Like Bailey, Thurlow was a lonely girl who found solace in hip Black music and the after-hours life. Though Thurlow was not in Bailey's league, she swung with a smooth, easy flow and had a pure, bell-like sound that was attractively innocent. "A few years ago, when I first heard Diane Schuur, I used to think of Janet Thurlow," said Fred Greenwell. "She used to sing like a record copy of Sarah Vaughan. Clear, and in tune, and muscular."

In the fall of 1950, Thurlow got her big break, and, as it turned out, she met her future husband, Jimmy Cleveland, in the deal.

> I was staying [in Portland] on the "other side of the tracks" with a Black family. It was a place where everybody came through town and jammed. Hamp was playing one night and he came over, and Jimmy came, too. When he took his horn out of the case and started playing, I said, "Man, I've never heard the trombone played

like that. I gotta meet him." Right after he finished playing, I walked up to him and told him I thought that was just great. He asked me if he could take me to breakfast.

Then I heard that Hamp was going up to Seattle to the Palomar Theater for a week. I invited Jimmy to dinner [in Seattle]. Hamp asked me to do a show with him that day. I was all excited and I got in my best evening gown. I went down and I did "Tenderly." And it went over good! Then I did "I Can't Believe That You're in Love with Me." That's the one I recorded with him. Five months later, they sent me a telegram and the money and a plane ticket to come and join them in Baltimore, at the Royal Theater.

Hiring a white singer was a deliberate experiment on Hamp's part, as he wrote in his autobiography: "It was [NAACP chief secretary] Walter White who suggested that I take an integrated band down South. He thought it would be a good thing to show whites—because I was doing a lot of concerts at white halls and clubs—that black and white can get along together. So I took a band down that was half white and half black. I even took a white girl singer with me, Janet Thurlow." Thurlow's anomalous position in the Hampton band led to incidents, however. Pony Poindexter, also in the group at the time, related that outside Lubbock, Texas, everyone was busted by a racist sheriff: "It turned out that since Janet Thurlow, our girl singer, was white, we were breaking Texas law by her working with us and by her riding on the bus with us. It took all day to get this straightened out. . . . Janet was taken to the airport and put aboard a plane for Chicago. Then the band was released."

Though Lionel's intentions were good, some of the material he gave Thurlow to sing made her less than comfortable, particularly an "Aunt Jemima"–type song, "Hominy Hoedown." But Hampton came from a generation of Black entertainers weaned on the grinning "Shuffle Along" school of Black entertainment, and he wasn't about to abandon it. As part of the same shtick, he picked up tap dancer Danny Alexander, an ace hoofer based in Seattle during the 1940s who had worked many a crowd at the Black and Tan. One of his specialties was picking up a table with his teeth.

Shtick or not, Thurlow was on the road with a name band, and on January 15, 1951, she came home to Seattle to prove it. Billed as the "white girl's singer of sultry songs," she sang her version of "Tenderly" at the Trianon. She was thrilled: "I said, 'Here I am, Seattle! I finally made it!' I felt real good that night. They compared me with Billie Holiday, Ella Fitzgerald." The following week, *DownBeat* praised her for her "amazing range and impressive styling."

Thurlow was in good company. She was appearing with one of the legendary Hampton groups, featuring, among others, Benny Bailey, Ed "Moon" Mullins, Jimmy Cleveland, Al Grey, Benny Powell, Bobby Plater, Jerome Richardson, Milt Buckner, and Don Lamond. "That was the Lionel Hampton band that everybody talks about," remembered Jim Gilles, a Seattle pianist who worked at the Black Elks Club and by coincidence once crossed paths with the Hampton group in Texas. Quincy Jones also came into the Hampton orchestra, thanks to Thurlow's prodding. "Janet Thurlow was sweet," Jones remembered. "She used to write me, 'Come on down to New York—Hamp wants to see you.' She kept bugging him about 'Don't forget about Quincy.'" Thurlow and Jones crisscrossed the country with Hamp. On August 31 and September 1, 1951, the two young musicians had the pleasure of seeing both their names on the marquee of the Trianon Ballroom. Even the newspaper ad took notice of a couple of homies making good:

> LIONEL HAMPTON
> Featuring two Seattleites
> Quincy Jones & Janet Thurlow.

While they were on the road with Hamp, Thurlow and Jimmy Cleveland decided to wed, an interracial marriage that would later inspire Charles Mingus to record Thurlow singing his brilliant ballad about such marriages, "Eclipse." Unfortunately, Hamp had a rule against married couples, so he dismissed the young singer from the band. She stayed in New York for a while, working with the Loumell Morgan Trio at Snooky's. It was at this point she became a Jehovah's Witness, a faith that has carried many other jazz musicians through hard times, including Andy Kirk, Benny Golson, Anna Mae Winburn, and Cozy Cole. "When I worked at the Baby Grand in New York City with Nipsy Russell," said Thurlow, "he called me 'the Bible Lady,' because after I left the stand I'd go in my dressing room and read my *Watchtower*!"

Thurlow dropped out of public performance for a long time, but got back into singing in 1974, after moving to Los Angeles. In 1983 she and Cleveland started working in a wonderful, eight-piece "little big band" that played at the Lighthouse, Marla's Memory Lane, and other Los Angeles venues. She performed a concert with Joe Williams in 1985. Sitting in the living room of her comfortable home with Jimmy Cleveland in LA, looking back on her Seattle days, Thurlow could still be the shy, modest, unassuming girl with the small, bell-like voice who got up and sang "Tenderly" for Hamp. In her view there was nothing particularly glamorous about her Jackson Street days, though she remembered them fondly: "It was just ordinary people trying to make it, that's all. Our hearts were in music, we were young and we were out there, gung ho, singing with this band, singing with that band, jamming—anything for exposure." Thurlow did not perform after Jimmy died in 2008; she passed in 2022.

———

Janet Thurlow advanced Seattle bebop by introducing musicians to one another and by alerting them to hot new records. Another vital source of the new sounds was Norman Granz's Jazz at the Philharmonic (JATP) series. Granz was the Los Angeles promoter whom Norm Bobrow had scooped by four years with his 1940 swing concert. In the JATP shows Granz attempted to re-create the fervent atmosphere of a nightclub jam session in a concert hall. The JATP shows got underway in the fall of 1944 at Philharmonic Hall, and the name stuck when Granz took the concept on tour the following year. JATP reached Seattle with tenor saxophonist Coleman Hawkins and pianist Thelonious Monk, among others, in December 1945, at the Civic Auditorium, although the show bombed, as both daily newspapers were on strike and word never got out. On April 29 and 30, 1946, Granz offered a slew of musicians on three shows at the Moore Theatre, each billed as "All-Star Jazz Concert." The lineup featured, among others, Hawkins, Lester Young, Meade Lux Lewis, Helen Humes, Ken Kersey, Charlie Drayton, Buck Clayton, and Shadow Wilson. A similar lineup, with Bobrow attending to on-site promotional duties, returned the following October, with the addition of Roy Eldridge. By November 1948, Charlie Parker had made it to town on a Granz extravaganza, along with a couple of beboppers on the LA scene—trumpeter Howard McGhee and altoist Sonny Criss—as well as vocalist Kenny "Pancho" Hagood, Flip Phillips, J. C. Heard, Tommy Turk, and Coleman Hawkins.

"That was like the Beatles, man," recalled Quincy Jones. "People screaming, just happening. It was killer. There was so much heat. People just dying to see that." The JATP shows brought modern stars in for a night, then they were gone. But before long, emissaries of the new music began to wander into town and stay a while too. Roscoe Weathers, Pony Poindexter, and Gerald Wiggins were among the first to arrive. Weathers was a somewhat mysterious character.

A likable fellow with a weeping mustache and sad eyes, he was originally from Memphis, Tennessee, and worked with Jay McShann and Horace Henderson before coming west. Most sources say he jumped off the Jay McShann band in Seattle. McShann played Seattle's Civic Auditorium in 1945; Roscoe's name first appears in a Seattle newspaper that same year, when he was featured with Vern Mallory at the Savoy Ballroom.

Weathers played alto saxophone with a raw, biting tone and an oddly off-kilter sense of pacing that sounds almost avant-garde today, the way it veers haltingly between angular bebop lines and stretches of sweet caresses. He blew away the locals. Wyatt Ruther referred to him as "the Charlie Parker of the Northwest." Leon Vaughn remembered: "He was the first inkling that we had of how far bop had gone. He could put such unusual combinations together. He really knew his horn. He had the trio that came on from six o'clock 'til nine o'clock at the Basin Street for four months or so. He'd come in and jam a whole lot at the Basin Street and also at the Sessions Playhouse and the Blue Note. He was a hell of a sax player. Nobody could compete or compare with him. He could play all night long on 'How High the Moon' and every chorus would be different." Weathers was messianic about spreading the gospel of bebop. Ken Boas, who worked with him for several weeks in Portland, remembered standing in Basin Street with Weathers, listening to the jukebox as it played Bird's "Scrapple from the Apple." Boas recalled: "I never will forget, Roscoe turned around to me and he had tears coming down his eyes. I said, 'What's the matter?' and he said, 'Oh, you don't understand. Those guys, it's just like they were praying.'"

Roscoe Weathers steps outside to have his picture taken in front of the Sessions Club, South Main Street near Twelfth Avenue South, ca. 1948.

Weathers was a generous teacher and didn't have a big ego. "There were a lot of tunes where they take the standard tune and put a different melody to it," Boas recounted. "He'd say, 'Here's what you do.' He'd know it just like nothing. He'd say, 'He goes up like this, and he goes down in chromatics and when he gets there, he stops, and he goes up,' you know? He'd show me on the piano, real slow." In the fall of 1949, Weathers and Kenny Boas rented adjacent rooms in the Woodson Apartments (where many musicians lived), around the corner from the Washington Social Club. Their "pad" became a place for beboppers to congregate and socialize. Said Boas: "That was one of the happiest winters I ever spent, the fall of '49. We would listen to music, and play gigs. Roscoe liked to cook. He'd get a pot, and everybody would bring something and he'd boil a bunch of stuff. Guys would come by to see him, like Sonny Criss and Gus Johnson. And Paul Quinichette, you know? They were all friends, from playing together. You could tell by the way they [acted] that they respected him."

Weathers played in a variety of pickup bands in Seattle. Bassist Buddy Catlett told of walking into Birdland one night and seeing the alto saxophonist smoking in a bebop group with Floyd Standifer (trumpet), Ray Charles (piano), Milt Garred (bass), and Jimmie Rodgers (drums). Despite his prowess and first-call status, Weathers's eccentricity and intensity made it difficult for him to adapt to making a living in music. "He'd come to work wearing these dark glasses with white rims with no glass in them," recalled Red Kelly. "In between tunes, he'd reach in and scratch his eye. I'd think, 'Is he doing that on purpose?'"

"He had a mind of his own about things," remembered guitarist Garcia McKee. "If it wasn't right, he'd walk off." Major Pigford remembered one night in particular:

> We were at the 102 Cherry and this drunk guy comes up and he's got this big old brown paper bag. He says he wants to hear Roy Acuff's "Blood on the Highway." [Pigford was referring to the 1942 country-and-western song "Wreck on the Highway."] Well, it just so happens that I happened to know the words to "Blood on the Highway." So Roscoe says, "Hey, man, don't you want to hear something by Charlie Parker?" And the guy says, "I don't know nothin' about that. I don't know no Charlie Parker." He wants to hear "Blood on the Highway." So I go up to Al [Pierre] and I say, "Look, Al, I know the words to one or two choruses of that thing. We can fake it." So we faked it and this guy took this whole paper bag and threw it in the kitty.

> It had eighteen hundred dollars in it. So I told Roscoe, "You wanted to play Charlie Parker. Hey, man, Roy Acuff gets you the money." You know, we split that together.

Pigford's anecdote is a paradigm for the dilemma beboppers were beginning to face: as their art became more and more complex, it became less and less accessible to the average fan.

The beboppers took a humorless, almost adversarial, attitude onstage, which sometimes translated as contempt for the audience's taste. As a result, many of the early bebop musicians who remained true to their art couldn't find work and ended up leaving music in despair. Weathers was among them. Though he had been a cupbearer to Seattle and remained there through the early 1950s, ultimately he dropped out of music as a career. He toured Europe with bandleader Archie Savage, played Bop City in San Francisco, and in 1958 played some fleet, Bird-like alto sax solos on an unusual album, *Stringin' Along*, featuring arrangements by Bill Holman, Benny Carter, and other notables. In the 1960s, Weathers also recorded an (uneven) album, *Rosco* [sic] *Weathers: His Sterling Flute & Piccolo*. When Ernestine Anderson ran into him in the mid-1970s in Los Angeles, Weathers had taken up jewelry-making and photography, though he continued to play on the side with former Seattle musicians Len Brooks and Garcia McKee. According to Anderson, Weathers died sometime in the late seventies.

Among the early westward bearers of the bop message must also be listed former Savoy Boy saxophonist Billy Tolles, who, by leaving town to go to A & T College in North Carolina, expanded his horizons to include both bebop and R & B. In the Southeast, Tolles played with young firebrands such as Lou Donaldson, James Moody, Dave Burns, and Joe Gales, who were stationed at a nearby Army post. Tolles made the transition to bebop easily. "We were playing 'Ornithology' and 'Billie's Bounce' and practicing every day," he recalled. "It didn't take us minutes to make the transition."

Tolles took a summer off from school in Seattle in 1945, gigging locally, but spent an even more important summer off in Newport News, Virginia, in 1947, working with the classic organ trio of Jack McDuff, as well as with Redd Foxx, Ruth Brown, and Jimmy Scott. In the East, Tolles not only picked up the new styles, he acquired an aggressive, professional punch that would set him far above most players in Seattle. Around Greensboro, North Carolina, he subbed with some of the best outfits on tour, including Louis Jordan, "Hot Lips" Page, Lucky Millinder, Benny Carter, Buddy Johnson, and King Kolax. In Boston he worked with Sabby Lewis, then briefly picked up the tenor saxophone chair in Billy Eckstine's band, playing gigs on the Atlantic coast all the way to the Apollo Theater, in New York. When Tolles returned to Seattle in 1948 for a longer stay, he scared people to death. "When I came back, I came racehorsing and bebopping like a sonofagun," he said. "Sonny and Gerald and all the guys, they'd say, 'Why you wanna play so fast, man?' ''Cause I can.' I'd been out in the world and I'd made it, man, and I'd played with everybody and I had an attitude. I'd been to New York City. I'd become twenty-one in New York, and I was really cocky, man, more than I should have been."

Tolles played a couple of times at the Washington Social Club with the Bumps Blackwell band, then started working with bassist Bob Marshall. For a brief time Tolles went back into the Army, at Fort Lewis, where he played with some of the other heavies stationed there (such as Earl DeWitt, Walter Benton, and Sir Roland Hanna). He also promoted jazz concerts at the theater on the post, including one or two shows with Ernestine Anderson. When he got out of the service in 1952, he went to Los Angeles and played for two weeks with Billie Holiday at the Tippin' In before returning to Seattle. At this point Tolles moved away from bebop and became something of a Seattle rock 'n' roll pioneer, forming a group called Billy Tolles's Four Question Marks, which Tolles liked to call "Seattle's first rock 'n' roll band."

In 1952 his group won the Combo Clash at the Eagles Auditorium, using Norwood "Pony" Poindexter and the magnificent trumpet player Kenny Dorham. (Dorham spent six months in Seattle, although he kept a low profile.) Tolles's Combo Clash sax man, Pony Poindexter, had been making his mark on Seattle jazz since 1946. He was a troubling figure, a versatile entertainer with a distinctively original style whose life was first plagued by drugs and crime, then consumed by anger and bitterness. A degree of the notoriety he craved came his way eventually, when he worked with Lambert, Hendricks, and Bavan, but to Pony it always seemed as if life gave him the short end of the stick.

Poindexter, who was born in New Orleans, grew up sitting in with Sidney Desvignes's combo on Bourbon Street and moved to Oakland, California, when he was fifteen. One of his first jobs in the Bay Area was with Vernon "Pops" Buford, the tenor saxophonist. Poindexter spent the war years playing hide-and-seek with the draft, squeezing in stints on New York's Fifty-Second Street, and playing a spell with Tiny Bradshaw, but he ultimately served in the Army as a musician in Naples, Italy. Poindexter then enrolled at the Candell Conservatory of Music, in Oakland, on the GI Bill. When he approached Ernie Lewis on the stand in 1946, Pony struck the older bandleader as not only feisty but remarkably advanced. The great saxophonist and flutist Jerome Richardson was playing with Lewis at the time. When an offer to go to Seattle came up, Richardson didn't want to go, so Lewis offered the gig to Poindexter. It was Pony's first tour. The gutsy Louisiana fire in his tone fit right into the mix of styles evolving in Northwest clubs.

"He just took Seattle by storm," recalled Ernestine Anderson. "He was on everybody's list. Pony, little Pony. Pony Poindexter. He was called the 'ditty man,' because his solos were made up of a lot of different songs." For the next ten years Poindexter divided his time between Seattle and the Bay Area, exerting an enormous influence on technical standards and expectations in the Northwest. He married a Seattle woman in the early 1950s and spent a good deal of his time in the Northwest until 1958. One of his most prominent forums in Seattle was the weekly series of all-star concerts produced by Norm Bobrow, Jazz at the Metropolitan. Starting in May 1946, nearly every Sunday for two years Bobrow presented jazz nights at the Repertory Playhouse, in the University District, and at the Metropolitan Theatre.

As he had for Gay Jones, Bobrow went all out for publicity, promoting his shows as a DJ on two radio programs, courting the local press, and cranking out a mimeographed, 8½-by-14-inch promotional sheet titled "Norm Bobrow's Northwest Jazz Letter." The first (and only discoverable) issue—datelined New York City, November 1946—conveyed Bobrow's sweet sense of regional advocacy in a breathless air of fandom and "hep" talk: "The Northwest JAZZ LETTER is this moment being born on Editor Eddie Ronan's typewriter at the offices of down beat—That's the musicians' newspaper, father. This sort of makes DB's editors Michael Levin, Bill Gottlieb and Ronan godfathers to the Letter, and that kind of company is jazzy enough for us. Critic Leonard Feather, young man with apologetic manner, asking with keen interest about Northwest Jazz when we were introduced. . . . Our Northwest jazz rates with the best in the country—I say that straight from 52nd Street. Norm Bobrow." Bobrow often participated in his own shows, singing tongue-in-cheek jive.

Bobrow promoted anyone he thought was a good musician (and his critical taste was quite sharp), but he had his favorites. One of them was pianist

Gerald Wiggins, another progressive voice who migrated to the area—if getting drafted counts as "migration." Wiggins spent four years in Seattle (1944–48), two of them at Fort Lewis and two of them in town, though his stretch at the camp was so light he was able to keep a Seattle apartment—with a grand piano. Wiggins's only obligation in the Twenty-Ninth Special Services Band at Fort Lewis—which included Wyatt Ruther on trombone, Louis Jones (from Tiny Hill's band) on trumpet, and Junior Raglin on bass—was to play at the USO every Saturday night. "I don't think I spent over two or three days [in a row] in camp," said Wiggins. The pianist started playing dates in town and became notorious in the jazz community for playing sizzling-fast solos at concerts—while reading a book. "The Norm Bobrow shows were fun," recalled saxophonist Fred Greenwell, another Bobrow favorite, "because they were just [Gerald] and I and a rhythm section. A lot of the fellas around here could only go so far. Wiggins was in full control of whatever the spread was."

Part of Gerald's book-reading act was sheer bravado. Though he was only twenty-two, Wiggins was a hip New Yorker who had already been on the road with Benny Carter and had appeared on the historic 1942 Les Hite recording of "Jersey Bounce" that featured the pioneering bebop solo by Dizzy Gillespie. Wiggins had been around the block, and he didn't mind letting the locals know. He also was just plain perturbed about being in the Army, which he had evaded until the MPs snatched him off the road in handcuffs. "I kept thinking about Benny Carter and all the cats having a ball on the strip," he reflected. "It took me a while to get over that." An Art Tatum disciple who could run harmonic circles around most any piano player anywhere, Wiggins quickly became known as the best keyboard man in town. "Nobody could catch up with Wig," remembered Ernie Lewis.

A short, puckish man with a scrunched-up face and a cagey sense of humor much like his oblique piano phrasing, Wiggins settled in Los Angeles after the war. In the 1980s he was living in a large, comfortable house. In his studio there was a photograph of Marilyn Monroe, whom he coached for the singing parts in her 1950s movies, and another of Cybill Shepherd, whom he also coached. "Wig," as he was affectionately known, seemed surprised and pleased during his interview that anyone was interested in his Seattle days, and also somewhat amused to look back on his crazy youth. He blushed to admit that he probably came on like a New York know-it-all when he first got to town, but said there was one musician who humbled him—Julian Henson.

> Usually in a city like Seattle, there's one good musician that everybody talks about. The rest of the guys kind of look up to him. I thought at the time I was there that Julian Henson was the best piano player in town. Because he was doing things that I just couldn't figure out. That automatically made me say, "He's got something going." He was ahead of his time. He didn't know it was hard. He didn't read or anything. But he was really doing it. He was heavy. And he was fast. Oh, he was fast. I'd listen to him quite a bit.

Wiggins worked five months with Al Hickey and the Jive Bombers at the Washington Social Club. He lived just two blocks away, at East Madison Street and Twenty-Third Avenue, but still he managed to come in late to the gig almost every night. The guys would tease him, but he had other things on his mind. One of them was the beautiful Seattleite I'Lee, whom he later married. The other was fishing. "About seven or eight blocks up Madison, up the hill, there was a little pond that had catfish in it," he said. "Little baby catfish. We used to go over there at three or four o'clock in the morning and catch them. I'd go catch some catfish and bring them home and put them in the sink. My wife would find them there in the morning and I'd hear a shriek." Wiggins was probably referring to the spring-fed body of water that eventually became the koi pond in the Seattle Arboretum. For a while he worked weekend gigs with his fishing buddy, saxophonist Tootie Boyd, in Portland. "He sure was a fast driver. He had an old Buick and it would do a hundred and twenty. And he'd get every bit of it every time. We used to go from Seattle to Portland in almost less than an hour. I was always afraid of riding with him. And you know he never got a ticket. People'd say, 'You're crazy for riding with him. He's a maniac.' And he was. But I was young and crazy and full of that juice. I didn't give a damn. 'Can't you go any faster?'"

While Wiggins was in Seattle, he recorded a bristling 12-inch 78 with Fred Greenwell and Wyatt Ruther that attests to the heat and quality of music-making going on in town at the time. An extended bebop line over the changes of "Just You, Just Me," taken at a fast clip, showcases Wiggins as a fleet, linear player in the style of Bud Powell who also throws in tumbling, whole-tone scales in the manner of Art Tatum. He swings like mad, and so does Freddie, whose easy phrasing and blowsy tone—dry, like Lester Young's but broader—still sound immediate today.

After Wiggins was discharged in 1946, he went back to New York briefly, then returned to Seattle. He worked at the Rocking Chair with Ruther, soloed in the Aero-Marine Club (at the top of the Sorrento Hotel), played duets with Julian Henson, and made an album with local vocalist Juanita Cruse. By 1948 he was ready to move on. Bassist Charlie Oden, who had played with Wiggins in the Army band, found a trio gig for them in the Bay Area. When Oden—along with guitarist/trumpeter Earl Boatley, from the Ernie Lewis band—was killed in a car crash, Wiggins struck out on his own, starting an illustrious career backing all the top vocalists, including Lena Horne, Dinah Washington, Helen Forrest, Eartha Kitt, Joe Williams, and Helen Humes. In the 1950s he found a niche as a Hollywood vocal coach. After many years of sitting just outside the limelight, in the 1980s Wig decided to "play for myself for a while." The result, a series of trio and solo albums for Concord and an expanded roster of dates that took him to all the major festivals, had been highly rewarding. A somewhat ornamental player, Wiggins had a harmonic conception and feel for a romantic tune very much in line with another pianist who spent time on the Seattle scene studying the licks of Julian Henson—Jimmy Rowles.

The Wiggins/Rowles/Henson connection is an interesting one. All three pianists, with their flowery ornaments and sympathy for sentimental popular songs, were disciples in one way or another of Art Tatum (though Wiggins, the youngest, played in a more modern style), and their paths first crossed in Seattle. The stylistic trail is a circuitous labyrinth of connections: Henson and Wiggins hear Tatum on record; Rowles learns firsthand from Henson in Seattle, then goes to Los Angeles and sits at the feet of Tatum himself. Wiggins and Henson duet in Seattle, then Wiggins also moves to Los Angeles, after Tatum dies, and carries on the tradition. Rowles and Wiggins, with their sensitive voicings and swing-era sensibilities, go on to become two of the greatest accompanists for jazz singers. Most interesting for the Northwest is that some of the qualities that made Rowles a great accompanist had begun to be transmitted to him by a bar pianist like Henson, on an obscure local scene like Seattle's, as early as 1937. This is part of the subterranean, unwritten history of jazz, the history that happens after hours and rarely gets acknowledged.

Though Ernestine Anderson was the most popular local singer during the 1940s, Gerald Wiggins thought enough of one of her competitors, Juanita Cruse, to cut a record with her in Los Angeles after they'd both left Seattle. It's not clear exactly how long Cruse was in the Northwest, but she was working with Elmer Gill at the Rocking Chair in 1946 and seems to have left sometime after 1948 with Jack McVea's band. Originally from Saint Louis, Cruse played trumpet in high school before coming to Seattle, where she began to sing professionally. She was exceptional. Fred Greenwell said without hesitation that his two favorite jazz singers in town were Ernestine and Juanita. Wyatt Ruther said Ernestine caught your attention faster, but Juanita was more mature: "Juanita Cruse worked all over that place. She was one of the most popular singers around Seattle at that time. Juanita was a cross between Dinah Washington and Billie Holiday. She was very good. She had her own style. She was one of those people that wouldn't sing a song exactly like somebody else sang it."

The album she made in Los Angeles with Wiggins, *Juanita!*, shows Cruse to be every bit as fine a singer as Greenwell and Ruther make her out to be, though not as expressive or individualistic as one might have expected. Critics ranked Juanita and Ernestine pretty closely. *DownBeat* awarded Cruse three stars (out of five) for her album in the same 1961 issue that Anderson received three and a half stars for *Moanin' Moanin' Moanin'*. She had a fine instrument, with true highs and a rich, raspy middle, and her conception of a song and execution were pristine. Cruse worked with Jeep Smith's band for eight years after she left McVea, then sang in Hollywood supper clubs. No information has come to light about her later career.

Another modern singer on the scene was Wanda Brown, who had followed her drummer husband, Vernon, to Seattle in 1944. A good-natured, gravel-voiced gal who could often be found with a highball in one hand and a cigarette in the other, Wanda was a much-loved figure with a slow Southern drawl who was still singing in the early 1990s. In her heyday locals compared her favorably to Billie Holiday, whose melismatic, emotionally direct style Brown seemed to have picked up independent of Lady Day. Though she did not scat, Wanda was an improvising jazz singer who wound her way through the melody according to how she felt, like a horn player. She could belt out a jazz tune with blues feeling as well as anyone in town.

Brown was born Wanda Robertson in Oklahoma City in 1919. Her mother was a pianist with whom Jack Teagarden occasionally played; her father played fiddle and her brother, bass. Wanda sang in the glee club at school and remembered joining the young Charlie Christian in Oklahoma City jam sessions. Her Holiday-like style, she said, came to her by chance, much as improvising did to Ernestine: "I used to sit in front of the nickelodeon and I'd listen to Ella Fitzgerald, whom I always admired, and still do. But she never, never sang in my key. I put nickel after nickel in, trying to learn the tune that she was sing-

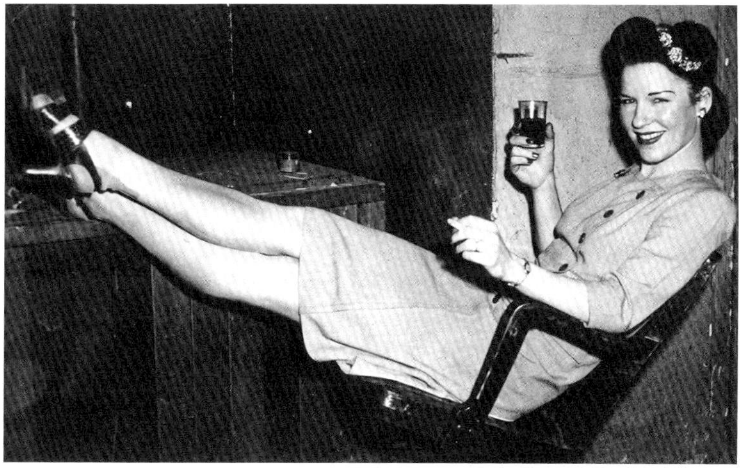

Wanda Brown.

ing. As a consequence of not being in my key, and me not knowing what key to sing it in, I sort of started singing around the melody. A lot of people I've talked with seem to think that is probably what makes me sound more like Billie Holiday. I admired Billie but my favorite was Ella Fitzgerald."

When Brown was fourteen, she walked into a burlesque house in Oklahoma and boldly announced she'd like to be in the show. She soon found herself posing in "scanty clothes" singing in the chorus line (but not, she said emphatically, working as a stripper). Two years later, she left home, bound for Minneapolis, where the scene was hot. In 1939 she met Vernon Brown working in a club in Milwaukee, and they got married in 1941. They moved to Detroit, where Vernon was called out to Seattle by Al Pierre in 1943. Wanda came out a few weeks later. She remembered having trouble at first adapting to the local custom of "table singing," which required vocalists to really belt out a song over the crowd noise, without a microphone. The protocol for Seattle's police raids was new to the singer as well. One night she and Vernon were working the Sessions Club when the place was busted. "We heard the raid coming. Everybody stood up while I ducked out the exit door. Then Vernon ducked out. I wound up over here on 14th and Yesler, walking around on the street, waiting to see if Vernon was going to come and pick me up. I didn't know whether he got put in jail or not."

Toward the end of the war, Brown left Seattle with an all-women band called Clarence Love's Darlings of Rhythm, but she only lasted about two months on the road:

> We had this sleeper bus, and the gal who played saxophone had the berth right above mine. She was alcoholic and her whiskey bottle kept falling down and hitting me on the head when I was sleeping. Several of the girls were definitely gay in the group and they were hitting on me all the time. I said, "This is not for me." In Klamath Falls, I said to heck with this noise. I sent Vernon a telegram to be prepared to

send money, that I was coming home. When D-Day came, I said, "Good-bye, this is my D-Day also," and I came on home.

After the war Brown worked at the Washington Social Club with Wyatt Ruther, then with Billy Tolles in a fabulous but short-lived venue called the New Orleans Club, near the old Longacres racetrack. The venue had a barbecue pit and a New Orleans chef; the band was as hot as the food. Billy's sextet had Neil Friel on trumpet, a trombonist from Los Angeles named Bones Robinson who could play like J. J. Johnson, Al Larkins on bass, and Gerald Frank on drums. There was a complete floor show and, for a while, big-time traveling acts, like the one-legged tap dancer Henry "Crip" Heard, performed there. One night in March 1949, when Ernestine Anderson was working the same show as Wanda, Billie Holiday dropped by the New Orleans. After hearing Wanda sing, she told Ernestine she thought Wanda must be Black, "because she couldn't sing like that if she wasn't."

Brown herself, who lived with Black musicians most of her life and believed in minimizing racial differences, scoffed at the notion that there are "Black singers" and "white singers." But Holiday's comment speaks volumes about the expressive and flexible style Brown used on such tunes as "All of Me," "The Man I Love," "Ballin' the Jack," and "Body and Soul." Brown worked in the Seattle area throughout the 1950s, occasionally as a chorus girl at the Rivoli Burlesque but usually as a jazz single. In the early 1960s she picked up a day job as a secretary for King County Animal Control, and she retired from professional singing in 1964. After Vernon died in 1966, Wanda lived with Gerald Brashear for about three years. In the early 1990s she occasionally appeared at Patti Summers's nightclub, much to the delight of fans both old and new. She died in 1995.

Wanda Brown's sometime-bass player, the big-framed, slow-talking Wyatt "Bull" Ruther, was another first-class musician (and future Basie-ite) who did his apprenticeship on Jackson Street. Ruther was playing trombone in the Special Service band at Fort Lewis when, like Wiggins, he decided to stick around the area. His first local job was with a fondly remembered seventeen-piece band Al Pierre put together. Ruther made some of his first arrangements for this band. When Wanda Brown asked him to play bass, rather than trombone, at the Washington Social Club, he decided to give it a shot. Ruther had started his conversion to bass at Fort Lewis when Charlie Oden left the Army band, so the transition was not difficult. Besides, his general musical skills were already high.

The Al Pierre rehearsal band at the Union Club, ca. 1948. Saxophones (*front row, left to right*): Ish Dotson, Joe Gauff, Terry Cruise, Jonas Weir, (first name unknown) Hobson; trombones (*second row*): Wyatt Ruther, *far right*; others unknown; trumpets (*back row*): Skeeter Evans, unknown, Bob Russell; bass (*far left*): Adolphus Alsbrook; piano (*behind bass*): Al Pierre; drums: Vernon Brown.

Ruther had attended the Pittsburgh Musical Institute, where he had learned to read both bass and treble clef, playing piano, xylophone, and trombone. When bass virtuoso and former Ellington sideman Adolphus Alsbrook came to town, he made Ruther his special project. "Adolphus Alsbrook taught me just about everything I know about bass violin," recalled Ruther. "In fact, when he died, he left me one of his fiddles. We were very close. He taught me how the instrument was supposed to be played."

Alsbrook's tutoring paid off for Ruther, who joined Ernie Lewis at the Black and Tan and accompanied him back to the Bay Area in 1948. Work followed with Dave Brubeck, Lena Horne, Erroll Garner, George Shearing, and Count Basie. In 1955, Ruther moved to Canada, where he spent much of his professional career. He made a milestone album there with Canadian swing revivalist Fraser MacPherson, *Fraser: Live at the Planetarium.* In 1972, Ruther made a rather lackluster album with Gerald Brashear, *Easy Living with the Ruther IV.* The bassist moved back to the Bay Area in 1984 and continued to work in the 1990s as a first-call sideman, traveling to festivals in Europe and throughout the United States. He died in 1999.

Ruther regarded his time in Seattle as a significant ingredient in his success. "I think it was very important to my musical career that I was there at that time," he said. "I was learning my instrument on the street. That's what a lot of us did. We learned how to play. If you walked in with an instrument, they'd call you up on the bandstand. If you could play, you stayed. If you couldn't play, you went back and you went to practicing again and came back when you could play. But you always had the opportunity."

Ruther's mentor, Adolphus Alsbrook, was a curious fellow. Originally from Kansas City, he had studied classical bass and harp and, according to Leon Vaughn, worked with Lester Young in Minneapolis and with Eli Rice on a Midwest tour in the 1930s. Julian Henson remembered working with Alsbrook at the Rhumboogie Club in Minneapolis in the 1940s, where he said the bassist also taught judo in the police department. Alsbrook gathered praise from many high places, including the memoirs of bassists Charles Mingus and Milt Hinton, so the quality of his playing is not in doubt. Gene Ramey, the renowned Count Basie bassist, reported that Alsbrook was one of the only musicians ever to quit Duke Ellington's band: "The bass player who preceded Jimmy Blanton with Duke for a short time was from Kansas City. His name was Adolphus Allbrooks [*sic*], and I used to see him walking across the viaduct from Kansas City, Kansas, to Kansas City, Missouri, with his bass on his back. He was a great bass player, but he complained that Duke was using all the wrong chords. He was a great arranger, too, but he didn't want to consider that Duke was creating a new sound in music. He became a professor up at the University of Minnesota."

Alsbrook came to Seattle at about the same time as Leon Vaughn and worked with Vaughn as a waiter on the Great Northern Empire Builder, which ran from Chicago to Tacoma. He subsequently played with Vaughn's band at Basin Street, and with Ernestine Anderson, Kenny Boas, and a variety of other players in town, including a brief commercial gig downtown with Wyatt Howard. Alsbrook had tremendous "legit" technique, with and without a bow. He also suffered from narcolepsy, a disease that seizes its victims with sudden brief bouts of sleep. He was notorious for dozing off while playing. Gerald Wiggins remembered Adolphus falling asleep as he walked up a flight of stairs. Despite the limitations caused by his affliction, Alsbrook was admired by musicians for his technical ability and his unusual intellect. "He was a very mysterious person," said Ernestine Anderson. "He was very sophisticated. He stayed at a hotel down in Chinatown. In his room, he had an upright piano and walls of books. Everybody was, like, in awe of him. He introduced me to pearl tea—hot water with cream and sugar. We worked together for years. He was very protective of me. We talked and talked." Years later, Anderson discovered she was Adolphus's cousin (her grandmother's brother was Alsbrook's father). When she excitedly told him this one afternoon in Los Angeles, he withdrew and never spoke to her again.

Alsbrook left Seattle for Los Angeles in the 1950s and enjoyed success there, playing with R & B sax master Earl Bostic as well as with Amos Milburn and Fats Domino. Alsbrook's path crossed with another Jackson Street veteran when he played on the Jesse Belvin single "Where's My Girl," accompanied by the Bumps Blackwell Band. Adolphus wrote music for Hollywood, including tunes for Herb Alpert's Tijuana Brass. He later moved to Vancouver, British Columbia, and died there in 1988.

Part of what made Jackson Street swing in the 1940s was its democratic embrace of gutbucket blues as well as jazz. There was little room for jazz snobs. "If you couldn't play the blues," said Wyatt Ruther, "you couldn't play in Seattle. That was during the time when the smaller bands would be patterning themselves after Louis Jordan's band. There was Jack McVea and his 'Open the Door, Richard.' Everybody did that one. You had to entertain."

A venue that well reflected this eclectic and tolerant coexistence of dance music and art was the Washington Social Club, where all of Seattle's prominent musicians held forth at one time or another. Ernestine Anderson, Ray Charles, blues man Clarence Williams, Quincy Jones, and Bumps Blackwell all performed there, as well as national blues and jazz groups, such as B. B. King, Arthur Prysock, Red Allen, and Wardell Gray. The club was owned by "the Good Reverend" Sirless "Sy" Groves of Montana, who gave it an air of legitimacy that distinguished it from other after-hours joints. Incorporated in 1944, the club was large and out in the open, for one thing—many after-hours clubs were hidden in back alleys—and it was also in the heart of the staid Madison neighborhood, just a block or two from Mount Zion Church. The building still stands at the corner of Twenty-Third Avenue and East Madison Street. Pianist Patti Bown remembered climbing up the stairs many nights as a teen. "I always remembered the eighteenth and nineteenth stairs creaked," she said. "I used to go from seventeen to twenty for good luck."

Though its full name—the Washington Educational and Social Club—sounds comically inflated, there were reasons to give it such a label. Although hard liquor was illegal, the state liquor board allowed private "clubs" to sell drinks to their members under special club licenses. Sy Groves actually had such a license, which made his place quasi-legitimate. To get in, you had to have a membership card. The membership-card system was essentially a scam, part of the look-the-other-way tolerance policy upheld by the police. According to *Seattle Times* columnist Johnny Reddin, "Most of my generation carried wallets fat with cards, each naming the bearer as a bona fide member of the 'Sahara,' 'Cavalcade,' or 'Blue Button' club, or numerous others." But the Washington Social Club did, in fact, serve community purposes other than pouring drinks. "It was sort of organized like the center of the Black community," asserted Sonny Booker. "Groves tried to do it right. They wanted to make it a social club. There'd be some women's meetings. They formed a young marching group for the parade."

Legitimate purposes notwithstanding, Groves still had to pay off the police, since he stayed open past the legal closing time, among other violations. Occasionally, of course, there were raids, some for show and some for real. It was an elaborate place. At the top of the stairs a long bar lined the entryway, separated by a wall from the main dance hall. Across the floor was the bandstand, with a little railing around it. The room was half-filled with long tables—there were also some booths along the sides—where some of the best fried chicken and barbecue in town was served. The waiters offered "setups"—ice and soda—and customers brought their own bottles of whiskey, which they kept under the table. For an exorbitant fee, you could also buy a bottle from the house. The hall held about 250 customers. Like Basin Street, the Washington Social Club had a floor show. Shake dancers with names like "The Flame" or "Princess Zenobia" (Zenobia Jefferson) traded sets with the musicians and the tap-dancing emcee Teddy Felton, who did comedy routines.

Two of the most familiar faces on the Washington Social Club bandstand during the late 1940s were both blues-oriented tenor saxophonists—Vernon "Pops" Buford and Al Hickey. Buford was a contemporary of Pony Poindexter in Oakland, California, and was the only musician from the Ernie Lewis band to actually settle in Seattle. Becoming a wheelchair user after 1977, when he had a stroke due to diabetes, which also required amputating both legs, Pops spoke with a severe disability that made him difficult to understand. His wife, Lillian, interpreted for him as best she could, a process that often led both of them into hysterical laughter. In 1989 he came across as a cheerful, upbeat man who still loved music and life. He wore a massive gold ring on one hand and laughed loud and long at life's vagaries.

Buford was the son of a flutist who played in the same World War I military band as Seattle pioneer Powell Barnett. Both of Buford's parents had died by the time he was eleven, so he was sent to Oakland to be raised by an aunt. A student of Jerome Richardson, by the time he was fourteen Buford was playing jazz up and down the state. Pops was a hard-swinging, blues-to-bop player in the style of Gene Ammons and Sonny Stitt, inspired as a youngster by the big bands of Erskine Hawkins and Jimmie Lunceford and by the solo styles of Charlie Parker, Lester Young, and Sarah Vaughan. He met Lillian in the Bay Area, and they moved to Seattle in 1946 when the Ernie Lewis band came north. When Lewis returned to the Bay Area, Pops and Lillian decided to stay in Seattle and raise a family. For a while, Buford made his living exclusively from music, working with Bumps Blackwell at the Washington Social Club and with Quincy Jones at the East Madison YMCA. He also worked in Bremerton, Washington, one night with Billie Holiday and in a hot quartet at the Black Elks Club.

In the 1950s, when work died down, Pops took a day job at a car dealership and later was an orderly at University Hospital. He continued to make music, playing with guitarist Mike DeFillipis, drummer Gerald Frank, and for several years pianist Winfield King at a downtown club called the Textile. Buford was good friends with guitarist Al Turay, who got him work in many white clubs in the North End that might otherwise not have welcomed him. In 1957, Buford christened Seattle's first real jazz club, Pete's Poop Deck; in the 1960s he became the premier R & B tenor-saxophone honker in town, working in the burgeoning Fort Lewis rock 'n' roll scene. Pops died in 1994.

Another exemplar of Seattle's heady mixture of blues and bebop was tenor saxophonist Al Hickey, who co-led a dynamic, Louis Jordan–inspired combo called the Jive Bombers from 1946 on. Though the combo suffered from continual personnel changes, the Jive Bombers were an extremely popular dance band in the Black community. Hickey came to his Seattle success by a circuitous route. Born in Virginia in 1921, he grew up in New York, where he heard Count Basie, Chick Webb, and other hot big bands at the Apollo Theater. But it was Louis Jordan, whom he heard while outside the door of a little Harlem club on

133rd Street, who made him want to play music. Hickey's description of how he taught himself to play is a dramatic illustration of how jazz is often handed down as an oral tradition.

> I went to a pawnshop and started out with a clarinet. It cost about two dollars. I got a fingering chart. It took me about two months, practicing the fingering on a broomstick while I paid the pawnshop fifty cents a week to buy the clarinet. Then I did the same thing with a saxophone. Then I went around asking musicians how you learn to play your horn. One person told me, "Learn your scales," so I went home and ran all the scales. Then another person told me, "Learn your chords." Well then—one, four, five, seven—I started learning the chords. Then one person told me, "What you need to do is not only play chords, but learn how to transition from one chord to the other." Pretty soon, if you were to sit down and call the chords, I would play. I didn't have to know the song.

Hickey joined a trio and played his first professional gigs in upstate New York, then got an athletic scholarship to Fisk University, in Nashville. Jimmie Lunceford was also at Fisk, playing in a twelve-piece swing band called the Fisk Collegians. Hickey made the band, and in it met his future Jive Bombers co-leader, a trumpeter from Ohio named Harry "Doc" Wheeler. Hickey and Wheeler wrote arrangements for the Fisk Collegians and gigged in swing bands around Nashville. In 1943, a year after President Truman integrated the military, Hickey and Wheeler were part of an integrated cohort of five thousand musicians recruited and sent to the Great Lakes Naval Base, just north of Chicago. There they met William Funderburg, a territory bandleader and reed player from Birmingham, Alabama, who had enjoyed success leading a swing band during the Depression. (Funderburg is honored with a display in the Birmingham Jazz Hall of Fame.) "All the musicians in the Navy started there," explained Hickey, who later retired to Portland following a successful thirty-year musical career. "They'd get organized and then they'd go off to where they're posted for," Hickey said. "Talk about jam sessions! Ernie Royal, Marshal Royal, Willie Smith, Clark Terry—everybody was there. Every noon, there was a jam session. There was also a seventeen-piece military band, which I wrote arrangements for."

While Hickey was stationed at Great Lakes, he, Funderburg, and Wheeler were part of a twenty-five-piece military band that toured naval bases. They also worked occasionally in Chicago in a small group they called the Jive Bombers. When their military band was transferred to Sand Point Naval Air Station in Seattle, Hickey, Funderburg, and Wheeler kept the Jive Bombers name alive as a Navy swing unit. Seattle bassist Bob Marshall, also stationed at Sand Point, joined them. The military band played USO shows with traveling stars, including Jack Benny. While the band was still a Navy group, the Bombers occasionally played local nightclubs, sometimes in uniform. In 1946, when Wheeler and Hickey were discharged, things had been going so well at the Washington Social Club, they decided to form a civilian Jive Bombers, with different personnel.

"We had about seven arrangers in the Navy band," explained Hickey. "When the band broke up we exchanged arrangements, so we had a book from everybody. Anybody that was planning on being a leader when they got out of the service had a book. I was writing. Doc Wheeler was writing. And Bobby Braxton was writing. We had a hefty book going." The core of the Jive Bombers was three horns and three rhythm, with Wheeler doing most of the arranging: Al Hickey, tenor saxophone; Doc Wheeler, trumpet; Bob Braxton, alto saxophone; Kenny Boas, piano; Al Larkins (later replaced by Wyatt Ruther), bass; and Duke Moore, drums. Wheeler left town in 1948 and became a high school principal in Oklahoma City. He was replaced by Dave Bradford; Gerald Wiggins played piano occasionally, and Johnny Moton replaced Boas on piano in 1951; John Willis inherited the alto chair from Braxton. Both Adolphus Alsbrook and Wyatt Ruther played bass with the Jive Bombers for a while as well. In the 1950s, Ralph Davis took over drum duties from Moore.

The Bombers were versatile entertainers. They did jive vocals in unison and jump tunes in the manner of Louis Jordan, and they got the crowd up dancing. Their version of "Flyin' Home," which sometimes went on for half an hour, included Hickey or Braxton—or both—"walking the floor" for dollar tips, which customers stuffed into their horns as they passed by. Braxton also sang ballads, in the Eckstine manner, and Hickey did some jive singing. Dave Bradford, a song-and-dance guy from New Orleans who also did comedy, was the front man. The band did popular Nat Cole arrangements, such as "Straighten Up and Fly Right."

One night the Bombers got into a "battle of the bands" with Lester Young, the "Pres" himself, who worked at the Washington Social with a quintet for six weeks in 1948. The group included Shorts McConnell on trumpet, Roy Haynes on drums, and possibly Argonne Thornton on piano. No one seems to remember who the bass player was, but he was from out of town. Lester was in a far-out mood. Ron Pierce recalled: "Lester had long, long fingernails and he had this zoot suit on. He stood up at the microphone and said, 'Now we're going to play "Tea for Two,"' and he bowed his head and played one note—*whooooaaa!*—then he fingered 'Tea for Two,' and you could hear 'Tea for Two' but he would just be blowing air through the horn. On breaks between sets, he would stand very silently next to people sitting at a table. He would just wander up and he wouldn't say a word." The "battle" between the Bombers and Pres's band took place on February 5, 1948, at the Civic Auditorium. Hickey added some ringers for the occasion—Gerald Wiggins on piano, Roscoe Weathers on alto, and Bobby Braxton on vocals—and renamed the group the Atomic Bombers. The Bombers reportedly gave Lester a run for his money.

Dave Bradford belting a "big note," ca. 1962.

By the 1950s the Jive Bombers had dwindled to a quartet. Finding that jobs were less plentiful in Seattle, Hickey took a trio to Anchorage, Alaska—as did many Seattle musicians at this juncture—with drummer Duke Moore and pianist Elmer Gill. When he returned, he took a day job at Boeing and played in a rehearsal band there led by Leon Vaughn, then took a group into Bremerton to play. In 1953, Hickey moved to Portland. Like many musicians of his era, Hickey looked back on his Seattle years affectionately as a great learning experience. "When they had those jam sessions," he said, "if you weren't up to it, you were going to look like a fool. And if you've got any kind of competitive spark in you, you're trying not to let that happen. There were high-quality players. Anyone coming out of that era can handle any job they go on." Hickey remembered one jam session in particular when he learned a lot, the night the great Los Angeles tenor saxophonist Wardell Gray performed. "Every tenor player in town came in and tried to blow out Wardell Gray," says Hickey. "Fools! They'd come in one by one, and disappear. About three hours later I said, 'Let's complete our discussion we had going, now that we've got rid of all them tenor players!' We sat up there on the bandstand, Wardell and I, talking all night long."

Before the decade was out, a new generation of Seattle beboppers would walk up the long flight of stairs at the Washington Social Club to continue the "discussion" begun by Hickey, Buford, Poindexter, and their cohorts. Quincy Jones, Patti Bown, Buddy Catlett, and Ray Charles—among others—would refine the Seattle mix of jazz and blues, shaping a music whose influence eventually would fan out to the rest of the world.

6 The Next Generation

Quincy Jones and Company

ON FEBRUARY 16, 1949, THE Dizzy Gillespie Afro-Cuban big band, with Cuban drummer Chino Pozo, played Seattle's Senator Ballroom. This was a Bebop Event of the first order. Forty years later, Gary Steele, a white saxophone player from South Bend—a remote town in the southwest corner of the state—still remembered convincing his parents to drive him up to Seattle—130 miles—to hear the band. Steele, a high school student who was familiar with Gillespie's quintet records, thought he was going to hear a small group. From a 1989 interview:

> Here I came from this fishing village straight into the best thing that was happening musically in the world. . . . The thing that struck me most was the offhand and casual way that these guys looked when they were playing this music. Slumped in their chairs just like it was nothing, throwing it away. The whole band was kind of framed around this carnival-style conga player. He played with a strap over his shoulder. He was kind of the focal point of the whole thing. He was just unbelievable. What he was doing with the band. You could hardly take your eyes off him. He was a charismatic creature. And this band was just this living, breathing monster thing. I remember every little thing that happened. I remember Lester Bass was playing and he was up on a riser and he dropped his hat down through the risers and it kind of clattered down through there. He never did get it again. He just shrugged his shoulders and the band kept on roaring and nobody cared.
>
> Diz sat in front of the band in kind of a straight-back chair and he had another straight-back chair in his hand this way. He was trying to make a top out of it. He was trying to make it spin. Like he was totally preoccupied, you know, like he didn't give a shit. They were playing "Manteca," and all these great tunes they are still playing today.

The night Dizzy's big band played the Senator (now home of Union Arts Center), the Bumps Blackwell Junior Band had a gig. No one in the group was too happy about missing Dizzy, least of all a young trumpet player named Quincy Jones. All through the job that night, he was thinking about going up to the Washington Social Club, where he knew some of the guys from the Gillespie band would probably fall by afterward. As luck would have it, a couple of them did. Recalled Jones:

> I never will forget, they had those big, furry coat collars and those hip, New York pimp hats, you know? Ray Brown came up. These guys were bringing the sounds. That's the only contact we had. I couldn't believe it. It was like New York. Heaven. See, there was no way to communicate [in those days]. There was no MTV or anything. And *DownBeat* was the only way you could get any word out in a big city, outside of word of mouth, talking to the guys in the band—"Man, what's Bird doing?" "Bird put some Benzedrine in Rubberlegs Williams' coffee, man." All these stories would come out of there.

Quincy Jones belonged to the young generation of modernists who would shape the next phase of Seattle music. Just sixteen when Dizzy came through town, Quincy was playing with a group of Garfield High kids originally led by tenor saxophonist Charlie Taylor before being taken under the wing of promoter Bumps Blackwell.

Quincy Jones's high school yearbook photograph, 1950, *Garfield Arrow.*

The Bumps Blackwell Junior Band is a legend in Seattle's Black community. Not only did the band nurture the young Jones, it also served as the staging ground for the careers of Buddy Catlett, Billy Johnson, and Tommy Adams. Because Bumps himself was a flamboyant character who also used Ernestine Anderson and occasionally Ray Charles, the band is a focal point in people's memories of the Jackson Street scene.

The Bumps Blackwell Junior Band was started by Charlie Taylor in the fall of 1947. Taylor was an intellectual whose influence on Jones as well as the scene at large has been unjustly overshadowed by the self-promoting Blackwell. Taylor was the son of Evelyn Bundy, the pianist who led the Garfield Ramblers in the 1920s. When he was growing up, famous touring musicians came to his parents' home to socialize or jam in the basement. "We used to have their pictures all pasted around on the walls," recalled Taylor, who earned a degree in anthropology and later ran a computer business. "They'd eat there and sign the pictures and we'd put them on the wall. Lionel Hampton bought me a set of drums."

The Bumps Blackwell Junior Band at the Trianon Ballroom, March 14, 1949. *Left to right:* Billy Johnson, Harold Redman, Charles Taylor, Buddy Catlett, Quincy Jones, Blackwell, Major Pigford, Tommy Adams.

Taylor didn't start playing music until he was seventeen. His description of how he came to music says a lot about the role of jazz in the Black community when he was growing up:

> All the Black kids I knew had a favorite instrument that they liked to listen to and could "pose" to. I liked to pose to a tenor saxophone, so that's what instrument I got. Everybody knew how to pose. We didn't really know how to play, but we just kept on doing it, so it went from posing to playing. We were listening to Jazz at the Philharmonic, Illinois Jacquet, Gene Ammons, Lester Young, and Coleman Hawkins. I could make sounds like all those different ones. The first thing was, you pose, then you can make some sounds. The first sounds you make are being able to sound like Lester Young or being able to sound like Coleman Hawkins or whatever.
>
> I got a saxophone for Christmas. I took lessons from Frank Waldron. For six months, I practiced about six hours a day. And when I couldn't play with a mouthpiece, when it got late, then I would just play with my fingers, fingering. Then the rest of the time I would just imagine it. At the end of six months of lessons—running chord changes and reading—I quit lessons and started a band.

When Taylor began to recruit musicians for his project, he turned first to his best friend, a kid who had just moved over from Bremerton, Quincy Jones. Jones was a handsome youngster whose spirit seems to have attracted good people and good projects from the start.

At sixty, Jones was as unpretentious and enthusiastic as he must have been that night sitting at the feet of his musical idols at the Washington Social Club. His great celebrity and wealth did not prevent him from being one of the most genuine and disarming personalities in the music business. In the 1980s he lived in a wood-sheathed hillside house in Bel Air, California, decorated in earth tones and warm surfaces more in keeping with jazz than with the glitz of the Los Angeles techno-pop he was producing at the time. His voice was sensitive and urbane, with a high, caressing edge. He touched when he talked.

Born in Chicago in 1933, Jones moved west with his family when he was ten, to the Navy town of Bremerton, about forty-five minutes by ferry from Seattle. His father had been offered a good wartime job as a carpenter in the naval shipyards. The family was placed in Sinclair Heights, a segregated housing project built for African Americans whom the Navy needed—temporarily. "They made sure it was way away from town," recalled Jones. "You had to walk three miles up this hill to get into town. They also didn't put phones in the homes. You had to go to a telephone booth. They didn't want the Black people to get so comfortable there after the war. They wanted them to get out. I didn't even realize this until someone told me that later."

Since those days, Bremerton has heartily embraced its Black heritage. In 2025 the city dedicated Quincy Jones Square downtown, which features a statue of the great musician and entrepreneur, as well as a mural down the street depicting other Black leaders. Jones attended school in Bremerton, where he received hit-and-miss musical instruction. His first instrument was French horn, an interesting coincidence in light of Jones's colorful use of that instrument as an arranger. He worked his way through piano, drums, and cymbals at Coontz Junior High, then played violin, tuba, baritone horn, E-flat alto horn, and trombone before he finally got to trumpet, his destination instrument, at the age of twelve. He had no private instruction, save some general pointers about music handed down by Eddie Lewis, a Bremerton barber whose son, Dave, later became an important figure in the Seattle rock scene. Jones, for whom arranging would become a more passionate concern than "chops" (that is, instrumental prowess), did get inspiration from Joseph Powe, a local school music teacher who had a dance band.

> I used to get butterflies when I stood in front of that band. They had real music, written by hand, with numbers on it, and copied out, not like the stock music that's printed. That was like big-time stuff, because that's what Woody Herman had. That's what Basie had. I used to baby-sit for [Powe]. I'd look at his Glenn Miller arranging books and it was just like walking into fantasy land, just to be able to look at those things with the trombones and how they worked. How you put the saxes and trombones and stuff together. I was just hooked on it. I must have been about thirteen. It took over my life.

Just before the end of the school year in 1947, Jones's family moved to Seattle. As soon as Quincy got to Garfield High School, he gravitated toward Charlie Taylor, who, like himself, was a natural leader. "Charlie was an only child," remembered Jones, "and came from a family where he was well-raised, so to speak, and he was well-loved as a child. He had a lot of high self-esteem. He was a big influence." Both Jones and Taylor played in the Garfield concert band, directed by Parker Cook, a teacher who was supportive of their extracurricular ambitions and who would answer their questions about theory, songwriting, and arranging. The two also took lessons from Frank Waldron. Jones was not an exceptional instrumentalist, but he had a fantastic ear for harmony. "Quincy had his lesson from Frank Waldron right before I did," said Ron Pierce. "Frank would say, 'Quincy, play me an augmented flat nine scale here.' He'd play it. 'Okay, play me a thirteenth scale.' He was very impressed with Quincy. Quincy was a good student."

Quincy agreed to join Charlie's band. Taylor then continued recruiting, this time going to two musicians whose lineage, like his own, dated back to Seattle's first jazz generation—alto saxophonist Oscar Holden Jr. and pianist Grace Holden; their father was Oscar Holden Sr., the veteran pianist from the 1920s. The rest of the chairs were filled by Eddie Beard, another Waldron student who Quincy said played the best tenor saxophone version of "Stardust" in town; Quincy's stepbrother, Waymond Miller, on drums, shortly succeeded by Harold Redman; and Billy Johnson on bass. Tommy Adams, who later became an innovative local drummer, did vocals. Said Jones:

> The first job we ever played was at the YMCA on 23rd and Madison, in 1947. We got seven dollars apiece. We played all of Louis Jordan's things and a little bebop. We used to rehearse at Charlie's house, in the basement, every day. We listened to records. We were very conscientious. I still have the minutes. We had a president, vice president, and a secretary/treasurer. All that stuff. We were really organized dudes. We used to have fines for drinking. If you were late, this happened, and so forth. I couldn't believe how organized we were as kids. We were really serious about it.

At first, Taylor's band played Garfield noon dances and the spring talent show. As the group moved on to gigs at Fort Lawton and other outlying areas, Grace Holden bowed out, supplanted by Van Lear Douglas. Major Pigford joined on trombone. Harold Redman replaced Waymond on drums. Billy Johnson started playing bass. Sometimes they were joined by a guitar player named Booker Martin, a seaman who was older than the kids and was into playing Charlie Parker solos on guitar.

Oscar Holden Jr. was soon replaced as well, by Buddy Catlett, another student of Waldron's who was also in the Garfield school band. Catlett was known later as a bass player, but in his youth he played alto saxophone. He was the premier instrumentalist in the Taylor group. Catlett, who like Taylor was a Seattle native, joined by serendipity. Recalled Buddy: "The alto player was a basketball player and he didn't show up for rehearsal. I dropped by Charlie's basement and they asked me to play. I had my tenor and I transposed the part. Charlie thought that was fantastic. The tunes were fairly simple and I'd heard both of them anyway. So I got hired. Oscar was six-foot-three or -four. My first uniform . . . they cut the sleeves off and that was all. I looked like Pee Wee Marquette!" Catlett's idol at the time was Johnny Hodges, whose warm, full tone he imitated. That tone, and Taylor's chutzpah getting jobs, soon had the Charlie Taylor band playing for functions all around Puget Sound. One night, Bumps Blackwell heard the band at a dance at Lake Sammamish. Blackwell had lots of connections and one of the only organized sets of written band arrangements in town. Knowing a good thing when he heard it, he offered to expand the band's bookings if the kids would change their name to the Bumps Blackwell Junior Band and give him a percentage. Taylor and his friends agreed.

Robert A. "Bumps" Blackwell, who later pioneered the careers of Little Richard and Sam Cooke, became an influential figure in the lives of his young protégés. Born in 1918, he was a 1936 Garfield graduate who had little musical training as a youngster but adopted the airs of a conductor, dressing and acting the part. In 1939 he mounted and performed in an original musical, *Ceremony in Swing*. But like many swing-era bandleaders, he could barely play his putative instrument, the vibraphone. "Everybody that was around Bumps, overall, was a better musician than Bumps was," Ray Charles commented. "But that didn't matter, because Bumps had the gig."

Bumps was the kind of man who always tried to make something dramatic happen, and often did. He had tremendous energy. Father figure, promoter, manager, uncle, counselor, and bandleader, he tirelessly promoted the Junior Band around the region, particularly at white society gatherings where Black leaders had not ventured before. A whole generation of white Seattleites grew up listening to Blackwell's various bands—at fraternity and sorority parties, for the cotillion in the exclusive walled-in neighborhood of Broadmoor, for dances in Leschi and Madison Park, at the Seattle Tennis Club, and at fancy resorts out of town. "Bumps Blackwell could talk his way into anything," remembered trumpet player Floyd Standifer, who arrived on the scene in the late 1940s. "Sometimes he talked his way out the other side, but he really was a showman. He had an inventive mind. This guy would never take no for an answer on anything."

In addition to the Junior Band, Bumps led a Senior Band and a group called the Big Band that combined personnel from each. Blackwell would send different combinations of musicians out on four or five gigs in one night, all under the Blackwell aegis, then drive around town to check up on them, like a booking agent. Elmer Gill, a pianist who sometimes worked for Bumps, didn't think much of his methods.

> He'd call any three things to play together. I remember one time he called me and we were playing out at the Knights of Columbus Hall. I got there—now, this was a formal dance—and it was me to play the piano, Dick Thorlakson to play trombone, and somebody else playing the guitar! That was it. Piano, trombone, and guitar. Bumps came in with a white jacket and a great long baton. Man, I went out the back door! He was standing up there with his baton, directing a trombone and guitar! No drums, no bass! And all these people in long dresses and tuxedos.

Blackwell kept his ad hoc music agency afloat from his butcher shop on Twenty-Third Avenue and Madison Street, within shouting distance of the Savoy Ballroom and the Washington Social Club. Remembered Floyd Standifer:

On any given day, you could walk over there and there'd be a whole bunch of people, most of them musicians, standing around at the meat counter. You might find young Ernestine Anderson. Quincy would be there. I was there a few times. Major Pigford. All these guys standing around waiting to hear about rehearsal plans and things like that. Bumps lived right around the corner, and everybody rehearsed at his place. He was kind of like a magnet. If you were at all any kind of a performer with any kind of pizzazz, Bumps had to attract you. He was really Mr. Show Business, as far as Seattle was concerned.

For a time Blackwell had a virtual music monopoly, according to Billy Tolles: "If you wanted to work, you were working in one of Bumps's bands. He would come and collect the money off of each gig, and pay you what he wanted you to have. He had the thing locked up."

The Charlie Taylor band thrived under Blackwell's sponsorship. Blackwell coached the youngsters to be total entertainers. They not only played, they danced, they sang, they did routines—they could put on a whole floor show. Jones recalled: "At the Seattle Tennis Club we played all the schottisches. Then we'd play at ten o'clock till about one at the Black clubs, where it would really loosen up, and get down and go into stuff like Eddie 'Cleanhead' Vinson's 'Kidney Stew Blues' and Roy Brown's 'Good Rockin' Tonight.' We had comedy acts. I used to sing 'Run Joe' with a big hat. We had the stock arrangements on 'Room Full of Roses,' we'd sing 'Blue Moon.' And we also had all the stuff that Dizzy was playing." The band's first gig under Bumps's baton was at the Civic Auditorium, playing opposite no less a figure than Cab Calloway. The band wore white jackets with no lapels. The date went over so well, Blackwell approached Lemuel Honeysuckle to reopen the Savoy Ballroom, which had been converted into a skating rink. Honeysuckle complied, and the Junior Band played there every Sunday. Blackwell also got the Junior Band gigs at county fairs in Yakima and Puyallup, at the Pacific National Exhibition in Vancouver, British Columbia, at nearby resorts on Shadow Lake and Angle Lake—even a regular weekend engagement at Island Lake Resort, near Bremerton. Jones used to tease Ernestine Anderson about the night in Vancouver she squeezed into a shake dancer's skirt and shimmied onstage.

Blackwell was on the lookout for the moral character of his young charges, offering them friendly guidance in the ways of the world. Recalled Taylor:

He took on the role of being a father to us. He would be telling interesting stories about [how] you got to watch this, and watch that, and make sure that you look at her bra strap—if it's dirty, don't have anything to do with her. He had all these little tales. He gave us lectures on dope. He would get upset if he thought we were smoking pot. And he would always point out all the people that had gotten into music and then gone down the tube by getting caught up in all the things that were peripheral to it. He spent a good deal of time on that. It didn't take much to turn the shoulder, you know. I remember I got in the cab with Bird once, on my way to the Social Club—it just happened we were in the same cab together—and I remember that he was incoherent. It wasn't hard to see what [Bumps] was talking about. It wasn't an abstract thing.

Blackwell's caution was perhaps warranted. One night, after a gig at Island Lake, on the way back to the ferry the band was pulled over for driving too slow, and the police discovered a joint in somebody's pocket. Taylor insisted the incident was a "setup," but the band spent the night in jail. The charges were later dismissed.

Another depressing object lesson in the perils of the jazz life came on February 12, 1949, the night the Junior Band found itself backing up Billie Holiday at the Senator Ballroom. Though most of the young men felt proud to be playing behind Lady Day, they vividly recalled how incapacitated she was. "She could barely talk," said Jones. "I remember she didn't show up for rehearsal."

The following year, Billie's accompanist, Bobby Tucker, came back with Billy Eckstine and requested the same backup band. "That was very, very important in terms of building confidence," remembered Jones. The Junior Band also opened for Nat Cole at the Civic Auditorium and worked the same stages as Mel Tormé and another important musical model, Louis Jordan. Blackwell units also traded sets with a parade of early rock groups that had started to come through the Washington Social Club: Bull Moose Jackson, Pee Wee Crayton, Joe Liggins, Roy Milton, and Lucky Millinder. Sammy Davis Jr. and Clark Terry also offered Quincy and his pals time and guidance. Said Quincy:

We'd hang with Sammy. Worry him to death! All day long. He had all these records—"Lemon Drop" and "Early Autumn," all this bebop, with "Birth of the Cool" and Miles and all that stuff. It had a tremendous influence. He was the first guy that had earphones and a record player. I had never seen that before. We used to play hookey and go down to the Palomar Theater. We dressed like we were old, so we could get in. We'd take our bags and go in there and pretend like we were part of the band. Clark Terry was [there] with Count Basie. I used to ask Clark, "How do you do this?"

Billie Holiday performing at the Eagles Auditorium on February 12, 1949, with the Bumps Blackwell Junior Band behind her. *Sidemen in rear, left to right:* Billy Johnson, Harold Redman, Charles Taylor.

After the Bumps Blackwell Junior Band had been together less than a year, an odd turn of events brought together many of the area's young white and Black jazz musicians in an unlikely setting that is still a source of amused pride for all concerned. The armed forces were segregated during the 1940s, but times were changing. The Washington National Guard decided to form a unit including Black men. Charlie Taylor got wind of this through a friend of his mother's and went to visit Bumps. Thus was formed, in October 1947, the Forty-First Infantry Division Band, Washington National Guard, with fifty-six musicians under Warrant Officer (Junior Grade) Robert A. (Bumps) Blackwell—temporary quarters, the Field Artillery Armory at Camp Murray. The band included Quincy Jones, Buddy Catlett, Major Pigford, Charlie Taylor, and just about anybody else in the neighborhood who could hold a horn. Trumpeter Floyd Standifer, who was attending the University of Washington, was also recruited. The members were issued free instruments (a big motivation for many of the kids) and uniforms, and they started to learn to march. "Not one of them could blow their nose," Blackwell later exaggerated affectionately. "I ended up bringing in men out of my big band."

One of the professional additions was Ish Dotson, a tenor saxophone player who had worked in Al Pierre's big band. Another was Ron Pierce. Soon, white musicians Al Pace, Dick Thorlakson, Bruce Ford, Dave Tuttle, Ken Boas, and a whole batch of others just out of high school, whom Bumps had been using in his various bands, also joined the unit. The National Guard band survived three summers at Camp Murray, running the telephones and communications and playing

The Forty-First Infantry Division Band, Washington National Guard, directed by Robert A. "Bumps" Blackwell, Camp Murray, 1947–48. *Far left:* Blackwell. *Front:* unknown. *Columns, left to right, front to back:* (1) Billy Johnson, Charles Taylor, George Brown, Quincy Jones, Harold Redman; (2) Major Pigford, unknown, Harold Hardy, Eddie Beard, Tommy Adams; (3) unknown, Clayton Harold, unknown, (first name unknown) Clark, unknown; (4) "Butch," unknown, Andrew Guyong, unknown, unknown; (5) Buddy Featherston, Oscar Holden Jr., Buddy Catlett, unknown, unknown.

for retreat parades and dances. The band was a boon for many kids, but it was also a firsthand preview of how badly the jazz life mixed with military regimentation, particularly when the guys tried to play gigs in town. As Jones recollected:

> We all had staff-sergeant ratings. We came back to camp late one time, and we all got busted. Including Bumps. I couldn't believe it. They were pissed. They said, "Good to see you, Sergeant, do you have any answer for this?" I said, "No." They said, "Well, Corporal, go over there." We'd been demoted. It got to the place where we were privates.
>
> I was supposed to be company bugler. I had to play reveille in the morning. We stayed out all night and I didn't get up until about 11 o'clock. The who-o-o-le base overslept. They were so pissed off at me they made me sleep with the MPs after that, so I'd get up with them and wouldn't oversleep.

Eventually Blackwell was replaced as leader of the National Guard band by sweet-band leader Jackie Souders, but not before he mustered out the kids to protect them from being sent to the Korean conflict.

Bumps Blackwell, who died in 1982 having achieved little national recognition, cared a great deal for the young musicians he nurtured in Seattle and afforded them many opportunities. Regrettably, as some of his protégés became famous, he exaggerated the magnitude of his influence on them. It was not uncommon for him in later years to boast that he had "given Quincy Jones his start," or led a big band with Jones, Ray Charles, and Ernestine Anderson. In fact, Blackwell's contribution to Jones's career was minor and he never led such a band—at least not on any but the most sporadic basis. Musically, Blackwell was neither an innovator nor even a quality bandleader. But he made his claims on Jones often enough that people came to believe them. Even Buddy Catlett, who remained a close, lifelong friend of Quincy's, surmised that Jones was inspired by Blackwell's take-charge attitude and dramatic sense of leadership, a notion that surprised Jones: "No. Not at all. Not at all! I was much more influenced by Charlie [Taylor] than by Bumps. But, you know, people write whatever they want. You tell them about Frank Waldron and they put down Clark Terry. You put down Charlie Taylor, they put down Bumps Blackwell."

If Charlie Taylor was Quincy's personal inspiration, Ray Charles was his musical one, since it was R. C., as he was then called, who fired up Quincy's arranging ambitions. The meeting of Jones and Charles on Jackson Street is one of the most important moments in the story of Northwest jazz. It began a lifelong musical relationship that had a lasting influence on both men. With all the millions of dollars that passed through their offices, Jones and Charles worked together without a contract. Neither seemed to remember exactly how or when they met, but it was soon after Charles's arrival from Tampa, Florida, in the spring of 1948. Quincy's first recollection of Charles was at the Elks Club, where Charles was singing on the stand: "Ray seemed o-o-o-o-old. He was so mature. And he was only two years older than I was! He was sixteen and I was fourteen. He had his own apartment, his own suits, and everything. Oh boy, did I look up to him. He was just so wise."

"Quincy tells lies!" Charles said, laughing out loud when he heard this quote repeated back to him during a Los Angeles interview:

You know why he says that about me, though, because I had my own apartment. I had a girlfriend that stayed with me and all this kind of stuff. I had a piano. I had a hi-fi. And my old lady, we were keeping house. He was a kid in school, so I guess I did seem like an old man.

Quincy was playing trumpet, but he really wanted to write jazz. So he asked me how to do it. He was a very enthusiastic fellow. Not only enthusiastic—you see some people that are extremely attractive, and that's the way Quincy was with me when we were youngsters. I was very, very attracted to him. Our chemistry just clicked.

You remember, we used to work from one o'clock till five in the morning and I didn't get to sleep till six-thirty. Quincy was the kind of a guy, he'd wake me up at nine. He wanted to learn how to write music. He liked things like "Emanon," with Dizzy Gillespie's band. And it just turned out that I knew how to write music. I had been writing music since I was maybe ten, eleven, twelve years old. So he would come over and I would show him things. I'd show him how to voice for saxophones, how to voice for the trombones and the trumpets, what the chord structures were, like a B-flat augmented eleventh, with an added thirteen, things like that, you know? And from that, he started to write.

Jones echoed the story, remarkably remembering the exact same chord:

I must have been fourteen years old and I wanted to write so badly. I used to listen to Billy Eckstine's band, "Blowing the Blues Away." I couldn't figure out how eight horns—four trumpets and four trombones—could play together at the same time and not play the same note. So Ray hit a B-flat-seventh in root position and a C-seventh, which is a real Dizzy Gillespie kind of sound. They always had that eight notes or seven notes [in the chord]. And bang! He just hit that thing. When I saw that, it was like that whole world just opened up. Everything from then on made sense. Just that one chord started to let me know.

After the *bang!* of that chord, Jones and Charles were inseparable, hanging out, comparing notes, staying up all night or playing together at the Washington Social Club. "I remember Quincy being so excited about this new thing that R. C. had shown him," said Ernestine Anderson. "All these new changes and the new chord structure . . . he was just so knocked out about R. C. and his music. Ray just sort of took him under his wing."

It's not difficult to surmise why the relationship between these two men ran so deep. They shared a lot. They were teenagers when they met, they were both going through formative, sensitive periods in their lives, and they got their first breaks at around the same time. Both were alive to the musical possibilities exploding around them, and both were extremely ambitious. Said Charles:

> A lot of people don't understand Quincy and my relationship. And I'll tell you something, if you look at Quincy, as a side note, and you look at me, you probably would never understand how we could be brothers, close to each other as we are, because our personalities are so different. I'm very—almost introverted. Some people think I'm antisocial. Whereas Quincy is more open, he's more around people. He enjoys that, and people love him. We're very opposite in our styles, and yet we are very together in our feelings.
>
> We don't work for each other. That's number one. I can't afford him! [*Laughs.*] He calls me and says, "Ray, hey, lookahere, I want to—," and I say, "Okay." And that's it! No contract, no nothin'. If it's something Quincy Jones wants me to do. He tells me. I do it. And it's the same thing. If I call him up and say, "Hey, Q, I want you to—" [*claps hands*]. That's it. Finish! So that's why we are the way we are today. This is not like all of a sudden we have got ulterior motives or we're looking for something, you know, it ain't that kind of thing. It's a true, genuine friendship, man. And it has lasted now for some forty-three years. That's a long time. I'm just thankful, because I love him so much, ever since we were kids. He's like my brother, and I really mean that sincerely. He's always been that way with me, until this day. If I got a dime, he's got a nickel. Honest to god.

"Ray and I are the only ones that have been in touch all the way through," confirmed Jones. "We've been working right up until now. As we get older, we're getting more sloppy and sentimental about our relationship. Before, we used to be kind of cool about it. There was always love, but you turned around and be cool. But now it's gushy and mushy and we just hug and hang out as much as we can."

From the start Jones had been more interested in composition and arranging than in the trumpet, but when he met R. C., a whole new world opened up. Jones's growing arranging skills attracted the attention of a young music teacher at Seattle University, Gus Mankertz, who recruited the young trumpet player for a progressive, seventeen-piece "jazz workshop" band. Mankertz was an oboist who had studied jazz and composition at the College of Puget Sound (later renamed the University of Puget Sound). For his workshop band he raided the Jackson Street clubs and Garfield High School, bringing in Quincy, Buddy Catlett, Tommy Adams, Floyd Standifer, tenor saxophonist Rollo Strand, and trumpeter Don Smith. The workshop band was ultra-modern, performing the hippest new bebop arrangements by Stan Kenton, Woody Herman, and Dizzy Gillespie.

While playing for Mankertz during his senior year in high school, Quincy composed his first major piece, *The Four Winds Suite*. On May 9, 1950, a month before Jones graduated from high school, the suite was performed by the workshop band. Don Smith, who would later join Kenton, played lead trumpet on the premiere. Rod Levitt, who would later distinguish himself as a composer, played trombone. Floyd Standifer, who also played trumpet on the piece's debut, recalled that from this moment on, Jones's reputation as an arranger began to soar: "With Quincy, you said to yourself, 'This cat, he doesn't play all that well, but man, he can sure write.'"

Besides learning to arrange, the other consuming passion for Jones at this time was to leave town with a name band. "Ernestine was our idol," he recalled. "She was out with Johnny Otis and those bands before anybody. Everybody was in awe of anybody that had gone on the road with a professional band. 'I'm on so-and-so's band,' 'I'm on so-and-so's band.' That was really hot." As it turned out, the arranging skills Ray Charles passed on to Jones would be Quincy's ticket out of town, though not quite as fast as he had hoped. The story of how Quincy left Seattle with Lionel Hampton after auditioning backstage has been told and retold—and embellished—but what really happened is known by only a few.

Hamp was in town. The year was 1950. As usual, Quincy had found a way backstage at the Palomar. He introduced himself, sat down at the piano, and played an excerpt from *The Four Winds Suite*. Hampton was knocked out. He invited Jones into the band on the spot. However, Hamp failed to clear his invitation with the band's business manager—his wife, Gladys. Jones recounted:

> I wanted to go with that band so badly. I never wanted to play with a band so much. Hamp had all these guys! Jimmy Cleveland and Benny Bailey and Betty Carter and Jimmy Scott and Sonny Parker and Porter Kilbert. Jerome Richardson. Incredible band! It was just like, "God!" you know, just "Please!" I wanted to leave home. I was

dying to leave home. I just wanted to go. I didn't want to finish school or anything. So when Hamp said, "You're with the band," I didn't want to take a chance! I just got on the bus. I had one of those little bebop things, the little leather cases. I was ready to go. I was gone. I wasn't even going to ask anybody. I didn't even want anybody to notice I was there, so they'd just leave town and I'd be with them. Then Gladys got on the bus and she said, "No. Get that kid back to school. Get him off the bus." I was so hurt. So hurt. I just wanted to go so bad.

For the time being, Jones had to settle for a scholarship to Seattle University, where he continued to play for Mankertz. He became a local celebrity. An article in the school newspaper—"Quincy Jones, Musical Prodigy, Studies at Seattle University"—captured the intellectually cool, button-down-collar image the young Jones had picked up hanging out with touring professionals:

> Though this is his first year here, freshman music major Quincy Jones made his debut in SU music circles last year when his descriptive suite, "The Four Winds," was played at the spring concert. He plays the trumpet and the piano. The same arrangement of "The Four Winds" is scheduled to be played by Lionel Hampton at "Bop City" in New York in the near future.
>
> When asked his plans for the future, he replied, "I would like to study at Westlake Music College in Hollywood, and later to write serious studies for the movies—mood music, they call it. . . . I appreciate the good in all classes of music, from boogie on up to the classics. However, at present I have a leaning toward popular dance music."

Jones spent only one semester at Seattle University. In the spring of 1951, having sent his *Four Winds Suite* ahead as an audition manuscript, he left Seattle for Boston, to attend the Berklee College of Music, then known as Schillinger House. "I liked Seattle University, because Gus Mankertz had this band there," remarked Jones. "But it was just a little bit square, that's all. I just really wanted to get out of town. I wanted to get away from home and get back to Boston so I knew I'd be close to Bird and Miles. And get me to New York. That's all I cared about. I knew I would never be home again. Never."

Jones had been in Boston but a few months when Lionel Hampton came through town. Janet Thurlow, the hip singer from Seattle, was with the group. She reminded Hamp he had once unsuccessfully tried to hire Quincy in Seattle. Hamp renewed the invitation. Jones needed little prodding to drop out of classes and jump on the band. This time—with Gladys's blessing—Quincy was allowed to stay. As the new kid on the block, Jones at first met with resentment from older band members. But his unique arranging talents soon won over the skeptics. By May he was recording with the band. The following fall, his name was on the marquee of the Trianon Ballroom, with Hampton's and Thurlow's. Most of the fans who came to see that show thought he'd been hired right out of Seattle, knowing nothing, of course, of the incident with Gladys or of Thurlow's role behind the scenes.

Once Jones left town—in fact, even earlier, when he entered Seattle University—the Bumps Blackwell Junior Band began to disintegrate. Charlie Taylor enrolled at the University of Washington and married a woman who discouraged him from pursuing music. Buddy Catlett contracted tubercular pleurisy and was hospitalized. Bassist Billy Johnson moved to Los Angeles, where he became a successful professional musician. (He appeared on an album with Roscoe Weathers.) Tommy Adams remained in Seattle, working with Billy Tolles as a drummer and becoming the most important single force in early Seattle rock 'n' roll. Major Pigford continued playing, then dropped out of music for over a decade, pursuing biology and accounting, only to come back to his trombone in the 1980s.

The Charlie Taylor/Bumps Blackwell Junior Band lasted fewer than three years, but Jones had intense affection for the days he spent with it. "It was one of the magic times in my life," he said. "We were finding out what makes sounds work and listening. Everybody was always trying to pick up new tunes and just learning and growing. All we cared about was getting better." And getting ahead. It's clear that raw ambition played a large role in Jones's youth. Charlie Taylor remembered sitting around in his basement with Quincy practicing how they would sign autographs after they became famous. Jones himself idolized bandleaders like Billy Eckstine and Duke Ellington, men who were not only great musicians but successful entrepreneurs. At a time when racism barred most African Americans from basic free enterprise, Black bandleaders were an attractive role model.

Jones's ambition may also have been a veil for his desperate unhappiness at home, a way of focusing his attention on something other than his difficult family situation. His parents had recently divorced—a stigma in those days—and his stepmother favored the children she brought from her previous marriage to live with the family. Jones's mother had become mentally ill. During his high school years Jones stayed away from the family home on Twenty-Second Avenue, just a block from Garfield High School, as much as he could. Quincy would often fall asleep in school, having been up until all hours the night before at the Washington Social Club. The image of the intense, heavy-lidded Jones, carrying his trumpet in a cloth bag, is conveyed by old friends in a tone that implies that Jones was, like most geniuses, eccentric in his intensity and single-minded in his devotion to music.

"I think about sitting in the attic of that little house," said Jones, who sometimes practiced his scales and arpeggios in a closet, for privacy and protection from criticism. And yet, if an unhappy home helped launch Jones into the world, it is also true that the middle-class life his family enjoyed in Seattle in the 1940s nurtured him. Jones himself has said that had he grown up amid the violence of Chicago's South Side, he probably would not have made the choices he made. "I came stone out of the ghetto in Chicago to Washington and it was just the antithesis of that whole thing. That really struck me early. I was lucky that I got a chance to deal with people one-on-one, and not by the road signs."

By "road signs," of course, Jones meant racism. Though there was much about race relations that needed to change in Seattle, Jones had the moral support of a strong Black middle class whose roots went back to that turn-of-the-century Edwardian community established by Powell Barnett, Horace Cayton, and others. The result was that when push came to shove, Jones had Charlie Taylor for a role model, Frank Waldron for a music teacher, and Bumps Blackwell as a booking agent (a ticket into white social life), not to mention the whole neighborhood support system that allowed the Junior Band and the various nighttime exploits Jones undertook to happen without incident. Had these strong figures and solid supports not been there, many of his experiences—the bust at Island Lake, for example—might have had entirely different results.

Quincy Jones was not the only Seattle musician of his generation to be ambitious and well-cared-for. Pianist Patti Bown, hailed as a prodigy at Seattle University in the same year as Jones, grew up in the heart of Seattle's upwardly mobile Black community too. Though she was not officially part of the Bumps Blackwell/Charlie Taylor band, Bown hung out with the guys, and her career converged with Quincy's on several important occasions after they both had left town.

Patti Bown was an outrageous character, one of the great eccentrics in contemporary jazz. An enormous woman who wore broad-brimmed hats and spoke in page-long sentences, Bown could hold forth on contemporary composition, spiritual healing, cosmetics, geopolitics, and the music business—and often did, all in the same breath. As a pianist, she was an oddity—a technical virtuoso who hewed to no stylistic camp yet combined an utterly individual approach with broad entertainment values. At her best as a soloist, she could entertain a cocktail crowd at New York's Village Gate, as she did for several years, without sounding cloying or pandering to bad taste. She could also hold her own with the best of the beboppers, "free"-jazz improvisers, studio pop musicians, or even rock 'n' rollers. Whitney Balliett, jazz writer for *The New Yorker*, once described a Bown solo on John Coltrane's "Giant Steps" as "an eight-minute lesson in how to make a piece of improvisation so tight and complex it would supply a dozen soloists for a week."

Bown's parents settled in Seattle's Central District in 1921. Ten years later, Patti was born and the family moved to an old-fashioned, two-family house on Twenty-Second Avenue. The Bown household was a center of social and cultural activity, where visiting Black artists such as Marian Anderson and Roland Hayes sometimes boarded overnight, because they were not welcome in white-owned hotels. Neighborhood musical gatherings were common.

> We had the whole ground floor of this big, old-fashioned house, with a big backyard and a lot of fruit trees. It was really a beautiful place, lovely flowers in it. Saturday night, we would have "at-homes." My mother and father were exquisite chefs, so they would cook unbelievable food. The bread was always homemade. There was fresh cake, dill bread, homemade booze. There would be music and people reading poetry and painters coming there to visit. Morris Graves named all his dogs after one of my sisters!

> My mother really encouraged us into the arts. We always had dance lessons, tap lessons. We were considered poor, [but] my mother always found money to take us to all kinds of concerts. We went to the museum every Sunday after Mass. Our mother used to paint. She took us to see Arthur Rubinstein, Marian Anderson, and Katherine Dunham.

The Bown girls were sent to Immaculate Conception School. The first to take up music was Edith Mary. A piano prodigy, she made her New York debut at Town Hall in 1950 and later studied at Fontainebleau with Robert Casadesus and Nadia Boulanger. When two of Patti's other sisters also got piano lessons, and her sister Florence started to dance, Patti was jealous. She began to teach herself to play. "I discovered that when they were going to school, I had the piano to myself," said Patti. "So all day long I could get these little goodies off the radio. I'd just make them up, and play games in my head. My mother had taught me the alphabet when I was about three, so I just started a form of writing on a piece of paper, where I would draw lines, to make myself remember where my melody was."

Bown started formal piano lessons when she was six. By the time she was eight, she too was being touted as a prodigy. She performed for Danny Kaye at the Overseas Press Club and got a job playing hymns in a funeral home. Like Billy Tolles, she also found her way into the Syvilla Fort studio—not as a dance student but as a rehearsal pianist. "Syvilla Fort was every Saturday morning," recalled Bown. "They had a little place where they had dance classes, and she always did improvisational dance. So it gave me a chance to make up original music. Which meant that every Saturday morning I had a chance to improvise jazz for the dancers to exercise and dance to. She'd count out a rhythm of how fast she wanted and I made up original music for it."

As with so many budding jazz pianists, improvisation—the freedom to create one's own melodies—was already important to Bown. Privately she had begun to take apart her classical lessons and "swing" them. Her rebellion from classical music and her mother's middle-class proscriptions was already underway. Her father took her to see Count Basie at the Trianon Ballroom. She skipped out of school early to hear Percy Mayfield at the Palomar Theater. Bown's sisters brought home records of Glenn Miller's "Slow Freight" and Duke Ellington's "Chelsea Bridge." When they put on a record by Lil Green, "Romance in the Dark," their mother, who played "pretty fair" blues piano herself, objected to it as “dirty” and “suggestive.” “My mother was still living out that old script from *The Jazz Singer*—‘I want a concert pianist, I don’t want you to go in those clubs’—that whole middle-class thing. Jazz was evil, jazz was the work of the devil. It was the music of gangster movies. My mother figured I was going to be a drug addict or an alcoholic if I stayed with jazz, because people who took classical music went into nice halls and they had prunes in their mouths. It was like a higher-class thing, a prestige thing. She was very socially conscious, you know? I naturally rebelled.”

As it had for Ernestine Anderson, the neighborhood along Madison, where the Savoy Ballroom and the Mardi Gras stood across the street each other, provided a ready temptation. “When I walked home from school, I passed the pool parlor and the Mardi Gras,” Bown recollected, “and they always had jazz playing. It was like, my mother was saying, ‘No!’ but the music was sensuous and it said, ‘Yes, come here!’ It was too exciting to pass.” The teenage Bown was soon making up stories to get out of the house, peeking into speakeasies in Chinatown and along Jackson Street. By the time she was thirteen, she was working with Pops Buford on the sly at the Officers’ Club at Fort Lawton. Some of her mother’s worries about drugs and jazz proved to be well-founded.

> I was singing and playing piano. Wearing rhinestone earrings and strapless dresses. Showing all my female pulchritude. It was on Sunday afternoon. The colonel would pay me the money at the end of the gig and he always gave me a bag of smoke. Yes. The guys in the band were delighted. I didn’t get high because I was a kid. We rode back from Fort Lawton in a convertible Cadillac. I probably got a contact high, for all I know. They were smoking away. My mother didn’t know I had this job. Eventually, I told her. We had some pretty rough periods there.
>
> I tried to look older, so I could get in a lot of places. That’s funny when you think about it, the nerve you have. But when I think back on it, it was the only way I could learn my craft. Today, the kids have the advantage of jazz programs in the schools. We didn’t have any of those things. To learn your craft, you had to get around other musicians and learn.

The adult atmosphere Bown was entering intimidated her, but she put up a bold front. When a friend brought Dizzy Gillespie over, Patti recalled being high-handed even with the king of bebop. “I got to the house before they brought Dizzy back,” recounted Bown. “I was in the bathroom and Dizzy knocked on the door and I said, 'Who is it?' He said, 'It's Dizzy Gillespie.' I said, 'Well, I'm Patti Bown and you'll have to wait.' Honey, I had a real attitude. I was shy underneath, but I had to act like I was ready."

In the summer of 1949, Patti won a music scholarship to Seattle University as a concert pianist. In 1952 she performed with the Seattle Symphony and transferred to the University of Washington, where she studied with August Werner, an authority on German lieder, and worked as a rehearsal pianist for opera singers. But by this time she had emotionally given up the idea of a classical career. Her sister Edith Mary had already made her debut, so some of the pressure from her mother was off. For the next four years Patti played concert music in the daytime and jazz at night, soaking up the best of both worlds, sometimes mixing the two. She worked with her old friend Billy Tolles, who led her to Ray Charles, saxophonist Floyd Franklin, Emmett Lewis, Jabo Ward, Vernon Brown, and Al Pierre—anywhere she could pick up another bit of knowledge. The club scene, with its stars and sessions, was dazzling to the young pianist.

"Being in Seattle in those days was like seeing this great movie that never ended," she said. "I'd be playing the piano like this, never looking at my fingers, and looking out, scared I'm going to miss something!" Two of her first mentors were Vernon and Wanda Brown: "I learned how to go out onstage from Wanda, and how to talk to the audience. I learned how to be calm, how to have fun. Wanda always made the audience feel good. Vernon would have a deep laugh in the background, sort of re-emphasizing the words she'd say as the emcee. They would guide me. People like that were very good to me." So was Ray Charles, whose jam sessions at the Washington Social Club with Billy Tolles, the Charlie Taylor gang, and visiting musicians such as Dexter Gordon were another proving ground. She explained: "That's how I learned to comp. Ray Charles and Dexter Gordon and Billy Tolles would have a tenor battle. They might play one tune an hour and a half or two hours. They would tell me, 'You're all over the keyboard, girl! You have to learn how to put those chords. Leave some space!' Telling me, showing me. There was no books. You had to learn by doing it. Those rhythmic licks, trying to figure what they're doing, how to feed a soloist, stay out of his way, give him space, do a little nice, rhythmic pulsing thing to give him encouragement."

Another early confidence-builder was Myrtle (Myrt) Francois, a woman from New Orleans who owned a nightclub on the corner of Twelfth Avenue and Yesler Way. She played drums and sang in her own house band, in the window of the club. Francois billed herself as the "Personality Girl" and later worked with pianist Melody Jones in an act called "Melody and Mirth." Female drummers were far more unusual in 1949 than they are today. Seeing a woman instrumentalist was encouraging for an aspiring girl pianist. Francois's club also afforded Bown an unusual chance acquaintance.

> One night, this man came in. He sat down in the back and ordered dinner. They had New Orleans food in there and it was kind of late, about eleven-thirty or twelve. I was playing Billy Strayhorn's "Lush Life," and he came up to me and said, "Did you like that tune you were playing?" And I said, "Yes, you know Billy Strayhorn is a genius." "Oh, well, why is he a genius?" "Because he knows how to write simple melodies that singers can sing and very complicated harmony on them." He looked at me and said, "What's your name again? I'm Billy Strayhorn." He was there because Duke Ellington's band was in town.

When Count Basie came through, Bown impressed his trumpet man Thad Jones at a cutting session at the Blue Note. "Thad Jones looked around the room and he said, 'We're going to play a blues in B-flat, and every chorus, we're going to raise it a half step.' Then he called an impossible tempo, like '*Dang! Dang! Dang!*'—real fast—and everybody's all over the keyboard. It got to the key of B, and some people dropped out. Finally, it was just me playing by myself, me and Sonny Payne. Thad dropped out. Everybody dropped out. They asked me what my name was and said, 'When you come to New York, you're going to do something.'"

Like Quincy Jones, Patti had stars in her eyes.

> When they would take me to see Katherine Dunham or Marian Anderson, in my mind that meant, "These people are from New York!" It was like in Never Never Land. Little girl me, about four, five, six years old, off I would wander. My mother would be talking to somebody, I would let go of her hand, say I'm going to the ladies' room or something, and keep on going until I got backstage. Get an autograph. Look at the person, they'd say, "It's nice, this sweet little girl." I'd say, "Take me to New York." I always thought of myself as being a star. Even when I was a little girl, I had hitched my wagon.

In 1955, Bown made her move, joining her sister Edith Mary in the Big Apple. The first trip proved to be little more than exploratory, but by the following year, Bown had become a permanent feature on the New York scene. It was a struggle at first. She sat in at Birdland, did gigs for a talent agent who sent her to businessmen's bars where the men pinched her on the rear, wrote commercial music for CBS television, and got a duo job playing with English bassist Peter Ind.

Patti Bown.

"In Seattle, I had never learned how to ask for a job, because everybody knew that I could play. I was shy. I learned to open my mouth and carry on a conversation. I was so poor I had to make two audition dresses. For a while, I lived in Harlem. That's where I wrote "G'wan Train" (a rhythmically propelled, churchy tune she later recorded with the Quincy Jones Orchestra). Patti was helped in her effort to break into the New York scene by her old friend Quincy, whose reputation as an arranger with Hampton had enabled him to start making a living as a freelancer in New York, beginning in 1953. One of the first things Quincy did when Patti got to town was to set up a recording session for her. It was a much-needed break. Nevertheless, she immediately ran into gender prejudice.

> Quincy brought me on this date because he was forming a band. He had a choice of anybody he could want. We went in the studio, and Ernie Royal—bless his heart, he's dead now—yelled real loud, "Oh, a B-I-T-C-H is going to play the piano." He said the word, and all the guys cracked up. I felt weird, because I was looking on them as heroes. Why were they doing this chauvinistic thing to me? Quincy came over and he put his arm on my shoulder and he said, "Why don't you just go on over there to the piano and warm up a little bit." So I went over and I started playing, and when I finished warming up, the whole room started clapping. Then they stood up and they just kept clapping. I was so embarrassed I couldn't figure out what they were doing. They were coming up to the piano and shaking my hand and putting their arm around me, "Say, baby, you can cook. You can blow. I'm going to get you some work."

In New York, Bown came under the stylistic influence of Horace Silver. In 1958 she made her first album as a leader, *Patti Bown Plays Big Piano*, a knockout of eclectic jazz piano that included "G'wan Train" as well as "Nothin' But the Truth," "Head Shakin'," and "Waltz de Funk." A year later, Jones invited her to join a special project in Europe that would involve two other Jackson Street veterans—Buddy Catlett and Floyd Standifer—and also would have disastrous consequences for almost everyone concerned.

In 1959, Jones had been invited to put together a big band for an unusual new Harold Arlen musical, *Free and Easy*. The path leading to this invitation had been one of frenzied activity for the young trumpeter-arranger, who in six years had risen from a section trumpet player in the Lionel Hampton band to one of the new stars on the transatlantic jazz scene. His reputation had begun in earnest with an arrangement he'd done for a small group in Europe, with Hamp, on the tune "Stockholm Sweetnin'," subsequently recorded by Clifford Brown. This had led to projects with, among others, Dinah Washington, Art Farmer, Jimmy Cleveland, and Clark Terry, as well as the leadership of two big bands for Dizzy Gillespie—one for a recording in 1954 and another for a State Department tour to the Middle East. (The latter included an old Seattle University pal, trombonist Rod Levitt.) Jones had also made an eighteen-month detour back to France under special assignment for Mercury Records, working as musical director for Barclay Disques in Paris throughout 1957 and much of 1958. While there, he conducted a fifty-five-piece orchestra for Frank Sinatra at Grace Kelly's annual benefit party at Monte Carlo's Sporting Club and studied theory and composition with the great French teacher Nadia Boulanger.

Now, in 1959, Quincy hooked up with his old Seattle friend Ray Charles, who had broken into the mainstream market with his infectious blues piece "What'd I Say," and together they produced one of the best albums of both of their careers, *The Genius of Ray Charles*, a jazz big-band effort that pulled out the stops on soul, jazz, R & B, and rock. Just as he was producing *The Genius* and writing scores for half a dozen other musicians, Jones was approached by the producers of the Arlen show. *Free and Easy* was one of the only big failures of Quincy Jones's career. The show itself had been tossing around New York for some time. Originally called *St. Louis Woman*, it had begun as a pastiche of old Arlen tunes, but over the years it had evolved into an experimental musical featuring jazz recitative (sung dialogue), stylized pantomime, and a full jazz band onstage in acting roles, an idea credited to Jones himself. The story was about a turn-of-the-century New Orleans jockey, Augie, and his love interest, Della. (Singer Patti Austin, then seven years old, was part of the cast.)

It was hoped that after the show completed its European tour, Sammy Davis Jr. would take the part of Augie. An opening was scheduled in Europe for December 7, 1959. To skeptics who feared that a show with jazz musicians acting onstage would never work, Quincy replied, "We're either going to rock the boat or sink it." His bravado was prophetic. The show opened in Paris on January 15, 1960, at the Alhambra Theatre. At about this time the Algerian crisis erupted, and France's attention turned to politics. Ten days later, *Free and Easy* closed; Quincy had eighteen jazz musicians on his payroll with nowhere to play. He called a meeting of the band and announced that anyone who wanted to go home had a ticket waiting for them. If they wanted to stay, he would book the band for a European tour. "It was a nightmare," he recalled. "It was one of the hardest things I ever did in my life, because I jumped into some water I didn't understand. I didn't have a manager. We had no agent. I was twenty-five years old. I didn't understand about the business at all. I felt a tremendous pressure. Guys like Clark Terry had left Duke Ellington to come with my band. At one point, Clark got a call from the Johnny Carson band. I said, 'Go. Do it, man. We're over here scuffling.'"

Desperate to keep the band working, Quincy patched together bookings from one week to the next in the former Yugoslavia, Sweden, Denmark, Portugal, Spain, Holland, France, and Austria. Patti Bown was often featured as a soloist to warm up the audience. She and Buddy Catlett went into the studio with Bill Coleman, the expatriate swing trumpet player, and made an album. The whole band recorded for Barclay Disques. At one point Jones booked a thirteen-city tour of one-nighters on the Orient Express, in remote towns in Eastern Europe. Catlett remembered: "I went to sleep in an empty car. When I woke up, we were going into Transylvania. It was a gray morning, it had been raining all night, and there was one of those twisted trees on a big cliff and there was a river down there and it looked just like Dracula was coming, like one of those old 1930s movies."

"When we got to Cannes," said Bown, "there were no hotels because it was the height of the season. I had to sleep on top of the grand piano." Catlett added, "We flew from Denmark to Rome in one of those English two-motor jobs. The plane was loaded down. We flew *through* the Alps, not over them. Nonpressurized. My ears stayed plugged up for three days." Bown remembered, "Near the end we had a bus with cellophane windows. Rain was on the floor this high. Everybody was coughing on the bus. People got sick." After nine months the pressure got to everyone, including Quincy: "I finally got to Finland and I just ran out of energy. That's the only time in my life I ever thought about suicide. I never saw the sun shine. I was upstairs, trying to figure out how do we survive the next week. We need new uniforms, we got to have new bandstands, we got to do this, we got to do that. I was just so tired."

In the fall Jones booked passage home, on the SS *United States*. For a while the group worked in New York as the house band at the Basin Street, but by 1961 the project fizzled. Quincy must have known that in 1960, big bands were economic dinosaurs. But he had grown up wanting to do what Basie, Hamp, and Duke had done. It's a shame that his big band didn't last. Many musicians on the scene, including trombonist Jimmy Cleveland, said that in terms of swing, drive, solo power, and sweetness of arrangements, Quincy was giving Basie a hard run for his money. According to Cleveland, "Basie came over there. We were playing a theater in Paris, and they were standing in the wings and we came off and he said, 'I don't know what you all are trying to do, but it looks like you're trying to put me out of business!' And there wasn't a smile on his face. This band was smokin'! And we didn't care who knew it."

A rare live recording of the band as it was constituted in Paris, *Live at the Alhambra '60*, was made just two weeks after *Free and Easy* closed. This is Quincy Jones at an all-time peak, with the knockout punches of Basie combined with open voicings for French horn and flute riding over big, airy chords with baritone sax at the bottom. "Walkin'" featured a fourteen-chorus solo by Buddy Catlett, a booming, entirely credible outing that came about, Catlett remembered, laughing, "because the band wouldn't come in." Patti Bown offered an appealing and novel chorus as well, with odd, angular intervals. But by far the most polished and representative recording of the band is *I Dig Dancers*, recorded in Paris after nearly a year on the road. The band made every tune in one take and breathed as if it were a single player speaking perfectly articulated, laid-back swing. Three more recordings were made back home (with slightly different personnel, and excluding Standifer): *Newport Live*, *The Birth of a Band*, and *The Great Wide World of Quincy Jones* (subsequently re-released as the two-record package *The Birth of a Band*).

The *Free and Easy* tour was a personal disaster for many of the musicians involved, including Jones. Musicians came home nearly penniless to wrecked families and detoured careers (Jimmy Cleveland described it as an "alimony band"). Catlett's plans to attend Juilliard did not materialize. Standifer came home to a new child who didn't recognize him. "Everything we had at home disappeared," recounted Buddy. "Wife, kids. Not only me, Floyd just made it back on time."

For Patti Bown, however, the exposure to Quincy's troupe of heavyweights turned out to be a catapult into the heart of Manhattan jazz. She became musical director for Dinah Washington, toured with Sarah Vaughan, and appeared at the Newport Jazz Festival with Jones. She was invited to record with George Russell, Roland Kirk, Benny Carter, Nina Simone, Charles Mingus, Sonny Stitt, Duke Ellington, and Aretha Franklin. She composed dance music for Joseph Papp's West Indian musical *Ti-Jean and His Brothers*, and fed tunes to Basie, Jones, and others. She also started "ghosting" in the studio, playing for a variety of projects, including rock records by Ben E. King and Little Anthony and the Imperials; Aretha Franklin's early, pre-rock album, *After Hours* (produced by Quincy); and the soundtrack of Norman Mailer's film *Tough Guys Don't Dance*, which features her famous belly laugh at the end of the film. In 1980, Bown was a guest on Marian McPartland's *Piano Jazz*, the celebrated National Public Radio show. The Duke Ellington Society presented a Patti Bown Night in 1982. In 1985 she became a member of the New York Jazz Repertory Orchestra, and the Mary Lou Williams Foundation gave her its Award for Excellence in 1986. The day Bown died, in 2008, Quincy Jones was in Seattle, eulogizing Charlie Taylor and Floyd Standifer at the opening concert of the Northwest African American Museum.

For Jones the *Free and Easy* disaster was a turning point too—one that, bit by bit, steered him away from jazz and toward a more eclectic, commercial approach. Over the next five years Jones learned the music business from top to bottom. In 1962 he became the first Black executive of a major record label when he took the job as vice president for artists and repertoire at Mercury. One week he was producing hit records by bubblegum-pop artist Lesley ("It's My Party") Gore; the next week it was an album with Count Basie, the classic *One More Time*, or Basie and Sinatra, *It Might as Well Be Swing*. On *Genius Plus Soul*, Jones paired Milt Jackson and Ray Charles. *The Great Wide World of Quincy Jones* initiated a sequence of albums under his own name that would establish him in the role of leader/presenter for which he would become known worldwide.

Back in his Garfield High School days, someone had given Jones a copy of Frank Skinner's *Underscore*, a classic treatise on writing music for films. He had often spent entire weekend afternoons watching films at downtown theaters, sometimes closing his eyes to see if he could guess who the composer was. Music had always been a visual experience for Jones anyway. "Even now," he told a reporter for *Life* magazine in the 1980s, "I think of primary and secondary colors first, and shapes and densities, before the sound comes." Jones broke into movie scoring with a jazz soundtrack for *The Pawnbroker* in 1964 and never looked back. *In Cold Blood*, *In the Heat of the Night*, *Cactus Flower*, *Mackenna's Gold*, *The Lost Man*, *The Anderson Tapes*, *The Wiz*, and twenty-five other films followed, earning Jones and his record albums twenty-eight Grammy Awards. One of them was for the 1989 Qwest Records album *Back on the Block*, which showed the aesthetic connections between jazz and hip-hop. Jones also launched a magazine devoted to hip-hop, *Vibe*.

Jones's gigantic success and his move away from an all-jazz program angered many of his colleagues, who felt he had sold out to commercial interests even as they were struggling on the artistic front lines for jazz. His 1974 move to no-holds-barred funk music, with gold records for the Brothers Johnson, and his subsequent best-selling album of all time, for Michael Jackson, *Thriller*, added fuel to the fire. But Jones stoutly defended his choices. "It always surprises me when I run into these beboppers and they're talking about, 'You sold out!'" said Jones hotly. "I've been playing this music all my life. A whole life. Everything. Concert music, swing things, rhythm and blues, gospel. I'm happiest that way because I got a chance to enjoy the best of all music."

Jones entered an even wider public imagination when he scored the music for the television series *Roots* and produced the gospel-inspired all-star album *We Are the World*, to assist with famine relief in Africa. After those projects he became a kind of American institution. He was memorialized in a series of *Doonesbury* cartoon strips and was engaged in 2008 as artistic director of the Olympic Games, in Beijing. Jones used his money, power, and influence to advance whatever caught his interest, and that wasn't always jazz. But those specialists who would disparage his contribution to the music have only to look at the work he did as an arranger for Hampton, Basie, and Clark Terry, the small group records he did with everyone from Oscar Pettiford to Dinah Washington to Jimmy Cleveland, and his own albums from the 1950s and 1960s. If populism or commerce—or perhaps a bit of each—prevented Jones from being an advocate for jazz in and of itself as an art music, separate from other Black traditions, then it must also be said, in fairness, that he made more people aware of Black traditions generally than most of his detractors.

A miraculous recovery from a double aneurysm in 1974 made Jones even more conscious, he said, of maintaining the "warm and fuzzy" things in life. One of those things was a determination to remain true to his Jackson Street roots. He regularly visited old friends and colleagues in the Northwest—particularly Charles Taylor—and made time for birthdays and special occasions, despite a schedule that perpetually had him hopping from one continent to the next. He also stepped up to the plate for his old friend Ernestine Anderson, producing two albums for her on his Qwest label, one of which was nominated for a Grammy. When Anderson was in danger of losing her Central District home, Jones came to her aid financially. He also gave money to Seattle schools' jazz programs when they were cut by the district.

In 2001, Jones conducted the Seattle Repertory Jazz Orchestra in a concert of his own compositions and arrangements at the Seattle Center Opera House (now McCaw Hall) and gave the band copies of the charts. In 2008 he was invited to deliver the commencement speech at the University of Washington, which included an adamant brief for jazz. By that time Quincy had begun to back up that rhetoric by scouting and recording a number of young jazz players, including the excellent blind pianist Justin Kauflin. The year Jones came back to Seattle to give his address at UW, Garfield High School named its auditorium the Quincy Jones Performance Center, which became the official home of Garfield High School Jazz Band. Jones died in 2024.

7 White Boppers and Ivy Leaguers

THE TRANSITION FROM swing to modern music is associated with a switch from big bands to bebop combos, but there were big bands playing modern music in the 1940s too. The Dizzy Gillespie group that Quincy Jones had so regretted missing in Seattle was a good example. So were Woody Herman's Second Herd, organized in 1947, which specifically addressed the new music, and Stan Kenton's orchestra, which aggressively marketed its "modern" sound. These groups, which ranged from seventeen to twenty-five pieces, looked like swing bands, but their music was aimed at hip listeners rather than ballroom dancers. In this they held a card in common with the bebop quintets, and like the boppers they also occasionally outreached their audience's grasp.

"Progressive jazz" bands, as they came to be called, exercised an enormous influence on young players all over the country in matters of both musical and personal style. The boppers brought Black pride to the Black community; the progressives brought a new image of the cool and crazy hipster—or "beatnik"—to the white community. Seattle and Tacoma, for some reason, seem to have spawned more than their share of "wild men," some of whom are legendary in regional lore.

The first Seattle group of wild and crazy progressives coalesced around Ronnie Pierce in 1946. Pierce had gone to Roosevelt High and played with the Noteworthies in 1943; he'd also played in Stanton Patty's Chevaliers. He was a white player fascinated with Black culture who operated easily on both sides of the color line. He had studied with Frank Waldron, hung out on Jackson Street, and played with Bumps Blackwell at the Washington Social Club. He was also a fast-talking, eccentric fellow who loved excitement and anything slightly loony, a sort of Spike Jones character with a grand sense of the absurd.

Raised in the carnival business in Puyallup and Seattle, Pierce was already playing after hours while in high school—with Bud Storm, at the Havana Club. (The bassist was Red Kelly; the pianist, Kenny Kimball; and the drummer, Don Manning.) In 1946, Pierce formed a band that tackled modern sounds—a brassy, ambitious bebop group with five trumpets, four trombones, French horn, five saxophones, four rhythm, and two singers. The roster was a virtual insiders' list of the best-known and best-loved white jazz musicians in the area. In the sax section were Pierce, Freddie Greenwell, Milt Price, Jimmy Shevenco, Irwin Adler, and Dick Sanders; trumpets were Marv Thomas, Dave Nelson, Walt Chamberlain, and Jim Freng; on trombone were Don Anderson, Dave Tuttle, Danny Reff, and Harold Spohr; Lowell Richards played French horn; Keith Purvis or Vernon Brown was on drums; bass was Red Kelly; piano, Kenny Kimball; and guitar, Glenn Thompson.

Local aficionados of a certain age will immediately notice trumpeter Marv Thomas in that list, who later owned the Seattle jazz club Parnell's, and whose son, Jay, is among the finest jazz musicians ever raised in the Northwest. Marv Thomas was the epitome of the hip generation of white kids who came up in the swing-to-bop transition of the 1940s. In 1942, when he was a sophomore at Franklin High School, Thomas's band, the Aristocrats of Swing, was playing Charlie Spivak's "Too La Loo Ra Loo Ral" and Slim Gaillard's "Flat Foot Floogie" for dances. Thomas recalled:

> We were cool little cats. We had our barber that we went to downtown and we had tailored suits. I saw Lester Young up at the Washington Social Club. . . .
>
> We used to go down to the Trianon. I remember being down there the night Neil Friel sat in with Les Brown. He was just a teenager, but he got close with Zoot's brother, Ray Sims, who played trombone. That band! You'd stand out in front and they'd play their theme and your hair would just stand on end.
>
> We also saw some of the Black bands down there—Jimmie Lunceford and I think Louis Armstrong might have come through with a big band. Later on, I played at the Trianon with Curt Sykes. Freddie (Greenwell) was in that band. When we were in high school, we also went up to the Rocking Chair (the after-hours club where Ray Charles got his start). There was another place where a lot of (touring) musicians would come down after the gig. Roy Eldridge came through one time.
>
> Then we got a connection with some people in West Seattle—(trombonist) Don Glenn and (saxophonist) Rollo Strand—and from there it went to (band leader) Vern Mallory. (Drummer) Don Manning played in that band, so did Red Kelly, and Ronnie Pierce and Don Glenn. The weird part with Vern was that we played up at the Savoy Ballroom, on 23rd and Madison (later known as Birdland) and it was an all-white band, except for Jabo Ward.

When Thomas was a high school junior, he and drummer Dave Stetler and saxophonist Rollo Strand went with a band to Spokane, then on to New York, where Thomas investigated the burgeoning bebop scene on Fifty-Second Street. Strand stayed in New York, but Marv came home to finish high school, then enrolled at the University of Washington, where he shared a few classes with Freddie Greenwell. "I remember we'd go walking across the campus and Freddie would light up a joint and I'd get sort of nervous. The teacher who had the stage band and the marching band was (trumpeter) Bill Cole. He'd been on Les Brown's band. Bill Cole was so good. Jesus! He was just a great guy, great player. He later taught up at Western [Washington University, in Bellingham]."

Thomas spent a year studying at Los Angeles City College but returned to Seattle, where he finished at the UW, then went to pharmacy school but continued to play in big bands, notably at the Spanish Castle and Parker's. Mallory hired him again, but this time for one of the new "tenor bands" forming after World War II, which played sweet swing for dancers at the Olympic Hotel. "We also had a steady gig at the Sand Point officers' clubs," recalled Thomas. "I added up what I made one year on my calendar and it was five grand!" Thomas had been raised by his mother in a modest apartment on South McClellan Street, near Franklin High School and the old Seattle Rainiers ballpark, Sick's Stadium. Coincidentally, one of the pickup bands he played with in 1957 opened at Sick's for Elvis Presley. Thomas retired after several decades in pharmacy and real estate and at the age of ninety-six was still showing up for his son Jay's gigs.

Another musician in the Ronnie Pierce big band who merits a mention was French-horn player Lowell Richards, who later played tuba in Seattle Dixieland groups and worked in the short-lived Norm Bobrow Little Big Band in the 1950s. Richards's wife, Phyllis Richards, became Seattle's first jazz critic, writing freelance under the name Maggie Hawthorn. Jimmy Shevenco and Don Anderson were top-notch studio musicians who became pillars of the 1960s scene, as did Dave Tuttle. Keith Purvis played in Dixieland bands and for touring shows and also opened a well-known drum shop. Freddie Greenwell became one of the top four or five players ever to come out of the Northwest. And bassist Red Kelly became a legend in his own right, perhaps the wildest of the Seattle-area wild men, during his many years with the Harry James and Woody Herman bands.

For a year or so, Ronnie Pierce's band had steady work, playing high school proms and such venues as the Palladium Ballroom and the Civic Auditorium, but as Pierce put it, "The band was geared more for the ears than the show." After a deal fell through with Sonora Records in Chicago, the band dissolved. It had been a brave experiment. "I guess you could say it was the dream jazz band of that era," said pianist Kenny Kimball. "You've got to give credit to Ronnie Pierce for trying to do in Seattle what Stan Kenton was doing in Balboa Beach about the same time. God, what a band that was! Great charts, marvelous charts!"

Pierce went on the road shortly after the "dream band" broke up. For a while he played third alto with a comic, Spike Jones–style nine-piece, in Billings, Montana, then in 1948 played in the pit at Seattle's Palomar Theater and with Frankie Roth's dance band at Dick Parker's ballroom, on Aurora Avenue. In 1959, Pierce helped bring music back to the Pioneer Square area, working in a "funny hat" comedy band at the Blue Banjo. He also played with Skinny Malone and the Hot Bananas at the World's Fair. Pierce went on to become one of Seattle's most colorful rock entrepreneurs, running a legendary go-go club called the Vault, at Second Avenue and Union Street.

Pierce's drummer, Don Manning, also played with Frankie Roth, which led indirectly to Seattle's first white bebop jam session, in 1946, at a downtown place called the Players Club, at Seventh and Pike. Manning remembered: "[Frankie Roth] called me from a place called the South Seas. His group was real commercial. At the same time, they open a place upstairs and call it the Players Club and make it a hot jamming joint. I was the leader at first. [Red Kelly and I] hired two guys that were older, [pianist] Jimmy Buettner and [tenor saxophonist] Norm Hoagy, who was just out of the service. Guys would come and sit in, whoever came through town, like Harry the Hipster [an early Los Angeles bebop pianist and comedian]." Tacoma trumpet ace Neil Friel confirmed the importance of the Players Club. "I date my whole Seattle experience from the time I went on a jam session with Les Brown's guys at the Players Club," he said. "That's where I heard Freddie Greenwell jam. The Players Club had acoustical qualities that just made a horn player feel like playing. You felt like you had gone to heaven."

Bassist Red Kelly, at the time just out of Queen Anne High School, called the Players Club a "milestone," noting that Purvis, trombonist Dave Tuttle, clarinetist Rollie Morehouse, and California bassist Willie Cain also made the Players scene. Norm Bobrow, who had revved up his Metropolitan Theatre concerts, sang at the Players from time to time, recruiting musicians for concerts, and eventually became manager of the place, renaming it the Stage, Screen and Radio Players Club. But the club soon succumbed to milder stewardship, as the wild men, Manning and Kelly, were forced out by the very sidemen they'd hired—Hoagy and Buettner. "They fired us," said Manning. "Can you believe it? They said we were endangering their livelihood and they were really concerned because we were so wild." Part of the problem was hard drugs, which were beginning to infiltrate the Seattle bebop scene. "It was common knowledge that heroin was present there," said Friel. "It was in the form of caps. I think they called them number two caps and they sold for as little as three dollars. Being a seaport town, Seattle had a reputation for having good-quality heroin." Drummer Dave Stetler, who had come up in the kid bands, recounted: "You know, when Parker and Diz broke on the scene, I knew a lot of young musicians around Seattle who were quite a bit younger than me, just out of high school, [who were] very impressionable. Charlie Parker had been on heroin, so they said, 'If this guy's a genius, then we'll be able to play like that.' Next thing you know, four or five of these kids are strung out so bad you can't believe. Some of those kids are dead."

Hard drugs were just one symptom of social change in a world that had gone from pre-atomic to post-atomic in one August day. The Cold War had begun, and the Seattle-Tacoma area was one of its military-industrial nerve centers. Everyone had the jitters. Seattle saxophonist Aaron Davis went mad trying to find the "atomic note" in his horn. One player after another succumbed to drug addiction, alcoholism, or madness. Major Pigford captured well how the atomic nightmare related to the musical mood: "Bop was frantic, ending on notes that people were unaccustomed to hearing, phrases and melodies that were kind of strident. There's an uncertainty about bebop. Your ears are satisfied with it, but it's not like the old Tin Pan Alley songs, where you usually knew where they were going. . . . To me, this reflected the hecticness and the uncertainty of the world we were in. We didn't know what was going to happen. Nothing was certain."

Given this emotional turmoil, it is not surprising that rebellious behavior became almost normal. "Outlaw" musicians such as trombonist Dick Thorlakson and trumpeter Bob McDermid competed with each other to see who could drink, shout, and burn more violently than the night before. Musicians like Thorlakson and McDermid were quite at home at Danny Woo's New Chinatown, up the hill from Jackson, at the northwest corner of South Main Street and Sixth Avenue South. It was an occasionally rough place patronized by sailors and prostitutes but very much out in the open. A large rice bowl with chopsticks hung from the corner of the building with a sign shaped like a whirl of steam rising out of it, dotted with incandescent bulbs. Below, a marquee announced the culinary and musical delights within.

The New Chinatown, corner of Sixth Avenue South and South Main Street, 1955.

Opened in 1940 by entrepreneur Danny Woo, a descendant of one of Chinatown's most prominent pioneers, Chin Gee Hee, the New Chinatown was an exceptionally large joint that could accommodate five hundred people for banquets. The formal bandstand had a wraparound railing and awning. Woo later became a pillar of the Asian community, helping found the Seattle Chinatown Chamber of Commerce as well as the Chinatown Seafair parade and donating a strip of land for a park and community garden that now bears his name, down the street from his old club. In his salad days, however, Woo was one of the biggest bootleggers in Seattle. For five dollars you could walk up the very steep stairs to the New Chinatown with a bottle purchased on the premises.

"I played there nearly a year," recalled Kenny Kimball, "and never suspected that we were a front for the illegal booze traffic downstairs." Bassist Buddy Catlett, who worked the New Chinatown with Terry Cruise, recalled something else unusual about the New Chinatown. "It had this huge kitty in the shape of a cat," he said. "A real kitty. It looked like Sylvester. Red nose. Sitting on the floor. It was almost as big as you are. You dropped money into its mouth." The kitty wasn't always full. Kimball recounted:

> Sometimes it got really lonely and we'd spend our time on the bandstand just shooting the breeze, but most of the time we went through the motions of playing sets and taking intermissions, just as if we had an audience. When the fleet was in, the place would occasionally get crowded with sailors and chicks, mostly prostitutes, and we'd be so thrilled to have someone there, even though they were mostly making boozy love in the booths and not listening to us, that we'd trot out our best tunes and try to play really inspired solos. Since we were an after-hours joint and

didn't even begin to play until 1 a.m., we'd have other musicians drop by after their gigs to socialize.

The bouncer at the New Chinatown was "Big Dave" Henderson, who also played piano. Musicians have described Henderson as a remarkable player whose sparse, natural style reminded them of Thelonious Monk's. Nearly every musician seems to have a drinking or brawling story about the New Chinatown. One perhaps apocryphal tale has the bouncer (not Henderson) throwing an obnoxious patron down the steep stairs to his death. Jimmy Shevenco, a hard-drinking clarinetist who moved to Seattle from Universal Studios in Los Angeles and then played in Ronnie Pierce's "dream band," led a group at the New Chinatown during and just after the war. Shevenco became notorious for drinking whiskey on the bandstand from a one-quart milk bottle. The New Chinatown survived the demise of the other Jackson Street clubs, though in later years the fare was more sweet than hot, staying open as a legitimate Chinese restaurant until 1975.

Into this rather seedy atmosphere, with its case of musical nerves, briefly ventured a white teenager from Wenatchee who would become the most notorious Northwest bebopper of them all—Don Lanphere. Though Wenatchee, at the eastern foot of the Cascades, was far from the Jackson Street hub, Lanphere kept in touch with the action while growing up, thanks to his father, who drove him over the mountains to Seattle every week for saxophone lessons with Johnnie Jessen, who had worked in Los Angeles with the Phil Harris band on the *The Jack Benny Program*. Lanphere's dad also took him to the Trianon to see the great swing bands. According to Lanphere's childhood friend (and excellent jazz critic) Doug Ramsey, by the time Lanphere stormed New York, even Miles Davis knew where Wenatchee was.

In his 1989 book *Jazz Matters*, Ramsey recounted that one night at the Jazz Gallery in New York, Miles came off the stand and sat down next to the writer at the bar. They made small talk for twenty minutes. When Miles got up to return to the stand, he asked, "Where are you from?"

"Oh, nowhere you've ever heard of—Wenatchee, Washington."

Miles paused. "Say hello to Don Lanphere."

Lanphere started playing when he was eight, after discovering his dad's saxophone in the attic. At thirteen, when the Lunceford band came through Wenatchee, Lanphere played his version of Coleman Hawkins's solo on "Body and Soul" and made Willie Smith and Joe Thomas smile. As a youngster, Lanphere collected two thousand jazz records, buying them in big batches through his father's music store. Ramsey vividly remembered intense listening sessions with Don. "That's where I first heard Miles," Ramsey wrote in a liner note to a Miles Davis album.

In the summer of 1944 the sixteen-year-old saxophonist got permission from his parents to live alone in Seattle. Working at the Olympic Hotel with Wally Anderson's tenor band, Lanphere lived in a downtown hotel and explored the after-hours scene. "I got introduced to life there," he recalled. "The war was still going on, so the Club Maynard was servicemen all night long. And yet, walking there at one o'clock in the morning at the height of the war, carrying my horn with a smile on my face, nobody ever bothered me." In 1945 he graduated from high school and headed for Northwestern University in Evanston, Illinois, with the intention of becoming a school music teacher. He was soon soaking up the sounds of Sonny Stitt, Jimmy Raney, and others on the scene. When Claude Thornhill had an empty alto/clarinet chair, Lanphere filled in for a few days. Other opportunities followed. Charlie Ventura needed a sub, and Don found himself playing in a band with trombonist Kai Winding. Another player who would later work in the Northwest showed up as well—pianist Betty Stitt (no relation to Sonny), who was also attending Northwestern and studying with Lennie Tristano. The two recorded an acetate.

For a while, Lanphere, trombonist Jimmy Knepper, and saxophonist Joe Maini roomed together. Maini had started to make illicit recordings of Charlie Parker at the Regal and Pershing Ballrooms. Lanphere caught the bug and joined the crowd of "Bird Watchers"—or "Ornithologists," as they would be memorialized in a later song title—who would make important recorded "sightings" of Parker throughout his career. Lanphere and Knepper joined a bebop septet led by swing bandleader Johnny Bothwell, which after three months took them to New York, into the Baby Grand, in Harlem. Lanphere dropped out of school; the year was 1948. The first night the septet played at the Baby Grand, a beautiful, dark-haired girl named Chan Richardson walked in with Bothwell. She left with Lanphere. The next day the jealous bandleader gave Lanphere notice. Chan was a hip follower of the new music who lived in an apartment above 7 West Fifty-Seventh Street. Musicians playing the clubs downstairs would come up during their breaks to get away from the crowds. Chan was another "Bird Watcher" and was good friends with Ross Russell, who was recording Parker on his label, Dial, and would later write a Parker biography.

"One night Ross Russell came in with Chan and said, 'Be at this place on a Friday at such-and-such a time and bring your horn,'" Don remembered. "So I walked in and I saw Max Roach and Fats Navarro, and I'm supposed to make a record. It was a bit of a shock!" This was Lanphere's first record date in the Big Apple, November 29, 1948—a vocal session led by Earl Coleman. The group waxed the very first recording of Denzil Best's new tune, "Move," which would shortly become a "cool jazz" classic. Lanphere learned "Move" on the set, soloing after hearing Fats run through it once.

After the date, trumpeter Navarro befriended Lanphere. The saxophonist was invited to do his own album for Bob Weinstock's New Jazz label, a subsidiary of Prestige. "Bob asked me who I wanted in my band," said Don, "and I said, 'Bird's rhythm section and Fats Navarro.' Of course I was joking. He said, 'All right.'" In September, Lanphere went into the studio with Fats, Al Haig (piano), Tommy Potter (bass), and Max Roach (drums), and recorded four sides, including a tune Don had written on the changes of "Pennies from Heaven" titled "Stop." These records are early bebop classics.

Between these two recording sessions, Lanphere did three months on the road with clarinetist Jerry Wald, then went out with Woody Herman's Second Herd. Lanphere was in the thick of the most exciting musical happenings in jazz. Jimmy Knepper and Joe Maini rented a sub-basement in a building on 136th Street and Broadway and fixed it up as a jam-session pad where Lanphere, Bird, Bill Crow, Gerry Mulligan, Warne Marsh, Bob Dorough, Seattle drummer Buzz Bridgeford—and even Lenny Bruce—would come by to play, at any time of the day or night. On one session, taped by Lanphere and later issued as *The Apartment Sessions*, Bird and Lanphere performed together. Another famous Bird "bootleg" album, *Bird at St. Nick's*, was also the result of a Lanphere recording session. "Playing with Bird was like lesson time," recalled Don. "He was very generous in showing us stuff and making little explanations."

Joe Maini started a jumbo-sized rehearsal band to showcase the arranging of Gene Roland that included Lanphere, Al Porcino, Red Rodney, Jimmy Knepper, Charlie Parker, Al Cohn, Zoot Sims, Joe Bushkin, and Tiny Kahn, among others. The group never performed, but it can be heard on the recording *The Band That Never Was*.

As Lanphere was soaking up the sounds of this extraordinary environment, he also was unfortunately absorbing some of the more deadly aspects of the bop lifestyle. He had already been exposed to heroin in Chicago. By the time he went to New York, he was an addict. To make matters worse, Chan Richardson had left him and moved in with Bird. Lanphere began to lead an increasingly reckless life. In 1951 he was arrested on the street in Detroit for scoring drugs and ended up in the county jail. He was twenty-two.

Lanphere spent the next six years back in Wenatchee, working in his father's music store, trying to get his life back together. In 1956 he and his childhood friend Doug Ramsey produced a two-day jazz festival in Wenatchee, bringing over pianist Paul Neves, bassist Larry Rockwell, drummer Gerald Frank, Patti Bown, and trumpet player Chauncey Locke from Seattle. The following year, he headed back to the East Coast with renewed confidence. For eight months he lived in Boston with Paul Neves. The following summer, he rejoined Woody Herman. More tours and recordings followed, with Charlie Barnet and Claude Thornhill. But in 1961, Lanphere's lifestyle caught up with him. He was arrested for possession of marijuana in Oklahoma. His parents bailed him out again.

For the next twenty-three years, Lanphere's horn lay nearly mute. In 1969 he was reborn a Christian, and he finally found an anchor to his life. By 1982 he felt he wanted to try to revive his career. "[My wife] said, 'You're sixty years old. If you don't do it now, you're never going to do it.'" Lanphere took her advice, and the jazz world was the better for it. The saxophonist started out with a few local gigs in Seattle, then got booked into the West End Cafe in Manhattan, and his career took off again. After that he released thirteen albums, beginning with *From 'Out of Nowhere,'* utilizing a nexus of Northwest musicians that usually included Jon Pugh on trumpet, Jeff Hay on trombone, Dean Hodges on drums, Marc Seales on piano, and Chuck Deardorf on bass. He also released collaborative albums with guitarist Larry Coryell and vocalist Jay Clayton, who lived and taught in the Northwest starting in the early 1980s. Lanphere toured Europe and Britain, played at the North Sea Jazz Festival, and performed regularly in clubs around the country. He had a large clientele of improvisation clinics at school jazz programs. Don Sickler, a Spokane native who makes a specialty of publishing jazz tunes, transcribed Lanphere's bop lines, published by Jamey Aebersold as *Lanphere Lines to Aebersold Tracks*.

In the 1990s, Lanphere was still a tough tenor whose swaggering, sinuous improvising bristled with the excitement of swing-to-bop discovery. His low-ing tenor tone was an extremely personal one, plaintive and hollow, through which the chuffing warmth of his swing-era roots still bubbled. After his religious renewal, Lanphere took up soprano saxophone, which he played with extraordinary sensitivity on ballads. Like most old boppers, Lanphere was in love with speed and loved nothing better than to flip expectations. At one point, he even recorded the swing dance tune "Take the 'A' Train" as a waltz. His speedy "Cherokee" takeoff, "Noble Indian Song Pt. 2," doubled back on itself with tricky rhythms that were nearly impossible to play.

Lanphere said in the 1990s he was having a lot more fun than in his frenetic Fifty-Second Street days, when he was driven by competitiveness: "I'm thoroughly enjoying this, because I'm not trying to impress anybody anymore." In his later years Lanphere performed often at Tula's jazz club, in Belltown, and was also a featured soloist with the Seattle Repertory Jazz Orchestra. For many years he and the late Bud Young, who ran a beloved jazz record store in Pioneer Square, had a show on the Bellevue College radio station KBCS. Lanphere died in 2003.

At one of Lanphere's all-night jam sessions in Manhattan, he had hooked up with Wayne "Buzzy" Bridgeford, the drummer who had played with Curt Sykes at the Trianon. Bridgeford was another great Seattle swing-to-bop–era musician. Buzzy was from Olympia, where his father, a prominent doctor, had worked for the state government. Friends and admirers paint a picture of the young Bridgeford as a sensitive Chet Baker–type who had many advantages growing up, among them the unfortunate one of getting his fingers into his father's pharmaceuticals. As a youngster, Bridgeford played in Brad Bannon's commercial swing band in Tacoma, then graduated to Curt Sykes's jazzier group. After the war he became a savvy hipster whose sense of rhythm was matched only by his sardonic sense of humor. Don Manning, who idolized the drummer as a guru and became his informal student, recalled the first time he saw Bridgeford, about 1944:

> The word went out that Buzz was going to take [the drummer's] place in Curt Sykes' band. There's this knock at the door and he walks in. I couldn't believe it. Here's this little guy. He had long hair almost like a girl. He was so frail. He acted real strange, a real hepcat. Buzz, he's gritting his teeth and frowning, listening to everything, you

know. He's looking down at the floor and he's going just like a Kerouac character. He's wigging out. I'm hanging on his every word. What's he gonna say? What's he gonna do? And the music stops and he says, "Don, goddamnit, if I ever overplay the band like that I want you to tell me." And he walks out and slams the door. The next day, he comes in and plays all the arrangements like he's already studied them.

Buzz Bridgeford, Tupper Lake, New York, summer 1950.

"He was a real natural, amazing player," according to Red Kelly. "Those guys, like Shadow Wilson, and Art Madigan, they'd hit a cymbal and it'd sound like a painting, Van Gogh or something. . . . Buzzy could do that." (A private 1955 recording of Bridgeford with a Seattle quartet bears Kelly out. Buzzy's cymbal sound was luxurious.)

Bridgeford enjoyed turning on other musicians to music and to his philosophy of life. He told Manning early on he had to decide whether he wanted to be a drummer like Gene Krupa (the aggressive, bashing type) or like Jo Jones (the subtle, understated power beneath the band, using shading and dynamics as well as force). Buzzy had already made his choice. Rollie Morehouse told of a night on the road with Curt Sykes, when the bandleader asked Buzz to put a little more backbeat into his playing, to make a particular tune a little more danceable: "I looked up and Buzzy was back there with a saw and a board, sawing on the afterbeat!" Kenny Kimball, who worked with Bridgeford in 1950, remembered, "Buzzy would get so frustrated with the people that wanted to hear corny stuff, the same old commercial tunes, like 'Tea for Two' and 'Ace in the Hole.' I remember one night Buzzy jumped out from his drums and he kicked the bandstand—*BANG! BANG! BANG!* He was so frustrated he couldn't stand it any longer."

Bridgeford left Seattle with Jan Garber, a commercial bandleader, played in trumpeter Jimmy Zito's band for a while, along with Seattleite Fred Greenwell, then joined Randy Brooks. For a couple of years, Brooks's sizzling modern big band—a good example of a swing unit taken over by young, bebop-hungry soloists—captured the imagination of jazz aficionados, scoring sixth in the 1947 *DownBeat* poll for best swing band. Bridgeford rode the critical wave, placing No. 15 in the best drummer category. At some point he became Brooks's manager, in which capacity he got into a severe car accident while driving the bandleader's Cadillac. This prompted a return to his parents' home in Olympia to recuperate.

Bridgeford was a fast talker and a born hustler. In Seattle, when he met and fell for the astounding Lennie Tristano student Betty Christopher (whom Don Lanphere had known in Chicago as Betty Stitt), Buzzy decided he had to play music with her. Christopher had come to Seattle with an all-girl orchestra. Bassist Bill Crow, who was attending the University of Washington at the time, remembered:

> Buzzy couldn't believe what he had found here. In the first place, he had eyes for her, and in the second, she was somebody who played very good piano and didn't know anything about anything except Lennie Tristano. Since he loved to hip people, he started hipping her to Bird and to Bud [Powell] and all these wonderful things. She was just sopping it up like a sponge.
>
> Buzzy manufactured a job at one of Russian John's clubs, the Filipino Veterans of Foreign Wars. I think they had some kind of Hawaiian band in there. Buzzy talked to the owner. "Look," he said, "you've got a rounders' club here. This is where all the high rollers and the pimps and the hookers and everybody that's hanging out after hours [goes]. You're supposed to have jazz in a club like that. This Hawaiian music isn't it." The guy said, "Yeah, maybe you're right." So he put a band together with Betty, Doug Goss on bass, and Freddie Greenwell on tenor. I used to take my valve trombone and bongos down.

In Tacoma, Bridgeford promoted a gig at a beer joint on Ninth Avenue and Pacific Street called the Pirate's Cove, easily the best white bebop band assembled to that date in the Northwest, with Freddie Greenwell on tenor saxophone, Don Ober on guitar, Hollis Sulser on piano, and Paul Binnings on bass. As Greenwell recalled: "That was really one of the best jobs I ever played in the Northwest. We had a real good swing bebop band there. We played blues and rhythm and blues and jazz. That piano player was absolutely one of the best piano players you'd ever want to hear in the world. He was like Hank Jones. He was really a gasser. That was quite a jazz experience down there. It was just really inspiring to play a steady job with Buzzy."

Like Lanphere, Buzz Bridgeford was into playing very fast. Dean Reilly, a bass player who also worked on the Tacoma scene, remembered bassist Traff Hubert and Bridgeford having "speed contests": "Buzz would say, 'Okay, here we go.' Just the two of them. I remember Neil Friel and Buzz and Traff once played 'Cherokee' for five or ten minutes as fast as it could go—it was breathtaking." Bridgeford played at the Black Hawk in San Francisco with Stan Getz in 1951. Later, he traveled east with bassist Bill Crow and played in a group with vocalist Dave Lambert. But his drug abuse was getting progressively in the way. He eventually came home in a shambles. Dave Stetler remembered filling in for Buzz at the Union Club when the sick drummer was sent home in a cab. Bridgeford died in 1956, one of the first of the drug casualties on the Seattle bop scene.

Hollis Sulser, the pianist on the Pirate's Cove gig and the leading bebop pianist in Tacoma, later went to Hollywood, where he joined Bobby Sherwood's big band. Tragically, he died young in an automobile accident in Tacoma in 1957. Bassist Paul Binnings left town and became a professional musician in Reno. Don Ober was a Charlie Christian–style guitar player who wore a big hat and pinstriped suit and smoked a cigar. In the 1970s he became a regular sideman at Red Kelly's club, the Tumwater Conservatory, and died in 1979.

When Buzz Bridgeford left the Pirate's Cove, the job had gone to one of the most unlikely, underappreciated musicians ever to work in the Northwest, trumpet player Neil Friel. An obsessive and zany character with a precocious enthusiasm for many of the themes adopted by the beat generation—Eastern mysticism, fringe therapies, and drugs—Friel is universally acknowledged as one of the best bebop musicians to emerge from the Northwest. A bent imp of a man in 1989, whose face had aged beyond his years, he was a gentlemanly, warm individual who possessed a gift for storytelling and a wry sense of life's ironies. Tracked down in Manhattan, Friel recounted his early years this way:

> I was born in the Black Hills of South Dakota, on February 27, 1930. My father, Monte Friel, played violin, trumpet, clarinet, and drums. When I was nine, he came west with a band led by Dale Fitzsimmons. They had their sights on the big time. They had four nights a week at the Crescent Ballroom in Tacoma. With one break or two, one way or another they could have made it.

My father wouldn't hear of anything else but that I should become a swing trumpet player. Bunny Berigan was his absolute idol. When I was nine, I started practicing. Within a few months, I was solo cornetist with the all-city orchestra. I had to practice two hours a day. I wasn't even permitted to think of anything else. My father used to take me around to hear Black jazz trumpet players. I heard one named Leon [Vaughn, probably] and another named Herman Grimes. Then, one Sunday, it came like a full-blown transcendental revelation. My friend Whitey Collier put on a record by Louis Armstrong one Sunday afternoon. I would always listen politely to the notes as that transpired and they meant nothing to me. All of a sudden, Louis Armstrong took this jazz break, improvised, and what he said in that break just illuminated me from the bottom of my spine. I lit up like a fluorescent tube! From that moment on, I've never wanted to do anything else in my life but play jazz trumpet. I think I was fifteen. I would run two miles home from Bellarmine High School at lunch hour in order to play Sonny Berman's trumpet chorus on "Sidewalks of Cuba."

Neal Ely and I worked with Brad Bannon at Five Mile Lake during the summer. Brad Bannon had the best band around. Louis Grenier played at the Top of the Ocean for thirty years. If I hadn't been so imbued with star eyes, I probably would have just stayed there and had quite a comfortable little middle-class career.

Then I saw Charlie Parker. It was 1948 at the Jazz at the Philharmonic show, down at the Moore Theatre. It was pure distilled magic. I decided I wanted to go to New York to see Bird and Diz and get in on the bebop. But there was another reason. One of my chief mentors at that time was Neal Ely, who had promulgated this system of Reichian analysis. He was worried about my becoming heavily neurotic. And there was no doubt about it, I had a little persecution complex going. It's obvious, looking back, to see what brought it all on. I was wearing long hair before it was popular. I ran into all kinds of heat, was called various names. I developed a hell of a chip on my shoulder. So Neal thought I should go through Reichian analysis. I was all for it. My family had been going through an internal scene that was just utterly unpleasant.

The Reichians had an approach dealing with life energy, which in terms of Indian mysticism and yogi teachings is the same thing they have known for centuries in the East as *prajna*. Wilhelm Reich was the Charlie Parker of psychiatry. Neal got an orgone accumulator. The first time I got in one, I didn't know one was not supposed to do yogic breathing in there and I just passed right out, within thirty seconds. I went to a Reichian analyst in Brooklyn named Dr. Chester Raphael. Dr.

> Raphael said, "Yes, you need help my son, and the sessions are fifty dollars an hour, minimum." In 1950, that was just hopelessly out of my range. He did give me some hope, some group therapy, but I wanted that one-on-one vegetotherapy. I thought it was going to unlock my personality. . . .
>
> New York was like being thrown into a bathtub of great music. Right across the street from my little room on 53rd and Broadway, every night at nine o'clock, the Tito Puente Orchestra would open up and play their theme song till hell wouldn't have it. It was an immensely exciting time. I got to meet Sonny Stitt. Don Lanphere was there. He was already a famous player. He had recorded with Fats Navarro. Music was coming out of the skyscrapers themselves.

When Friel returned from his first trip to New York City in 1950, at age twenty, he was one of the few musicians in the Northwest who had actually jammed on Fifty-Second Street—Fred Greenwell was another—and the only one who had picked up on the nascent "beat" movement. He immediately began to spread the word. Quincy Jones recalled: "Neil had a big influence on me philosophically because he was real far out. We were dealing our little homemade orgone emulators, out of tin foil and stuff. And we were enlightening the teachings of the masters of the Far East. We were into L. Ron Hubbard, Dianetics, and all that stuff. Fourteen and fifteen. There were about four or five of us who were into this real spiritual quest." Friel and Jones became friendly competitors: "Quincy was further advanced than me when it came to writing. Trumpetwise, we seemed about even. We were both into playing bop. We played together in this one band and he and I still talk about it. It was Fourth of July. We went out to this lake and that band did not do anything but swing, a la Dizzy Gillespie's Orchestra, right from the get-go."

Friel hung out on the Tacoma and Seattle scenes for a year or so, playing after hours and with various commercial dance bands, when his pal Charlie Johnson, another avid bebop trumpeter, gave him a call to join Darryl Harpa, a debonair Latin bandleader with whom Red Kelly and Don Manning had left town. Harpa was Seattle's mambo man throughout the late 1940s and gave nearly a dozen local jazz musicians their first taste of the road. Originally from Los Angeles, where he had led a floor show–style rumba band, Harpa worked at Seattle's El Rancho, on Aurora Avenue, in 1947, a roadhouse that had started out as Doc Hamilton's Barbecue Ranch. Harpa billed his band as "Musical, Both Americas," a reference to the group's two sets of arrangements, one Latin and one swing. His bongo player was Dacito (David) Niego, a showboat Cuban who danced in front with Harpa's wife, Myrna. Pianist Eddie Diamond, a Hawaiian who worked in Seattle in the late 1940s, wrote the band's Latin book. Pianist Jim Gilles, who worked with Harpa in 1950, said he learned authentic Latin style in the band, but Red Kelly characterized Harpa as a "con artist" who "didn't know anything about music." Kelly was right about the "con artist" part. On his Midwest tours Harpa never played the same hotel twice, because of the gambling debts he left behind.

In early 1951, Harpa was playing in Washington, DC, and he needed both a trumpet player and pianist. Friel and Gilles took off like two bullets aimed at their dreams. As Friel remembered it, "Jimmy Gilles and I rode across the country on a Greyhound and joined the band at the Wardman Park Hotel. Darryl taught us all we know about Latin music." On the road Manning and Kelly defected from the band, but Friel stayed on, recording a tune with Harpa in 1952 called "You and the Night and the Music," with Marana Page on vocals. After the Harpa tour Friel spent some time in Los Angeles, working as a copyboy for the Associated Press during the day and jamming at night wherever he could, including sessions on Central Avenue with Wardell Gray, Sonny Clark, Frank Morgan, and Max Roach. Friel also began a laborious reconstruction of his trumpet embouchure and technique in Los Angeles, studying with symphony player Louis Maggio.

When Friel came back to Tacoma, he hired bassist Traff Hubert and pianist Jimmy Gilles for the gig at the Pirate's Cove, on Pacific Avenue. Friel was still having trouble with his trumpet embouchure, so he took up drums. His trio, called the Cosmos, toured the Northwest throughout 1955. Friel then got a show job as a drummer in Great Falls, Montana, and switched back to trumpet for a gig with a group called the Fabulous Woodsons. By this time Friel felt he was ready to go back to New York to try to get on with a name band as a trumpet player. Returning to the Big Apple in 1960, he got a call from Billy May, a bandleader who was making a career of reviving the big-band sound with some integrity. For the next ten years Friel worked with plenty of name bands—not only Billy May but also Woody Herman, Les Elgart, Charlie Spivak, Jimmy Dorsey, Glenn Miller, and Claude Thornhill. In 1965 he recorded with Si Zentner, and in 1967 with Woody Herman at the Monterey Jazz Festival, getting off a dizzy trumpet solo on Bill Holman's "The Horn of the Fish."

Friel drifted from one band to the next, getting fired and rehired, as he alternately got straight and fell off the wagon. Eventually, in 1971, he left the fray and moved to the Catskills. He played at Grossinger's in a show band for over four years. After Friel came home to Tacoma in 1976, he played at Seattle's Roosevelt Hotel with pianist Johnny Lewis. In the early 1990s he was living in the small village of Jamestown, New York. Looking back on his career, Friel was poignantly honest: "The traveling and doing one-nighters with a big band—that was all we ever wanted. Once I had reached that, I didn't have any other goals. I had never thought of myself as becoming a jazz star. All I ever wanted to do was just play for a big band." White saxophonist Chuck Stentz remarked, "Neil was his own worst enemy. He never got his personal thing together. But he played great. And he played very warm." Sadly, Friel returned to Tacoma and died there of a heroin overdose in 1999.

Things turned out better for Fred Greenwell, whose career bore striking parallels to both Friel's and Buzz Bridgeford's. All three came up as swingers then turned to bop. They all played in some of the hipper postwar big bands, and all were diverted from music by drugs and alcohol. They are also among the top ten musicians ever to come out of the area. One solo by Fred Greenwell could stand by itself as justification for a book about Seattle jazz. He was a burly, soft-spoken man who counted among life's great pleasures music, large mugs of tea with sweetened milk, purebred cats, and the close, shrouded environment of the rainy Northwest. Fred lived in the 1990s in a tranquil neighborhood on a hill near Green Lake in Seattle and liked to look out his window at the soft contours of the city, with its evergreen trees and constant cloud cover. It was an image that matched his playing, which had the soft and swirling attack of his contemporary Stan Getz but with a slightly acidic edge.

Few players elicit the unqualified endorsement Fred Greenwell did from his contemporaries. Said drummer Dave Stetler: "Now there's the giant of the saxophone. When I first heard that guy play, I was fortunate enough to play in a session with him. He would take a chorus, then he'd take another chorus, and then another one, and every one would get more beautiful than the last. He would just take you on a trip, have you sailing on the clouds. He was so full of soul, this guy, you couldn't believe it."

Greenwell was born in Wilmington, Delaware, in 1924. His parents were both musicians. During his youth he went to all the shows coming through Wilmington at the Black Odd Fellows Hall—Duke Ellington, Cab Calloway,

Fred Greenwell sitting in with Charlie Parker at the Spotlite Club, Fifty-Second Street, New York, 1946. *Left to right:* Stan Levey, Leonard Gaskin, Sir Charles Thompson (partially hidden), Parker, Greenwell.

Andy Kirk, Earl Hines, and Count Basie. Black swing was his passion. "I used to have to walk past the Black ballroom to get to high school," recalled Greenwell. "I'd go in early and watch those guys set up. I was eighteen years old and studying the clarinet real hard. This was really an education, that style of music. I had a lot of desire to be in the field of modern music that those guys represented."

When the war broke out, Greenwell was accepted into the Navy music school, where he received conservatory training and wound up in bandleader Claude Thornhill's detachment. (Seattle clarinetist Rollie Morehouse was also in the band.) Thornhill was one of the progressive bandleaders introducing the sounds of modern classical harmony to the white big bands. Greenwell toured the South Pacific with Thornhill for a year, then was stationed in New York. He naturally got into Manhattan as often as he could to hear the boppers on Fifty-Second Street. (Hanging on Greenwell's wall was a picture of him jamming at the Spotlite Club with Charlie Parker. Another showed him in a tenor duel with Wardell Gray.)

After his Navy stretch, Greenwell moved west. His mother, who had been born and raised in Prosser, Washington, had moved back to Seattle and started a successful music studio, where she taught piano and violin, in the Greenwood neighborhood. Morehouse had also encouraged Greenwell to come to Seattle. Fred entered the University of Washington music department but soon dropped out. To keep cash flowing, he joined Morehouse in the Curt Sykes band, but he reported Sykes's commercial arrangements "bored me out of my skull." A six-nighter with the celebrated Texas trombone player Jack Teagarden made life more livable. So did Greenwell's discovery of the few like-minded souls in Seattle who were hip to what he'd heard on Fifty-Second Street; these were the friends who introduced him to the after-hours joints where the real music was happening. He became an instant regular.

> As soon as I could get through at the Trianon, I would go down to Jackson Street, which was just roaring. You couldn't get in the Rocking Chair very easily at all. That's where Ray Charles worked. He never seemed to want to let anybody sit in, but I would still try to do it, because I knew he was really good. I enjoyed being able to play at least along behind him. Milt Garred [Charles's bassist] would talk Ray into letting me play. They always had good music. If you were known, you could get in as a white. But most white people wouldn't want to even go there. They're not interested in really relaxing and having a good time and being up at that time of night. They're out running the banks.

Though Greenwell had absorbed the latest licks in New York, his goal at this time was to learn more tunes so he could make a living playing with commercial combos. He set about getting an education on the street. "I made an effort to go to a lot of different places where I knew they were going to play some different tunes," he recalled. "I found you could always get ten dollars out of playing 'Ace in the Hole.' Another one was 'Squaws on the Yukon,' and if you can sing it, even better. I learned ballads that later guys would say, 'Where'd you ever hear that?'" Greenwell soon became an in-demand player, welcome everywhere—except, of course, by other tenor saxophonists. Al Hickey, tenor man with the Jive Bombers, recalled:

> One night, Paul Quinichette came to town. He said, "Hickey, get your horn and let's jam." We played at this club for a half hour and then we'd go to the next club and jam and the next club, and then we got to the Rocking Chair and Freddie Greenwell was up there. I said, "You go and get your horn out and I'll be right up there." Boy, he got up there with that Freddie Greenwell and I thought that cat was about ready

Fred Greenwell and Wardell Gray, Jack's Basket Room, Los Angeles, 1948.

to throw away his tenor. He said, "What you doin'?" I said, "Look, I have to deal with this every night!"

What knocked out other musicians about Greenwell was not only his natural ability but his individual voice, something all jazz musicians strive for. Like Dick Wilson before him and white saxophonist Denney Goodhew after

The Norm Bobrow Little Big Band, ca. 1952. (*Center*) Norm Bobrow. *Clockwise from upper left-hand corner:* Floyd Standifer; the Signatures; Mike DeFillipis; Don Conway (seated, alto saxophone) and Fred Greenwell (tenor saxophone).

him, Greenwell was a Seattle saxophonist who played in a personal and completely accomplished style of his own. Chuck Metcalf, a bassist who as a young man worked in the Bobrow Little Big Band, added perceptively: "The tenor saxophone players [in Seattle] sounded different from one another. Gerald Brashear and Billy Tolles had markedly different styles, and Freddie Greenwell had another different style. He was a highly evolved, Les Young–style player of those first kind, like Herbie Steward and Stan Getz and Zoot Sims. One of the highlights of my career here was first hearing Freddie Greenwell play."

When Fred wasn't knocking out other musicians at concerts, he worked casuals with Vern Mallory and sat in wherever he could, including a blues joint near Twelfth Avenue and Yesler Way, where Palmer Johnson's old drummer, Gilbert "Punkin" Austin, and pianist Dave Henderson worked. After a couple of years on the Jackson Street scene, Greenwell was picked up by Jimmy Zito, a hot Les Brown trumpet man who had started an eleven-piece big band and needed a third alto player who could also play good clarinet. (Bud Shank, who would move to the Seattle area in the 1980s, was playing lead alto and flute.)

The band recorded with vocalist Helen O'Connell for Coast Records and toured San Diego, Albuquerque, and other points close to Hollywood, where most of the players were based. For several months Buzz Bridgeford played drums.

Greenwell was based in Los Angeles for about a year, where he played with Wardell Gray, scat singer Leo Watson, and Zoot and Ray Sims, and did some occasional studio work. But Greenwell was uncomfortable in the laid-back southland. In 1949 he found a ticket out with Alvino Rey, the electric-guitar pioneer. After two or three years touring with Rey, Greenwell was hired by Buddy Morrow, an excellent bandleader who eventually became extremely successful in Hollywood. Greenwell made twenty or thirty records with Morrow (playing in section, not soloing), including *One Mint Julep* and Morrow's monster hit, *Night Train*. Throughout the 1950s, Greenwell moved back and forth between Seattle and New York. His itinerary is sketchy. Like Buzzy Bridgeford, his personal habits were beginning to catch up with him. In 1951, Greenwell was in Seattle for a spell, playing with Bridgeford, Ken Kimball, and bassist Bill Crow. When Crow and Kimball left for New York, Greenwell joined them. The following year, he was back in Seattle, where he joined Norm Bobrow's Little Big Band.

In 1954, because he thought a change of scenery might help him stop drinking, Greenwell moved to Tacoma. The band he worked with there, at the Pirate's Cove, was the legendary Tacoma bebop ensemble that also featured Bridgeford. Greenwell and the men were so inspired by one another that after the gig, they would drive out to the countryside and continue playing. "We'd pile into two or three cars at one-thirty or two o'clock in the morning and we'd go out to the Straits, way out in the fields—no homes, out in the forest, the great green, wet Northwest—and we'd have our instruments, and in the middle of fields we'd play. Far out, boy. We had some wild times."

During the 1950s, Fred hung out a lot with the other great bebop tenor saxophonists from Seattle, including Gerald Brashear.

> We usually took the bus to my house, just about dawn. I usually had long hair and it was real kinky. Once Gerald told me, "You know, one time we were coming out here, Sunday morning, the two of us were sitting in a bus that was pretty empty, and these two blue-haired ladies were going to church and they were looking at the two of us and they looked at me and they said, "He's one of those white black guys." Gerald thought that was good.

We'd go down to my basement room and just sit around. We never would drink or carry on, just try to be quiet. I'd play him some of the things I'd been listening to. I really liked him. He was really good. He had that kind of sound and feeling in his playing—alive, alert, swinging.

In 1956, Red Kelly got Greenwell onto the Woody Herman band for nine months, but Fred didn't get along with Woody or pianist Nat Pierce, who was running the band. After that tour Greenwell was in New York, where he participated in the famous jazz loft on Sixth Avenue run by David X. Young and photographed by W. Eugene Smith from 1957 through 1963. Smith recalled a night when Greenwell came in after midnight and jammed with drummer Ronnie Free on a Sunday night and continued to play "until Friday. . . . It was an amazing show of determination." This was a "very constructive" period, said Greenwell, in which he played with Zoot Sims and Herb Geller, worked weekend casuals, and hung out with Don Lanphere. He also subbed in the Artie Shaw group, "before Artie fired the whole band," and rehearsed with the Benny Goodman band for two weeks.

After New York, Greenwell spent the next two decades fighting the monkey on his back, moving first to Charleston, South Carolina, in the 1960s, then to Dallas in the 1970s, still working parties and country clubs but having put ambition aside. In 1980, after pulling himself together, he came back to his beloved Seattle. "I've always liked the natural environment here," he said, looking out his window. "I think it's there, in people's playing." Greenwell continued to play casuals and made the occasional festival appearance, but not nearly often enough to satisfy an older generation of listeners who knew he was one of the greatest musicians ever to arise from the Northwest. Unfortunately he made no commercial recordings as a leader, so his reputation has largely circulated among fellow musicians. One of them, Seattle bassist Pete Leinonen, hired Greenwell often when he came home and in 1988 recorded the saxophonist privately with a local group. Greenwell's solo on a medium-fast rendition of "After You've Gone" lives up to the praise heaped upon him. Playing lithe, serpentine lines from the basement to the attic, in a manner clearly inspired by Lester Young, but with a grittier tone and more percussive surprises, Greenwell spits out one sparkling idea after another, chorus after chorus, a few of them a cappella, with swashbuckling ease.

When Red Kelly learned there was to be a book about Northwest jazz including him and Fred Greenwell, the bassist said, "I want this to go on record. I think Freddie Greenwell is the greatest living jazz saxophone player. Period. I don't think there is anybody that comes close. Not even remotely close." Greenwell died in 1994, having suffered for many years from diabetes.

Red Kelly was probably best known to Washingtonians as the whimsical, red-faced, publicity-prone prankster who, in the grand tradition of Vic Meyers, started a tongue-in-cheek political campaign and wound up getting a ton of votes—in fact, the largest minority vote in Washington history. On a lark, in 1972, Kelly and a couple of politico friends submitted an official slate of jazz-musician candidates. Kelly ran for governor; his wife, "Fast" Lucy, ran for secretary of state; pianist Jack "Clean as a Hound's Tooth" Perciful, another Harry James alum, ran for state treasurer; guitarist Don Ober was on the ballot as commissioner of public lands; and trumpeter Floyd Standifer ran for Congress on the OWL Party ticket (Out With Logic, On With Lunacy).

But Kelly was more than a political clown. A Queen Anne High School kid from Seattle, he worked on the road with some of the best big bands in the business, including Harry James, Stan Kenton, and Woody Herman, and his locomotive bass is legendary among drummers and sidemen. "Red" was born Thomas Kelly in 1927, in Shelby, Montana, and moved to Everett, Washington, a mill town with a Boeing airplane factory and, back then, a Navy base, just north of Seattle, when he was six months old. During the Depression, Red's parents were forced to place him and his brother in an orphanage in Great Falls, Montana. Kelly's first exposure to playing music came from there. "I found out if I could get in the drum-and-fife corps I could get out of working in the laundry. It's amazing the talent you develop overnight with that incentive. I found that it came easily. When I came here [to Seattle] to go to high school, there was a bass at Queen Anne and nobody played it, so I just took it home. That way, I could play in the band. I never had a lesson." Kelly saw very quickly that the life of a professional musician was a way out of the regimentation and poverty he had experienced at the orphanage. "I didn't want to get up at eight o'clock in the morning, ever. I don't ever want to get involved in an environment that's remotely like school. Ever since we got out of the caves and somebody invented something we can see in the nighttime, I don't see why we got to get up the minute the sun comes up. We got light, you know?"

Red Kelly.

Musically Red was what jazz musicians call a "natural." Without knowing the first thing about music, he made his way into the business through chutzpah, a great sense of time, and a phenomenal ear. "I remember watching him start to figure it all out," recalled Don Manning, who knew Red in high school. "We were sitting in my car and the radio was playing and Red starts singing the low tone and he realizes that he's got a gift, that he can find the notes. He always knew something that would fit underneath."

When he was sixteen, Kelly was recruited by a Dixieland band playing at the China Pheasant, the prosperous roadhouse out by the Duwamish River (near the present-day Boeing Developmental Center) where Dave Stetler had worked in Bob Harvey's band. In the time-honored jazz tradition of passing on the music hand to hand, Kelly learned to play bass on the job. He couldn't have had better teachers. Joe Darensbourg, Seattle's jazz pioneer from the 1920s, was the clarinetist; Johnny Wittwer, a remarkable musician who would record with New Orleans trombonist Kid Ory in 1945 and become part of the San Francisco Dixieland revival the following year, was on piano; Tacoma doctor Neal Ely, who'd introduced Neil Friel to Reichian therapy, was on saxophone; Evan Humphrey or Pete Carrabba played trumpet; and Keith Purvis was on drums. The gig attracted the attention of a national magazine, Art Hodes's *The Jazz Record*, which praised the band for its authentic revival of New Orleans jazz. Darensbourg described Kelly's first night on the job: "We held the rehearsal and this big red-headed, freckle-faced kid came out there. He had a nice smile and plenty of enthusiasm. Johnny said, 'Now we got a bass player, we gonna start our rehearsal. Are you tuned up, fellers?' So Red says, 'Tuned up? What do you mean, tuned up?' We nicknamed him Jimmy Blanton, after the greatest bass player in the world. He got the biggest kick out of that."

The China Pheasant was a classic roadhouse—a huge place parked in the middle of a cow pasture by the river, complete with a rickety back porch, where musicians slipped out for a swig or a toke, and an elaborate casino concealed behind the kitchen. White bandleader Bob Harvey, who had worked as an arranger for Ted Weems, led a society band there throughout the 1940s and 1950s. National acts such as Johnny Otis and the Wardell Gray/Howard McGhee sextet worked there on occasion. The club eventually became the spearhead for Seattle's Dixieland revival. Owner Harry Lew was a Chinese operator who played a continuous game of cat and mouse with the authorities; the club was raided often. *Seattle Times* reporter Johnny Reddin recalled one botched, slapstick bust when "three carloads of sheriff's deputies . . . (broke) down several doors, arrested the proprietor and two employees, and . . . confiscated the most complete assortment of gambling paraphernalia to be found this side of the ornate establishments in Reno and Las Vegas."

Kelly thought it was all good fun, but after working at the China Pheasant for nearly a year, he was soon swept into the national maelstrom of swing. "Red was the first to go," said Manning. "He was just gone, overnight. This is the way it was then. They'd stop a guy on the street, some kid coming home from school with a music case: 'Say kid, you wanna go on the road?'" Kelly's departure with bandleader Tiny Hill was the beginning of a lifelong career on the road, a cascade of names and places and one-night stands that later all ran together in Kelly's mind as he tried to remember hopping from town to town, band to band, and hotel to hotel. Kelly toured with Hill a few months, then got a telegram from Ted Fio Rito, on Manning's recommendation. Don Trenner, the pianist who would later lead the band on Steve Allen's television show, was in the band; so were trumpeter Doc Severinsen and alto man Ward Swingle, who later created the Swingle Singers. This was 1945.

One night on Fifty-Second Street, Kelly played with Charlie Parker. Apparently Bird approved, because Kelly got a good "review": "I remember the first tune we played was 'Slow Boat to China,' and I thought, 'Boy, oh boy, here I am and Bird's playing, wowee!' So I played and that night we went up to Joe Maini's house and I walked into the apartment and Bird was there. Bird looked up—he was talking to somebody—and he got up and came over, gave me a big kiss on the cheek and hugged me and then went back and sat down."

When the war was over, Ted Fio Rito's band broke up and Manning and Kelly returned to Seattle. Kelly took a commercial gig with Wyatt Howard at the Town and Country Club and played with Curt Sykes. Then Buzz Bridgeford called from New York. "He said there was an opening in Randy Brooks' band. So I went back to New York. Then I got a telegram that said, 'Be in Brooklyn tomorrow night. Sam Donahue needs a bass player.' Sam Donahue was the white Jimmie Lunceford, right? Oh, shit, that was a band! It would knock your hat off, that band." The stint with Donahue led to one of Kelly's most exuberant musical experiences, playing with the legendary Chubby Jackson, who had turned from playing bass with Woody Herman to leading his own band. Of all the shrill, frenetic big bands that rose and fell with bop after the war, Jackson's best communicated the sizzling intensity of the genre. Kelly fit right in. As a bassist, he was in the vanguard of a new wave of big-band players who replaced the four-four "thump" of swing with a more complex, sinuous feel that complemented bebop rhythms.

When Kelly joined the band at the Royal Roost, in New York, all the bass players in the audience—including big names like Eddie Safranski and Oscar Pettiford—wore red to honor his arrival.

> I got out my bass and right in front is Eddie. I thought, "What in the hell am I doing here?" We worked all the Black theaters. There were only two ballads in the book, so everything was just a screamer. It was powerful as hell. Twelve-piece band—three trumpets, two trombones, four saxophones. It was just astounding. That was really my entrance to the wild, great, frenetic, marvelous jazz band. Chubby played out-and-out jazz music. But there isn't much else you can do with that kind of a band. It was about 1949, and the dancing, the frenetic jitterbugging and all that, was over. Everybody kind of wanted to sit back and get over the war.

Like Ronnie Pierce's local "dream band" back home, Chubby Jackson's group succumbed to a lack of bookings. Kelly joined Herbie Fields, a hot saxophonist who had been with Lionel Hampton and had formed a septet. Red worked with Fields around the Midwest for about six months, then replaced Eddie Safranski in Charlie Barnet's band. "That Barnet band was where the expression 'We saw the big man tonight' came from. Which meant that you go into that thing where it was so powerful that you don't even know what your name is or what the tune is. It's just one big instrument, it's not a bunch of guys there. 'We saw the big man tonight.' Now once you do that, you spend the rest of your life trying to do it again. And you do, maybe once or twice a year. If there's a religion, that's mine."

Kelly left Barnet and toured to Hawaii with one of the era's historic small groups, the innovative Red Norvo Trio, with vibist Norvo and guitarist Tal Farlow. But big bands were his first love; he was replaced in the Norvo trio by Charles Mingus. "I don't know if that was the wisest move, looking back. It would have done more for my career had I stayed with Norvo. [But] I got homesick for horns. One night in San Diego, I got drunk with Barnet. It was his wedding night. We went out on a boat, and Barnet invited me to join a new band he was forming. Woody says if it ever gets to where it's not a hobby, you don't want to do it." Music apparently became less than fun for Charlie Barnet too; he abandoned his new group. Kelly returned to Seattle, where he shared an apartment on Capitol Hill with Fred Greenwell. The peripatetic bassist was soon back out on the road, this time with Darryl Harpa. In a Nashville bar one night a Woody Herman sideman told Kelly that Claude Thornhill was looking for a bass player. "I loved Claude," said Kelly. "He had a whole book full of Gil Evans, long before Miles Davis ever thought of getting into that stuff. The band was just one continuous party."

Kelly toured with Thornhill a year, rejoined Woody Herman's Third Herd, jumped off Woody's band in Seattle, and went to work with Norm Hoagy at the Showbox Theater.

> Woody kept calling, but he would replace me with Chubby anytime Chubby wanted the job back, so I said no. Finally, Woody called and said, "Okay, the job is yours from now on." Somehow, I got the dates screwed up. I was supposed to meet him in Knoxville, Tennessee. A saxophone player and myself were out celebrating my imminent departure. Somehow, we lost track of the days. Somebody said, "You're supposed to be playing when?" I said I'm supposed to be playing the night of the 20th or whatever it was. Tomorrow night. Well, this is the 20th. Holy Christ. So [he] said, "Go back by plane." So I just throw a bunch of stuff together and grab my bass and go out and I jump on the wrong plane. I wound up in Minneapolis. Fortunately, I did leave a day ahead of time. So they ran me down to Chicago and stuck me in a hotel. Right downstairs there was a joint where a bunch of guys were playing. I went down and got loaded with them and sat in and, you know, the next day I got to Knoxville and walked into the lobby and there's [Bob] Brookmeyer, and he says, "What are you doing in Knoxville?" I said, "I'm going to join Woody," and he says, "Well, so am I."

By this time Kelly had had enough of the road, at least for a while. After playing with Woody, he returned to Seattle, where he worked at Norm Bobrow's new nightclub, the Colony, and at the Lake City Tavern in a group called Don Anderson's Seattle Rhythm Kings.

In 1956, Kelly got a call from saxophonist Med Flory, who was working with Maynard Ferguson. Red worked with Maynard a while, then went with Stan Kenton for two years. Afterward, he tried doing studio work, but he missed the camaraderie of the road and the big bands. He worked briefly in 1960 with Les Brown ("Kind of Boy Scout," he said); then Harry James called—twice. "I kept thinking every time I heard his band, he always had one of those really white-sounding bass players. Really short notes and really stiff rhythms. I like Jimmy Blanton, with that big ring. So I figured Harry ain't gonna like me. But it turned out he did like me and we had a lot of fun." That's an understatement. Kelly worked with James for the next fourteen years. Every other month, they played the Flamingo Hotel in Las Vegas and three weeks in Lake Tahoe. Pianist Jack Perciful, who had grown up in Idaho and settled in Olympia, and Corky Corcoran were also in the James band.

Kelly worked with Phil Harris's outfit for a while, in Las Vegas, and jumped off the James band from time to time to work shows in Lake Tahoe and Reno with Sonny and Cher and others. It was during this period that he took up the electric bass, using a special instrument made for him by Ampeg, a "Red Kelly" fretless bass with more resonant pickups than a Fender. The idea was to sound more like an acoustic bass.

In 1974, Kelly finally left the road and opened his own club, the Tumwater Conservatory, near Olympia, the staging ground for the revival of Ernestine Anderson's career as well as the site of the OWL Party's genesis. In the 1980s he opened another club—Kelly's—in Tacoma. Musicians all over the country knew about Kelly's, but for most musicians the bass player's name will always be associated not with a nightclub but with one of jazz music's most famous road stories. Known affectionately as the "Red Kelly Story," the "Red Kelly Dog Story," or the "White Room Story," it goes like this: One night, Kelly was invited to visit a wealthy woman whose home was furnished all in white—white carpets, white furniture, white walls. During the course of the evening, Kelly got drunk, and at some point wandered off to find the bathroom. On his way he bumped into a writing desk and spilled a bottle of black ink all over the rug. His attempts to clean it up only made the mess worse, and eventually he fled from the house, leaving a trail of black footprints. The next morning, he woke up and felt so guilty he decided to go back to the house and offer to pay for the damage. A maid answered the door. She asked him to sit down while she went to fetch the lady of the house. Kelly sat down to wait. He heard a sickening yelp beneath him. Inadvertently he had smothered the woman's little dog. Completely undone, he hid the dog in the grand piano and ran away from the house, never to return.

This story has been repeated by musicians on the road thousands of times. Northwest novelist Tom Robbins even borrowed it for his book *Still Life with Woodpecker*. Of course, as Bill Crow explains in his entertaining collection *Jazz Anecdotes*, as with other "urban legends," the Red Kelly dog story never happened. In fact, Seattle trombonist Mike Hobi originally told Kelly the story while driving to a gig; Kelly, always fond of a humorous tale, started telling it to everyone he met. Over the years musicians began to associate it with Kelly until he became the protagonist. As Kelly told Crow, "Total strangers would come up and say, 'Are you the guy that sat on the dog?' After years of going through this, it got to where I finally resigned myself. . . . I didn't even deny any complicity in it at all. People would come up to me in Florida or someplace and say, 'Are you the guy with the dog?' 'Yeah, that's me.'" As Crow also points out, it's the kind of story that *should* have happened to Kelly, and that's why it stuck. A fellow who started out joining the fife-and-drum corps in an orphanage to get out of doing chores, who took his first gig without knowing how to tune his bass, yet wound up traveling around the world with Woody Herman, probably has a right to think the world is just a trifle upside-down.

Kelly never stopped laughing at life. The Tumwater Conservatory closed after four years, but in 1986 he opened Kelly's, with a sign on the back door that said "Musicians Dressing Room." The door led to a wooden porch with a view of Tacoma. Kelly could usually be found sitting in the darkest corner of the room, behind the bar, asking patrons in a raspy voice why every other joint in town had a sign celebrating a guy named "Nosmo King." In 1998, Kelly celebrated his seventy-first birthday by throwing a party for himself at the club. The best musicians in town came by. Whenever sidemen from modern big bands came through town—Herman, Kenton, James—they always dropped by Kelly's and pulled out their horns. After the music they'd pour themselves a drink and tell all the old war stories. It was an education for the listener, and it was the closest you'd ever find Red Kelly to a school. Kelly's closed in 2003 and Kelly died the following year.

———

Kelly's accomplice in the James gang, Jack Perciful, was another white "renegade" whose career touched on Jackson Street. In *The Swing Era*, Gunther Schuller lists Perciful as one of James's "outstanding" soloists, along with Kelly, Corky Corcoran, Buddy Rich, and Willie Smith. Perciful's credentials as a Pacific Northwesterner date from his Idaho days and a brief stint around Fort Lewis during the war years. The pianist was born in 1925 in Moscow, Idaho, a small university town just six miles across the border from Pullman, Washington. After taking classical piano lessons, Perciful started to learn jazz and pop from a college student who rented a room from his parents. "He got me into the college band," Jack said. "I got into playing a lot of boogie-woogie. Albert Ammons. Pete Johnson. Jay McShann."

When Perciful enrolled at the University of Idaho, he had already been playing with the school band for three years. He was drafted out of the university in 1943, which brought him to Camp Roberts, where he worked in a combo behind Red Skelton. After the service Perciful returned to Moscow to complete his degree. For most of 1949 he toured the West with a funny-hat band called the Jay Makers, led by Red and Jeanne Thompson. (Red Ingle, who later did most of the vocal sound effects in the Spike Jones band, played with the Jay Makers as well.) Perciful completed his degree in classical music and theory, then worked in a trio out of Spokane for a year and a half. As he remembered it, "The leader, Howard Robins, kept telling me, 'Don't go down there to L.A., they'll eat you alive, you'll never make it.' I got tired of hearing that, so I said, 'Howard, find a new piano player. I'm going to L.A.'"

This was November 1962. Perciful immediately found work in the California Club, a Black nightspot in East Los Angeles. After the gig musicians hung out at an all-night barbecue place. "That was the greatest learning process in the world, education right off the street," said Perciful. During this period Nat Cole and Spokane native Jimmy Rowles were Perciful's biggest influences: "Jimmy still is a big influence. I think he's the most creative player there is right now. Whenever I get depressed, or I just get stale or I'm bored, I just put on some Jimmy Rowles and listen to it for about an hour and I feel great." Perciful counted Jess Stacy, Teddy Wilson, Fats Waller, Dodo Marmarosa, and Bud Powell as other influences. He stayed in Los Angeles until 1956, then went to Las Vegas to play with Milt Herth, an old-time organ player from the 1930s. After five months he was just getting ready to leave the gaudy city in the desert when Harry James's manager asked if he would audition. Convinced that auditioning was for beginners, Perciful refused.

> I sent a demo record. Harry liked it and called me back. They sent me a plane ticket, which I cashed in because I was broke. I took a bus to L.A. I was scared to death. I went to the first rehearsal at the Palladium. Harry says, "Jack, you just got here, so you don't know, but be at Capitol tonight at 6 p.m. We're doing an album." It was my first recording of any kind and I was with my heroes. I was twenty-eight, had no idea what I had gotten myself into. I had no intention of staying with the band. I was married and had two kids still in Vegas. But we went on a six-week tour

> and got a Fourth of July three-day shot at the Flamingo Hotel in Las Vegas. That gig was so successful they hired us for ten years.

Perciful worked for James for the next eighteen years, ten of which were at the Flamingo Hotel, three to six months a year. During the rest of the year the band toured the world—South America, Japan, Europe. One of the best musical moments came around 1964 in Lake Tahoe, when he, Buddy Rich, and Red Kelly were the rhythm section. Gary Moore, the comedian, was doing his television show in Tahoe and had brought in his whole crew. "Our band was hot," Perciful said. "Harry laid about an hour-and-fifteen-minute set on them and they were just in tears. . . . The highlight of the James era was the five years with Buddy Rich on drums. This affected me musically more than anything in my whole life—harmonically, lyrically, professionally, attitude-wise." Perciful wrote charts for the James band, including "James Gang," recorded on the *Double Dixie* album, and can be heard on twenty-five records with the bandleader. His favorites were *Double Dixie* and *In a Relaxed Mood*, a sextet album.

Perciful left James in 1974 but stayed on good terms with him, playing in the band in 1980 and 1981 in South America and, later, on a Texas tour. He also did cruises with the James ghost band as well as a public-television special. He said he missed the travel and camaraderie, but "musically, it wasn't that great near the end. I can't really put my finger on it, but it had deteriorated. Harry knew it but didn't do anything about it." While Perciful and Kelly were playing with James, they became roommates and fast friends. When Jack left the band, he joined Red at the Tumwater Conservatory. When the Conservatory folded, Perciful got a job at the Capitol Bar and Grill, in Olympia, playing solo piano. Five years in Olympia gave way to a job with trumpeter Fred Radke (who became leader of the James ghost band) at Seattle's Four Seasons Hotel. In the early 1990s Perciful was playing with Olympia vocalist Jan Stentz and with the excellent Buddy Catlett Trio at the Thirteen Coins, a lounge near Sea-Tac International Airport. Perciful was active as a player locally until a year before he died, in 2008.

———

The wild men—and women—of Seattle's bebop era were not the only white musicians to embrace the new music. While Perciful, Kelly, Greenwell, and the rest were taking their knocks out on the road, another school of beboppers was forming in the ivied halls of the University of Washington. Many of the musicians who were part of this scene—Chuck and Joni Metcalf, Bill Crow, Kenny Kimball, Chuck Mahaffay—forged significant relationships with musicians on Jackson Street that would become the crucible for the jazz culture of the next decade. More than four decades after he wrote it, clarinetist and drummer Mahaffay's article in the July 15, 1949, *DownBeat* still serves as a fine introduction to what came to be known as the Annex Sessions:

> In the last few months, the staid atmosphere surrounding the older buildings on the University of Washington campus has been somewhat shaken by a series of flatted fifths and fast choruses of "How High the Moon." Although these sounds do not carry too far, many students walking through the campus have stopped and wondered if the music they heard was coming from a small building that houses practice rooms for University musicians. Every Friday afternoon, when the rooms are usually empty, a group of campus jazzmen move in and make the most of two or three hours of freewheeling, modern jazz.
>
> The sessions were started early in January. . . . Since then, however, they have become a gathering place for the best musicians on the campus who like to hear and play bop. Those that come have a genuine appreciation for each other's ideas and ability and, as a result, some of the finest modern jazz in the Northwest is being played by this unique group of university students. . . .
>
> A typical Friday meeting starts about 4 p.m. when pianist Kenny Kimball arrives and starts playing a few warm-up choruses. . . . He started the original sessions in January and has since penned three or four of the bop tunes that the boys use for material.
>
> Since the start of the weekly sessions, attendance of both musicians and interested onlookers has greatly increased. This in itself serves to keynote the rising trend toward more bop and modern jazz in the Seattle area as well as on the University campus. . . . One of the more worldly listeners at a recent session remarked, "These guys are the young pioneers of Northwest bop."

Musicians who participated in the Annex Sessions included Chuck Metcalf, bass; Dick Mandle, trumpet; Bill Crow, valve trombone; Ed Jenkins, trumpet; Bernie Bursett, tenor saxophone; Joni Swartz (who would later marry Metcalf), piano and vocals; Floyd Standifer, trumpet; Ernestine Anderson, vocals; Gerald Brashear, saxophone; Bill Dement, a bassist who later went on to become

The Annex Sessions at the University of Washington, 1948. *Left to right:* Dick Mandle, Bill Crow, Bill Dement, Kenny Kimball (piano), Dick Nelson, Bernie Bursett.

a leading dream scholar at Stanford University; Armand Boatman, bass; Bob Dyke, piano; Jim Giles, a tenor saxophonist who became a psychiatrist and also played in local big bands for decades; Al Pace, piano; Kayo Shelton, guitar; Rod Linden, trombone; Rod Levitt, the arranger who would later work with Quincy Jones on Dizzy Gillespie's Middle East tour; and Mahaffay himself, on clarinet. Of these participants, Metcalf and Standifer would become the most important players for the region, but Kimball was the innovator of the Annex scene.

Kenny Kimball had come up through the kid-band circuit with Ronnie Pierce, in the Noteworthies, then studied piano and composition at the University of Washington. While he was leading the Annex Sessions, Kimball also took casual gigs downtown. One day he wandered into Al Siedel's record store and met the great go-between Janet Thurlow, who introduced him to Ray Charles as well as Quincy Jones, Ernestine Anderson, and the rest of the Jackson Street crowd. The pianist fondly recalled leaving the Washington Social Club one night in his 1934 Plymouth with Quincy, Ernestine, and Charlie Taylor in tow. As he became a Jackson Street habitué, Kimball picked up the beboppers' lingo. He said he had to remember not to talk too "hip" at home. Recalled Kimball: "I led a Jekyll-and-Hyde life. In the daytime I was a full-time student at the university. Then at night I'd go on into the jazz world and I'd talk a different language. I had to keep them separate. One of the expressions we had then was that when something was really great, it was 'gone.' One night I forgot myself at the dinner table at home and I said to my dad, 'This pie is gone, Dad.' And he said, 'It is? I thought we had plenty.'" Besides being initiated into the night world of jazz, Kimball had the opportunity to learn an authentic Cuban piano style working with a group at the Olympic Hotel led by Darryl Harpa's former percussionist, Desceito Niego. When Kimball sat in with another Latin bandleader, Raymundo Val, Val asked him to go on the road, which he did, but Kimball soon tired of playing commercial dance music night after night and returned to school.

Kimball graduated in 1952 and began pursuing a master's degree in music but was drafted the following year. He was assigned to the cryptography room of NATO, in Paris—a move that allowed him to fulfill a lifelong dream of studying with the great Parisian composition teacher Nadia Boulanger. As it happened, Quincy Jones had also moved to Paris. Kimball spent an idyllic year (1954–55) in the French capital, cracking codes, studying composition, meeting the woman he would later marry, and hanging out with his old friend "Q." "We went to all the great little clubs," Kimball recalled. "I got a chance to hear Lucky Thompson and all these other marvelous players I'd always heard about. They would sit at the table and talk to Quincy, you know, basking in his glory. I was able to go down and jam at places like the Ringside Club, which I wouldn't even have known about otherwise. I owe an awful lot to Quincy."

That summer, Kimball and his fiancée married in England and came back to the United States by way of New York. Quincy, who was now working for Mercury Records, was on hand to host him again. Ernestine Anderson was in the Big Apple as well. "I remember us walking down Broadway. Quincy had this big coat on, with fur lining just around here [the neck]. I thought, boy, this is real living. All these guys were playing that I'd worshipped all my life. Like Art Farmer, Kenny Dorham, Lennie Tristano, Horace Silver. Art Farmer was going with Ernestine in those days. She was singing at a place called the Page Three down the street in the Village. Quincy and Art took Audrey and me down there to see Ernestine. That was a thrill. Oh, it was just a marvelous night." Kimball returned to Seattle, finishing his degree at the University of Washington in 1955. That same year he took a job teaching music at Centralia College, from which he retired in 1990. Kimball died in 2003.

One of the other lucky university musicians to be initiated into Jackson Street by Janet Thurlow was bassist Bill Crow. Crow, who was playing valve trombone at the time but would later record as a bassist with the Gerry Mulligan Quartet, was, like Kimball, a native Washingtonian. Crow grew up in Kirkland, then a small bedroom community across Lake Washington from Seattle. He'd gone to high school with trumpeter Dick Nelson, who also played on the Annex scene. Crow started on piano, switched to trumpet, then to baritone horn—a small, tuba-like brass band instrument—which he played through the end of high school. He discovered bebop, and the valve trombone, in the Army. In 1949 he decided to enroll at the University of Washington but soon discovered that "the only thing I was interested in was the jam sessions that were going on after school." As students, Crow and drummer Dick Mandle shared a houseboat on Lake Union, which became another key site for the Annex crowd. "Our routine for a while was to get up in the morning, somebody would put the coffee on, and we would start playing while we were still in our pajamas," recalled Crow. "We would play until everybody had to go to class."

Sometime during this idyllic collegiate period, Crow, like everyone else, ran across the hip lady behind the counter at Al Siedel's Music:

> I was looking through the Charlie Parker records, and the girl that was working behind the counter came over and said, "Are you a musician?" I said, "Yes." Her name was Janet Thurlow. She asked me if I had ever been up to the Washington Social and Educational and if I'd met Bumps and if I'd met Ray Charles and if I'd met Quincy. Of course I hadn't, so she took me right up there and introduced me to everybody. Ray Charles was sitting at the piano playing kind of like Bud Powell. I had no idea there was something as good as that going on in Seattle. There was a good band on the stand. Everybody was laughing and dancing and carrying on. I thought, "My god. There's a world here that I never knew about."
>
> Quincy was nice. He said, "Oh, man, we got this big band that I'm writing for. Bumps got a couple of gigs for it. Why don't you come over and rehearse? We need a trombone player." So I came over and I think I was the only white guy on the band. It was the first band like that I'd ever worked with. It was sloppy and out of tune, but there was this strong musical impulse. Everybody had the phrasing down. As soon as I came, Quincy wrote a new chart that had a trombone solo in it on my

part. It was like, "Welcome to the band." It was funny. Everybody in Seattle felt like if you were a musician, you were automatically a member of a secret society and everybody should know everybody.

In 1949 or 1950, Crow and Kimball got a gig with saxophonist Paul McCrea's quartet at the Cirque Club, in the old Broadway Theater at Madison and Broadway. At one point Duke Ellington's vocalist, Ivie Anderson (who recorded "It Don't Mean a Thing If It Ain't Got That Swing"), worked with them for a week. Crow then joined a band with his first great mentor, Buzzy Bridgeford.

> Buzzy was the one who showed me the difference between just keeping time and swinging. I didn't know there was a difference. He danced it out for me one night while playing me some records. It was just like these scales fell from my eyes. I saw what the whole idea was. I have a soft spot in my heart for Buzzy because he really turned my musical life around. He couldn't believe that I had never heard the Basie big-band records with Lester Young. He got out all these records and played them for me. That really added to my education tremendously. He showed me what the rhythm sections were doing. He showed me what Jo Jones was doing, how Shadow Wilson did it differently, and showed me what different drummers did about kicking certain figures. Those were issues that had never occurred to me before.

One night, Buzzy turned to Crow and said, "Look, if you want to be a musician, you got to go where the music is. Let's go to New York." Crow recalled: "I think I only had about fifty dollars cash, my trombone, and a small suitcase full of clothes. We got on the Greyhound bus and came to New York. January 1950." There, Bridgeford introduced Crow to his friend Dave Lambert, who later started the great Lambert, Hendricks, and Ross vocal trio. Buzzy found them a summer job in upstate New York with trumpeter Gene Roland and pianist John Benson Brooks. Fred Greenwell came out from Seattle and also joined the band. Crow started out on trombone, then switched to bass.

Later that year, Crow moved to New York City and entered the mainstream of jazz history. Stan Getz hired him in 1952 and they recorded some excellent sides; Crow went on to work for Claude Thornhill, Terry Gibbs, Marian McPartland, and Gerry Mulligan, with whom he stayed from 1957 to 1965. It's a neat coincidence that Mulligan's famous quartet came to feature Bob Brookmeyer on valve trombone, since Crow had started out on that unusual instrument at the Annex Sessions. Crow recorded several excellent albums with the Mulligan Quartet, including *Live in Boston at Storyville*, *Newport Jazz Festival*, *What Is There to Say?*, *Live at the Village Vanguard*, *The Gerry Mulligan Quartet*, and *Night Lights*. When work slowed with Mulligan, Crow settled down to the life of a jazz and pit-band musician in New York City, playing five years with trombonist Kai Winding at the Playboy Club and eight years in the pit of the Broadway production *42nd Street*.

In 2025, at age ninety-eight, Crow was still playing and was well-known not only as a world-class bassist but also as a superb jazz writer. His monthly humor column for *Allegro*, the journal of Local No. 802, led to the publication of a hilarious and critically well-received compilation, *Jazz Anecdotes*, as well as an autobiography, *From Birdland to Broadway*. Crow's style as a bassist is light, accomplished, swinging, and melodic—qualities that clearly attracted Mulligan and Getz to him. It's tempting to link Crow to the "West Coast" style associated with those saxophonists, given Crow's dues-paying in Seattle, but it would be a misleading connection. Neither the Annex players nor the Jackson Street scene at that point was influenced significantly by the "cool" school. The Seattle scene was steeped in tradition, not in experiment. For Crow, however, the stylistic influence of Seattle is less poignant in his memory than is the milieu of the jazz life generally. "Seattle was where I first began to realize that there was a community of musicians that were supportive of each other and would teach each other stuff and were looking for the fun in the music—a wonderful grapevine of information about jobs and the music itself. It was really the springboard that got me going. It seems ironic that I spent so much time during my school years in the thirties and forties wishing I could be on the jazz scene in New York, when there was so much going on right across Lake Washington that I never knew about."

One of the ironies of the Annex scene was that, although it unfolded on the UW campus, few of the musicians involved were music majors. One of its most important figures, Chuck Metcalf, was studying architecture. Metcalf pointed out perceptively that for him as well as for others in his circle, it was almost a matter of principle *not* to become a professional musician. "Everyone seemed to think they didn't want to make music their career," recalled the bassist, who did not become a bona fide professional himself until 1960. "And if you wanted to be a star, that was bullshit. I never, ever practiced. This is the absolute truth about me, I never practiced the bass until age thirty. That was my idea about my life, that I was going to be an architect in the daytime and a musician when it suited me."

For a guy who started out not wanting to be a professional musician or a star, Chuck Metcalf traveled a rather remarkable distance. A veteran of both Dexter Gordon's and Anita O'Day's groups, and a first-call bassist in San Francisco during the 1970s, Metcalf wound up as one of the dozen or so Seattle musicians to be recognized by anyone but locals. Metcalf was born in 1931 in Grand Rapids, Michigan, and moved to Pasadena when he was six. As a teenager, he attended the historic Gene Norman concert that included Corky Corcoran's "Stardust" solo. His parents, both public-school music teachers, moved to the Northwest in 1946. Metcalf started on violin and piano as a youngster. "When I was eleven or twelve," he said, "I discovered boogie-woogie piano—Meade Lux Lewis and Albert Ammons." "My mother used to come in from the kitchen and say, 'Charles, come to a cadence!' She couldn't understand those unresolved dominant sounds! When Bird's records came out, I was fifteen. I went up to the record shop and I heard it and immediately it was as if Charlie Parker captured my soul. Stan Kenton was on the charts then, so I started listening to that stuff—Woody Herman and Dizzy Gillespie—and I was off into it. Bebop caught my ear right away."

Chuck Metcalf.

Metcalf started to play the bass that year, taking lessons from his mother. At Highline High School, south of Seattle, he played in the school orchestra and in a swing dance band. In 1948 he entered the University of Washington and immediately fell in with the bohemian crowd around the Annex. A trip to San Francisco that year, during which he sat in on piano at Bop City, gave him a vivid and enticing image of *la vie bohème*. "Hey, I was a beatnik in college," he said.

> I was dap. I had my Mr. B collar and my peg pants, a flannel suit with wide rolled lapels and my wide knit tie with a Windsor knot. I was cool. I meant business. I had a pad at 3809 Brooklyn which was actually one of the scenes in the fifties. I had the whole Stan Kenton band over to my pad in 1951 or '52. It was a building dated from Victorian times, probably from the Alaska-Yukon Exposition. It had a [defunct] grocery store in the first floor and an apartment up on top. I just cleared all the shit out, finally put a toilet in the back. The meat locker, I turned into a giant clothes closet for myself. I put foreign newspapers all over the walls and ceiling and

I had apple boxes as a divider. It was kind of like a Mies van der Rohe, beatnik-style thing. I moved a piano in. The people upstairs were kind of intellectual types, so they didn't mind the music. We used to have sessions. Lee Konitz was with the Kenton band when they came up.

Meanwhile, Chuck met Janet Thurlow, who sent him to the East Madison YMCA, where the Brashear brothers were playing.

You can't imagine any more green, naive seventeen-year-old, out of the suburbs, never been around any Black people, totally enthralled by the actual shit happening right in front of his very ears. They let me sit in. They told me not to rush and so I got some of my early training. I knew the tunes and I could play the right notes and that was a rarity among bass players at that time. A bass player that actually played the right notes, the roots of the chord, and knew what they were. Pops Buford, Mike DeFillipis, Traff Hubert, and Floyd Standifer—those four in particular really became role models for me. I just admired them tremendously and found them to be very warm, extremely intelligent, and hip, you know. Almost immediately, I was in demand. I was playing gigs. I quit my job as a busboy at the Roosevelt Hotel because I was making so much more money, and pretty soon I was putting myself through college as a musician. I was having a ball.

In 1951, Metcalf got one of the choicest gigs on Jackson Street—Friday, Saturday, and Sunday at the Black Elks Club, with pianist Paul Neves and drummer Jimmy Raymer. The music at the Elks was on the cusp between bebop and swing, less fiery than East Coast bop but bluesier than California jazz. "See, the Black people could dance to the up tempos," Metcalf explained. "The rhythm sections were basically going *chug-chug-chug-chug-a-chug*, [but] a lot of the tunes were actually bebop." (A 1947 live recording of one of Norm Bobrow's concerts illustrates Metcalf's point nicely. As Pony Poindexter flies over lines inspired by Charlie Parker, drummer Chris Tull plods along in straight swing time.) As a bassist, Metcalf developed quite differently than Bill Crow. The fat tone and raunchy swing attack of club players such as Milt Garred and Al Larkins were Metcalf's main influences, with the recordings of Jimmy Blanton following a close second. "They were playing by the Pops Foster method, which was [to] grab with your whole fist for each note, and go for it. [As for] left-hand technique, I didn't bother with it, because I saw that they weren't. I knew that was the ‘correct’ way, but I was in revolt against classical music, because my parents came from an extremely uptight scene. It was only later that I realized that I really should have taken stuff out of it.”

While he was at the University of Washington, Metcalf fell in love with Joni Swartz, a singer/pianist who had attended Lincoln High School in North Seattle and entered the university in 1949. She was studying music—classical voice—and had been playing jazz and pop piano since she was a teenager. She started to fall by the jam sessions at the Annex. For many years Chuck and Joni Metcalf’s “pad” in the University District—with its grass mats and grand piano—was the center of the scene, and for many Seattleites this couple was what local jazz was all about. Joni’s reminiscence of those idyllic college years appeared as a handwritten prose poem on the back of one of her locally produced albums. It evokes the feeling and spirit of the times better than any press clipping could:

> There were jam sessions every Friday at the U of W HUB. Who could resist? Kenny Kimball and I crawled through an unlocked window in Meany Hall one nite and gave a concert from the darkened stage. Bob Dyke shocked everyone at faculty-student parties with his wild improvisations. I sang over KUOW on a weekly air show produced by Chuck Mahaffay. Ray Charles was working in a small club downtown, and we called him R. C. then. Everyone was digging the Cecil Young Quartet. One night a bass player sailed on Green Lake on his aluminum bass. Jack Korsaw had wild-wild parties on his houseboat every Saturday nite. I married Chuck Metcalf. Our “honeymoon cottage” was an old abandoned store in the “U” District.

Joni Metcalf’s mention of Ray Charles—as yet an obscure lounge pianist—and her own subsequent success as a jazz-inspired cocktail vocalist are a reminder that in the 1940s and 1950s, jazz wasn’t just a matter of bebop quintets and dream bands. As the wild men and women of the beat movement and their ivied cousins at the university pursued the frenetic muse of bop, working musicians on Jackson Street also beat time to a more subtle, accessible culture of commercial trio music. Often their music had as much jazz content as its more obviously jazz-oriented relatives. Ray Charles, among others, forged his early career within that culture.

8 "Straighten Up and Fly Right"

Ray Charles and the Nat Cole Influence

BEBOP AND BLUES DROVE THE imaginations of musicians after World War II, but another influence equally as mighty shaped postwar music, and that was the piano trio. As Pete Barrington suggested earlier, in his comments about the new, peacetime mood, a demand for intimate, romantic music—particularly with vocals—rose after the swing era, perhaps to accommodate soldiers who had come home to their wives and girlfriends. Technology played an important role too. Finally, after years of thumping along in the background, the bass could be heard through a microphone as a melodic instrument, and the amplified electric guitar could soar above a big band. Early piano trios featured either bass and guitar or bass and drums. With all the instruments clearly audible, a new orchestral sound could be created by just three players.

The most influential piano trio of the 1940s was led by Nat Cole. Though Cole later became known as a crooner, he started out as a jazz pianist and virtually invented the piano trio during the 1939–44 period. His trio featured the great Oscar Moore on guitar and Wesley Prince on bass. Moore raised the ante for guitar players by employing sophisticated, "open" voicings, leaving just enough notes in a complex chord to suggest the harmony. The interplay between Cole, Moore, and Prince captured the ears of musicians everywhere. A November 1943 hit record, "Straighten Up and Fly Right," captured the public. By the 1950s, Cole would be an international pop star with his own television show.

Cole's influence over the next twenty years of jazz history has been oddly underplayed, probably because disappointed jazz critics became sidetracked over his defection to pop music. But the issue never was Cole's popular success, it was his ensemble innovation, which, while it has encouraged its share of corny cocktail pianists, also spawned an enduring new genre that has inspired a multitude of fine musicians over the years, among them Diana Krall, the most popular jazz vocalist in the world. Piano trios inspired by Nat Cole flourished in postwar

The Elmer Gill Quartet at the Rocking Chair, 1946. *Left to right:* Juanita Cruse, Gill, Johnny Warren, Jonas Weir.

Seattle. Pianist and vibraphonist Elmer Gill led one of the most durable, helping define intimate, small-group jazz locally.

Gill came to Seattle in 1946 and played there through the end of the 1950s, establishing one of the most important venues in town, the Ebony, along the way. Guitarist Milt Green, a friend of Cole's who had come to Seattle from Minneapolis and later played with Gill, led another prominent trio. A third Nat Cole imitator, R. C. Robinson, also came to Seattle as a youngster to hone his nightclub skills. Robinson was later known as Ray Charles.

Elmer Gill was such an accomplished Cole imitator that Quincy Jones's crowd sometimes referred to him, affectionately, as "Char"—short for "charcoal," the tone of Nat Cole's complexion. Like Gerald Wiggins, Gill came to Seattle after being discharged from Fort Lewis. A short, stocky man full of sparkling energy and a continuous line of talk, Gill spoke in a quick, halting clip, with a hint of a lisp. He grew up in Indianapolis, Indiana, a few blocks from the Montgomery brothers (Wes, Monk, and Buddy), studied piano from the age of nine, and attended the Cosmopolitan School of Music. He formed his first band as a senior in high school and enrolled as a chemistry major at Indiana State Uni-

The exclusive Old Rocking Chair Club, at 115 Fourteenth Avenue South.

versity in 1942. Erskine Hawkins on the jukebox, big bands on the road, and church music filled the gaps in his musical education. Gill recalled: "Some of the first experiences I remember with something that swung [were] in a vacant lot about five blocks from our house. They would set up one of those 'holy roller' churches in a tent. Boy, we'd go down there, my brother and I, they'd be inside of this church and they'd have tambourines and everything. The preacher would be preaching, man, and they would be swinging like you wouldn't believe. You felt like telling them to take another chorus."

Gill had no intention as a youngster of becoming a professional musician, but two years in the Army changed all that. When he found himself unemployed in Tacoma in May 1946 with two other ex-service musicians, bassist Johnny Warren and saxophone player/vocalist Jonas Weir, the three formed a trio and got a job at the newly opened Rocking Chair Club, on Fourteenth Avenue South, just off Yesler Way. Later they added vocalist Juanita Cruse. Before they knew it, each of the band members was making $100 a week in tips. "I started in playing there and I've been in the music business for forty-two and a half years," laughed Gill. "The first fifteen years, I wasn't out of work six weeks."

The Rocking Chair started out in 1933 as the Blue Rose, operated by Bill Bowman, the Chicago promoter who kicked off the early jazz scene up in Vancouver, British Columbia. In 1945, "Big Lewis" Richardson opened the Old Rocking Chair in the same building. Richardson was an old friend of Count Basie's. When Basie was in town, he and his men would often drop by the Rocking Chair after hours. It was an exclusive place. Situated in a tall house with a fake-brick exterior and a tall chimney, the tiny club had a small bandstand with an upright piano. The decor was red and black, with leather-upholstered booths and an elegant bar. Customers dressed up. Downstairs was a bar, kitchen, and bandstand; upstairs, a card room. The club ran from midnight until morning and was hard to get into, unless you knew someone. You had to pass through two doors to get in.

The bar at the Rocking Chair, late 1940s. *Third and fourth from right (seated at bar):* Bruce Rowell, who worked for Noodles Smith, and Bob Frazier, a club bouncer.

At the entrance, "Cabdaddy" would hail taxis and watch for police. If there was a raid, the doorman pressed a button under the carpet. "It would make all the lights flash inside in the bar," according to Gill. "They'd pour all the whiskey down the drain and everybody would be drinking Coca-Cola when they'd get in there." The Rocking Chair crowd loved the blues. "Sometimes," Gill remembered, "we'd start in playing the blues at twelve o'clock, and at four o'clock in the morning we were still playing the same blues. Everybody would come up and take their turn singing or playing. In those days, man, we just played for the playing. There wasn't any categories like they're having now. People played from their soul."

Gill stayed at the Rocking Chair until August, then went back to school in Terre Haute, Indiana. When he realized he could make more money in a weekend playing music than college graduates were earning in a week, he got more serious about becoming a professional musician. After returning to Seattle in 1947, he worked in Portland with guitarist Al Mitchell, then was back in Seattle at the Sessions Playhouse (the old Entertainer's Cabaret, where Jelly Roll Morton had played), first with Al Hickey and Al Larkins, and later with Johnny Warren and guitarist Buster Coates. Gill then took a steady job after hours at the Black and Tan for ten months. The tips were so good, he never even opened his pay envelope.

The Question Marks at the Spinning Wheel, ca. 1952. *Left to right:* Elmer Gill, Bob Braxton, Duke Moore, Milt Price.

Gill had a knack for finding good jobs. He also refused to fall in line with a system that kept Black musicians working after hours for tips. For the next two years he ensconced himself at the Spinning Wheel, downtown on Second Avenue, in a group called the Question Marks, with Bob Braxton (alto saxophone and vocals), Duke Moore (drums), and Milt Price (guitar). By this time Gill was playing marimba and vibes as well as piano and had turned into an all-around entertainer, doing vocals, leading the band, and writing arrangements. *Billboard* magazine reported, "Braxton's . . . billing as 'Seattle's Billy Eckstine' is not unwarranted. He's better than good." (Braxton lived up to such praise with a luxurious vocal on his own record of "Summertime.")

In the summer of 1952, Gill was lured to Anchorage, Alaska, with Al Hickey and Duke Moore, in hopes of earning big wages. The pay was excellent, but Gill disliked the cold weather and raw pioneer edge of the town. He gave notice and flew back to Seattle. With cash in his pocket, no commitments, and nowhere in particular to go, he bought a car, filled the gas tank, and headed for California. In San Francisco he jammed with Pony Poindexter at Jimbo's Bop City, then continued down the coast.

> I drove to Los Angeles. I was just driving down the street and I looked up at the Paramount Theater and here was a sign that said Lionel Hampton's orchestra was playing there. I knew Quincy was with the orchestra, so I wheeled into the parking lot and I go backstage to the theater. The band was out on the stage, playing. I waited until they got off, and I spoke to Quincy. Quincy told me, he said, "You know, Milt Buckner's just left the band. If you think you'd like to have a gig, I'll introduce you to Hamp." So Hamp had them bring his vibes back. He had a little piano back there and he asked me would I play "Tenderly," I played "Tenderly" and he hired me right then! I put on a uniform and played the very next show with them, at the Paramount. . . . I stayed with them the next year and a half.

Ernestine Anderson joined Hamp while Elmer was still with the band. Quincy, Gill, and Ernestine all played for Dwight D. Eisenhower's presidential inauguration. In New York, Hamp decided to take the band to Europe; however, the terms of the tour were so fuzzy that Gill and Ernestine decided against the trip, fearing they might get stranded abroad. Gill returned to Seattle, where he would be instrumental in the struggle to integrate the Black and white musicians' unions.

When Gill was playing at the Black and Tan, another jazz trio, led by guitarist Milt Green, also was becoming known around town, at the 908 Club, Doc Hamilton's old stomping grounds. Green grew up in Minneapolis in the same neighborhood as pianist Julian Henson, where he had also known Leon Vaughn. Green was a light-skinned, fine-featured fellow who had blue eyes and sometimes passed for white. "He modeled himself on Charlie Christian—real crisp, and trying to keep it melodic," recalled Vaughn. Green arrived in Seattle in the late 1930s. Guitarist Al Turay remembered jamming with Green and Junior Raglin. In 1945 Green persuaded Henson, who had returned to Minneapolis, to come out and form a trio with bassist Bob Marshall for the 908 Club. It turned out to be a good move. Their recording on Seattle's Linden Records of "My Last Affair" showcased the trio's elegant, Nat Cole style, with Green's insouciant vocals answered by Henson's twinkling piano. Said Henson: "We went to work at nine o'clock and very rarely got off before four or five. One night, we made fourteen hundred dollars in the kitty."

Elmer Gill collage with Lionel Hampton band, 1952. The band featured several Seattle musicians. Center circle, Gill (*left*), Hampton (*right*); (*bottom center*) Ernestine Anderson; (*left side, in trumpet section, second from right*) Quincy Jones; (*below trumpet section*) Monk Montgomery.

The 908 Club had changed since Doc Hamilton had gone to prison for his dice games. By 1946 the club had been bought by Dick Ruffin and Nixie Smith, who toned down the gambling but kept the refined atmosphere. "The 908 Club was one of the finest," recalled Henson. "They had the old dining-car waiters and a chef in the kitchen called Honeysuckle that could make a piece of cardboard taste fine. Steaks and chicken, you never tasted anything like it in your life. Fine service. And they had these nice, dark lights. We played nice, soft music. It was a nice atmosphere." In this lounge-style ambience, which was to set the tone for the 1950s, Ruffin and Smith catered to rich whites and celebrities, just as Doc Hamilton had. Dave Beck, leader of the Teamsters union, was a regular. Judges and lawyers came by frequently. Actress Diana Barrymore had been seen there. So had many entertainers—including Nat Cole himself, whom Henson met at a concert one night:

> Nat Cole came to Seattle and the microphone went wrong, so he went down underneath the stage and I followed him in there. I asked him if he wanted a drink and he said, "No, but my bass player needs one real bad." We told him where we was working at, so from that time, he'd come out to the 908 Club whenever he was in town. He was a real gentleman, a sophisticated, nice person. With no advertising at all, it was unbelievable, he would come to the club and it would be just packed. I don't know how it got around! He was gracious to people. He would play.

Sometimes Cole would socialize after the gig. "When King Cole came to Seattle, after the show, he came out to Milt's house," said Leon Vaughn. "I can kick myself now for not having recorded King Cole all night long with the songs that he sang and played, as we were drinking and telling lies and stuff about our one-night stands."

Seattle's early lounge trios broke up and regrouped over the years. Julian Henson moved to Portland in 1948, where he pursued a successful career as a lounge player. Green stayed at the 908 for seven or eight years. Between 1952 and 1958 he worked R & B social-club dates with tenor saxophonist Floyd Franklin and opened a pool hall, Milt's Recreations, at Twelfth Avenue and Jefferson; by 1964 he had relocated to Twenty-Third Avenue and Union. Green was a regular on Norm Bobrow's extravaganzas and often worked with Elmer Gill, first at the Spinning Wheel, then at the Caballero, on Sixth. Gill, Bob Braxton, Duke Moore, and Green played in Vancouver, British Columbia, at the Pacific National Exhibition in 1951. Green died in 1983.

The lounge era affected the focus of solo piano players as well as jazz groups. There had always been a market for "singles," as they are known in the business—Oscar Holden and Palmer Johnson were good examples—but early solo pianists were all-around "piano professors," playing a variety of material from Tin Pan Alley tunes to light classics. After the war a new, "mellow" style of cocktail pianist/singer emerged, in the style operative today in hotel lounges. Though the majority of the players who worked in this vein were, and continue to be, purveyors of pianistic clichés, there were a few local singles with jazz backgrounds. One of the most important was Ernie Hatfield, a delightful swing-era pianist and vocalist who worked two years with Ella Fitzgerald and performed at the Seattle Tennis Club into the 1990s.

Hatfield, among many other accomplishments, had the honor of being one of the first musicians ever to appear on television. It was 1940, and he was working with a vocal quartet called the Four Keys, which would later back up Ella Fitzgerald. "There were only 300 [television] sets in the whole country," stated the affable pianist, who in 1987 was still remarkably fit. "It was a station in Philadelphia—WPTZ. It was so hot under those lights it wasn't even funny. The monitor they had was a huge cabinet with about a six-inch picture." Hatfield, who was born in Chester, Pennsylvania, formed the Four Keys with his classmates the brothers Bill, Slim, and Arthur Furness. The group became well-known in the Philadelphia area and had a weekly radio program featuring spirituals. Said Hatfield of the era:

> At that time, there were lots of trios—the Andrews Sisters, and so forth—then all of a sudden they became quartets—the Mills Brothers, the Ames Brothers. Slim wanted to get this real deep and close quartet harmony, like the Modernaires were doing at the time. After about three years we had a call from New York because Chick Webb had died. Ella had been with Chick's band. They put her with the orchestra after he died, but the men in the band didn't respect her, so now they were looking for something to put with her. So we went up there and the man said, "Just sing something." So we sang "I've Got It Bad and That Ain't Good," and everything just blended right together. Moe Gale—he was the manager of the Ink Spots—said, "That's it!" and he pulled the bottle out of his bottom drawer and sealed the deal.

Hatfield and the Four Keys worked with Ella two years (1942–43), touring the Eastern seaboard and making eight records for Decca, among them "I'm Gettin' Mighty Lonesome" and "Mama Come Home." Hatfield had fond memories of those years in New York. He recalled one night when Ella and the Four Keys spontaneously composed a song he remembered as "Fuji Boo" while driving to a gig. Another evening, Jay McShann accidentally introduced the group as "Ella Keys and the Four Fitzgeralds." Hatfield worked with Clyde McCoy's band and at the Onyx Club, on Fifty-Second Street, on the same program as Billie Holiday.

The Four Keys disbanded in 1943 and Hatfield was drafted. After three years in the service he returned to play piano around Philadelphia in a quartet called the Dial Tones. One day he received a call from drummer Jimmy White, who had been working across the street from him in Atlantic City. "Jimmy said he was putting together an act to come out west because he'd married a girl from here," Hatfield recalled. "They guaranteed us fifty weeks out of the year. We piled into the car—it was a brand new Buick Roadmaster, so I knew we wouldn't have any trouble getting out here—all three of us, and drove out in three days."

Hatfield found the musicianship in Seattle stood up pretty well to New York's and Philadelphia's, but, like Roscoe Weathers before him, he was appalled by requests from customers for country music. "You don't find anybody in Pennsylvania that goes for western music. Nobody." The Jimmy White Trio—with White, Hatfield, and Duke Johnson on bass—worked all over Washington, Montana, and Colorado, and up and down the West Coast. When White decided he wanted to take the band to Southeast Asia, Johnson went to Hawaii, instead;

Hatfield was stranded. "I had to get a job," he said. "I had just written to my wife and six-month-old baby to come out, so I went down to Boeing and got a job as a mechanic." Two and a half years later, Hatfield got on as an evaluator with the State of Washington, where he stayed until retiring in 1977.

Like so many other musicians trying to make ends meet, when Hatfield finished his day gig, he changed clothes and went back to work. One of the first players he met was Stan Payne, an outstanding tenor saxophonist who had recorded several sides in 1939 with Billie Holiday, including "Them There Eyes," "Strange Fruit," and "Fine and Mellow." Hatfield and Payne started working at Fort Lawton every Sunday at the Officers' Club, then moved to McChord Air Force Base. Hatfield also worked with Payne and drummer Myrt Francois (Patti Bown's inspiration) at Coe's Tavern. During the 1980s he was the senior member of a swing-to-bebop group, the Inner City Jazz Quartet, with Jabo Ward (tenor saxophone), Terry Morgan (bass), and Peter Madsen (drums). In the early 1990s Hatfield worked at the Seattle Yacht Club two nights a week and occasionally played casuals. He died in 2002. His son, Bryan "Jammin On Cuts" Hatfield, carried on the family musical legacy in the 1980s as a member of Seattle's first generation of hip-hop artists.

One of Hatfield's favorite musicians in Seattle was another "single" pianist, Winfield King, the son of LeEtta Sanders King, an important early piano teacher who had moved to Seattle from Yakima, Washington. King was playing in Seattle groups by the late 1930s, when he succeeded Palmer Johnson at the Two Pals and sometimes subbed for Al Pierre. Pops Buford remembered working with King for several years during the 1960s. In Pops's opinion King was one of the best musicians in the area. King died in 1976.

The other important piano single in town was Derneice "Melody" Jones, a Seattle institution who worked regularly in the early 1990s in the foyer lounge of Lofurno's Italian restaurant, one of the last places where the old Jackson Street flavor persisted, until it closed in 1993. A heavy-set, modest but tough woman with a cute voice and a wonderful sense of humor about life, Melody was a trouper whose life was a slice of jazz history that could be heard through her fingers. She was born in Chicago in 1907 and moved to Harrisburg, Pennsylvania, where she started piano lessons at age seven. After graduating from high school, Jones moved to New York City, where she lived with her aunt in Harlem. She learned to play Bach on the organ and to accompany movies on the Wurlitzer, at the Alhambra Theatre. She also played at the Lafayette Theatre, where Fats Waller was featured. (When Waller went on a binge, Melody sometimes sat in for him.) After the stock market crash of 1929, Melody began to get "hands-on" lessons, literally, from Waller at Harlem "rent parties."

> Mr. Waller used to play house-rent parties. He would book five or six of them and have me and other piano players go and keep the music going until he could get there. The house-rent party usually ended up with some kind of jam session sometime during the course of the party. A man like Waller, who knew a lot of musicians, would draw big crowds. He used to put out a card that said, "Talk, Mr. Rabbit; Skip, Mr. Bear; and Mr. Thomas Fats Waller will positively be there."
>
> Fats called me "Baby Sis." People thought we were some relation, because we were both so fat! He took my hands in his and showed me the walking bass and how to play tenths. One of his hands was as big as my two together. He told me, "Pay strict attention to your left hand, but whenever you play your right hand, let your melody stand out."
>
> Fats taught me one or two of the tunes that he had written so that if people asked for them, I could play them. Many were double-entendre tunes. In those days, in the cabarets they always featured one singer who did what we called the dirty songs, the double-entendre songs. While the orchestra and the show were resting, we moved the piano up to the side of the table where there was a party that wanted to hear something like that, and we would play and sing just for them. They had a piano with a short keyboard. They called us "floor girls."

When Franklin D. Roosevelt was elected president, Jones got work with federal theater projects as a rehearsal pianist and accompanist. In 1941 she worked with USO shows up and down the Atlantic seaboard and all through the South. The following year, she entertained troops in the Far East, working in the Philippines, New Guinea, Indonesia, and the South Pacific. In the Philippines, Jones met a warrant officer from Seattle who asked her to marry him. He also gave Jones her nickname: "When he heard me play the piano, he said, 'You sound something like Fats Waller.' I told him what Fats had said about playing the melody and he said, 'That's just the name for you—Melody.'" When the war was over, Jones's fiancé suggested they move to his beloved hometown of Seattle. Melody was unenthusiastic. She had been there on her way to East

Melody Jones at the Showbox Theater, 1947–48.

Asia and hadn't been impressed. "I got here at the time of year when it was rainy season. They had a camp down there in the middle of Fourth Avenue called Camp Jordan. Our building was at Jefferson Park, which was a mud puddle. We had to make fires in open stoves, with wet wood. We tried to heat the water to take our baths so that we could do the shows. We worked in three feet of mud and rain. When I met my husband and he told me he was from Seattle, I said, 'You couldn't give me a telegraph pole in Seattle.'" Reservations aside, Melody made the move and things turned out better than expected. Her husband's uncle, it developed, was Gus West, who booked the Black Elks Club, on Jackson Street. Gus introduced Melody to Al Pierre, who hired her to play pipe organ afternoons at the Showbox Theater, before the band came on. The Showbox gig ended early. Afterward, Melody and some of Pierre's men would occasionally work after hours at the New Chinatown. Other nights, Melody subbed for Elmer Gill in Johnny Warren's group at the Black and Tan. Despite abundant local work, Melody and her husband shipped out again, to Asia. From Japan she broadcast "foxhole shows" over Air Force Radio to Korea and played in Pusan for the Air Force. The Asian stint was followed by four years in Europe. In 1956 she settled in Seattle for good.

By the time Jones had returned to Seattle, piano bars had come into vogue, and Melody, a swing-era player with a Harlem-stride background, found work in hotel lounges, among them the Mayflower, on Pine Street. Sometimes she worked in a combo with Al Larkins and Milt Green; she also played with white drummer Dave Coleman and Pony Poindexter at the Ebony. Jones counted Larkins as her biggest influence in Seattle. "I had known [pianist] Ellis Larkins in New York, so when I met his brother out here it was like sort of a reunion," she said. "Al Larkins introduced me to the musicians. Just before he died, we started giving jazz concerts in schools. He was teaching at Franklin [High School]."

As part of her concerts, Jones lectured the Franklin kids about the struggles she experienced as a woman instrumentalist in jazz. In the early days of jazz, she told the students, women were relegated to the "girl singer" role. At the time of her interviews in the late 1980s, Jones had been in the trenches for five decades fighting that stereotype. She also pointed out that dark-skinned girls like herself were often shunned in show business, even by Black promoters, who preferred "high yellows," the light-skinned Black women favored as chorus girls at the Cotton Club and elsewhere during the 1920s and 1930s. In Seattle, however, Jones said she found neither racial nor gender prejudice to be as deeply ingrained as elsewhere. She also found several strong women players in Seattle.

> There had been a girl here who played with Bumps Blackwell [probably Patti Bown]. She had done quite well. Then there was another girl named Elise Blye, who lives now in Portland. She was a very fabulous woman pianist. I worked also with this girl Myrt Francois. She played the drums. We formed a team one time and called ourselves Melody and Mirth. We worked all through Montana. Ruth Rhymer was a drummer who came to the Washington Social Club with Elise Blye. At times, Ruth would work for Terry Cruise. And Bea Smith worked at the Colony for a long time. Beatrice Smith. She was a great blues singer.

Two other female "singles" found an enthusiastic following in Seattle in the cocktail lounge era, although neither was part of the Jackson Street scene. Thurston County pianist Ruby Bishop, who led a band called the Centralia Buccaneers in 1932, brought a lilting, filigree style to the Mayflower Hotel in the 1960s. After an Asian tour for soldiers in Korea and Vietnam, she became a popular fixture at the Roosevelt Hotel. Bishop was a multitalented woman who also worked as a court reporter, beautician, and cabinetmaker. She remodeled the kitchen of her home in Leschi, which had a magnificent view of Lake Washington and walls festooned with sheet music. The display echoed the wry sense of humor she sometimes manifested onstage. One of the tunes pasted on her living room wall was the 1906 hit "If the Man in the Moon Were a Coon." After a late-life comeback at the popular Madison Street bar and restaurant Vito's, Bishop was inducted into the Seattle Jazz Hall of Fame in 2016. She died in 2019 at the age of ninety-nine.

Merceedees Walton (born Mercedes Welcker) was more of a torch diva than a jazz artist—*Seattle Post-Intelligencer* columnist Emmett Watson once excoriated fellow journalist Doug Welch for daring to tarnish Merceedees Walton's name with the label "jazz"—but she conveyed deep feeling with a rich alto voice that, in Watson's apt words, was "full of winter nights and rainy streets and far away places." A couple of reel-to-reel tapes she left behind reveal an unremarkable stride pianist who did not play flashy solos, but whose time and flow gracefully underpinned the music-hall-flavored songs she favored, many of which she appears to have written herself. (Before she came to Seattle from New York, two of her songs had been recorded by Jimmie Lunceford and Glenn Miller.) Working under the stage name Merceedees, she became a Seattle institution with her own show for several years on KING-TV. Sadly she fell into a deep depression in the 1960s and lived as a recluse until she died in obscurity in 2000.

Melody Jones, by contrast, continued to perform long enough to collect the acclaim she well deserved. In 1993 she was inducted into the Seattle Jazz Hall of Fame, three years before she died, in 1996. While Jones was held in high regard, one of her most important contributions to Jackson Street went largely unacknowledged. In 1948, while working at the Black and Tan, Jones was indirectly responsible for the arrival of the greatest Nat Cole imitator of them all, Ray Charles. Jones recounted:

> One night, a fellow named Garcia McKee came into the Black and Tan. He told me that he was looking for work and he was a guitar player. I was getting ready to leave [for a USO job in Germany]. I said, "There's plenty of work here. I could give you four or five spots if you could get a piano player." Garcia said, "I have a friend who's a marvelous piano player. He imitates King Cole, but he plays beautiful piano and he sings well." I said, "He would do well here. Can you get him? If you can, I'll pass

> this job that I'm working on over to you." So he got in touch with his piano player. I loaned him the money and Ray Charles came up here on a Trailways bus.

Thus began a new era in Seattle music. Nine months after Quincy Jones moved to Seattle, and four years after Ernestine Anderson came up from Texas, in March 1948, Ray Charles embarked on a project that would turn the world of American popular music upside down. Blind, ambitious, and a mere seventeen years old, Charles spent just over two years in Seattle, forging many close alliances, both musical and personal, as well as making his first appearances on radio and television and recording his first single. Although he wasn't yet performing in the rock style that he would invent and become famous for, Charles would exert a profound musical influence on the Seattle scene. Likewise, the city's high-rolling nightlife gave him the opportunity to develop into a well-rounded musician.

Ray Charles Robinson was born in 1930 and raised by his mother in a country shack in Greenville, Florida, near the Georgia border. He was not born blind. His sight was claimed by glaucoma, a deteriorating disease that could have been treated had he been raised in different circumstances. By age seven he was totally blind. Charles learned Braille and how to play the piano and clarinet at the Florida State School for the Blind, in Saint Augustine. He spent summers at home, where his mother prepared him well for independence, treating him as a sighted child, teaching him to chop wood, haul water, and do chores. In his autobiography *Brother Ray*, Charles wrote that he even rode a bicycle around the countryside; once, for the sheer thrill of it, he started up a tractor in the school parking lot.

When Charles was fifteen, his mother died, and the young man struck out on his own. He moved in with friends of his parents in Jacksonville, then spent two difficult years on his own, scuffling in blues and jazz bands, at one point going on the road through the South. Even at this early phase in his career, Charles was an eclectic, versatile player, comfortable with gospel, blues, swing, and commercial crooning. In the fall of 1947 he moved to Tampa and worked in a seven-piece, Louis Jordan–style band led by Charlie Brantley. It was in Tampa, in 1947, that R. C. met guitarist Garcia McKee, in a summer rehearsal band at Florida A&M University. The band included in its ranks bassist Sam Jones and alto saxophonist Julian "Cannonball" Adderley. Charles and McKee played together as a duo at Drew Air Force Base for about six months. McKee had worked up an imitation of Oscar Moore's complex harmonies and steady beat, and R. C. was singing as close to Nat Cole's crooning as he could. Said Charles in *Brother Ray*, "During all these years I was imitating Nat Cole. To me, it was practically a science. I worked at it, I enjoyed it, I was proud of it, and I loved doing it. He was a guy everyone admired, and it just made sense to me, musical and commercial sense, to study his technique."

The club owner at the base was impressed by the young duo and encouraged them to take their act out of town. But Charles was skeptical: He had just moved in with a girl named Louise, and he didn't want to leave her behind. He was also somewhat apprehensive about leaving the South for points unknown—a not-uncommon attitude for Southern Black folks at the time, even more understandable for a blind teenager. However, Charles eventually agreed to leave town with McKee. "I told Ray Charles," said McKee, "I said, 'Listen, let's get away,' and he says, 'Where?' and I said, 'Well, I'll get a map!' and I went and got a map and we decided we wanted to go as far away from Tampa as we could go, so we wouldn't know nobody!" Together, they found a town in the upper left-hand corner of the map—Seattle—which seemed faraway and exotic. "I didn't know anyone living up there, and I hadn't heard a thing about the town," explained Charles. "It just seemed like a reasonable place to go. All mystery and adventure. I also liked the fact that it was way on the other coast—real far away. That term—West Coast—was appealing to me. I came from the woods, and the idea of heading west was enticing as hell."

McKee left first. As soon as he got to Seattle, he went to the Black and Tan, where he met Melody Jones. Melody's uncle Gus booked a room at the Coast Hotel for Charles and loaned McKee $100 to bring Ray out. Garcia left a message for Ray at a Tampa pool hall. After five days and nights on the bus, the hot, sweaty, tired seventeen-year-old arrived at the depot, unannounced. He had no idea how to find McKee. Always the survivor, Charles called the police department and several radio stations, asking them to broadcast McKee's name, and to say that his friend R. C. had arrived. McKee remembered:

> A guy who had seen me around told me, "You know, there's a blind guy down at the bus station looking for you." So I went down to the bus station and they said [they] had told him I lived at the Coast Hotel. I went on back there and that's when I found him, sitting down, waiting for me. I let him get some sleep, we went and ate

> at a little place up on Jackson Street that was open twenty-four hours. Then I took him down to the Black and Tan that night . . . because Melody told me that's where she was going to be. Elmer Gill was playing piano, Johnny Warren was playing bass, and a Caucasian boy was playing guitar [probably Al Turay]. Nice group. Melody introduced us to all the people and asked us to play. We went into our act. This is the very first night. We played all these pretty tunes, didn't need nothing behind us. That's how we got the job at the Elks Club.

"We were astounded at how young he was and how well he played," recalled Melody.

Charles and McKee played as a duo at the Black Elks Club for several months. It was a popular place. Unaffiliated with the more widely known Elks Club, which did not admit Black people, the Black Elks Club was part of Seattle Lodge 109 of the African American organization called the Improved Benevolent and Protective Order of Elks of the World (IBPOEW, for short), which had begun presenting holiday dances in Seattle as early as 1919. In 1943, not long after moving its home office to South Jackson Street, the organization opened one of the city's most popular late-night music venues. It was situated on the north side of Jackson, between Maynard and Seventh, upstairs, in the ornate white building called the Rainier Heat & Power Company Building, which is still standing. A large, smoky, low-ceilinged establishment peppered with cocktail tables, the Black Elks offered people a place to socialize in an atmosphere where they could also drink. The kitty was a cigar box. A huge elk's head that musicians used to duck behind to smoke joints was mounted near the piano. The place could accommodate about two hundred people and was known for its excellent barbecue sandwiches and as a place where name entertainers often dropped by after their gigs; the clientele was cool enough not to make a fuss over them when they did.

The Black Elks Club had a running card game; other vices could be satisfied there as well. Leon Vaughn remembered being introduced at the Elks to *yen pah*, a concoction made from the scrapings from an opium pipe, which were then poured into a drink or put on the lip and sipped with coffee. The crowd at the Black Elks was racially mixed but mostly Black. "The lady that did the cooking at the Elks Club was named Georgia Kemp," recalled Melody Jones. "Ray used to sing that song to her, 'Georgia.' She liked him very much. I rented a room at Mrs. Kemp's house. I was leaving, so Garcia asked me, 'When you leave, Mrs. Jones, can we have your room for Ray?'"

The Black Elks Club, 662 South Jackson Street.

Charles moved into Kemp's house on Twentieth Avenue, near East Madison Street. She had a grand piano, and she enjoyed letting musicians rehearse on it. She also liked to take care of players who were down on their luck. She was from the South and frequently cooked one of Charles's favorite Southern comfort foods, red beans and rice. Comfortably ensconced at Georgia Kemp's and secure with his new gig, Ray played with McKee at the Elks Club throughout the spring of 1948. The young Floridian soon convinced his girlfriend, Louise, to come out and live with him. Life was good. R. C. Robinson began a youthful idyll in Seattle, working one of the best jobs in town, "keeping house," as he put it, with Louise, and making friends with local musicians. Charles recorded his first impressions vividly:

> The entertainment business was in something of a boom. Competition was fierce. Many cats had just left the armed-forces bands—and don't think those outfits couldn't play. In one respect it was just like Tampa: There were lots of musicians roaming the streets who'd blow your ass off the stand if you gave 'em half the chance. . . . Cat called Bumps Blackwell had a well-known combo around Seattle. . . . And there was also my good friend Gerald Brashear. . . . There were a lot of faces around Seattle, and I tried to make mine familiar so I could keep working. The McSon Trio [Charles, McKee, and bassist Milt Garred] played all over—Fort Lawton, Kirkland, Tacoma, and places in Seattle like the Washington Social Club or the 908 Club. . . . I could see that in a city like Seattle—a place which was more sophisticated and open than what I was used to—my act was going to pay off.

Nearly everyone from the period remembered Charles as a versatile musician and a playful, remarkably independent person. "Everybody liked him," said Elmer Gill. "He didn't make any special deal about his being blind. He was just one of the boys. He'd walk all over town, never had a cane. Never used a dog or nothing. He'd come in always smiling and carrying on." Sonny Booker remembered: "I'd see him walking downtown. He'd be by himself always—and he'd walk right alongside of the curb, just as fast as anybody else, just—*boom! boom! boom!*—there'd go Ray. And you'd say, 'Hi, Ray,' and he'd say, 'Hi, how're ya doing?' and he'd just keep on going." Buddy Catlett added: "We went on for about a year before we knew that he was an orphan. He'd keep saying his parents were on vacation. He wouldn't tell anyone he was taking care of himself."

The Maxin Trio, 1948. *Left to right:* R. C. Robinson (Ray Charles), Garcia McKee, Milt Garred.

In the summer of 1948, Charles landed a regular job at the Rocking Chair. As Elmer Gill had discovered two years earlier, the crowd there demanded raucous music. Charles and McKee hired a bass player to drive the group. Milt Garred was twenty-four years old, a friendly, round fellow who had moved to Seattle from West Virginia. A monstrous swinger with a huge, booming sound, Garred became an immensely important figure on the Seattle scene. Fred Greenwell described him as "the Seattle Wilbur Ware . . . gigantically talented," and Traff Hubert, bass player and longtime connoisseur of jazz history, counted Garred as his "favorite bass player of all time." Charles agreed. "He was a real funky bass player. He had that old nasty sound. Milt was a very strong player. I would say that Milt was the glue of the trio, I really would, honestly. I was the quote, star, unquote, of the trio, but Milt was the glue." After Milt joined, the group changed its name to the McSon Trio—a combination of the musicians' names, McKee and Robinson. (Later, the name was changed to the Maxin—then the Maxim—Trio.)

The ensemble played at the Rocking Chair for most of the rest of 1948. It was a plum gig, one of the only regular-paying jobs in town where the salary was worth as much as the kitty. "All the rounders, pimps, and the working girls would come and throw the twenty-dollar bills for us to play 'Nature Boy' and 'To a Wild Rose' to the women," remembered McKee. In addition to blues and progressive numbers in the style of Nat Cole, one of the McSon Trio's specialty numbers at the Rocking Chair was a version of Frankie Laine's "Mule Train," a novelty number that featured the rhythmic "snap" of a whip against the hide of a mule. Recounted McKee:

> Ray Charles got him a cap pistol and we got a belt, and whenever we would play "Mule Train" he would take the belt and hit on the piano like it was the horses and he would take the cap pistol and shoot it. That was our act. But [one day] Ray was out of caps, and instead of asking me to get them for him—he was so independent, he wanted to do it himself, and he never did use a cane or a dog, never did in his life—he went downtown and he was waiting for the bus to come along and he had the pistol in his hand, and the police came along there and told him to "Get back up against the wall!" The guys who were standing there, they said, "Man, that guy's blind!" And of course they were red-faced. And he said, "That's just a cap pistol. I wasn't attempting to rob that place. I just need some ammunition. Yessiree!"

Charles continued to add new tunes to his repertoire at the Rocking Chair. The house singer, Juanita Cruse, and another Rocking Chair vocalist, Bea Skaggs, introduced him to some of the material he would later become famous for, including "Just for a Thrill." Charles said he didn't remember Skaggs, but everyone remembers the smooth and sexy blues Charles himself added to his repertoire, in honor of the club—"Rocking Chair Blues." Charles and McKee both claimed authorship of the tune, though neither seemed to care enough to argue about it. The lyrics are mostly generic, and the fictional characters, such as "Dubonnet Judy" and "Gin Fizz Flo," bear no relation to the actual people who worked at the club, though there's one line that pegs the blues in soggy Seattle: "If you don't have your rubbers, take a taxi down." It's fitting that Charles commemorated the Rocking Chair with a blues song, because the McSon Trio is largely remembered for shaking the rafters there with house-rocking music.

The new demand for shuffle tempos and "down-home" blues reflected the demographic changes occurring in Seattle, as Southern Black people moved north. During the prewar and war years forty-five thousand African Americans came to the Pacific Northwest to work in defense jobs. Seattle's Black population grew from 3,789 in 1940 to 15,666 in 1950, which for the first time made it the largest nonwhite racial group in the city. An informal sample by the Seattle Urban League from the period showed that the majority of Black people living at the Delridge Housing Project were from five Southern states—Texas, Louisiana, Oklahoma, Arkansas, and Missouri. For a while there was friction between the older Black community and the new arrivals. “I was quite ashamed of them,” confessed LeEtta King. “They looked so bad. Dungarees weren’t worn on the street by women, but these women would be wearing them. Their big shapes—and their heads tied up with a handkerchief. I was so ashamed. And they were noisy. I just tried not to see them. . . . [Before they came] we could eat in any restaurant we wanted to. . . . The parks were always open and the theaters were open. You bought a seat in the theater and it didn’t matter where you sat. . . . There was a feeling of the people that were here of resentment against them.” Others, like Powell Barnett, were simply condescending. “I actually saw a man eating watermelon on the street curb,” he recounted. “But I felt that was all the more reason to extend a helping hand and help these people adjust to western ways.”

Though no one dared speak publicly of it, there was also an issue of skin tone within the Black community. The new immigrants, largely from the Southwest and the South, were not only more rural, less educated, and “ill-mannered,” they were also darker-skinned. “They used to call us ‘cotton-pickers,’ and ‘sharecroppers’ when we first came to Seattle,” recalled Leon Vaughn, the trumpet player who came to Washington from Nebraska in the early 1940s. “The only people that were any good were those that had been here for years and years and years, the light ones that could fit in.”

Political cartoon, the *Northwest Enterprise*, September 5, 1943.

Buddy Catlett’s family had been in the area for half a century before the Black migration west began, so he understood why older, established families were upset. On the one hand, he said: “You don’t want to see so-called ignorant people coming in your domain, because that means the whites you have to deal with are going to look at you in the same manner. When you get halfway cool, you don’t want nobody to come around and rock the boat.” On the other hand, Catlett saw that the people who came up from the South actually put him in touch with his own culture. “We were fortunate; [before they came] we were isolated. I mean, it’s the people in the fields that bring this culture value, that bring the spices to the stew. That made jazz what it was. A lot of people resent the harshness of the blues, an intrusion on the values they already got set up. The Army, the war, the shipyards, Fort Lewis brought the culture up here. That's why you had so many musicians that could play. We're fortunate. We'd just be non-white whites in a sense [if it hadn't happened]."

The division between North and South, urban and rural, created a double bind for African Americans, who needed to stand together against discrimination from the white community but felt also culturally divided. Nowhere was this cultural split more evident than in music, where the new styles of the Southerners and Southwesterners—house-rocking blues and sanctified church music—were as new to most Seattle Black people as they were to white folks. "I didn't know what Ray Charles was doing," declared Al Hilbert, the bartender at the Basin Street Club. "But I liked it. I took him down to this place that a friend of mine owned to see if he would hire him. He just laughed. The guy that owned the place, he was from Memphis. He said, 'Yeah, people don't know anything about that kind of music here.'" Buddy Catlett told another story that suggests Charles knew that his accent and brash in-your-face Southern style embarrassed northerners. Catlett said R. C.'s idea of a good joke was to start playing some gutbucket blues, real loud, over at Catlett's house just as a girlfriend would call—or worse, just as her parents answered the phone—and he was trying to impress her with his best uptown English. "He'd try to f—— your act up," laughed Catlett.

The whole issue of blues brings up the question of whether Charles was performing in his signature, gospel-inflected style—the way he later sounded on "I Got a Woman" and "What'd I Say"—while in Seattle, or if he was still just an imitator of Nat Cole and a so-so jazz pianist. Bill Crow, the former Gerry Mulligan Quartet bass player who grew up in Kirkland, Washington, observed: "When I heard him at the Washington Social, I thought, 'Well, he sounds like a fairly decent imitation of Bud [Powell], but he doesn't really have it down.' Then everybody was saying, 'Ray, sing the blues! Sing the blues!' So finally Ray sang the blues and he tore my head off. I never heard anything like that in my life before. When I met him later, I said, 'Ray, how come you don't do that all the time?' And he said, 'Oh man, you can't make a nickel singing like that.'" In *Brother Ray*, Charles wrote that his looser vocal style, which wedded the gospel sound of Clarence Fountain with the rolling beat of Kansas City blues, definitely had not jelled in his Seattle days. Many of the recordings of the McSon Trio, such as "Rocking Chair Blues," "Honey, Honey," "Ain't That Fine," and "What Have I Done?" bear him out. As a singer, Charles was still imitating the smooth stylings of Nat Cole and the restrained blues inflections of Charles Brown. However, two cuts he recorded in 1947 in Tampa, "Walkin' and Talkin'" and "I'm Wonderin' and Wonderin'," and his 1951 Los Angeles recording "Kissa Me Baby" show unmistakable trademarks of his later style, complete with aching gospel inflections and cries, suggesting that Charles may have been singing occasionally in his mature style even in Seattle.

According to Buddy Catlett, Charles had already come up with the germ for this style, without even knowing it. "It wasn't until after he went to Los Angeles that he began that gospel style," said Catlett. "Here, he would only do that for fun. I mean, gospel was involved in church. It was sacrilegious. So he would like poke fun at it. I didn't know he was serious!" Sonny Booker confirmed: "I was surprised when he really *made* it doing the blues, [because] it was always like a joke. We'd say, 'Ray, do your thing,' you know, and he'd do his fun thing—joke thing—going into the blues which really made him famous." The notion of the young Ray Charles privately "gospelizing" tunes in Seattle as a joke, then discovering later that this was what people wanted to hear and that this was his truest musical self, is an appealing and plausible one. One 1960 review of "What'd I Say" noted that "many of Charles' gospel blues songs are virtually parodies of gospel songs."

Ray Charles had a puckish sense of humor. Things tickled him. It's easy to imagine him getting a kick out of the attention his Southern accent and sanctified vocalizing would evoke from a Northwest audience. As Albert Goldman perceptively pointed out in his (otherwise unpleasant) biography of Elvis Presley, there was an element of parody in the best early rock 'n' roll, which set it apart from the blues proper. Charles, a guarded, private soul who maintained a firm first line of defense between himself and the public, was inconclusive about this notion. Sitting on a stool in 1991 in his huge, private studio on the second floor of his South Central Los Angeles offices, mug of tea and whiskey in hand, he laughed at the idea. "I don't know. When you're that young, you just do things, especially when you're around musicians I'm sure that they are right . . . so I'm sure I could do takeoffs. . . . [But] if you were to say to me, 'Ray, could you give me specifics?' I can't remember that."

Pinpointing the origins of Charles's style may be chronologically slippery, but there is no disputing that he was a fairly accomplished bebopper in his early years. Traff Hubert, a bass player who worked with Cecil Young, recalled being mightily impressed by Ray Charles one night in 1949 at the Tuxedo Club, across the street from the New Chinatown: "I thought he was the best piano player I had ever heard. He played piano, bass, drums, and sax, and he really did it. He'd demonstrate a different guy—'This is Bud Powell. This is Tatum. This is whoever.' Then he'd say, 'This is me,' and he'd play the blues. This was 1949." Said Buddy Catlett: "Ray sounded like Bud Powell. He was a bebopper. Except he was always commercially minded. He liked to play saxophone and when he'd come off his job somewhere, working someplace with a small group, he'd come up to where we were working after hours at the Washington Social Club and he'd always grab my horn—'Let me play your horn!' I walked into Birdland once and Roscoe Weathers, Floyd Standifer, Ray Charles, Milton Garred, and a drummer named Jimmie Rodgers were playing. That was really a good bebop group."

Charles also began to work on another musical innovation on Jackson Street—the use of electric keyboards. In 1948 or 1949 he bought a tinny electric piano made by Wurlitzer, the same company that made jukeboxes, and began to experiment with the sound. Floyd Standifer remembered this well: "He just beat all the keys off it, he played it so hard." Contemporary musicians sometimes use electric keyboards for convenience and as replacements for live instrumentalists, but Charles said he bought the electric piano strictly because he liked the sound, not to take to work. His fondness for his little Wurlitzer led to a revolution in music, beginning with his hit record "What'd I Say," which helped popularize the instrument. Charles chuckled to think how even fellow musicians laughed at him when they saw his little keyboard. "Later on," he said, "when I got to Atlantic, the people were laughing. 'What you going to do with that little piano, man? That little toy?' They used to call it a toy. Then I made 'What'd I Say' and everybody got one of these little 'toys'!"

The most important personal connection Charles made on Jackson Street was with Quincy Jones. It was a musical relationship that had a lasting influence on both men, particularly on the young and impressionable Quincy. They continued to collaborate musically until Charles died in 2004. Charles signed a three-record deal with Jones's label, Qwest, and contributed to Jones's 1989 hit album *Back on the Block*, with the track "I Be Good to You." Before that, there were many other recordings, including *The Genius of Ray Charles* and Jones's *Black Requiem*, for symphony orchestra, dedicated to Charles.

When Ray Charles and Quincy Jones first met in Seattle, both young men were hungry for knowledge and success. But whereas Jones had to go east to find his big break, success came courting Charles on Jackson Street, first in the form of a radio show, then with a primitive television appearance, and then—prize of prizes—a record deal. A few short months after the McSon Trio started at the Rocking Chair, the group was offered a fifteen-minute "pay-to-play" spot on Saturdays for KRSC radio. ("We gave Garcia's phone number over the air in the hopes of finding some gigs," Charles recalled.) Soon afterward, the trio was asked to perform on KING television, on what must have been one of the earliest live broadcasts in town. Though it was a one-shot deal, it brought attention to the group, which was subsequently asked to play when United Nations dignitary Ralph Bunche came to town.

But more important for R. C. was that all over the country, independent labels were beginning to record the new styles of Black music that had cropped up after World War II. In Los Angeles, Specialty, Swing Time, Modern, and Black and White were just some of the labels capturing the new sounds. Just as they had in the 1920s, these new "race record" labels sent out scouts to find and record new talent. Unbeknownst to Charles, a Los Angeles record executive named Jack Lauderdale had heard about the McSon Trio from saxophonist Jack McVea a couple of months after the group started at the Rocking Chair. When Lauderdale offered the trio a record date, they thought he was putting them on. McKee recollected: "Ray and I got together and said, 'This guy thinks we damn fools!' I told Ray Charles, 'This guy is talking about records.' Ray says, 'Oh, man! He's full of bull!' And I thought so, too. We didn't know he was serious, because we didn't know nothing about recording. He kept on persisting, and persisting, and finally he got us down to this station and then that's when we did our first tune. We had about three or four days to get these things together. We recorded them downtown, at a studio, down around Second or Third."

"You know," added Charles, "when something comes along that you've been wanting and you really have a strong desire for it, and somebody just sort of puts it in your lap, you don't quite believe your good fortune. We just couldn't believe that—we're going to get to make a record and we're going to make it in Seattle." The trio made two sides, "Confession Blues," by Charles, and "I Love You, I Love You," written by Charles's friend Joe Lee Lawrence. The session occurred in late 1948, only six months after Charles hit town, and the record, a 78, was released in early 1949. Though "Confession Blues" was not a hit, it sold respectably enough that Lauderdale brought the trio down to Los Angeles to record again. Several records were waxed, including "Ain't That Fine?," "Honey, Honey," and "She's on the Ball." Within a year or so, Lauderdale's Swing Time sessions would lead to R. C.'s first national hit on the Black charts, "Baby Let Me Hold Your Hand," a languid, Charles Brown–style number. The Los Angeles sessions would also lead to the breakup of the trio. Lauderdale, who was interested only in Ray Charles, let bassist Garred go. Recounted McKee:

> The second [trip to Los Angeles], Jack Lauderdale didn't send Milt a ticket. I think Milt faulted me a little, but I couldn't do nothing about it. While we were down here making the second batch of records with another guitar player and a drummer, he gave me enough money to buy a car. I bought me a '49 Chevrolet, and Ray Charles and I drove all the way back up to Seattle. We almost froze to death, because we didn't have no heater. But we had transportation! We got back to Seattle and Georgia Kemp loaned me money to buy a heater in the car.

It was around this time that McKee also anointed Charles with his first pair of sunglasses, which would become one of his signatures. Oddly, in the first promotional picture showing Charles wearing shades, the glasses were drawn in, like a bad cartoon. McKee explained: "Once the guy recorded us, we had to have a professional picture taken. I had some pictures taken at the radio station where we were paying to play, but I didn't know what I was doing and they weren't good enough. What happened was, they drew the sunglasses on that one when I sent the picture to Jack Lauderdale. They are drawn on him on that picture. Right after that, Len Brooks [Seattle pianist and photographer] said, 'Let me take some pictures,' and I said, 'Let's put some [actual] glasses on him.'"

Despite tensions created by Lauderdale, the Maxin Trio remained together through 1949, moving from the Rocking Chair into the Washington Social Club, where it played intermissions. McKee saw to it that the trio had gigs at the university, playing fraternity parties, socials, and dances. In June 1949, Charles played an unusual novelty show at the Trianon Ballroom, inspired by the musical shenanigans of Slim Gaillard and probably produced by Bumps Blackwell, who, if indeed he produced the show, billed himself as "Julius MacVootie." Called "French and Be-Bop," the program featured Ray with the brothers Brashear (Gerald and Buddy), Floyd Standifer, and Al Larkins; the ads claimed that MacVootie would sing "French Jazz. See you hipsters Sunday."

But the trio was starting to break up. When Jack Lauderdale recorded Charles with guitarist Oscar Moore and other top-flight studio musicians,

McKee began to get the picture. Sometime in early 1950, the guitarist headed for Great Falls, Montana, where many entertainers were finding work on the "silver circuit" in Las Vegas–style nightclubs run by the mob. McKee connected with bassist Eddie Cole—Nat's brother—and they formed a comedy and music group called Three Loose Nuts and a Bolt, which, said McKee, transformed him into an entertainer. In Great Falls, McKee also met his future wife, actress Lillian Randolph (*Amos and Andy*, *The Great Gildersleeve*), with whom he formed a family band that played Hong Kong, Honolulu, and Army bases all over the world. The act worked on cruise ships for a while, and McKee eventually turned away from entertainment, becoming master chef for a cruise line. McKee had retired by the early 1990s and was living in Los Angeles. If he had any hard feelings about the breakup of the band with Ray Charles, he masked them well. "We wasn't mad," McKee recalled. "No, no, no, no. Because next time I saw him, he was doing good with his blues, and had his band, in Philadelphia, and Lillian and I had our family act. We felt good about it. It was the best thing to do."

Charles agreed. "It wasn't anything bitter or angry. The trio thing just wasn't happening, and Milt and Gosady [Garcia] ran out of bread. . . . Jack was primarily interested in me." Charles had other reasons for leaving Seattle. His girlfriend, Louise, had returned to Florida. At about the same time the police had begun to crack down on the drug trade in Seattle too. One of the sorrier legacies of Ray's Seattle period was the beginning of his heroin use. Charles described his early addiction openly:

> Didn't take me long to figure out that before a gig, the cats might be doing something besides smoking reefer. Or if we were at someone's house, I'd hear them doing something in the kitchen. Before long, I discovered that they were cooking up "horse," and I wanted to try some for myself. . . . There wasn't no pusher hanging 'round the back alley who enticed me into it. . . . I wanted the shit bad enough so I found a way to get it. I went back to bugging the other musicians. . . . One of the cats finally said, "Give the kid some shit just to keep him quiet." . . . And that was how I got my first hit.

Buddy Catlett remembered the change that came over Charles when he started using hard drugs: "Ray moved to an apartment on 12th and Jackson. I went by to see him there one day. He had a record on and he was sitting in a big, overstuffed chair. He had slumped to the floor and he was just sitting there—listening, scratching. I could see where that euphoria that dope gives you just lightened his whole load. He could then focus on what he wanted to do, and do it. In his case, it seems, the ends seemed to justify the means. But he could afford it. He didn't have to go to the street to find it." Charles remained addicted to heroin for several years. Perhaps because of the addict's perennial fear of being busted, he seems to have been prepared for a swift departure from Seattle at any time. Ernestine Anderson said, "He told [his group], 'One of these nights, I'm just going to disappear. I'm going to get on a train and I'll be gone.' And he did. He just left in the middle of the night and nobody knew." McKee commented: "Things got a little hot, as you may have heard." By February of 1950, two years after he had arrived in Seattle, Ray Charles had left the city and started working in Los Angeles.

In April, Lauderdale put Charles out on the road with label-mate Lowell Fulson, the great Los Angeles blues man. Through working with Fulson, and traveling as a single through the South for the next two years, Charles found his true voice, which came from his rural blues and gospel roots. In 1952 he signed with Atlantic Records, where the promotional genius Ahmet Ertegun guided him to success. The Atlantic deal was R. C.'s first honest contract in the music business: in the three years he had worked with Lauderdale and Swing Time, he never earned a nickel in publishing royalties for his songs. Charles was philosophical about this:

> Jack Lauderdale, [to] my mind, is a great man, to this day, because he provided for me the one thing that I felt I had been wanting ever since I knew what music was, and that was to record a record. This was the ultimate in life, I thought, at that age. So who in the hell knew anything about royalties and stuff? And Jack Lauderdale was not any different from most record companies. They didn't pay no artist no royalties. A lot of record companies, what they would do for artists is go buy 'em a car. But then in the end, they would still take the money out of their royalties.

The rest of the Ray Charles story is well-known. Along with Lowell Fulson, Pee Wee Crayton, Guitar Slim, Jay McNeely, Roy Milton, T-Bone Walker, and others who played the Washington Social Club, Ray toured up and down the West Coast and throughout the South, continuing the fusion of jazz, blues, and gospel that would become contemporary rhythm and blues. Eventually, in

1954, that fusion would result in the groundbreaking record that announced to the world Charles's gospel-rocking signature—"I Got a Woman." Five years later, "What'd I Say" put him over to white audiences and the nation in general. Ernestine Anderson vividly recalled hearing those records and trying to square them with the R. C. Robinson she had known in Seattle: "Ray left first. When he resurfaced again a few years later, it was a different Ray Charles. It was the Ray Charles that we know now. The style was totally different. He had added this gospel thing to it. It was like a whole different person. It was like, 'He had that in him?' I was just so awed! Amazed at the difference. I knew he was going to be bigger than life, as soon as I heard it. Yeah, this will fly. He was the first person to do that. He was the originator. The pioneer."

Ray Charles was a pioneer in another sense, too, in that he never bought into the then-popular misconception of the blind as dependent. On the contrary, he seems to have taken delight in shocking people with his ability to function without assistance, enough so that some Seattleites became convinced he wasn't blind at all. Sonny Booker once saw Ray sitting on the floor, repadding a clarinet, an intricate task that involves gluing tiny, button-sized pieces of fiber onto the underside of small metal keys. Ernestine Anderson also had her doubts: "One time, he had the radio all taken apart on the floor. He said to me, 'Watch out. Don't step on that!' and I'm—'Can he see, or what?'" Both Anderson and McKee swear that on different occasions they each watched Charles, alone, drive a car. "I saw him drive a car in Houston," Anderson said. "With my own eyes. At a motel where the drive was a round kind of thing that went around in a circle. There was a big thing in the middle with flowers and cement and curb. Fathead Newman had just bought a car. Ray got into the car and drove it around this circle. I'm standing there in the doorway watching the whole thing. I saw it. I saw it."

Leon Vaughn and bassist Bill Crow, among many others, reported that Charles always knew where he was when he was being driven somewhere, and would audaciously tell drivers when to turn right or left. Continued Anderson:

> Ray used to have his checks sent to my house. One night, when he called to let me know he was coming, my dad got up and was standing on the landing to watch for when he came in, because he was going to go out and help him. We were both standing there, looking out the window. You could see the street clearly. Ray got out of the cab, a Yellow Cab. The cab did not park where you could just walk straight

> up the walk [to the house]. Ray walked along the curb and then got to the walkway, turned, and came into the house. We were both standing there with our mouths hanging open. He came up on the porch and we opened the door. So everybody used to think he was putting us on. My dad, he just [said], "Nawwww, he's not kidding me. He can see." But he couldn't.

Emmett Lewis, the agent for Local No. 493, told a similar anecdote:

> I used to tell my wife that he could see. Because when I come in the door, he would say, "There's the business agent coming in from 493. Get your money ready." At the Eagles Auditorium, I saw Ray Charles leave the piano on the bandstand, walk out the front, and go right straight up the aisle. Didn't hit nobody, and got in a cab and went home. The first intermission. Got him a cab when he got through, come back. Walked straight back through the crowd, got on the bandstand. Sit down at the piano for the next three, four hours. Now, there's no way to prove that if you hadn't seen it, but I was there. The other two guys with me is dead. I used to tell him about it and he'd laugh and say, "Oh, will you stop kidding me."

Charles explained away most of these tales in his autobiography. For starters he admitted he had always had a near-suicidal attraction to motor vehicles. On summers off from school, a neighbor taught him to drive. He also asserted that he would meticulously go over familiar routes on foot, listening for variations in the sound of his footsteps, so that later he could walk back over the same route at a confident clip. As for giving drivers directions to his house, many vision-impaired and blind people use the same technique: memorizing bumps in the road—or sounds that come from certain corners—so they always know where they are.

Garcia McKee, who surely knew more than anyone about Ray during this period, stated categorically and emphatically that Charles was "stone blind." What's more interesting than raising questions about Charles's blindness is that in the process of proving he could take care of himself, he slighted McKee, the man who gave him so much over the years. For it was McKee—not Charles himself, as he claimed in his autobiography—who auditioned at the Black and Tan and got them the job there. It was McKee who first came out from Tampa on the bus. It was McKee who borrowed the money for Ray's bus ticket. And despite the amazing independence that Charles displayed as a teenager in Seattle, it was again McKee who looked out for him during their stay there. “He knew that I was going to see that he was taken care of, no matter what,” said the guitarist. “Even though he was alone, he had that confidence. He knew I was there. No matter where he was, he knew I would be there.” Leon Vaughn is less equivocal: “Everywhere he went, Garcia went.”

Ray Charles, like Quincy Jones, became a millionaire several times over, long before he died in 2004. A canny businessman as well as an ambitious and talented man, he became a national hero, part of American folklore, and was one of the first few African American musicians to crack the lucrative TV commercial market with his ads for Pepsi-Cola. In 2001, at the Kennedy Center Honors, he brought Quincy to tears with a heartbreaking version of the song, “My Buddy.” Charles received the National Medal of Arts and was also inducted into the Rock and Roll Hall of Fame and the Country Music Hall of Fame. Looking back at his Seattle days, after warming to the subject, and hearing again of his experiences as a struggling teenager, making his first record, meeting Quincy Jones and Ernestine Anderson, Charles became philosophical, even sentimental: “What do they call this—bar mitzvah?—where you come out as a man? I think Seattle was kind of like that for me. The reason I put it to you that way is because in Seattle, at that point, all of a sudden I had to become a man. I started keeping house—like Quincy says—I had an apartment, a piano, a big radio, hi-fi set, telephone. Cookin’. There ain’t no doubt about it. I became a man.”

9 Jackson Street Glitters, Then Goes Dark

THE YEAR 1950 EXPLODED ON Jackson Street with the debut of the most successful bebop unit ever to grace the neighborhood—the Cecil Young Quartet. Young's group took Seattle by storm, enjoyed a regional hit record, then traveled to New York, where it played Birdland. Folks lucky enough to have seen the quartet witnessed Jackson Street at its very best. Young was a vaudeville entertainer from New Haven, Connecticut, who came to town on a Palomar Theater date, part of a thirty-week series that featured Sarah Vaughan, Billy Eckstine, and other stars. The Palomar was a living testimony to Seattle's historic passion for theater—the last vaudeville house in town, it ran four shows and a movie daily, until 1956. The ebullient Norm Bobrow was hosting the series. "One of the acts that came through was called Young and Williams," he recalled. "The guy that was the dancer out front was Williams, and Cecil Young, a young guy, quite balding, was his stand-up piano player, who would mug. We hit it off, Cecil and I. He says, 'You know, I want to break away from this ridiculous vaudeville act.' So he stayed and I became his patron."

Cecil Young was like no one Seattle had ever known before. A short, stocky man with a wicked sense of humor, Young was a hipster and a hustler who spoke with a rabbity stammer. He was also the genuine item—a modern piano player with East Coast fire. Young spent two years at Yale's School of Music and lived for a while at the Cecil Hotel, in Harlem, where he met and jammed with Charlie Parker, Dizzy Gillespie, and other early beboppers. Cecil had a white girlfriend who drove a Bentley and used a Vassar vocabulary. He liked to put people on. Continued Bobrow:

> Cecil was "fly"—you know, an old synonym for hip. He was one of those "fly cats" from the East Coast. Cecil was a guy who just out-hipped the world—a very, very bright man.

Sometimes he would affect a little mintiness. I remember once someone called me to ask if he would play a private party in the Highlands [a fancy neighborhood in North Seattle]. I said, "I think that Mr. Young would like to look at the place in advance." So we went out there, and indeed it was beautiful. Cecil was dressed in a gray flannel suit and he was carrying an umbrella. It was a sunny day. The only thing that would have added to that image would have been if he were wearing a derby. And he's walking like this [*affects strut*]. We get in there and there's this huge living room with French windows that open out to the terrace lawn. And in this huge room there's statuary, almost like a Venus de Milo kind of thing. So Cecil is standing there leaning on his umbrella, and he says to this woman, maybe in her fifties or so—"I think that statue ought to go."

Cecil Young, ca. 1950.

Chuck Metcalf considered Young one of his most important "gurus." Cecil turned on the impressionable bassist to Jimmy Blanton but also to such exotic musical influences as Ravi Shankar and Edgard Varèse. Once Young decided to stay in Seattle, his first move was to drop by the New Chinatown, where Dave Henderson, the bouncer/pianist, had recently played. Cecil got the gig. He assembled a quartet, drawing on tenor saxophonist Gerald Brashear, who had been around since the Savoy Boys days and was now sounding a bit like a young Sonny Stitt; white bassist Traff Hubert, a new kid on the block from Tacoma; and Jimmie Rodgers, also new in town, a slick drummer originally from Detroit. The gig skidded, but the quartet took flight, securing a slot at the Black Elks Club, where Ray Charles had made his start. Once the word got out, the Elks became the place to be. "They were hanging from the rafters," said Hubert. "Billy Tolles and Ernestine Anderson came by to sit in. It really took off." Norm Bobrow asserted categorically, "The band was the number one turn-on of any musical group that I've ever heard. Nothing has been more exciting in this town."

As a pianist, Young played in a sparse but nervous, harmonically hip style, a combination of Basie and Horace Silver. But what made the group so extraor-

The Cecil Young Quartet, ca. 1951. *Left to right:* Jimmie Rodgers, Traff Hubert, Gerald Brashear, Cecil Young.

dinary was its rhythm section. This was the New York heat that hadn't yet appeared on the local scene. Young's "comping" was legendary. So were the tempos he and the quartet undertook. "Cecil Young's quartet would play some tempos faster than the fastest thing recorded by Charlie Parker, if you can imagine that," recalled Neil Friel, who sat in with Young at the Elks. "Jimmie could just sit there like nothing could give him pause."

One night, Nat Cole dropped by the Elks. "Cecil's quartet was on the stand," remembered Bobrow. "We're having some drinks, just the two of us, nobody bothering Nat. A little bit into it, Nat grabs me by the belt buckle and he says, 'Norm, that drummer's *walkin'*! He is *walkin'*!' Oh, Jimmie Rodgers was a bitch!" Bobrow promoted Cecil Young relentlessly on his radio show and eventually became the group's quasi-manager. The quartet played Spokane and Yakima, then Bobrow approached 908 Club owner Dick Ruffin about bringing in the group. Ruffin agreed. The Cecil Young days marked another golden period for the 908. Bobrow hosted the place as if it were his own living room. The menu sported a woodcut of the quartet, etched by Bobrow's wife, Pat Ward, and life-size caricatures of the musicians along one wall, also drawn by Ward. In the shell of Doc Hamilton's speakeasy, Seattle had the beginnings of its first modern jazz temple, where hipsters and bohemians, night people and nomads, came to listen—instead of dance—and talk about Zen and Camus, all in an atmosphere of reverence and cool.

"We used to close the place at five o'clock," said Bobrow, "and go to the 411 [he means Basin Street], where Ernie Lewis and Pony Poindexter and Ernestine Anderson played a breakfast show, which started at seven o'clock, six days a week. We always went there for breakfast, then we went home to bed." As the group gained notoriety, Bobrow began to book Young as a headliner in theaters.

The quartet brought a sense of razzmatazz to Bobrow's concerts that tickled the New York impresario and bowled over audiences. Young was a total entertainer, a tap dancer and clown who excelled at barn burners such as Dizzy Gillespie's "Salt Peanuts" and "Oop-Pop-A-Da." With Young doing his showbiz routines, Gerald Brashear playing congas as well as saxophone, and both Brashear and Young scat-singing, the group was a sensation.

"When you went to their concerts," said Ernestine Anderson, "you came away feeling just really elated. They put so much into it, so much energy." Gerald Brashear's conga-playing was no small part of the act. Brashear had taught himself to play in the style of Dizzy's Cuban percussionist, Chano Pozo. Buddy Catlett said Brashear "played like a Cuban," he was that good. The bass player in the Young quartet, Trafton "Traff" Hubert, originally from Puyallup, Washington, was an unusual character who had transformed himself from fan to musician, seemingly overnight. Hubert confessed: "I was a jitterbug originally. I was obsessed with jazz. I had about three thousand 78s. When Dizzy Gillespie and Charlie Parker first came out, I almost went crazy. I thought that was the greatest thing I had ever heard."

Traff was avid. In 1945, when he heard Charlie Parker was playing at Billy Berg's, in Los Angeles, he drove south, where he saw Bird and met Harry the Hipster, who would later appear at Seattle's Players Club. "I asked him, 'Is it true that you take Benzedrine all the time?' He said, 'No, man, only when I can get it.'" Back in Seattle, Traff was initiated into the local scene by (who else?) Janet Thurlow, whom he'd met at (where else?) the record store. Janet introduced him to bassist Adolphus Alsbrook. Traff started playing. "I had some friends in Tacoma who had a band and they didn't have a bass player, so I rented a bass from George Greenwood at Tacoma Music and bought a Bobby Haggart bass book and taught myself how to play."

"He just decided he was going to play bass," recalled Traff Hubert's childhood chum Dean Reilly, also a bassist. "He didn't know anything about music, was never in a band or anything like that. But he had a great record collection, so he knew what was supposed to happen." Hubert jammed with locals, ventured out to after-hours clubs on Tacoma's Broadway, then went on the road for five months with an unlikely group called the Wen Shu Orchestra, led by a German. When Hubert came home, he was a seasoned road bassist. He hooked up with Billy Tolles, who got him onto some rhythm-and-blues gigs at Fort Lewis; then, again through Tolles, Hubert broke into the Seattle scene, working after hours with Billy and Jimmie Rodgers. Traff also worked at the New Chinatown with Dave Henderson. Gerald and Cecil heard him there: thus was born the Cecil Young Quartet. The group was known for its comedy as much as its music, particularly when Young and Brashear went on a tear. Said Ernestine: "Gerald had a dry sense of humor. The two of them together were just craziness on the loose. Cecil was always playing crank jokes on people. A prankster. We used to wonder when he slept—he'd always be doing something, no matter what time of day or night it was. He reminded me of an overgrown kid. He never grew up, in that respect. You had to laugh when you were around these two people. I mean the Marx Brothers was nothing compared to these guys." Recalled Neil Friel: "Cecil would go into his gay act—'Gerald, you bitch, you stop that!'—and Gerald would pretend to be very embarrassed and raise his eyebrows. And Cecil just wouldn't let up on it. And always with a smooth front. I never saw him up a tree. He was one of the wildest operators I have ever known."

As funny as he was, Cecil Young was deadly serious about making it big in the music business. When Sid Nathan, president of King Records, came to town looking for Ray Charles (who was in Los Angeles cutting sides for Swing Time), Cecil convinced Bobrow to pitch the quartet. Bobrow agreed, and in one of his greatest gambits whipped up a Tuesday-night crowd at the 908. "This Sid Nathan had never seen anything like this where he'd come from," remembered Hubert. "Jumping so heavy on a Tuesday night!"

Tapes of the quartet had been made earlier at the Ladies Musical Club (which later housed the Harvard Exit movie theater) and the Metropolitan Theatre by Bert Porter, a local sales representative for Ampex and stereo-recording pioneer. Porter played the tapes for Nathan at a party and the record exec decided the quality was high enough to master a 10-inch album and ten 78s. The Cecil Young Quartet album, released on King in 1951 as a 10-inch LP under the title *Concert of Cool Jazz*, was the first local record since the Maxin Trio's to make an impact outside of Seattle. The quartet's influence reached even further when Los Angeles promoter Gene Norman released the crowd-pleaser "Who Parked the Car?" backed with "Jumpin' with Symphony Sid," as an EP. The Norman record showcased Gerald Brashear and so impressed San Francisco jazz critic Ralph Gleason that he encouraged local disc jockeys to play the cut, writing that Brashear's scat solo on "Who Parked the Car?" was the best scat solo ever recorded.

Gerald's solo is incontestably in a class by itself, Eddie Jefferson and Jon Hendricks notwithstanding. Frenzied, articulate, witty, and dazzling, it is a nine-chorus tour de force that includes quotes from *Flight of the Bumblebee* and the *Hungarian Rhapsody No. 2*, a perfectly in-tune recitation of the cycle of fifths, and a comic, conversational call-and-answer between high and low ranges that Clark Terry later used with great success. "Who Parked the Car?" was reissued in Seattle on a 12-inch LP titled *Jazz on the Rocks* (Audio Lab), which featured four cuts from the King album—"Race Horse," "Stompin' at the Savoy," "The Campbells Are Coming," and "Jumpin' with Symphony Sid" (retitled "Tribute to Al Benson")—plus four others. It is a West Coast classic that cries out for reissue. Its bebop intensity, hip wit, and classical and avant-garde allusions epitomize what the early 1950s were all about. Brashear weaves curlicue Lestorian solos with an appealingly dry, woody tone, fluid, fleet phrasing, and spitfire tonguing. Cecil blows cool and clear, with even-noted melodic ideas and ironic classical allusions, going "out" with a sonic landscape a la Varèse at one point, with variations on a drone followed by dense block chords. Jimmie Rodgers keeps light, swift time, and Traff follows suit.

On the strength of the album, the Cecil Young Quartet was signed to the William Morris Agency and booked on a national tour, playing Birdland in New York, Chicago's Blue Note, and Boston's Hi-Hat. "As far as I know, we were the only band to go directly from Seattle to Birdland," commented Traff. At Birdland they played on the same bill as Sarah Vaughan and "Wild Bill" Davis; Hubert and Rodgers accompanied Vaughan. The quartet members were ecstatic. In Chicago they worked beside Vaughan, Teddy Wilson, and the Delta Rhythm Boys and stayed at the Pershing Hotel, where Hubert remembered hearing an unknown pianist named Ahmad Jamal playing in the lounge. Because the group was racially mixed, the members often had to stay in Black peoples' homes. Hubert, the only white musician in the band, said, "I learned to eat hot soul food and learned about the illegal Black cabs called jitneys, who would act as your personal taxicab. It was an education. Some Black people asked me, sincerely, if I was crazy. I said, 'I'm here because I like the music.'"

Ernestine Anderson heard the Cecil Young Quartet play at Birdland while she was on the road with Lionel Hampton. "They were hot," she recalled. "We would hang, you know. It was a good feeling. They really made it big, and fast. Maybe a little too fast. As soon as this record was released they just [*snaps her fingers*] took off like a rocket." Unfortunately, the New York trip proved to be no more than a tease. The quartet's record never caught on nationally. Work dried up, and the members became impatient and discouraged. Some fell into drug use. According to Wanda Brown, who lived with Gerald Brashear after Vernon Brown died, the New York trip was devastating to the saxophonist: "He was disappointed. He thought that they were so great they were going to knock New York dead. And it didn't work like that. He didn't want to come back. Some friends back there bought him a bus ticket and put him on it and told him, 'You go home. This is not the place for you.'" The quartet soon disbanded. As fast as it had risen, the Cecil Young Quartet fell.

Young himself never came back to the West, though he apparently continued to play until his death, in the 1970s. Jimmie Rodgers died young after succumbing to the street culture around Times Square. Hubert played for a while with Elmer Gill and Neil Friel, but gradually moved into work as a DJ and record distributor. Loath to follow in the footsteps of his contemporaries, Hubert got sober in 1983 and worked as an alcohol and drug counselor at the Lakeside-Milam Recovery Center. The hipster bassist continued to play, notably in China, where in 2002 he had a long-term gig in a high-rise hotel in Guangzhou. In a conversation after he came home, Hubert said the authoritarian atmosphere there reminded him of the 1950s in America. "There was a sign in the elevator that said 'Don't Do Anything Immoral in This Hotel,'" reported Traff. "That's what it was like in the States in the '50s, this feeling that there was some power looking down on you from above. That's what we rebelled against." Hubert died in 2001.

Cecil's white-hot but short-lived Seattle career turned out to be a last hurrah for Jackson Street. Over the next five years a variety of forces conspired to scuttle the scene, and the action began to shift downtown and to the North End. The initial cause for the change was a drastic liberalization of state liquor laws that rendered the after-hours clubs almost obsolete. Shifts in popular taste, the rise of R & B, and perhaps most important, the integration of the Black and white musicians' unions also contributed to the district's demise. All through the late 1940s, the state legislature had been edging toward legalizing hard liquor. With the war years it had become obvious to everyone that there was a demand for public social drinking. The population had become more diverse and sophisticated, and the pioneer generation of antisaloon reformists had died off.

In March 1949, Initiative 171 legalized hard liquor by the drink, and 235 establishments in Washington legally began pouring vodka, gin, whiskey, and rye over bars where spirits had been served illegally for years, if not decades. The police and the state liquor board began to work together with a reform-minded Jackson Street Community Council to stamp out the "bottle clubs." Club patrons and owners had seen the writing on the wall for years. Even before Initiative 171, the Seattle Police Department had relentlessly pounded the after-hours clubs. In 1947 the police raided the Yukon Club five times. The Clover, Beaver, Sessions, Breakers, Rocking Chair, 83, and Owls clubs were hit the same year. The Clover Club fell to the baton and the ax again, as did the White Hat Club and Club Lido. In 1948 there were still more raids. On June 12 ninety-two people were hauled away from Basin Street. The club was padlocked and remained dark forever. On October 8, 1949, in the largest arrest ever made in a Seattle speakeasy, 166 people were herded down the long flight of stairs of the Washington Social Club, packed into paddy wagons on Madison Street, and booked. After Ray Charles left the Rocking Chair in 1949, its doors never opened again. An era was ending.

The attack on the Jackson Street "joints" was motivated by greed as much as it was by a desire to uphold the law. Liquor was an extremely lucrative business. Once it was made legitimate, the bottle clubs were not only illegal, they were competition to legitimate operators. The state had no intention of sharing the spoils with the old speaks. The city fathers were enthusiastically supported by the Teamsters union in the effort to stamp out the competition, as the union recruited bartenders into the hotel-and-restaurant-workers local. Since the new law allowed only restaurants and hotels to sell hard liquor, it was in the owners' and union's best interests to make sure they maintained a monopoly on liquor sales. On the street this meant a shift in the action from Black-owned Central District joints to Italian-owned—and union-controlled—cocktail lounges. In the 1950s jazz fans began to find themselves in downtown clubs with names like the Italian Village and Rosellini's Four-10.

To many Black patrons, this shift of venues had the air of discrimination, particularly since the new lounges continued to engage in other illegal activities, such as gambling. (As late as 1968, gambling rackets constituted one of the largest industries in the state, with profits of $50 million a year.) The payoffs continued; so did raids on the Black clubs. After the massive arrests at the Washington Social Club in 1948, the veteran establishment was formally abated in 1950. The big neighborhood club, where so many of the great figures of the 1940s had cut their teeth, became a tangible focus for community outrage. Owner Sy Groves took out a full-page advertisement in the *Northwest Enterprise*, addressed to prosecutor Charles O. Carroll, asserting that the establishment was a legitimate enterprise employing twenty-two people and was being singled out because it was a Black business. Citizens of the Central District signed a petition to keep it open.

Not everyone in the Central Area sided with Groves, however. The Republican editor of the *Northwest Enterprise*, Prentice Frazier, took out a reply ad, arguing that there had been many complaints about the Washington Social Club and that the prosecutor was "entirely free of bigotry." In the end, Groves lost. Mabel Williams reopened the establishment for a while, but by 1951 the Washington Social Club was gone. The Black Elks Club followed in December 1952, when 117 people were arrested there. Prosecutor Carroll, for his part, was later indicted as part of a conspiracy to maintain the payoff system and protect illegal gambling, although he was not convicted.

Unhappily for jazz musicians, the change in Washington liquor laws also coincided with profound shifts in musical taste that contributed to a severe shortage of work. In the early 1950s popular music entered a bland stage that featured such vapid songs as "How Much Is That Doggie in the Window?" and catchy tunes by scrubbed, "girl-next-door" goddesses like Patti Page. Hot swing was dead. Even nationally the biggest name bands were having trouble staying on the road. Duke Ellington was wracked by the departure of Johnny Hodges and several other important sidemen (though Ellington did record an album in Seattle in 1952, released on Victor and titled simply *Seattle Concert*). Count Basie disbanded for the only time in his career, and Charlie Barnet threw in the towel. Crowds stopped coming out. A 1954 booking of the Dorsey brothers, who in the 1940s had drawn six thousand people to the Civic Auditorium, sold fewer than five hundred tickets. Local swing bands began to fall apart as well. Al Pierre couldn't draw a crowd at the Showbox; neither could commercial tenor saxophonist Norm Hoagy, the bandleader who succeeded him. Bob Harvey's band at the China Pheasant started to cut back its hours.

Swing's stylistic successor, the complex and demanding bebop, wasn't accessible enough to take up the slack. Roscoe Weathers's refusal to play "Wreck on the Highway" for a drunken customer had turned out to be a harbinger of the growing isolation many jazz musicians would feel as they strove to assert their status as artists rather than entertainers. Ray Charles, always alert to the marketplace, had noticed this development in Seattle even before 1950: "The one thing which bothered me about some players I met around that time was their strange attitude: They'd say to a crowd, 'This is my music. If you like it, cool. If not, fuck it!' I thought that was wrong. People give you their bread and are entitled to some kind of musical return on their dollar. I don't mean you got to give them exactly what they want. But you do have to keep them in mind." Whether or not one agrees with Charles's conclusions, his recognition of the situation was on target. In the new lounge-oriented climate of the 1950s, Seattle jazz musicians would either have to adjust to the new audiences or find somewhere else to play.

White musicians who made the adjustment often managed to create lounge jazz with some verve and integrity. One of them was Norm Hoagy, a Kansas City saxophonist and vibes player whose strong tone and sinuous, swing-era phrasing had graced the band of Shep Fields. Hoagy (originally spelled Houge) moved to Seattle in 1946, where he worked steadily at the China Pheasant for many years. Starting in 1951, he headed a six- to eight-piece band at the Magic Inn, at Sixth Avenue and Union Street. (The Magic Inn had begun life as the Magician's Club in 1946, a front for gambling and hard liquor.) In 1952, Hoagy released a rockin' R & B single, "Showbox Boogie," showcasing his tough, throaty tenor. It's a Northwest gem. Hoagy's bands remained a refuge for hot jazz players throughout his life. Some dismissed him as a hack; others admired his arranging skills. There's no question Hoagy could swing, as a player and an arranger. He died in 1985.

Gene Sargent, Gene Boscacci, and Frank Sugia also stood out on the lounge scene and remained well-respected by jazzers. Sargent had played guitar in Woody Herman's famous Second Herd, the bebop ensemble that made Stan Getz and the Four Brothers famous. Boscacci, who was playing at the Washington Athletic Club in the early 1990s, was a pianist and vibes man who studied with Sugia and also found a niche playing jazz accordion, which enjoyed a faddish vogue in the late 1940s. Sugia, who grew up in Rainier Valley in the 1920s and 1930s when it was still an Italian neighborhood, learned classical piano and accordion in his youth but as a teenager, in 1936, started playing dance band music with Jackie Souders. After a stint with the radio station studio orchestra of KGO, in San Francisco, Sugia came home, where he became an institution on accordion, playing in jazz-savvy lounges. During the 1950s, Sugia held forth at the Italian Village, on Fifth Avenue, and became popular playing with violinist Joe Venuti and Floyd Standifer at his own club, the After Five, in 1968. This group also became known to locals as the Dickensian, top-hatted gentlemen who played Christmas music for the now-defunct downtown department store Frederick & Nelson. Sugia's sister, Lola Sugia, who married Gay Jones

The Norm Hoagy Orchestra at the Showbox Theater, 1951–52. *Left to right:* Sal Carrabba, Dave Stetler (*lower*), Red Kelly, Jim Weaver, Norm Hoagy (piano), Wayne Saxe, Dave Tuttle, Stan Keen.

saxophonist Floyd Tebelman, also enjoyed the Seattle spotlight as a crisp vocalist for sweet bandleaders such as Wyatt Howard and Jackie Souders as well as the more swinging Norm Hoagy. Her teen-oriented 1960 pop single "Blue Tears" was a local success.

Frank Sugia sometimes played at another lounge where jazz was welcome—Norm Bobrow's large supper club, the Colony, opened in 1955 on the site of the Clef, a club that had been operated by Seattle Symphony Orchestra bassist Mori Simon. At the corner of Virginia Street and Fourth Avenue, the Colony was a Broadway sort of place, in part thanks to Bobrow's open invitation to visiting theatrical figures from the nearby Moore Theatre. Singers were a specialty. One of them, Pat Suzuki, went on to Broadway fame in the show *Flower Drum Song*. Many of the area's finest white players worked at the Colony, including Red Kelly, Walt Tianen, Al Pace, Bud Schultz, Dave Stetler, and Don Conway.

Conway, who had worked in Bobrow's Little Big Band, was an excellent alto saxophonist in the feather-toned, Lee Konitz manner.

The downtown lounge scene was a viable compromise for white musicians, but as long as the unions remained segregated, Black jazzers had to make do in the vestiges of Jackson Street. Two of the clubs that hung on for a while were the Elks Club and the old Local No. 493 clubhouse, the Blue Note. At the Black Elks, Cecil Young was succeeded by a young musician from Boston, Paul Neves, regarded as the best jazz pianist in Seattle during the 1950s. Neves had studied in Boston with Madame Chaloff, the famous music teacher and mother of saxophonist Serge Chaloff, one of the original "Four Brothers" from Woody's Second Herd. (Neves's brother, John, achieved some notoriety as the bassist for pianist George Shearing.) Paul Neves was a quiet man with a sweet disposition and a natty wardrobe. Bassist and tenor saxophonist Gary Steele remembered him as the first person he ever saw in Seattle wearing a porkpie hat, Lester Young's trademark. Neves, who originally came to Washington courtesy of the Air Force, enrolled in the early 1950s at the University of Washington as an English major. While going to school, he worked after hours at the Elks in the trio with Chuck Metcalf and white drummer Jimmy Raymer.

In August 1955, Neves played at the Lake City Tavern with Fred Greenwell, Buddy Catlett, and white drummer Bill Kotick. He also worked often with Pops Buford. Tenor saxophonist Chuck Stentz remembered working with Neves at the Congo Club, in Tacoma, in 1955. Neves's work impressed locals as particularly advanced, a stylistic step or two beyond Cecil Young. Private tapes of Neves's playing from the mid-1950s reveal him as a cool, linear bopper with a light touch and great time, with flashes of harmonic daring and a sense of when to leave open space in a chord. At one point Neves's advanced harmonies cost him a job with saxophonist Coleman Hawkins, who found him too far out. "Paul was before his time around here," said Buddy Catlett in the 1980s. "He would be perfect for today's music." Neves left Seattle in 1957. In the early 1970s he and his brother John taught in Boston at Jack's Drum School. He also roomed for a while in Boston with Don Lanphere, and at some point moved to the Bahamas, where he became musical director of a hotel. Neves died in the late 1980s.

After Neves left town, the piano chair in the Raymer group went to Jimmy Gilles, a Tacoman who had jammed with Cecil Young at the New Chinatown and worked off and on with Billy Tolles. Of these rocky times in the early 1950s,

Gilles recalled: "The principal job that kept me [going] was the colored Elks Club. It would start about eleven or twelve and go to four or five. Then we all wandered up to the [New] Chinatown and got out of there about eleven or noon. It was a four-piece band. Pops Buford played tenor. Pops was a neat guy. I just loved Pops. The rest of the band there was white guys, which was unusual, because this was a Black joint. We were probably the most swinging, most hip band in town at that time, except Billy Tolles." After a stint on the road with Darryl Harpa, Gilles returned to Seattle in 1953. He worked with bassist Traff Hubert in a duo for a time, but jobs were scarce. The Black Elks Club had closed. "Things had wound down a little," he said of the era. "Everybody had scattered." Gilles eventually went to Montana with Hubert in 1956, then on to Las Vegas and Los Angeles, where the pianist moved into rock and commercial music. During his Seattle rock 'n' roll days, Gilles was known as "Mandrake," because of his pointed beard.

The other mainstay for Black musicians during this difficult period was the Blue Note at Jefferson Street near Thirteenth Avenue. The final headquarters for Local 493, the Blue Note was purchased with the help of a fundraiser on May 29, 1951, at the Senator Ballroom that featured a stellar showcase of Seattle jazz. The "1951 Orchestra Cavalcade" featured the Vernon Brown Orchestra, the Joe Gauff Band, the Bob Marshall Sextet, Billy Tolles's Combo-Clashers, (pianist) Len Brooks, the Bumps Blackwell Orchestra, the Jabo Ward Combo, (vocalist) Merceedees Walton, the Four Question Marks (with Elmer Gill), the Cecil Young Quartet, and Al Hickey's Jive Bombers. The new union hall did triple duty as an office, nightspot, and social club. It was a hub of fraternal camaraderie, hosting sessions on Friday and Saturday nights. Every member of Local 493 had a key to get in and was allowed one guest. Drinks were twenty-five cents, and there were no union agents around to stop the jamming, because the club *was* the union. Next door was a little restaurant where you could have a T-bone steak after the gig for $3.95. Name players showed up often, not only to jam but also to hang out, relax, and meet the locals. Floyd Standifer recollected:

> That's where I first met—and heard—Johnny Hodges. That's where I first met Thad Jones. These guys would come in and they'd know a few people in town already and they'd just be so happy to walk into a joint where it was, "Hey, man, Hodges is here, how you doing, man? Say, I want you to meet Johnny Hodges. Oh, man, I've admired you for a long time. Say, bartender, give my man a double." They weren't

on a star trip, no. They were on the road. All that was beaten out of them. They were among friends. You talk about fraternalism, those guys brought new meaning to the word.

"All the guys would come around there," said Elmer Gill. "Sonny Criss, Lee Konitz, Thad Jones, anybody that happened to come through town. They used to have some sessions in there that would be fantastic. We used to stay there all night long, walk out the doors and the sun would be shining bright, nine, ten o'clock in the morning. That was a great place."

The Local 493 union office on South Jefferson Street near Thirteenth Avenue South, known to musicians as the Blue Note.

In the 1980s the Blue Note became a modest lunch counter named Debbie's. On the tile floor you could still make out a faded pattern of blue tiles in the shape of an eighth note. The building was later torn down and replaced with an apartment block.

The Mardi Gras, one of the first legitimate, Black-owned taverns in town (it had opened in 1943), also continued to present jazz during these lean years and remained open well into the 1960s. Part of the reason for its success was that it presented R & B–influenced organ trios, part of the "funky" trend of the 1950s. Bob Braxton led a group there in 1954; Pony Poindexter, Gerald Brashear, Jabo Ward, and Billy Tolles played the Mardi Gras as well. One of the star attractions at the club was Gerald Frank, the best drummer in town after Jimmie Rodgers died. Originally from Detroit, Frank drifted from music in the 1960s into a go-go girl operation in Pioneer Square, then into a lucrative real-estate business.

Despite their convivial spirit, the Mardi Gras, Blue Note, and Black Elks could not sustain a jazz scene by themselves. As club after club closed, and the music in the lounges became more watered-down, musicians began to pack their bags or take other jobs to supplement their incomes. In 1950 and 1951 alone Al Hickey, Ray Charles, Ernestine Anderson, Janet Thurlow, Quincy Jones, Cecil Young, and Bumps Blackwell all left town. Dave Stetler, Floyd Standifer, and Jabo Ward took day jobs. It was a desperate period for jazz. It's no surprise that this was also the bleak era when many jazz musicians turned to hard drugs. In 1954, Stan Getz and fellow tenor saxophonists Zoot Sims and Wardell Gray were working their way up the coast with a Seattle rhythm section (drummer

Bill Kotick, white pianist Bob Alcivar, and bassist Larry Rockwell) when Getz attempted to rob a downtown Seattle drugstore for morphine. Getz was taken to jail, where he downed sixty grains of barbiturates in a suicide attempt. Charlie Parker, too, brought his problems with him, performing in 1953 at the Metropolitan Theatre in a drugged and drunken stupor. Parker, who had spent the whole day drinking, in one of his periodic attempts to kick heroin, was discovered backstage, before the show, getting a "fix" from Pony Poindexter.

Ironically, just as the bottom dropped out of Seattle jazz, Tacoma's Pacific Avenue, a sailor's strip along the dark edge of town by the water, exploded with bebop clubs catering to soldiers being shipped back and forth between Fort Lewis and Korea. The Pirate's Cove, where Buzz Bridgeford had played, plus the New Yorker, the Tiki, the 1306 Club, the 1515, and the 1518 all hosted jazz. In South Tacoma there was the Hi Hat and the Players; elsewhere were the Towers, the Congo Club, the Broadway, Ping's Gardens, and the Union House Club. "There was a lot going on around Tacoma in those days," remembered white saxophonist Bill Ramsay. "Good Seattle musicians would come to Tacoma for sessions after their gigs." The atmosphere was sometimes rougher than in Seattle's after-hours clubs. In Ramsay's words: "There was quite a bit of Mafia control in those days. A lot of the clubs were owned by the families. The godfather of the Northwest was a Tacoma resident by the name of Vito Catone. Many times I remember playing at the New Yorker and it was like some B movie, where the place would be full of people and a couple of Vito's boys would come in and clear the place out. They'd lay a long table right in front of the band. Then Vito and his family'd come in and we'd end up playing 'Come Back to Sorrento' all night long."

Among the Tacoma players who moved freely between the two cities on the Sound were Ramsay, Chuck and Jan Stentz, Dean Reilly, and Gary Steele. Ramsay was one of the best. A huge, imposing man with a big voice, alert eyes, and a driving energy, he chewed phrases off his saxophones—alto, tenor, and baritone—with the gritty energy of bop players who have swing flowing in their veins. A native of Centralia, Washington, about one hundred miles south of Seattle, Ramsay taught himself to play saxophone as a youngster and learned to play jazz while he was stationed at Fort Lewis, from 1948 to 1952. The young saxophonist gained early experience at the Evergreen Ballroom outside Olympia, working with Art Doll (the saxophonist who had done the brilliant Lunceford transcriptions for the Men About Town), saxophonist Chuck Stentz, Traff

Hubert, Buzzy Bridgeford, Neil Friel, and white bassist Paul Binnings. He worked at Tacoma's 1306 Club for a year, then moved to the 1515, while Fred Greenwell and Buzzy were down the street at the Pirate's Cove.

Like so many swing-to-bop musicians, Ramsay played in combos but yearned for the power and punch of a large group. In 1958 he put together a short-lived "dream band" that left behind an extraordinary tape recording from a 1961 concert at Bremerton's Roxy Theater showcasing a tasty, New Testament Basie-style band driven by the locomotive rhythm section of Dick Palombi (piano), Chuck Metcalf (bass), and Bill Richardson (drums). In 1979 he got a call from saxophonist Buddy Tate, asking him to sub in the Benny Goodman band. Five years later, Ramsay was offered the baritone saxophone chair with Count Basie. The thrill of that assignment gave way soon enough to fatigue, however, particularly after Basie did three coast-to-coast round trips in six days. Ramsay quit in 1985. He continued to enjoy an active musical career in the Northwest and on the road. In 1991 he recorded a CD, *Entre Nous*, with ex-Basie saxophonist Frank Wess. (Mel Tormé's *Night at the Concord Pavilion* also featured the Wess band.) Ramsay occasionally performed in a monster saxophone group, Tenor Dynasty, with Olympian Chuck Stentz and Seattleite Denney Goodhew, and led his own band. In 1995, when saxophonist Michael Brockman and drummer Clarence Acox founded the Seattle Repertory Jazz Orchestra, they recruited Ramsay to anchor the sax section on baritone. The big jazz man played with the band for twenty-two years and served as its go-to adviser on all things Basie—and beyond. Ramsay also led a ten-piece band that played the intricately swinging arrangements of Milt Kleeb, later kept in circulation by multi-instrumentalist Jay Thomas. Ramsay was named to the Seattle Jazz Hall of Fame in 1997 and lived to enjoy that honor until 2024.

Chuck Stentz was another musician who entered the local imagination during the Tacoma boom of the early 1950s. For two or three years he worked at the New Yorker club with Art Mineo and every Sunday with Paul Neves, Buzz Bridgeford, and Floyd Standifer at the Congo Club in South Tacoma. A no-nonsense "musician's musician" who described himself as "a born sideman," Stentz was a self-taught player who joined the Air Corps after high school, then used his GI Bill to attend the New England Conservatory, working and studying with pianist Nat Pierce and saxophonist Charlie Mariano. Stentz toured New England with Pierce, Johnny Bothwell, and Shorty Sherock. In 1949 he returned to Olympia. For a while, he played in a big band at the Evergreen

Ballroom that included hot, white Tacoma trombonist Art Mell. In the mid-1950s Stentz went to work at Yenney's Music Company in Olympia, which he later bought and turned into a musicians' hangout. Stentz played with more of a beboppish rhythmic edge than Ramsay but still had a vestige of the hollow, woody sound of Lester Young's disciples. In the late 1980s Stentz developed a generation-crossing collaboration, called Bebop Revisited, with white saxophonist Bert Wilson, a remarkable California avant-gardist who moved to Washington's capital in 1979.

In 1955, Stentz married one of the area's top vocalists, Jan Swenson, a romantically charged balladeer who swung with the light touch of such jazz singers as Lee Wiley and Chris Connor. Like many women of the era, Jan Stentz put her career aside when she had children, but in the mid-1970s she started singing again, at Red Kelly's Tumwater Conservatory. She then began a long musical relationship with Olympia pianist Jack Perciful; in 1981, Jan worked with another local white piano man, Barney McClure, at Port Townsend's Manresa Castle. She recorded a sparkling album for McClure's BAM Records, titled *Profile*. In 1989 she worked briefly with the Harry James band but found she was no more fond of the road life than her husband was. She continued to work locally with Jack Perciful. She died in 1998; Chuck, in 2021. Both were named to the Seattle Jazz Hall of Fame.

The Tacoma scene also nurtured Traff Hubert's friend bassist Dean Reilly, who first surfaced nationally in recordings by the Vince Guaraldi Trio. Reilly had put in a short stint with Jimmy Buettner at the pioneering Seattle bebop haunt the Players Club, before enrolling at the University (then College) of Puget Sound, where he studied for two and a half years. In 1950, Reilly joined Neil Friel and Jimmy Gilles on the road with the Darryl Harpa band, which took him to San Francisco. From that time on, he worked there as a first-call sideman with everyone from Georgie Auld to Helen Humes and recorded with guitarists George Barnes, Earl Hines, and Cal Tjader.

Gary Steele, the small-town kid who was so knocked out by the Dizzy Gillespie big band in Seattle, was another important Tacoma bopper. Steele was known in Seattle as the stalwart electric bassist who played behind his wife, the superior vocalist Patti Summers, at their cozy basement nightclub at the Pike Place Market, but in his Tacoma days he was a tough tenor saxophonist. Steele worked his way through Tacoma's University of Puget Sound, playing gigs at night, then spent two years in a Seventh Army Special Services unit. When he came home in 1956, he started playing bass in a lounge trio with Bud Schultz, an excellent pianist/vibist who used to show up on the Annex scene and later worked with "mood music" maestro Martin Denny. Summers and Steele closed their club in 2005 but continued to play from time to time. Steele died in 2026.

Many other strong players worked in Tacoma, including "Sonny Red" Norman (tenor sax) and white musicians Bill Baty (trumpet), Bob Schlicte (tenor sax), Dick Morehead (drums), Ford Collier (trumpet), and Shelby Zollman (piano). One of the ways Tacomans got experience was by playing with seasoned Black musicians stationed at Fort Lewis or McChord Air Force Base. The most important of those soldier/musicians was Eric Dolphy, who would later become an avant-garde innovator and introduce the bass clarinet to modern jazz. Dolphy was stationed at Fort Lewis from 1950 to 1952, having joined the Army in Los Angeles with his friend Walter Benton. While in the Northwest, Dolphy played clarinet and bass clarinet in the Tacoma Symphony, jammed on the local scene, and often showed up in the back room at Tacoma Music, where owner George Greenwood kept a jam room.

Dolphy was a master technician, even then. Gary Steele remembered: "The first time I heard Eric Dolphy play was at the NCO club out at McChord Field. The tune was 'Idaho.' You had to really know what you were doing to get through the tune. It was usually done at some kind of ferocious tempo. I walked in and Eric's playing it. You could hear horn cases slamming shut all over the room. No way would anybody get up there with him." Bill Ramsay, who rehearsed some legitimate woodwind compositions with Dolphy, says he was an unusual player even at this early stage of his career, with a penchant for playing notes "outside" the normal chords and scales. Steele reports that because the Tacoma scene was racially regressive, he and Dolphy—and other Black musicians—could not play regular gigs together in the same clubs: "Black musicians and the whites had to come out to the college to play, where there were practice rooms where you could jam, or you had to go out to the NCO club at McChord. Eric and I got thrown out of places."

Official racism notwithstanding, there were some great jam sessions in those days at the Congo Club and at Ping's Gardens. The great pianist Sir Roland Hanna, also stationed at Fort Lewis, was known to show up, as was Wilbur Hogan, the cooking drummer Ray Charles would later hire for his big band. Granville T. Hogan, another drummer who later worked with Bud Powell, also came by. So did Walter Benton, Dolphy's childhood friend and an excellent "groove" tenor saxophonist; Leo Wright, the keen-toned alto saxophonist and flutist who worked many years with Dizzy Gillespie; pianists Earl DeWitt and Ernest Crawford; and white trombonist/composer Tom McIntosh.

While bebop had a burst of glory in Tacoma, the scene continued to deteriorate in Seattle, in part due to the growing popularity of rhythm and blues. Still confined at this stage to an African American "race" market, R & B nevertheless was making its way into the hearts of teenagers like the ones who had been hypnotized by swing a generation earlier. This is the period when Roy Milton, Jay McNeely, and Amos Milburn, among others, were thrusting the double shuffle of Lunceford and the amusing backbeat of Louis Jordan into a new dance genre, which after a few years would cross over to the white market and be dubbed "rock 'n' roll." The jazz musicians who had the biggest hand in bringing rock to Seattle were Billy Tolles and Tommy Adams. "When I got back from college," recalled Tolles, "nobody was popping the sock cymbal two-four. They were all just kinda leading their sock cymbal, hitting it a lick or two. Back East, boy, they were popping that sock cymbal. I got [Tommy Adams] doing that, and that brought a whole new thing of drums to Seattle. I brought that from back East. That's what set everything on fire! That tight backbeat, man. We kicked ass right from the beginning. We were playing those heavy shuffles. Tommy Adams had such a raw sense of rhythm, boy. He'd be chopping wood, and there'd be wood all down up under the snare drum, where he'd been hitting that rim stick." In what would become a harbinger of things to come, Tolles's little rock 'n' roll combo won a "battle of the bands" at the Eagles Auditorium against the best jazz groups in town. "We were all raggedy-looking, and the rest of the bands were all dressed up," he recalled. "Cecil Young was on that thing and Elmer Gill and they were so sophisticated and intellectual, and so on, and we came on there with that blues and that 'Flyin' Home' and just walked off with that $150 prize."

Tolles formed his first rock 'n' roll band in 1951. He worked at the 908 and at dances organized by social clubs, such as the Royal Esquires, which set up shop in 1947 on one of the blocks of South Washington Street later occupied by the Bailey Gatzert School playfield. Such clubs continued the legacy of the Washington Social Club. In 1951 and 1952 one of the hot spots for these Black dances was a room on the second floor of the Chamber of Commerce building, on Marion Street between Second and Third Avenues. The atmosphere was essentially unchanged from that of the old bottle clubs. People brought their own liquor. Sometimes the dances were held at Washington Performance

Hall, at Fourteenth Avenue and Fir Street. Tolles presented a showcase quintet sometimes known as Billy Tolles and the Four Tolls, a funky, hard-driving rhythm band in which the front line later sang hits like "Sh-boom, Sh-boom!" and did dance steps. As Tolles remembered:

> I was playing the style that I learned with Louis Jordan. He made everything just happy, you know, playing those little shuffle rhythms and the blues and keeping it comedic and high-octane. I went and got Floyd Standifer, Buddy Catlett, Tommy Adams, and Elmer Gill, and we formed a singing group that set Seattle on its ear. If I could have six pieces, I would use Floyd Standifer and Rod Levitt. Then I started using another white boy playing trombone, Dick Thorlakson. That band survived for several years. We were singing songs like "Mother in Law" and the Mills Brothers. Me and Floyd Standifer fell out about something, so I brought Jabo Ward into the band, and he'd sing Floyd's parts.

In 1955, Tolles streamlined his R & B concept to a trio, using Tommy Adams and keyboard man Mike Taylor. The following year, he and saxophonist Floyd Franklin moved into Ayers Cafe, at 1311 Yesler Way, possibly Myrt Francois's old place. White students from the University of Washington flocked to the neighborhood. The Sessions Club (which had become Sessions Playhouse) was two blocks away, and the Esquires Club had found a home around the corner. The streets were rocking. "I could just honk," Tolles recalled, "and walk through the joint, jump from tabletop to tabletop, honking on my low B-flat, walk the bar, [go] outside and come back in the back door, and all that kind of stuff. That really got us over. Those white kids, they'd be in there clamoring for that."

While Tolles was at Ayer's, Dave Holden, Oscar Holden's son, replaced Mike Taylor on piano. Dave was just out of Garfield High School and attending Everett Junior College on a basketball scholarship. He started using an electric keyboard called the Organo, playing a walking bass line with the left hand and a honky-tonk riff with the right. With Adams's drums and Holden's electric piano, the new trio quickly became a local attraction, working at the Mardi Gras and Dave's Fifth Avenue. As Tolles threw himself more and more into rock, many local jazz players turned their noses up at him, regarding his forays into dance music as rank commercialism. A private 1956 tape recording made at Dave's Fifth Avenue sheds some light as to why. Playing with an all-star local jazz band consisting of Jabo Ward (baritone saxophone), Paul Neves (piano),

Monk Montgomery (bass), and Tommy Adams (drums), Tolles plays a mix of R & B and jazz that features an embarrassing vocal trio rendition of the faux-sweet novelty waltz "From the Vine Came the Grape," a 1954 jukebox hit by the Gaylords.

It's not clear which instrumentalists are singing in the trio Tolles calls out as "the Three Tolls," but it's probably Billy, Tommy, and Jabo. They also play a long, wailing version of the timeless Bill Doggett classic "Honky Tonk (Part 1 & 2)," with Ward sounding decidedly uncomfortable as he solos over a rock beat. Unsurprisingly, the set includes a rollicking excursion on "Flyin' Home," the Lionel Hampton hit with the athletic Illinois Jacquet solo that had inspired Tolles to pick up the tenor saxophone in the first place, as well as another Jacquet-like barn burner written by Tolles, "East Chester Flat," with Adams hammering the backbeat. For all its rock energy and lounge act schmaltz, the set is a fascinating illustration of just how fluid the relationship was between rock and jazz at this time in Seattle. Tolles's band may have been playing rock, but Neves, Ward, and Montgomery were among the heaviest jazz cats in town. Did they just need the work? Possibly. But they also sound like they're having a damn good time. As on Jackson Street in the old days, the line between R & B and jazz was still not especially strict. At the end of the set, Billy trolls the crowd to see if anyone wants to sit in—a jazz tradition—and calls out the great bass player Freddy Schreiber. Apparently the jazz cats weren't just onstage; they were also right there in the crowd. Clearly Dave's was the place to be in 1956.

Tolles could blow most Seattle jazzmen out of the water at their own game, so he bridled at any snobbery he encountered: "Everybody was ridiculing us. I was the best jazz player in town, but here I was, playing rock. They were saying, 'Oh, man, you playing that funky butt stuff.' But boy, we had the joint packed, jammed up, man. And we were getting grand-theft money. Everybody was coming, them included, because they'd be getting off their jobs early because all the people would be at our jobs. I said, 'To hell with what you think.' When I was doing dance music, I played rhythm and blues, and when I was jazz, I was all jazz." Not only did Billy play Seattle's first rock, he was hired by promoter and club owner Wilmer Morgan to book rock and R & B shows. Between 1952 and 1955, Tolles brought T-Bone Walker, Earl Bostic, Fats Domino, Pee Wee Crayton, Jay McNeely, and James Brown, among others, to the Eagles Auditorium, the Trianon Ballroom, and the China Pheasant. Sometimes his own band opened the shows. In 1952 he and Morgan presented

T-Bone Walker at Birdland for one of the first editions of the annual city-wide celebration known as Seafair. Walker played a street dance on the corner. Tolles didn't forget his jazz roots. He also brought up James Moody, his old friend from North Carolina, who had just come out with his hit "Moody's Mood for Love." Tolles boasted, "I had Moody at Birdland and Earl Bostic at the Eagles Auditorium the same weekend."

At one point, Wilmer Morgan owned Birdland, the Mardi Gras, and the China Pheasant, where he booked Percy Mayfield and Amos Milburn. Bob Summerise, an ardent jazz fan who also owned a record store at Twelfth Avenue and South Jackson Street called World of Music, worked with Morgan and was the first local DJ to play R & B, on Bremerton station KBRQ, in 1947. Many Seattle musicians and fans grew up on the intelligent mix of R & B and jazz on his *Cool Breeze* show. His theme song was "Tonsillectomy," by Boyd Raeburn, but he'd often follow a jazz cut with a tune by the Spinners or the Ravens. Summerise promoted several jazz concerts and also wrote a column for the *Northwest Enterprise*, in which he touted new sides, chatted about the local scene, and sometimes waxed philosophical about music. Summerise felt, as Tolles did, that jazz and rhythm and blues were part of the same tradition and needn't be at war.

Nevertheless, the money was increasingly in rock, and Tolles went for the gold. In 1956 his promotional talents led to a television show for teenagers, *Rock 'n' Roll Party*, on Channel 13. The show was a local version of *American Bandstand*, live from Parker's Ballroom. Dave Lewis, a keyboardist who had become popular by this time at Birdland, and the Frantics, a twanging R & B group that included white bassist Jimmy Manolides, were two of the popular acts on the Channel 13 show.

Tolles eventually decided to give up booking and go south with his trio to get in on some of the action. The Tolles Trio, with Tommy Adams and Dave Holden, played first in Santa Clara, then in San Francisco and Las Vegas. While Billy and Tommy and Dave were playing the El Morocco in Vegas, Dave's younger brother, Ron, hit the rock 'n' roll jackpot with a single, "Love You So." (The record reached No. 7 on the 1960 *Billboard* charts.) Dave left Tolles to join his brother on the road. Tolles continued working in Las Vegas with Earl DeWitt, the keyboard man he had first met at Fort Lewis, making periodic trips to Seattle to work at the Mardi Gras and the Downbeat, a new club in Pioneer Square at 110 Third Avenue that later became the Pink

Pussycat. During the 1962 World's Fair in Seattle, Tolles tried to open a club in Pioneer Square, but it never got off the ground. In 1966 he went to Denver to visit DeWitt and, except for a period when he toured the world as a regular for the Playboy Club circuit, settled there. Tolles enjoyed a long career in Denver as a revered local jazz musician, starring in his own show at a club called Dazzle. In 2002, Tolles returned to Seattle for an emotional reunion at Experience Music Project with Floyd Standifer and Dave Holden. That same year he released a lively album recorded at the venerable Denver nightclub El Chapultepec, titled *Chapulteset*. Tolles died in 2005.

Tolles's pioneering drummer during this period, Tommy Adams, did not fare as well as Billy. Tales about Adams's behavior have circulated among Seattle musicians for years. Many of the stories are true. Most people do not know, however, that Adams's erratic antics were caused by the onset of diabetes, which for many years he did not know he had. Born in 1930, Adams was a natural musician who came up in the swing-to-bop era, first as a singer in the smooth manner of baritone Billy Eckstine—performing with Quincy Jones in the Bumps Blackwell Junior Band—then as a drummer in a manner all his own. Adams and Tolles had been friends since the old days at the Washington Social Club, when they had jammed with Bumps's bass player, Billy Johnson. In 1950, Adams also played briefly in the Gus Mankertz workshop band at Seattle University. His hard-driving backbeat marked the local transition from jazz to rock. Dave Holden described it like this: "All the drummers in the area would come to hear Tommy. Tommy had one high hat and one cymbal and a snare drum. That's all. None of these other cymbals. Tommy was a swing drummer, but he was a swing-shuffle drummer. He gave swing a new feel because he'd shuffle through every swing piece. He influenced all the drummers that ever heard him in the Seattle area."

Slim as a young man, in his fifties Adams began to put on weight, earning the nickname "Fat Daddy." He loved to cook and enjoyed feeding his bandmates rich, fattening foods, probably the cause of his eventual diabetes. On edge, Adams began to get into fistfights, shout hysterically in clubs, and play so ferociously that it scared people. Sometimes he would jump up and down on his drums, run around the club, and tear his shirt off. He acquired a fetish for Native American regalia, donning a warbonnet, feathers, and a sash. At first, people put up with Adams's behavior, labeling it simple eccentricity, but in time, owners became leery of hiring him. The end came with a nasty incident in South

Tacoma, near Fort Lewis, when he was playing with Dave Holden and Gerald Brashear. By this time Adams had learned that he was sick; a doctor had put him on a severe diet, and he had lost eighty pounds. Recalled Holden: “The last night, Tommy started jumping up and down and running around and pushing people out of his way and running through the crowd and doing a *whoa-hoa-hoa*–type Indian thing in the middle of 450 people, in a beer tavern. This was a military place in South Tacoma, right down the street from Fort Lewis. Jam-packed. It got so bad at that point that we couldn’t handle it. Nobody could handle it. He was gone, mentally. The owner called the police because they had to restrain him. Tommy was down on the ground with handcuffs and they took him off to jail.” Adams was taken to the mental hospital at Steilacoom. When he realized where he was, he ran away. Adams died in 1965 while living with his mother in Detroit, after another severe bout with his illness.

Rhythm and blues cut severely into the market for jazz—later, rock would hit jazz even harder—but the most significant change affecting Jackson Street in the 1950s had nothing to do with musical style: it was the merger of the Black and white locals. By 1955 integrated bands were already working at the Lake City Tavern and at the Flame in the North End. “Mixed” bands were tolerated at the Black Elks Club as well, because they were under the jurisdiction of Local 493. But Local 76 still did not tolerate integrated contracts in the lucrative downtown clubs north of Yesler Way, the unofficial color line. The 1950s would be the decade in which, finally, there’d be some changes made. No one was more ready to start making these changes than pianist and club owner Elmer Gill.

Gill bitterly resented the way legalized racism had held down Black entrepreneurs in all fields, and how the terms of the racial discussion were consistently shifted by white people to tolerance and integration, when the issue for Black people was also money—the ability to make a living and succeed. More clearly than anyone else on the scene, Gill seems to have understood that while Black musicians might earn $100 a night in tips at the Black and Tan, Jackson Street was still an economic ghetto. He had first run into racial discrimination in the music world when he worked in 1952 with the Question Marks at the Spinning Wheel on Second Avenue, just north of the color line. As he remembered it:

The Spinning Wheel was a white-only place. I didn't know that at the time that I went in there. This friend of mine and their whole party and his wife came down there and they were standing at the door. I was up there playing and I could see that there was something going on. After a while, this guy came out from behind the bar and he says, "Uh, Elmer, [there's] some friends of yours back there and they want to come in. You go back and tell 'em," he says. "Tell them what?" I said. "Uh, you know the score!"

I caught on right then what he was trying to do and I went back there and I said, "Hey, man! What you doing standing out there! Come on in!" The guy almost fainted. From then on, when I played in Seattle, I used to put in my contract that anybody, regardless of race, creed, or color, as long as they were acting in accord with the place, and the policy of the place, and so forth, then they could come into the place while I was playing. You'd be surprised at the number of people that wouldn't sign that contract.

Gill's next solution to racial discrimination was to open a room of his own. In 1953 he bought part ownership in the Ebony Café, on South Jackson Street just east of Fifth Avenue on the ground floor of the Governor Apartments, where Phil Moore had lived. The Governor was one of two beautiful white buildings on the strip erected by the Rainier Heat & Power Company. Though it was just a block away from the shuttered Elks Club, Gill made an all-out effort to dissociate himself from the now-discredited after-hours scene, if not completely from the public that had made it lucrative. He wanted his place to be considered "legit" and aimed for a "classy" image in the new atmosphere of legalized liquor. He built a small stage and moved in a grand piano. The kitchen served full dinners and drinks. More than thirty years later, tellingly, Gill was sensitive when anyone referred to it as a club. "It was a *restaurant*," he insisted. "It wasn't a club at all. It used to make me mad. People would come in and they'd say, 'Where's the gambling?' We used to have a terrible time trying to make people drink up the drinks: 'Oh, this is Jackson Street, you don't need to be worried about that. You go all night here, don't you? Where's the back room?'"

For the Ebony, Gill formed an excellent, Nat Cole–style trio, hiring Al Larkins on bass and Al Turay on guitar. Larkins, whose brother, pianist Ellis Larkins, was one of New York's finest café jazz players, was one of Seattle's two or three best bass players in the 1940s and 1950s. An accomplished tuba player and a solid swing bass man who could play intricate solos with a bow, Larkins played for a long time with the Rainy City Jazz Band, a Dixieland group, and eventually became a math teacher at Franklin High School. For his service to the community, the city named a park at Thirty-Fourth Avenue and Pike Street after him when he died, in 1984.

Gill's choice for guitar, Al Turay, was known mostly to Seattleites in the 1960s as a teacher who ran a guitar studio in Wallingford, but the mild-mannered, lanky bassist/guitarist had been kicking around since the late 1930s, when he used to jam with Milt Green and Junior Raglin. Since that time, Turay had worked on Alaska cruise ships for a couple of years with white pianist Art Barduhn and white drummer/vibist Jimmy Sutton in a group called the Rhythm Rascals, followed by a gig at a downtown club called the Forty and Eight. After the war he was in a jazz trio with Al Pierre's bassist, Bill Rinaldi, and pianist Jimmy Buettner at the Roll Inn, a downtown tavern on Eighth, near Pike. Turay also did a stint with Norm Hoagy at the Magic Inn.

The Ebony Café was located on South Jackson Street just east of Fifth Avenue, inside the beautiful white Governor Building, which still stands today.

Recordings of early Seattle jazz musicians are rare, but a 1957 Corky Corcoran album released by Seattle's Celestial Records, *Sounds of Jazz Volume One: Corky*, showcases Turay's crisp, thoroughly modern, single-note guitar style to good advantage, offering a glimpse of the cool vibe that was probably on offer at the Ebony. With Gay Jones on piano, Dave Coleman on drums, and Milt Garred on bass, *Corky* is a gem.

Turay was working early hours at the Colony when he happened to drop by the Ebony to check the place out. He sat in, and one of Seattle's most popular groups from the 1950s was born. "That thing jelled right from the start," he said. "That was strictly a jazz thing. We used to have them lined up halfway around the block to get into that place there. I think I enjoyed that just about as much as any gig I played. We had a good feeling. We could sense what each individual was going to do." Another rare record featuring the trio playing "Al-ley Cat Noise," released on the Rube-K label, supports Turay's recollection of the trio's simpatico feel and also showcases his fleet-fingered bebop lines. As the Black Elks Club had been before it, the Ebony became the hottest spot on the street, running successfully until 1957 and reopening in 1959 with another trio that featured drummer Dave Coleman. Touring jazz musicians dropped by after their gigs, among them Dizzy Gillespie, Oscar Pettiford, the Modern Jazz Quartet, and Ben Webster.

One of the reasons celebrities came was to check out a strange gimmick Gill had created. A few months after the Ebony opened, perhaps out of a perverse reaction to those customers who kept asking where the "after-hours" action was (or because the liquor board forced clubs to stop selling booze early), Gill started to present jazz on Saturdays—from 6:00 to 9:00 a.m.! He titled the sessions "Jam for Breakfast." The concept was a smash. Recounted Gill:

> It always bothered me that they always wanted people to play music from nine o'clock to one o'clock in the morning. So I told these people, "Look, you can sell booze starting at six o'clock in the morning. Why not on Saturday morning?" They thought I was absolutely crazy. But I was so sure [it would work], I paid the musicians myself. The thing immediately took off. We did that for almost two years, every Saturday morning. There'd be a line out in front. We'd get people before they would go to the golf course, or maybe doctors and nurses that had been working all night long. You had people that would come all the way from Vancouver, every week. Make a day of it, go shopping and everything.

"Jam for Breakfast" was such a success that other clubs started imitating the concept, and Gill eventually was forced to copyright the name to protect himself from unfair competition. But having a successful concern on Jackson Street did not satisfy Gill, as long as the downtown lounges were still closed to Black musicians and fans. In 1956 he decided to challenge the whole rotten system of union segregation. The climate was ripe. Two years earlier the US Supreme Court had forcibly integrated schools in Little Rock, Arkansas. People had watched televised reports of fire hoses beating back demonstrators. Though many Black musicians struggled for equality in Seattle, Gill's story is worth singling out, first because he pulled in a musician from outside who would later have an enduring love affair with the Seattle jazz public, but also because the likable and popular Gill was so forthright and organized—yet disarming—in his demands. To Gill, it just seemed obvious that he should have the same opportunity as anyone else to play downtown, just as it had seemed obvious that he should sell alcohol at six o'clock in the morning if the liquor board prohibited selling it at one o'clock.

In August, recruiting his Ebony trio mates Larkins and Turay, Gill offered to play in the upscale Brigadier Room of the New Washington Hotel, a downtown establishment on Second Avenue and Stewart Street, a bastion of the white union local, just a block from the Bon Marché department store. The hotel was owned by Gene Autry's Doric Hotel chain. No Black group had ever played there before. When the management discovered not only that Gill intended to bring a racially mixed trio into the lounge but that his contract specifically stipulated the management could not refuse entry to anyone on the basis of race, creed, or color, they balked. Remembered Gill:

> This guy called me. He was the manager of the hotel. He whispers to me, "What they're worried about is it's gonna [bring in] the 'Jackson Street element.'" I said, "Well, I don't know what you're talking about the 'Jackson Street element,' but if this is a first-class place, a bum is a bum. It's no more than getting the Skid Row element from First Avenue. If he's a bum, then that's not in accordance with the policy of your place." I knew what he was trying to say, but I wasn't going to let him. So they called a meeting of the board of directors in Los Angeles.

The board of directors was somewhat more progressive, it developed, than their Seattle managers. They took a look at Gill's proposal, shrugged, and stamped their approval on the contract. After all, Nat Cole had been on television with his own show; Black artists were demanding their rights. Besides, this was good business. Gill had a popular trio. The board said it thought Gill's integrated group would be just fine.

The same year Gill challenged Seattle's odious segregation customs, Parker's Ballroom also bucked the union. In decidedly white union territory, on Highway 99, the club booked Dave Lewis as an opening act. Such landmark "invasions" of white territory took on new luster when Larkins and Turay, who didn't like the restrictive atmosphere of the Brigadier Room, went back to the Ebony and Gill replaced Larkins with Monk Montgomery, the electric bassist he had worked with in Lionel Hampton's band. (Milt Green took Turay's place.) Elmer and Monk were both from Indianapolis, and while they hadn't known each other there, they had the same attitudes about music and the inequities of the racial situation. Indianapolis was particularly backward at the time, so Montgomery had been anxious to leave. "When Elmer called me," recalled the bassist, "it sounded like music to my ears. I was very depressed."

"We were the first Black group to play in a first-class hotel downtown in Seattle, the first one," boasted Gill. "Len Brooks played solo piano down at a place that's now the Moore, but there wasn't any other." Gill's "outlaw " contract at the Brigadier Room went counter to the unwritten policy of segregation at

Local 76, but in fact negotiations were already underway to integrate the two unions. By the time the trio finished its engagement at the Brigadier Room, Seattle's segregated unions would be history. Previous attempts by the Black union to force amalgamation, in 1936 and 1950, had been brusquely rebuffed by the American Federation of Musicians, but with Little Rock pushing a new agenda, the national leadership had begun to promote mergers rather than resist them. Ernie Lewis, the bandleader from Basin Street who had reestablished Seattle's Black union local in the 1940s, had risen in the national union's ranks and was now assistant to the AFM president, delegated to represent Black locals in all merger proceedings. At a 1954 meeting in Chicago aimed at bringing the unions together, Lewis worked with Local 493 delegate Powell Barnett, the man whose determination to join the white local in 1909 had inadvertently given rise to the Black union in the first place. Barnett came back with a plan. Each Seattle local was to form an amalgamation committee to consider the issue, then present it to their membership for a vote.

Perhaps surprisingly, the majority of white musicians favored the merger. Though some feared for their jobs, most musicians saw the move as a positive social step. Tiny Martin, Gay Jones's former bassist and then a member of the Seattle Symphony and president of Local 76, endorsed the effort of the amalgamation committees. An unsigned editorial in the December issue of *Musicland* (probably penned by pianist John Wittwer, who was on the amalgamation committee) appealed to local pride and moral uprightness: "Not only can we steal a march on our 'Frisco friends by desegregating now, we can join in a sweeping nation-wide trend which gives the lie to the white supremacy bilge prevalent throughout much of our ethically decadent and crassly ignorant South. . . . On December 11th, let us give our resounding approval to the efforts of the two committees, to our own long history of tolerance among musicians everywhere, and to that precious principle: 'All men are created equal.'" Emmett Lewis, president of the Black local, contributed a mild but firm statement: "Generally, the Negro musician has proved no exception to an accepted pattern and for years his best source of livelihood was in the least desirable places. . . . We feel that joining your local will benefit both unions as a group, our members and their families, and the community as a whole."

On December 15, 1956, the Black union voted unanimously for the merger. The white union followed suit, passing the issue with a large majority. It took a little more than a year for the details to be hammered out. On January 14, 1958,

Lewis deposited a check with Local 76 and all members of the Black union became members of Local 76. Lewis was elected to the board of a new, integrated local. Local 493 was no more. The Seattle merger was part of a groundswell around the country that quickly integrated musicians' unions everywhere. In 1955, Ernie Lewis had had fifty-five Black locals to service. By 1957 the only segregated union on the West Coast was San Francisco's, which soon followed Seattle's lead. Between 1960 and 1966 the AFM merged twenty more locals. By the end of the decade union segregation was a thing of the past.

The effects of amalgamation on the Seattle scene were complex and took some time to play out. The rationale behind the merger, of course, had been fairness. When the unions joined, Local 493 had just over one hundred members, of whom perhaps eighty or so were active (Ray Charles and Quincy Jones, long gone, were still on the official list). The new, racially mixed union, it was hoped, would open the best-paying jobs in downtown lounges and theaters to those eighty players, who had been barred from them for more than half a century. In practice, however, this did not always happen. For while their membership in Local 76 made Black musicians technically eligible for jobs downtown, there was nothing in the new rules that forced the lounges and hotels—or, for that matter, white bandleaders—to hire Black musicians. Sadly, for many of them the post-merger world was in some ways worse than the pre-merger one. As the years went by, many Black musicians felt hoodwinked; a sour wake of bitterness developed. Tenor saxophonist Jabo Ward observed: "At our own local, they called us. When we went into 76, we got crumbs. We didn't get the show jobs—like when the Ice Follies came, they didn't call Black musicians. Didn't call us for certain artists coming in town to play the background music for them down at the theaters. No, we didn't get those jobs. We had our own buildup of clients that we dealt with, but 76 didn't do anything for us. Just made us pay more money into another local. It hurt. I'd say it hurt, yeah."

Chuck Metcalf agreed.

> I think it turned out to be a bummer for the Black musicians because they didn't get any more work, but they had to pay higher dues. . . . Okay, so Floyd Standifer . . . started to get calls to play in some big bands. But guys like Milton Garred wouldn't be hired by white musicians. Or Jabo Ward. The social patterns had already kind of congealed. There was a certain group of white musicians that went to play with

Black musicians and that stayed the same. But there was a certain group of white musicians that had just never played with Black musicians and it wasn't that they were racist or anything, it was just the way the scene was at that time. They didn't know them as friends. They had no reason to hire them, and so they didn't.

The problem wasn't only with the ingrained patterns of white bandleaders. Hotel managers and club owners often resisted integrated groups. Recalled Elmer Gill: "The Sorrento Hotel used to have a place up at the top. The guy came down to the Ebony and he wanted Turay and Larkins and I to play. He offered me a good deal, more money than I was making down there. I went to talk to him about signing the contract and we were sitting at the bar talking and as I got up to leave, I was shaking his hand and thanking him, and he says, 'Oh, one more thing. By the way,' he says, 'you got to get rid of the guitar player.'" Gill eventually became so fed up with the American racial situation that he moved to Canada. In the early 1960s he began to divide his time between British Columbia and Basel, Switzerland, where he played in a four-star hotel.

It's a pity Gill did not stick around to enjoy the legacy of his labors. With his "Jam for Breakfast" and early-hours jazz dining concepts, he successfully broke the local stereotype that jazz had to be played in an after-hours atmosphere or a cheap tavern, thereby gentrifying the context for jazz and closing the door on its old bootlegging-and-gambling image. Ironically he had done this right on Jackson Street. The clubs that emerged downtown in the modern era from the ashes of Jackson Street—integrated, upscale, and catering to hip listeners—owed much to Gill's efforts.

Unfortunately, the new social attitudes that allowed these clubs also drove a stake into the hearts of the old ones. Without a Black musicians' union, there was no support system for the most lucrative work Black musicians had ever had—in the Jackson Street venues. The first blow had been thrust by the state legislature in 1949, when it legalized hard liquor. The second had come from the neighborhood itself, which had sought to squelch the clubs in the name of respectability. The third had come from changes in popular taste, which created markets for lounge music and rock 'n' roll. Now, finally, in 1956 the very social structure that had made the whole scene necessary—segregation—was caving in.

One by one, the Black "bottle clubs" succumbed. Even diehard joints that had cut new deals with the police began to close. Mayor Gordon Clinton, in a fit of gratuitous moral reform, had his picture taken in front of the 908 Club, holding an ax. It closed in 1956. The Blue Note, where Local 493 convened, trickled on for a spell, some say until 1959; the New Chinatown lasted until 1975, though with a diet of sweet music. The last bona fide after-hours place to close, according to Dave Stetler, was the 605 Club (at 605 King, formerly known as the Kun Ming). "It went for quite a few years," said Stetler, "and I really don't know how." As Floyd Standifer put it, "As long as there was 493, there was a center. When 493 disappeared, it took away the focus for jazz. People began to spread out. Instead of having someplace to go, where you could find all the musicians in town at any given time, there was no place for this sound to be concentrated anywhere."

10 After the Bottle Clubs Closed

WHEN JACKSON STREET COLlapsed, it did not spell the end of jazz in Seattle, nor did all the great musicians who had been nurtured there hang up their horns. On the contrary, Seattle jazz experienced another golden period in the late 1950s and early 1960s, as new, legal nightclubs sprang up and a fresh, young audience came to patronize them. As the best musicians moved from the "bottle clubs" into the new racially integrated venues, elements of the old underground were absorbed into the "overground" culture at large. Floyd Standifer, the musician whose career best represented this transition during the 1950s, explained: "Musicians Black and white began to filter together. There became this great interchange. People began to spread out—and rightly so, you know, rightly so, because that other scene was built on something that was socially improper and intolerable. The jazz scene began to benefit."

As Standifer pointed out, amalgamation was progressive socially—however, like all assimilations, it involved losses. With integration, the music moved away from its roots in the community, as nightclubs relocated from the Black district to downtown. Audiences changed. The mood of performances shifted from comfortable neighborhood affairs to commercial exchanges. But there were gains too. Clubs were no longer raided, wages were regulated by the union, working conditions were (usually) improved, and—perhaps most important of all—a great musical tradition was made accessible to a wider spectrum of American society. The music played in the new clubs was more sophisticated than what had been offered on Jackson Street as well. Local players improved their command of bop, and the new styles of modal jazz and hard bop became a part of the regional vocabulary. National touring acts began to stop over on a more regular basis. By 1962, with the coming of the World's Fair and the establishment of modern jazz clubs such as Pete's Poop Deck and the Penthouse, Seattle (and by extension, Seattle jazz) would become thoroughly cosmopolitan.

Many Jackson Street musicians enjoyed their most productive years after the district's heyday. Ernestine Anderson, Pony Poindexter, and Buddy Catlett left town and forged important careers in the national mainstream. Floyd Standifer, Jabo Ward, Chuck Metcalf, and Elmer Gill worked throughout the 1950s in a handful of venues that were the prototypes of the modern jazz club, where people came to listen to the music rather than to dance or socialize. Two of the most important clubs—the Flame and the Lake City Tavern—opened in the North End, where the audiences were mostly white. Elmer Gill's Ebony Café, on Jackson, continued to draw a mixed crowd of professionals and working people. The short-lived but influential Northwest Jazz Workshop, in the University District, tried to fill the void left by the closure of the Blue Note. By the end of the decade the energy from these hubs would, in Standifer's words, "filter together," and a new jazz flowering would replace the old Jackson Street scene.

It's useful to look briefly at how this transition occurred, since Jackson Street was not some exotic, ahistorical event, but an era whose characteristics have profound links to the present. It would also be a disservice to leave unfinished the stories of those players whose careers blossomed after the decline of the Jackson Street era. A case in point was George James "Buddy" Catlett, who had started out with the Charlie Taylor band in the 1940s. Having a musician of Catlett's caliber in a town the size of Seattle was one of the rewards of being a jazz listener in the Northwest. Catlett had a round, firm acoustic-bass sound, the type that can only be achieved by plucking with real force against a string braced high above the fingerboard. After Milt Garred, Catlett's sense of time was the standard against which that of all other local bassists was measured—so were his walking blues lines and his note choices in a ballad. He sometimes got unfairly typecast as an "old-fashioned" player—indeed, his roots were in Basie—but anyone who listened carefully to his solos knew that he was every bit as versed in modern harmonies as bassists who succeeded him on the scene.

A short, stocky man, Catlett masked a deep, analytical intelligence behind his amiable smile. A good sense of humor about himself and life's vagaries was always a hallmark of Buddy Catlett. Though he was born in Long Beach, California, he came from a Washington pioneer family. His first musical memories were of his mother Natalie's wide-ranging record collection, which included Basie, Lester Young, and Nat "King" Cole; only later did he discover that his father played passable stride piano. The first live music he recalled hearing was at a picnic near Black Diamond, a small town in the foothills of the Cascades. "A guy named Banjoski [Adams] played guitar and Joe Darensbourg played clarinet. I was about eleven years old. They were really good players. The first big band I ever saw was Count Basie. My grandmother took me to it. They had dances every Thanksgiving here at the Civic Auditorium. I almost fell out of the balcony. J. J. Johnson was in the band, Illinois Jacquet, Shadow Wilson, Lucky Thompson—I never heard nothing like that in my whole life." Catlett learned to dance first, then took up cornet, on which he mastered a Louis Armstrong blues. When he was twelve, Catlett moved from trumpet to tenor saxophone, purchasing an instrument with money he'd earned as an usher at a Ballard movie theater. Lessons from Frank Waldron put him in touch with an early jazz style that would later prove valuable when he played with Armstrong himself.

Catlett played alto saxophone in the Charlie Taylor band; in 1950, however, he was struck with a severe case of pleurisy that doctors feared was tuberculosis—common at the time, and also incurable. The doctors instructed him not to play saxophone under any circumstances: blowing into the horn might make him sicker. For a teenager who sounded like Johnny Hodges and whose whole identity was wrapped up in music, this was devastating. Catlett was forced to spend his last two years of high school in and out of the hospital. "When I got out, I still wanted to play music. I had decided that in junior high school. But I'd lost the momentum and I was scared of it, really. I approached Elmer Gill about taking lessons from him. Then the bass player Billy Johnson went into the Air Force and his bass was at home. I knew his parents. They said, 'Well, Billy's bass is here, you want to use that?' That's when I started playing bass. I took lessons from Tiny Martin. I started playing with Billy Tolles, Freddie Greenwell, Paul Neves, and Buzz Bridgeford."

Catlett got his first gig as a bass player at an after-hours spot called the Aurora Country Club, where Floyd Standifer led the band. Buddy worked days at the university bookstore and jammed after hours, "going over those things over and over again," as he put it, "until it starts to make sense and you can hit it from any angle." One musician remembered seeing Catlett at the Lake City Tavern in those early years, playing "until his fingers bled." In the early hours Catlett played the Lake City with Paul Neves; after hours he worked in Billy Tolles's rhythm-and-blues band at the 908 Club. Catlett could have stayed in town and made a good living playing rock 'n' roll with Billy, but when veteran bandleader Horace Henderson (Fletcher's brother) scouted the 908 one night, Catlett promptly signed up. That was May 1956.

Horace Henderson was a jazz pianist, arranger, and bandleader who made some forays into R & B; he has been described by Gunther Schuller as "one of the most talented yet most neglected and enigmatic of figures in all of jazz." Catlett worked with Henderson until the spring of 1957, doubling as a copyist and teaching himself some of the principles of composition and arranging. The tour wound down in Denver, where Henderson was based, and Buddy, who had since married, joined his wife in the Mile-High City. Denver had a thriving jazz scene in the 1950s, and Catlett immediately found work in a band playing opposite Art Blakey at Sonny's Lounge. The group featured saxophonist Booker Ervin. Buddy also worked in Denver with Johnny Smith, the great guitarist. In 1959, California vibist and drummer Cal Tjader hired Catlett, an experience that gave him a chance to learn Latin music from Tjader's sidemen Willie Bobo and Mongo Santamaria. "Willie and Mongo helped me a lot to understand Latin rhythms, which I didn't understand then at all," Catlett recalled. "I had to go by Willie's place every night because I was playing the conception of Latin music all wrong. I was playing swing music. That perpendicular feeling was just too bad!"

Catlett was willing to take seriously any music put before him. But like many jazz musicians of his generation who had missed formal training, he had come to realize that to grow, he needed to acquire musical tools only available from a conservatory. When Quincy Jones invited him to Europe, one of the reasons he went was so he could attend the Juilliard School, in New York, after the tour: "Learning on the bandstand is one thing, but it leaves a lot of gaps, when it comes down to important music. What I wanted to do was stop and practice and study someplace. But I couldn't. When we came back, we were supposed to go on Broadway, and that would give me a chance to go [to Juilliard] or Manhattan [School of Music] in the daytime. But none of that took place. I stayed on the road."

When Buddy got to New York, he made his first recording, *Under Paris Skies*, with Jones and Andy Williams. While the *Free and Easy* band was in rehearsal, Catlett also worked in Harlem with the great pianist Red Garland. After the European tour, which lasted ten months, Catlett did return to New York. But instead of going to school, he went right to work with pianist Junior Mance, followed by stints with Chico Hamilton, Eddie "Lockjaw" Davis, and Johnny Griffin. When Count Basie needed an anchor man, Quincy recommended Buddy. By this time Catlett had been around long enough to know most of the players, so while it was an honor to get on the band, he was no longer in awe of them. He also knew the music, inside and out. "I had listened to

Basie since I was old enough to walk. I knew what it was supposed to sound like. There was a guy that lived in West Seattle, he's a retired ferryboat captain. We went to a Basie concert ten years before and we taped the whole concert at the Civic Auditorium. I had that tape for ten years, so I knew every tune they had. I knew it like I could do it upside down. So when I started, it was great. [People thought,] 'Wow, he's reading his ass off!'"

While Catlett was with Basie, the band recorded an album with Frank Sinatra, *Sinatra-Basie: An Historical Musical First*, and appeared on television numerous times. But the moments he remembered as highlights were when the band hit an ineffable groove:

> We were doing a Polish dance on the North Side of Chicago one night. We were playing "Little Darlin'" so slow that it actually would stop if you played it any slower. And the whole band was doing it. For everybody to function at that level was really an incredible feeling. The whole band, the dynamics of the thing—just diamond perfect. I think that's the most memorable time. Oh, there was one other time, on an arrangement called "Mama Devil." That was the first time I ever felt a band that large just get up and sit up off the ground. I mean, you feel it, it's like your hair stands on end when that happens. You're not even playing anymore. The whole thing has taken on a life of its own.

Buddy stayed with Basie until early 1965, then settled down in Brooklyn, where he played with the Maynard Ferguson band a while, then with Coleman Hawkins. One night at the Five Spot he looked up and saw Paul Neves and Norm Bobrow. "They were sitting there with their arms folded," he recalled, "like 'The jury is out.' It was quite a pleasant surprise." Working with Hawkins was "like a sociology course. You could tie up what you heard your parents talk about—the past. You could see how things were and how they were changing. To me, that was the important thing about it. Just playing the licks is superficial." After working with Hawkins, Catlett formed a group of his own, at Birdland, then was hired by Louis Armstrong. It would be Satchmo's last regular group, and Catlett stayed with Louis until the trumpeter died, in 1971. Armstrong's combo consisted of Billy Kyle (followed by Marty Napoleon), piano; Buster Bailey (followed by Joe Muranyi), clarinet; Danny Barcelona, drums; and Tyree Glenn, trombone. The Armstrong band toured Europe once a year and even played Tunisia.

For twenty years Catlett had been fighting a losing battle with alcohol. When Armstrong died, Buddy's personal problems, combined with the scarcity of work brought on by the rock revolution in the 1960s, finally brought him to a halt. He worked around New York for a spell, playing Beatles tunes in lounges, but got disgusted and lost his heart for music. For several years he stayed home and took care of his and his second wife's new baby. Catlett remembered spending a lot of idle time in those days, sitting on the terrace of their Brooklyn home, drawing sketches, not knowing what to do next. In 1973 he left New York to live with his brother in Connecticut. An offer from Dizzy Gillespie to go to Europe slipped by. Catlett drifted. In 1978, when he moved back to Seattle, he didn't even have a bass.

It was a call from a commercial contractor that got Buddy to pick up his brother Bobby's electric bass for a gig. Remembering that he enjoyed playing more than anything else, he decided to put music in front—and leave alcohol behind. For a while he worked in a funny-hat band with Ron Pierce called the Salmon City Seven as well as for swing bandleader Mickey Martin. In the early 1980s Catlett became the sideman of choice for many out-of-towners, from Eddie "Lockjaw" Davis to Art Farmer. In the early 1990s he worked regularly in a trio with Jack Perciful at a hotel and at Lofurno's, and toured Europe a couple of times with Elmer Gill. He also anchored the Seattle Repertory Jazz Orchestra and the Local 493 Reunion Band, which honored the Jackson Street legacy for many years at the New Orleans Creole Restaurant. An early inductee into the Seattle Jazz Hall of Fame, Catlett recorded his only album as a leader, a deeply, soulful and straightforward outing titled *Here Comes Buddy Catlett*, in 2004, for Seattle's Pony Boy Jazz Records.

Catlett never stopped studying music. He practiced clarinet and bass every day and gave lessons to a variety of students in a small studio in the back of his house. A blown-up photograph of the Bumps Blackwell National Guard band looked down over his practice chair. Along with Bumps, the ghost of Catlett's childhood saxophone teacher, Frank Waldron, probably stared down at him as well. As old Frank listened, leaning over to sip his vodka, he was probably saying severely, "Buddy, keep on practicing and you'll be with Duke Ellington." Old bald-headed Frank called it pretty close. Catlett lived long enough to be properly celebrated. Pianist Marc Seales recalled working at Tula's nightclub one night when trumpeter Wynton Marsalis showed up. "I came down to play with Buddy Catlett," said Marsalis. Buddy died in 2014.

Another Jackson Street veteran whose career took her around the world and back to Seattle was Ernestine Anderson. After the Johnny Otis tour that brought her home in a shambles from Los Angeles in 1949, Anderson went back to California for a second shot at fame. Marriage and motherhood soon interrupted her career. Based in Seattle, she worked in Fairbanks, Alaska, for four months on a double bill with tap dancer Emily Foster. But when Stan Kenton offered her a job in 1951, she realized that her next child, daughter Shelley, would have been born in the middle of the tour, so she turned Stan down. When Lionel Hampton came to town the following year, Ernestine's husband encouraged her to go. She recalled: "My husband at the time had heard that Betty Carter was leaving Hamp's band and Lionel was looking for a singer. He told me to go audition. I didn't want to go, because our children were young. But he kept encouraging me: 'I think you should do it, because I don't want you years from now going to bed thinking or wondering, "What if . . ." If you're going to do it, I think you should do it now.'"

Anderson set off to Georgia Kemp's house on Madison and Twentieth Avenue—Hamp's home away from home in Seattle—for an audition. Ray Charles's trio, which rehearsed at Georgia's house, backed her up. Guitarist Garcia McKee remembered the afternoon well: "She auditioned with 'Body and Soul.' She sounded beautiful. He hired her on the spot. The only thing we laughed about was that 'Body and Soul' is written in five flats [key of D-flat] and she said she wanted to sing it in B [five sharps]. [But] she wasn't nervous. She was a young girl so, naturally, once she started singing, that professionalism came out. Just a young girl, but she could sing."

This was in the fall of 1952. Ernestine spent the next fifteen months on the road with Hampton, "paying her dues" with her first real name band. Any loneliness or road blues the young singer may have felt were soon mitigated by the circle of friendly faces from Jackson Street: Quincy Jones was in the trumpet section, Elmer Gill was on piano, and Pony Poindexter was playing alto saxophone. She also got to know Monk Montgomery. Still, there were some bad times. On the way to Indianapolis, Anderson was thrown out of an equipment truck; her severely broken arm required a metal plate and a two-week hospital stay. Later, Hamp's band was booked to play Dwight D. Eisenhower's presidential inauguration, which led to a famous incident. After the inauguration the band played in a park along the Potomac, on the site where the Kennedy Center now stands. There were three acts—Louis Armstrong, Illinois Jacquet, and Hampton. As Ernestine remembered it:

> Since Louis was on first, Hamp was worried about getting upstaged, so he told Illinois Jacquet not to play "Flyin' Home," and it made Jacquet mad. "I'm the one that made 'Flyin' Home' famous," said Jacquet. "I'll play it whenever and wherever I please." [Jacquet] goes out there [and plays "Flyin' Home"], so by the time Lionel came on, none of his stuff worked. He jumped up on top of the drums. He did his sticks—he caught them and he clapped his hands. But it was over.
>
> Monk [Montgomery] told Quincy, "Now, when we play 'Flyin' Home,' I'm going to jump into the Potomac." He said, "I'll hand you the bass," or something. So sure enough, Monk went. Lionel looked up, and if you could have seen the look on his face—"What the hell is going on?" But when he did that, the crowd went wild! From then on, Lionel was like, "Yeah! Yeah, yeah!" Like it was planned. He didn't say nothing to Monk about that. In fact, I think he was really grateful, because he thought Monk did it to save the day. He had no idea what was going on behind his back.

When the band got to New York in the late fall of 1953, Ernestine, along with Elmer Gill and several other musicians, balked at a proposed trip to Europe. The trust level between Hamp and his musicians was low. Gill, Anderson, and some of the others presented a petition to Gladys Hampton, the band manager, requesting that the itinerary be pinned down to a specific timetable, pay scale, and return date, and that passage home be guaranteed. According to Anderson, Lionel responded by calling an old friend in Chicago, a union boss, who threatened the mutineers with revocation of their union cards. Several band members defected. Quincy traveled to France—an influential move in his life that eventually resulted in his job at the French record company Barclay Disques.

Ernestine, for her part, returned to Seattle to raise her children, at least for the time being. In a touching article in the *Seattle Post-Intelligencer*, previewing an appearance at the Metropolitan Theatre, she told columnist John Voorhees, "I had a postcard from Quincy. He said they'd be playing in Paris this weekend." Anderson's wistful tone, along with her decision to come home, spoke well to her profound ambivalence about pursuing the limelight. Throughout her career she repeatedly made thrusts into the national arena, only to walk away from the business a few years later. The issue for Anderson did not seem to be one of confidence, as it was with so many musicians who found the national scene frighteningly competitive, but rather some basic "homebody" spirit that constantly pulled her back to the house where she grew up, as if her sister, Josephine, were still calling her name from that windowsill. (Norm Bobrow, who knew Anderson well, later confided privately that it was indeed her devotion to Josephine that kept bringing Ernestine home.) It was an issue she would not resolve until much, much later, after suffering a good deal during her first remarkable successes in the 1950s.

For while Ernestine told the *Post-Intelligencer* in 1953 that she had come home to raise her family, she had in fact already decided to go back to New York. Her first job there was at a gay nightclub called the Page Three, where vocalists Sheila Jordan and Morgana King were also just getting started. Anderson made her recording debut during this period, in November 1956, on two tracks of an album with Gigi Gryce, *Nica's Tempo*. Art Farmer, Oscar Pettiford, and Art Blakey played in the band. After a couple of years of struggling in New York, Ernestine took an offer to tour Sweden with Swedish trumpeter Rolf Ericson. She wound up staying there six and a half months, recording an album for Metronome with Harry Arnold. When Metronome sold the masters to Mercury, Ernestine assumed that she would come home to the release of her first American album. It wouldn't be quite that simple.

Anderson spent the early part of 1957 working in Seattle, waiting for the record to come out. She sat in with her old Hampton bandmate Monk Montgomery at a new Seattle club, Dave's Fifth Avenue, in a promising new group called the Mastersounds. Soon afterward, she moved south to San Francisco with Monk's new group, where she caught the avid attention of San Francisco jazz critic Ralph Gleason, the same writer who had raved about Cecil Young and Gerald Brashear. Wrote Gleason in the *San Francisco Chronicle*: "To me Miss Anderson has it made. She's by all odds the best girl singer I've heard in years, with an individual style and no overtones of other singers. And she swings like mad." Gleason got Ernestine booked into the very first Monterey Jazz Festival that fall, and began to pressure Mercury to bring out her album. The pressure worked. Record company representatives began to offer deals. The ever-supportive Gleason stepped in again, advising Anderson to hold out for the best contract. In early 1958, Anderson, who by now had moved to Los

Angeles, signed a deal with Mercury, where Quincy Jones was working as an executive. *Hot Cargo*, her first record under her own name, was finally released.

The response was tremendous. John S. Wilson of the *New York Times* wrote, "Miss Anderson is a singer who disdains mannerisms, who respects both tune and lyrics and who seems to feel that a melody should fall pleasantly on the ear. . . . She displays an approach in ballads that in warmth, directness and sensitivity invites favorable comparison with Ella Fitzgerald." Twelve years after Norm Bobrow had been chastised by a local critic for making the same comparison, the Seattle promoter's enthusiasm had been vindicated. John Tynan, writing for *DownBeat*, followed suit: "She's good, darn good, and stands head and shoulders above the covey of cool-ies who have gained exaggerated prominence since June Christy set the style."

Ernestine Anderson's first album, released in 1958 on Mercury Records.

On August 4, 1958, *Time* magazine ran a glowing profile of Anderson, pronouncing her "the best-kept secret in the land" and "the best new voice in the business." The journalists were not exaggerating. *Hot Cargo* is an excellent album, and particularly instructive for listeners who know only Anderson's later work. Though the record is decidedly a period piece, featuring lush, stagey ballads with strings and alto flute that in the 1950s would have been quaintly termed "mood music," Anderson's pure tone, true pitch, artful dynamics, and control of her instrument are downright startling, on a par with Ella Fitzgerald, Sarah Vaughan, and Carmen McRae. Her relaxed vocal control is even more impressive on her fourth Mercury LP, *Moanin' Moanin' Moanin'*. It's interesting that Tynan thought to compare Ernestine to June Christy. The Stan Kenton songbird had recently popularized an erotically stripped-down, "cool" ballad style that was setting the pace in the marketplace. To that minimalist environment Ernestine brought a firmness of intention and earthiness that must have set listeners on their ears. On *Hot Cargo* her voice was lighter—the drawling, molasses-like quality of later years wasn't there, except perhaps as a hint of sexy amber in the lows—and there was an ingenue quality, an innocence. Her treatment of "Autumn in New York" featured a fetching turn that later vanished from her style; there was a sense of deep conviction on "Little Girl Blue."

For a couple of years after *Hot Cargo* was released, the public couldn't get enough of the singer from Seattle. At the end of the year she played a successful engagement at New York's Village Vanguard, following a two-week stint at Bobrow's Colony club. The *DownBeat* critics voted her New Star of the Year in 1959, and the next year Anderson was running third only to Ella and Sarah in the magazine's Critics Poll. Ronnie Scott, the prominent British saxophonist, recruited her for opening night at his posh new London club. Ernestine took a second apartment in New York, dividing her time between there and Los Angeles, then settled in Manhattan in 1959. Mercury continued to release new albums—she made six in all—and she continued to tour. But the record-buying public is fickle, and Mercury never could find the right formula to keep her records on the charts. Her popularity started to slide. When the Beatles began to transform the record business into a rock 'n' roll monopoly, said Anderson, "most agents didn't want to know you. It was either sing rock or don't sing at all."

She decided to take her chances in "swinging London," the new rock capital. For a moment she flirted with pop, recording a dreadful album called *The New Sound of Ernestine Anderson*, but soon she returned to jazz. For a while, Anderson was successful in Europe. She toured the Scandinavian countries, Spain, and Germany. But this was the beginning of a prolonged disillusionment with the music business. Discouraged by Mercury's failure to push any but her first album, and by the bleakness of the jazz scene in general, she dropped out for two years (1966–68). A last-ditch foray to Los Angeles to give it one more try was a bust. "I just couldn't get going. I tried a few gigs and it was like my heart wasn't in it. I did not feel it. I had nothing more to say. I was just dry. So I thought, 'It's time to hang it up.' I didn't really know what I wanted to do, but I knew I didn't want to sing anymore. I didn't have anything more to say. It was a bad time of life all around. For some reason, it got to me, kids taking dope and dying, all that. I had reached the point where I just wanted out."

Anderson fell into a deep depression. Afraid to go out on the streets or into a crowd, she retreated from the world. She would do her supermarket shopping only late at night. At about this time four friends told her, independent of one another, about the healing qualities of Buddhist chanting. She took it as a sign and attended a meeting. "I wanted to get in touch with myself. Find out who and why and what I was all about, as a person. Which I had never done before.

I'd always been too busy concentrating on a career, ever since I was thirteen years old."

That was in 1969. Anderson began to chant morning and evening as a regular practice. It would be several years before she felt ready to perform again, but in 1974 the jazz critic for the *Post-Intelligencer*, Maggie Hawthorn, coaxed her out of retirement, escorting her to Red Kelly's new club in Tumwater. The following year, Elmer Gill invited Anderson to sing at a "Jazz Weekend" on Vancouver Island. She reconnected with her old friend Ray Brown, who offered to produce a record for her on the new label he was recording for, Concord Jazz. In 1977 she was back on track with a new career, debuting with a fine album, *Hello Like Before*. "Before, there was a war. I couldn't put the two together—the homebody and the show singer. This Buddhism has allowed me to try to find out who I am, what my relationship is to the rest of the world. There's more to me than show business. I'm a mother, a daughter, a sister, a friend—I'm even a grandmother."

Anderson released eleven albums on Concord, earning Grammy nominations for two of them—*Never Make Your Move Too Soon* (1981) and *Big City* (1983)—as well as two for Quincy Jones's label, Qwest. Late in her career, she moved to HighNote Records, where she brought out three more albums. She also rekindled her touring career to a worldwide heat that included annual tours of the United States, Europe, and Japan. The contemporary Ernestine had a more rambunctious, raunchier style, put to particularly good use on her superb album of blues, *When the Sun Goes Down*, though she could still mesmerize an audience with the breathtaking purity of a tune like "Old Folks" or Hoagy Carmichael's "Skylark." Anderson's signature song became a long, talking-blues version of "Never Make Your Move Too Soon," a worldly-wise poem that reflected her maturity, wit, and wisdom. One of the most hilarious stories she told in that song recounted the afternoon she was stranded on the San Francisco Bay Bridge during the 1989 earthquake and ran all the way to Oakland, holding her high heels in her hands.

Like Jones, Anderson remained true to her hometown, generously offering services for the Garfield High School jazz program and encouraging young artists. Before she died in 2016, HighNote released a live recording of her at Seattle's Penthouse nightclub in 1962, a refreshing reminder of her salad days. Anderson was honored generously before and after she died. The Smithsonian Institution included her in its *Jazz Singers* anthology, and along with such notables as Alice Walker and Shirley Chisholm she was featured in photographer

Brian Lanker's tribute to African American women, *I Dream a World*. Anderson was in the first cohort of the Seattle Jazz Hall of Fame, and in 2012 the Low Income Housing Institute named one of its Seattle projects Ernestine Anderson Place. In 2016 the City of Seattle named the stretch of South Jackson Street between Twentieth Avenue South and Twenty-Third Avenue South Ernestine Anderson Way.

Like Ernestine Anderson and Buddy Catlett, little Pony Poindexter, the alto saxophonist who had first come up from Oakland with the Ernie Lewis band to play at Basin Street, also found success after his Jackson Street days. In 1947 he joined Billy Eckstine's orchestra—whose personnel also included Miles Davis. Poindexter made his first record in San Francisco during this period, coincidentally with Seattle bassist Red Kelly backing him up. In 1950, Poindexter joined Jack McVea for a tour to Salt Lake City, came back to San Francisco, and went to work with Dexter Gordon at Bop City. In early 1951 he played around the Bay Area with Vernon Alley before joining Lionel Hampton. While on tour with Hampton, Poindexter recalled jamming at the Club Alabam in Los Angeles with Dexter Gordon, Wardell Gray, Hampton Hawes, and Ernestine's old lookout, Shifty Henry. Like many musicians at this time, Poindexter started injecting heroin. "Pony used to get so high, man, he couldn't get away from the microphone," remembered Quincy Jones, who got Pony into Hamp's band. "Bless his heart. He was a legend in his own mind."

Pony left Hampton in 1952 and returned to San Francisco, where he traded sets with Bird at the Say When and played at Bop City with no less than three great trumpeters—Dizzy Gillespie, Miles Davis, and Kenny Dorham. At about this time Poindexter and Dorham came up the coast and hung out together in Seattle for several months, staying at Billy Tolles's place. This was the period when Tolles put together his remarkable group with Dorham and Poindexter, which won the battle of the bands contest in 1952 at the Eagles Auditorium. Neil Friel recalled running into Poindexter and Dorham one morning at a breakfast session. The two brilliant young musicians told him they were on their way to Alaska to seek work as bricklayers. "I stopped them," Friel recounted. "I showed them an article in the newspaper telling unskilled laborers not to come to Alaska."

Pony continued to gravitate back to Seattle year after year. Part of the attraction was a woman he had met, his future wife, Marie, but he also came back because he thought Seattle was a "cool" place for addicts, where the police didn't bother you as much as they might in, say, San Francisco and Los Angeles. It was an assumption that would nearly prove to be his undoing. Poindexter's Seattle arrest and subsequent prison term in the Monroe Reformatory are recounted in his autobiography, *Pony Express*. It is a bizarre and dreamlike tale in what is overall a fanciful, angry, and bitter book—so bitter in fact that it is hard to know how much of it to believe. According to Poindexter, he had just gotten off the road with T-Bone Walker and was living in San Francisco when he discovered that his name mysteriously had become part of a federal "secret indictment" list.

He decided to flee to Seattle. On his way he stopped to play a gig at the Swing Club in Portland with trumpeter Bobby Bradford; he wound up staying there, until February 1954. Next, Babs Gonzales, the vocalist who composed "Oop-Pop-A-Da," invited Pony to Seattle for a gig with saxophonist James Moody and vocalist Eddie Jefferson at the University of Washington. Poindexter claimed that one night, following a jam session in a roadhouse that sounds like it might have been the China Pheasant, he was arrested in a motel room for being there with a white woman, brutally beaten in an elevator by the police, and taken to jail. Poindexter was sent to Monroe for fifteen months, for what he called a trumped-up charge of grand larceny.

The Seattle Police Department was not known for racial tolerance in the 1950s; Poindexter may well have been beaten. And he definitely spent time in Monroe. But it was not for integrating a motel bedroom and it didn't happen when he says it did. In fact, Poindexter had already been convicted of second-degree burglary in Seattle—likely for one of the thefts he committed in search of drug money—and had been paroled in 1954. The incident he described in his autobiography most likely is a glamorized version of an arrest for breaking parole. Whatever the details, Pony was sent to prison in October 1956, where he remained until at least the end of the year, possibly until the spring of 1957. While there, he played in a jazz group—and also kicked his heroin habit. Paul Gonsalves and Ray Nance, then of Duke Ellington's band, also paid him a visit.

When Stan Getz was arrested in Seattle, his story made front-page news. Poindexter's catastrophe barely rated an item. That the press cared more about white musicians than Black musicians was nothing new. Such things were not supposed to happen to nice, white Jewish boys, even if they did play jazz, while the arrest of yet another Black musician was perceived as routine. In the 1950s, however, such racial bias took an ominous twist that was particularly exasperating for

Black bebop musicians. The roots of the conflict went back to 1949, when Miles Davis recorded *Birth of the Cool*, an album inspired by the arranging of Gil Evans and Claude Thornhill, who in turn were having great influence on other white musicians working in Los Angeles, such as Gerry Mulligan and Shorty Rogers. At the same time a young composition student at Mills College, in Oakland, named Dave Brubeck was beginning to come on strong. When Brubeck, Mulligan, and Rogers began issuing a slew of even-edged, carefully arranged, dynamically "cool" jazz records in the early 1950s, the movement called "West Coast jazz" was born.

Though never really a school, the concept nevertheless caught on with the press and the public, particularly college students. Brubeck made the cover of *Time* magazine. White audiences, who had left swing behind but had been perhaps confused or turned off by bebop, embraced jazz again. There was only one problem. As the term "West Coast" took on stylistic as well as geographic meaning, the media ignored anything from the West that wasn't "cool," or else assumed that if music came from the West, it must be cool. Black bebop pioneers in the region—like Pony Poindexter—suddenly became invisible. Perceiving the cool school as a racial conspiracy to rip off Black people, Poindexter became angry and paranoid. He accused Neal Hefti, who had written a musical homage to the saxophonist, "Little Pony," of stealing his lick for the tune. He claimed Brubeck appropriated his "special arrangement" of "How High the Moon." Spending over a year in jail did not improve his mood. When he was released, he went to work at the Mardi Gras, the soul lounge on Madison that had been keeping the Jackson Street spirit alive, but complained that he was ill-received.

"The Black musicians in Seattle were mostly cold," wrote Pony in his book, "but I overwhelmed them with sheer talent. Of course, most of them thought that I'd just go back to using skag right away and go back to the prison. Some of them sent dealers to me, offering free skag, which they had paid for. But I froze. Much to their surprise." Poindexter makes no mention here of his wife or of Pops Buford, who had loaned him his horn, or of any other Seattle musicians. Pony played at the Mardi Gras off and on throughout the latter half of 1957 and early 1958 and, once he cleaned up his act, headed into the most fruitful period of his career. He returned to San Francisco, where he worked with Cal Tjader and Dizzy Gillespie, played on poet Kenneth Rexroth's famous "Poetry and Jazz" shows, and recorded with both Wes Montgomery (*Beginnings*) and Jon Hendricks (*A Good Git-Together*), who liberally featured his New Orleans–style singing and soloing.

"The following week," Poindexter wrote in his book, "I did another album with Wes, his brothers and Harold Land called *Montgomery Land*. Because of the West Coast jazz movement, I hadn't been able to buy a record date for nearly ten years. And now, in less than two weeks, I had made two albums with some of the best musicians in America—all Black musicians." He noted with glee that soulful, Black-oriented "funk" music by Cannonball Adderley had finally started to supplant cool: "That marked the official end of West Coast jazz. Cannonball and his group had put the nails in the coffin. I was a delighted pallbearer at the funeral."

Pony enjoyed a flurry of albums under his own name and others', plus dates at Carnegie Hall, the Newport and Monterey jazz festivals, and every major jazz club in the country. His album *Pony Express* and his work with Jon Hendricks on the landmark *Evolution of the Blues Song* secured him a niche in jazz history as a lively original who successfully incorporated New Orleans roots and bluesy entertaining skills into a bebop imagination. In 1964 the combination of an established reputation and depressing racial tensions at home catapulted Poindexter to Europe, where he worked and recorded successfully for fourteen years, returning to the Bay Area in 1977. An album for Inner City done the following year, *Poindexter*, suffered from a poor rhythm section, but Pony's tone was still fierce, his articulation Bird-like, and his humorous "ditties" fully in place. He moved back and forth between the Bay Area and Europe until he died in 1988.

Why does one musician turn to the road and another stay at home? The knee-jerk response is that those who reach for recognition are better musicians; only the mediocre stay home, where life is safe. But as anyone knows who has spent time listening carefully to a local scene, such a simplistic answer is often misguided. Issues such as family, economics, and temperament often lead excellent players to work on a local scene. In Seattle several of the best musicians stayed put, including Floyd Standifer, Jabo Ward, Chuck Metcalf, Elmer Gill, Jerry Gray, and Dave Coleman. Their refusal to leave home had a salubrious effect on Northwest jazz that still can be felt. Working through the 1950s in a handful of local venues, these musicians and others pioneered Seattle's modern jazz scene.

Floyd Standifer in many ways was the quintessential Seattle bebop musician, capable of hot and furious chromatic improvisation of the first order, but also influenced by the steady and evenhanded shapeliness of Fats Navarro and Miles

Floyd Standifer at the Trianon Ballroom, summer 1948.

Davis. With his fat sound, absolute control, and sly sense of timing, the mature Standifer arrived at a bag that was part Art Farmer, part Carmell Jones, and part Lee Morgan—a hard-bop modernist with a cool undersurface. Standifer was born in 1929 in Wilmington, North Carolina; he came to Portland, Oregon, as a child in 1936. Though his father had a comfortable income as an African Methodist Episcopal-Zion preacher, with the Depression on, the Standifers wound up picking strawberries three years later. Floyd's father bought a farm about five miles outside of Gresham, Oregon. Standifer grew up learning solid values and respect for the land, milking cows, slopping hogs, and walking two and a half miles to school if he missed the bus. He and his father plowed with a mule, planted fruit trees, and cleared land with a grub hoe.

Back in 1939 there wasn't much jazz around Gresham, though there was all kinds of Black music at home: "My father sang and played guitar. He loved Josh White. Leadbelly. He'd have that guitar around the house and he'd sit around and do what he called 'frammin'—just grab something and play. My mother was a schoolteacher. She did church singing. I told her on two or three occasions, 'Mother, you sound just like Bessie Smith,' and she said, 'Oh pshaw, go away from here, boy, that's blues, that's trashy music.'" Like Elmer Gill, Standifer counted his experience in the AME-Zion church as his first exposure to swing. "I'm talking about swinging singing. Handclapping, shouting. I got so I could tell when they were getting ready to shout, because that beat would start getting insistent. It would build, just like a good jazz set. You could feel the intensity. I was hip enough at the age of three or four to understand. I'd slide up under Mama because I knew somebody someplace was getting ready to shout. When you come up in that kind of atmosphere, swing used to be second nature."

Floyd was first exposed to instrumental music in 1937, when he played drums in a Works Progress Administration (WPA) kid band in Portland led by a teacher named Bert Turner. Standifer had no other formal training. He plinked out melodies on the piano at home, imitating Basie, and took tunes off the radio. In high school Standifer was interested in the trumpet, but because his music teacher thought he'd never make it on that instrument, the young musician was assigned the tuba. Meanwhile, Standifer taught himself to play a friend's alto saxophone. He finally got a trumpet of his own in his mid–high school years: "I used to play it in the fields. It was a beautiful echo. There was about a two-second delay. You could play and then the note would come back. This was on a hillside. You'd play a scale and then you could hear whether or not you played it right." Radio brought the sounds of swing into the Standifer home—Harry James, Glenn Miller, Count Basie: "We had this one long room. My mother and father slept at one end, my baby brother slept next to them, my two sisters slept in this bed, and my middle brother and myself slept over here.

At dinnertime, I would ask the family to be quiet so I could listen. There'd be these remotes coming in from L.A. Frankie Laine was brand new on the scene. People from Jantzen Beach and Portland. There was a western band that came there and they were bebopping."

Floyd soon found a group of peers at Gresham Union High School, and they formed the Hot Club of Eastern Multnomah County. Exchanging precious copies of *Bandstand* magazine, they listened to records by Basie, Tommy Dorsey, Bunny Berigan, and Joe Thomas. Standifer remembered reading a story about young Corky Corcoran getting picked up by the Harry James band. Standifer worked in a cannery, stacking five-hundred-pound barrels of frozen strawberries, to earn enough money to buy a secondhand turntable that would hook up to the family's Atwater Kent console radio. The purchase led to his discovery of bebop. A friend brought him a Charlie Parker record, and from then on Dorsey and Berigan were supplanted by Dodo Marmarosa and Miles Davis, Roy Eldridge and Anita O'Day, the Gramercy Five and Nat Cole. A friend dragged Floyd into Portland for a Coleman Hawkins all-star show in 1945, where they heard pianist Thelonious Monk. This was Norman Granz's first tour of his groundbreaking Los Angeles revue, Jazz at the Philharmonic, though it was not billed as such; the show also played Seattle.

The boys in the Hot Club of Eastern Multnomah County were clean-cut achievers. Standifer was vice president of his class, and college bound. His father had been recently transferred to Seattle; the family was to follow the next year. In 1946, Floyd headed for the University of Washington—and his future. Standifer's father had a little white church with green steps at Twenty-Third Avenue and Olive, a stone's throw from the YMCA where Ernestine Anderson had first sat in with Gerald Brashear in 1944. Standifer soon fell in with the same crowd. As he remembered:

> One afternoon, I was walking down Madison. I had my horn with me. Right on that corner was a little restaurant, and right next to it was something that used to be a skating rink and was eventually called Birdland. I was walking past this, and in this building there was this group playing. I said, "Man, that sounds just like that stuff I heard off those records." I stuck my head in there and I listened. It turned out to be Gerald Brashear and Buddy Brashear, on drums. I don't know who the piano player was. But they were playing bebop. I introduced myself to them. I said,

"I'm going to school and man, this is the first time I've ever heard anybody play that stuff like on records." Gerald laughed.

Gerald took Floyd over to the YMCA near his father's church, and Floyd started to jam there on Saturday nights for the kids' dances. They earned ten dollars a night apiece. It was there that he met Ernestine, Quincy, Buddy Catlett, Major Pigford, Charlie Taylor, Bumps Blackwell, and everyone else on the scene. For the next six years Floyd worked with just about everybody in town, including Quincy, Billy Tolles, Bumps, and Ray Charles, plus musicians on the Annex scene. Throughout, he tried to keep his studies together, primarily at the University of Washington, then at Seattle University, then back at UW. Stylistically, he said, the years 1947 to 1950 were the ones that formed him. Rhythm-and-blues shuffles with a bebop accent, played with fellows at the YMCA, were his foundation, followed by the influence of Fats Navarro on records.

The Fats Navarro style, which applied an elegant, even pressure to all registers of the trumpet and emphasized continuous eighth-note scales (unlike Dizzy's flamboyant, angular melodies), would become the dominant trumpet style of the 1950s, associated with the "hard bop" movement. Navarro's style was popularized by a young virtuoso named Clifford Brown. Standifer remembered Kenny Kimball calling him from New York, excited about Brown: "He said, 'Hey, man, there's a cat out here that sounds like you." Chuck Metcalf held Standifer in similarly high esteem: "Floyd Standifer was on a very high level. Floyd was a bebopper. Stone Fats Navarro, right away, highly evolved." Being a more complex music, bop required not only fast reflexes and a sensitive ear but also a working knowledge of theory and harmony. Standifer never studied theory per se, but he gradually figured out what was going on. Many swing musicians at the time were still untutored, able to improvise in only three or four keys at best, and not hearing the extensions and relationships between chords the beboppers used. Beboppers played in all twelve keys, and no chord progression was too complicated—or at least that was the goal. Standifer remembered when he noticed that he had reached this level: "[We] were rehearsing 'Valse Hot,' by Sonny Rollins up at Birdland. And these cats pulled this new tune. I listened to it the first time, because I didn't know it. Somebody played the first solo and then they looked at me. Well, I had long ago figured out that if you could separate two-five-ones, you can convert that back to the scale, so you don't need to know the chords. So it was the same old two-five-ones. I just played it. Then I got arrogant on the second chorus and I decided I'd do a third one, just for the hell of it."

Standifer emphasized that despite the superior standards of the boppers, Seattle's music scene remained open to many levels and types of players. The kinds of tensions that developed between beboppers and swingers in other cities, for example, and between jazz musicians and commercial players, though they existed, were much less pronounced, possibly due to the smallness of the scene. "If you played R & B, the cats still dug you. Cats like Al Hickey were considered to be good jazz players. 'Big Jay' McNeely would come and we used to laugh, because he used to wear gloves with fluorescent lights and stuff like that. But we knew it was a show. Once you got Big Jay into the light, took off those fluorescent gloves, Big Jay could get out and play you some horn. He could flat play, man. Just because a guy played commercial, we didn't knock it."

Standifer wasn't above taking a little commercial work himself. In 1957 he played on Seattle's first rock record, "Rock and Roll Radio," with a group called Joe Boot and the Fabulous Winds, acquitting himself nicely as a soulful, throaty tenor sax soloist. Pianist Ernie Hatfield and drummer Kenny Smith were also in the band. Standifer's willingness to play in all situations led him to most of the spots on Jackson Street, and the tight corners they sometimes led to. He had a warm, humorous memory of the after-hours scene, including an especially vivid recollection of the Sessions Club, one of several iterations of the Entertainer's Cabaret, where Jelly Morton had played:

> The weekend started on Thursday and it didn't stop until Monday morning at about eight o'clock. There was the Sessions Club. A guy named Jimmy Linegan ran that. This cat would play E-natural all night long. He kept a pistol on top of the piano. Later we'd go in there and play for people like Zenobia, or George Bernie, a cat who'd dance on tables. Pick tables up with his teeth. After these little acts, they'd "chase" the act off with "Lester Leaps In." That's why they call it a "chaser." Variety entertainment.
>
> The first thing I learned, don't ever stand next to anybody in a raid. Keep your hands in your pockets. Don't take them out until you're told to. And when you do, make sure nobody's next to you, because you never know what'll end up in your pocket. Those were the days when I started carrying my horn either in a shopping bag or something light, because you could always keep it under your arm when you were running.

> There was a camaraderie, a fraternalism, that doesn't seem to be here anymore. That's when unionism was really a fraternal thing. Then, if you played any kind of jazz at all, you were a member.

The fraternalism Standifer cherished would never really return. It was a product of the special circumstances created by the Black musicians' union and Washington's peculiar alcohol laws. In 1955 a group of enthusiastic musicians, including Floyd and Chuck Metcalf, briefly attempted to fill the void left by the demise of Local 493 and its "clubhouse" by banding together in an organization they called the Northwest Jazz Workshop (NWJW). In an old house on Roosevelt Way, north of Forty-Sixth, they taught lessons, ran rehearsal bands, jammed, and staged concerts. The NWJW also produced a gala, locals-only concert at the Moore Theatre, tied in with Seafair, then a five-year-old, fledgling citywide summer festival. Dubbed the Seafair Jazz Festival, the concert took place on August 5, 1956, and featured Don Anderson's Dixielanders, the Paul Neves Quartet, Jimmy Glover's big band and Afro-Cuban septet, the Signatures, the Highlanders (a Renton youth quartet that sang on a locally produced television show, *Sheriff Tex*), Patti Summers, Don Lanphere, and Floyd Standifer. Eight hundred people attended. The NWJW persisted for a couple of years, even broadcasting a live weekly radio show on KUOW-FM, courtesy of Chuck Mahaffay, from the old Annex crowd. The workshop folded, said Mahaffay, because Paul Neves, who was a prime mover in the effort, went back to Boston.

Though the old 493 era could never quite be recaptured, as the 1950s wore on, quality local jazz musicians such as Standifer and Metcalf began to form bonds in a series of new clubs that made the transition from the old Jackson Street scene to a more modern one. One of these transition venues was Elmer Gill's Ebony. Another was the Flame Tavern, an unpretentious watering hole at 110th Street and Roosevelt Way with a horseshoe-shaped bar and a big fireplace. From 1954 to 1959, Standifer made the Flame his home base, thanks to a call from keyboard man Milt Price. Standifer was still trying to put himself through school, undecided as to whether he wanted to study physics or music. He also had taken a day job, with the Military Sea Transportation Service. With the birth of his first son, in 1953, he began to get eyes for a steady "six-nighter"—a commercial gig where the check would be steady. One day, Price got hold of him: "Milt was playing organ and guitar out at the Flame Tavern. He'd heard me play saxophone and he asked me if I'd come play. I said, 'Sure.' I went out to the Flame in December of '54, middle of the month. That's the greatest Christmas we ever had."

For three years the power-jazz trio of Milt Price, Dave Stetler, and Floyd Standifer kept the fires alive at the Flame, blowing nearly every instrument known to jazz. Standifer doubled on saxophone; Price was a multi-instrumentalist who played piano, alto and tenor saxophone, flute, guitar, and drums. He had grown up in Chicago with Ralph Davis, the drummer who had worked in the Jive Bombers. In Seattle by 1946, Price worked with Darryl Harpa, Bud Storm, Elmer Gill, and Billy Tolles. Price had a deep blues background and liked to play hard and funky. Drummer Dave Stetler, for his part, had been making a smooth transition from swing to bop. Since his days with the "kid bands" and his 1945 trip to New York, he had put in time with Harpa, Wyatt Howard, and a variety of jazz combos at the New Chinatown, the Black Elks Club, and the 908. In 1951, Stetler was at the Showbox with Norm Hoagy; right about this time he played on a fluke local country hit, "Navy Hot-Rod Boogie." The slow scene in the early 1950s forced him to take a day job at the Bellevue Post Office, where he stayed for fourteen years. Stetler leapt at the chance to play real jazz with Floyd and Milt at the Flame, a period he counted as among his most musically satisfying: "We had one grand time. It was one of the most fun jobs I ever played. Even as tired as I was when I was playing at the Flame, I had more inspiration playing there and more fun, just straight-out, stretched-out, hard jazz, as hard as we could play, every night. We brought it up from somewhere. We were all tired, but we went ahead and did our thing and went home and collapsed. I had more fun with those guys than I've ever had with any musicians in my life." Price, Stetler, and Standifer had a good time, but they also played advanced modal bop. Discussing how the new approach mystified some of the old swingers, Standifer said, "This was the era when Corky [Corcoran] would come by and he'd say, 'How come you guys are playing all them scales?' Those were the days when we were searching. We were starting to get away from bebop and finding that hard modal-bop thing. Started to slide off into the Dorians and Phrygians." DJ Bob Summerise did a remote broadcast on KRSC from the Flame Tavern, helping bring in the crowds. "I used to tell people they were only ten minutes from downtown," laughed Standifer. "I had guys coming in waving speeding tickets in my face."

Milt Price left the Flame in 1957 to form a more lucrative "one-man band" that would herald the canned music of lounges in the 1960s. Standifer continued at the club until 1959, with pianist Ernie Hatfield and, after Stetler moved over to the Colony, with drummer Kenny Smith. Stetler continued playing until his death in 2002, backing up touring stars, playing casuals, working in traditional jazz groups, often with the wonderful clarinetist and saxophonist Ham Carson. Standifer joined Quincy Jones for the *Free and Easy* jaunt to Europe, where he subbed for Clark Terry on Paris club dates. When he returned in 1960, he "walked the bar" for a while, playing rock 'n' roll tenor saxophone with drummer Gerald Frank and pianist Dave Holden at a "go-go" dance club called the Pink Pussycat (the old Downbeat), on Third Avenue.

Standifer worked in 1962 with Norm Hoagy at the World's Fair. The following year, he returned to the fair site (Seattle Center) to perform his beautiful jazz liturgy for octet, *Postlude*, an open-voiced suite inspired by the sonorities of Quincy Jones and Gerry Mulligan, which Standifer reprised at the 1987 New Jazz, New City concert series presented by Earshot Jazz. Standifer then supplemented work in the Cornish Jazz Sextet with lucrative commercial jobs in groups led by Frank Sugia and white violinist Joe Venuti. From 1965 to 1970, Standifer taught at Cornish College of the Arts, followed by six years as an instructor at Olympic College, in Bremerton. In 1990 he led his own group at the New Orleans Creole Restaurant and worked as the dean of humanities at the Northwest School. Inducted into the Seattle Jazz Hall of Fame in 1990, Standifer performed with the Seattle Repertory Jazz Orchestra and kept the memory of Jackson Street alive for twenty-five years at the New Orleans, in Pioneer Square.

Standifer was also called upon to teach workshops in Saskatchewan, Canada, and recorded two albums, *How Do You Keep the Music Playing* and *Scotch and Soda*, which captured his musical excellence on vocals, sax, and trumpet and his easy style with a crowd. He freely shared his knowledge of the jazz tradition and the jazz life with young musicians who were serious, a generosity that did not go unnoticed. "He inspired me to play music in the first place," said drummer Patti Padden, who worked with Floyd at the New Orleans. "He was a dear friend, a great teacher and a class act. I just can't think of anybody else like Floyd."

The Flame held on to its jazz policy through the early 1960s. Ernie Hatfield took the gig for several years, and in 1961, Gerald Brashear had a trio there with drummer Gerald Frank, whose group at the Mardi Gras was so popular. While the Flame was at its peak, another important transition venue sprang up in the North End as well—the Lake City Tavern. A barn of a place on the

Dave Coleman.

corner of 130th and Lake City Way, where students carried pitchers of beer to other college kids sitting at long picnic tables, the club was opened in 1955 by two University of Washington law students. It spawned a variety of memorable groups. One of the best-loved was the Signatures, an upbeat white ensemble inspired by the hip, close harmonies of the Hi-Lo's, and featuring Bob and Ruth Alcivar, Lee Humes, Cathi Hayes, and Gus Mancuso. Hayes and Mancuso, a multi-instrumentalist and vocalist, also put together an innovative white jazz band at the Lake City Tavern called Gus and Us, with drummer Dave Coleman, tenor saxophonist Joe Romano, and pianist Jerry Gray.

Traditional jazz enjoyed a revival at the Lake City Tavern too. Seattle's Rainy City Jazz Band played there often. Rainy City formed in 1946 and the following year was recorded by Seattle radiologist Frederick "Doc" Exner, the same trad fanatic who had waxed John Wittwer with Kid Ory in 1945. The original members were Gordon Greimes, clarinet; Boots Houlihan, cornet; Jack Sheedy, trombone; Lowell Richards, tuba; Dolph Bleiler, drums; and Barry Vye, piano. A less strictly traditional white group also formed at the Lake City Tavern—the Seattle Rhythm Kings, named with tongue-in-cheek bravado after a classic early jazz band, the New Orleans Rhythm Kings. The group was led by trumpeter Don Anderson, who was from Yakima, Washington, but had worked for years in the MGM studios in Los Angeles and played in the original Spike Jones Orchestra. (This Don Anderson, who died in 1986, is not to be confused with the other Seattle Don Anderson, a trombonist who grew up in Seattle and played in Dixieland groups such as the Island City Jazz Band.) In addition to trumpeter Anderson, the Seattle Rhythm Kings included Rollie Morehouse, clarinet; Mike Hobi, trombone; Red Kelly, bass; John Wittwer, piano; and Dave Coleman, drums.

John Wittwer spent some time in San Francisco, where he played intermission piano for Earl Hines at the Hangover Club. He also became friendly with

Kenneth Patchen, who along with Kenneth Rexroth had started a vogue for reading poetry to live jazz. This and other beat-era styles moved north to Seattle and became major ingredients in the modern jazz clubs that opened there. Jerry Rosen, a San Francisco–based author (*Blues for a Dying Nation*, *The Carmen Miranda Memorial Flagpole*) who spent a year in Seattle as a young man in the late 1950s, wrote a novel set in Seattle's beat scene in which he captured with Kerouac-like verve the quality of feeling suddenly at large during that era. As he walks into a Seattle jazz club, Rosen's protagonist says: "Jazz clubs were the only institutions in America in which I did not feel alienated at that time. The jazz people were my nation, the clubs our temples. . . . Jazz was not, for many of us, simply another form of entertainment, but it constituted rather a last sanctuary, our only hope, the underground religion of a racially integrated subculture, where Blacks and whites could engage in the ceremonies of welcoming each other to the new color-blind society which we felt was coming into existence before our eyes."

Pete's Poop Deck, the Penthouse, and Dave's Fifth Avenue were the first Seattle nightclubs to fulfill the sacred function Rosen describes and as such were the city's first true modern jazz clubs. Dave's Fifth Avenue was opened by Dave Levy in 1956, across the street from where a new city landmark would soon be erected for the upcoming World's Fair—the Space Needle. At Dave's fans gathered to hear Billy Tolles, Ernestine Anderson, and occasional touring acts such as Jay McNeely and Cal Tjader. Stars like Miles Davis and Dexter Gordon dropped by to jam. "The rest of Seattle was out on their boats," said Rosen, "and we were inside this dark tavern on a sunny afternoon, listening to jazz. We felt like we knew about something everyone else had missed."

One of the most important "inside" events at Dave's was the birth of the Mastersounds, which would outsell any jazz group that had so far come from Seattle. The Mastersounds was the pet project of bassist Monk Montgomery, who had left Elmer Gill's gig at the New Washington Hotel. The quartet featured Monk, his brother Buddy on vibes, plus Indianapolis drummer Benny Barth and Montana pianist Richie Crabtree. The Mastersounds opened at Dave's Fifth Avenue in January 1957. The group was an instant success, holding the crowds for three months. Mixing jazz tunes such as "Dexter's Deck" and "The Chase" with standards and songs from Broadway shows, the group opened each selection with an arrangement that carefully melded the sound of piano, vibes, bass, and drums. The sound was mellow and dynamically controlled, but the emphasis was more on straight-ahead swing, unlike that of the Modern Jazz Quartet or the Dave Brubeck Quartet.

A local engineer named Chet Noland brought his equipment into Dave's Fifth Avenue and recorded the Mastersounds live. Monk drove south and sold the tapes to Pacific Jazz Records, which released them in 1957, as *Jazz Showcase*. Between 1957 and 1960 the group made a series of extremely popular albums, the most famous of which was *The King and I*. (Broadway jazz albums and original cast albums had become a fad, as the musical comedy enjoyed a comeback.) The Mastersounds disbanded in 1960 but not before introducing the world to guitarist Wes Montgomery, who played on several of the albums and went on to revolutionize jazz guitar.

The Mastersounds left their mark on Seattle by introducing the college crowd to modern, arranged jazz. Before the Mastersounds there had been the arranged trio music of Elmer Gill and Ray Charles and Milt Green; there had been the big bands of Al Pierre and Bumps Blackwell; there had been the raucous jazz-jamming of groups such as Floyd Standifer's at the Flame; and there had been the burning tempos of Cecil Young's bebop. But there had been nothing like the Mastersounds, a modern, four-piece group that incorporated the latest developments in jazz into listenable, swinging music of the highest caliber. Part of the beauty of this was that the jazz listeners in Seattle knew the group had been spawned on their own ground. It gave them the same sense of participation and ownership in the national jazz scene that Ernestine Anderson had. As a jazz town, Seattle was growing up.

Seattle jazz took another leap forward when Pete's Poop Deck opened in the Pioneer Square district at the foot of Main Street, under the (now demolished) Alaskan Way viaduct. Pioneer Square was not a fashionable club-and-restaurant area in 1957, but a dreary, down-and-out mission district, so Pete's was something of a bold gamble. The Poop Deck was opened in the fall of 1957 by a clever twenty-year-old jazz fan and bartender named Pete Barbas. His establishment was the first self-consciously styled modern jazz club in Seattle, mingling a "beatnik pad" decor of orange crates, wooden benches, and peanut shells on the floor with a seagoing motif of fishnets and blown-glass floats. Local painters hung their oils on the walls; a mannequin sculpted into a mermaid hung from the ceiling. Poets came to recite their work, artists sketched in

Pete's Poop Deck, 1958–61. *Left to right:* Jerry Gray, Bob Winn, Milt Garred, Jabo Ward, Bill Richardson.

the corner, and the bearded Barbas himself worked behind the bar. Every once in a while, during a set, a train would go by under the old viaduct elevated highway and disrupt a quiet ballad, but that too was part of the ambience. The place could only hold 140 customers or so, but during its five and a half years on the scene, Pete's Poop Deck was rarely empty.

"People used to sit out in the rain with newspapers over their head and have to wait till the set was over so they could probably get in and sit on a soapbox," recalled saxophonist Jabo Ward, who put in some of his finest work at Pete's. "Pete didn't care what you played as long as it was jazz. And everybody that came there—that's what they wanted to hear, was jazz. And the place stayed packed." Barbas was a masterful publicist, securing items in the dailies on a regular basis. (The club even found its way into a Sidney Sheldon potboiler, *Rage of Angels*.) Pete's hosted the finest jazz musicians in town—as well as presenting out-of-towners such as Cal Tjader, Chris Connor, Barney Kessel, and Mongo Santamaria—establishing a standard for jazz clubs that would follow. Pops Buford led the club's first local group; the band that succeeded Pops's was fronted by a saxophone/flute double-threat of Jabo Ward and Bob Winn, a white newcomer from Detroit; with Jerry Gray, piano; Milt Garred, bass; and

Jabo Ward, 1959.

Bill Richardson, drums, also from the Motor City.

Pete's was the staging ground for the high point of Jabo Ward's career. Since leaving Al Pierre after his disastrous Alaska tour in 1949, Ward had led his own groups at the Far East Veterans Club, with Dee Dee Hackett doing vocal chores, and at the New Chinatown. In the Poop Deck era Ward was smitten by the innovations of tenor saxophonist John Coltrane, who had pushed jazz harmony and improvising intensity to a new level. Attempting at first to decipher on his own the complicated ins and outs of Coltrane's approach, Ward sent for a mail-order course from the Berklee College in Boston, Quincy Jones's alma mater. In 1955, Ward also began playing flute, studying with Victor Case of the Seattle Symphony and Joe Lazire, a local flute repairman. Jabo took his newly won chops into Pete's in 1958 and for the next three years knocked over audiences there. "Everything came together there—people, place, owner, the music—it was terrific," Ward recalled. "Pete let us play anything we wanted, and we wanted bebop. Working for Pete for two years, like I did, there was never anything said about what I played or when I played. Nothing."

Ward's style was ferocious on tenor, mixing Coltrane, Lucky Thompson, and the note-happy aggression of Sonny Stitt into one big-toned, expressive, well-executed style, solidly in the tradition. For the Poop Deck gig Jabo played flute and alto and tenor saxophones. His flute duets with Bob Winn at Pete's on "My Funny Valentine" and "Little Girl Blue" were still fondly remembered years later.

After Pete's, Ward gave up being a leader and started to cut back on his jazz work. He had taken a day job in the 1950s, driving, delivering, and repairing golf carts. In 1966 he went to work for Texaco Oil. In 1964 he started giving private lessons and worked private parties and occasional special events. During the

1980s he was part of a popular cooperative, the Inner City Jazz Quartet, with Ernie Hatfield, white drummer Pete Madsen, and bassist Terry Morgan, which played festivals and opened for national acts, such as Freddie Hubbard. Ward's appearances fell off in the late 1980s, and he died in 2004. But even late in life, the Jackson Street veteran could still be raised to the heights of enthusiasm about music. "What you do through your horn is project your own feelings," he explained. "Whether it's slow, fast, or medium, I'm still projecting feelings, see. And soul is one of the greatest things to have in music. SOUL . . . SOUL. Project your inner self through the bell of that instrument."

At some point Jabo was replaced in the Poop Deck band by Gerald Brashear. Brashear took a breather after his Cecil Young Quartet days; going forward, as with his pal Milt Garred, drugs and alcohol made his career erratic. But at the Poop Deck he became famous for a melodic solo he played on congas with his elbow, as well as for his remarkable tenor and vocal chops. Brashear worked throughout the 1960s, at the Colony, the Flame, the Seattle Jazz Society venue called the Jazz Gallery, and the Doubletree Inn. At one point he backed up Zenobia, the shake dancer, at Earl Mack's club. By then, he too had picked up Coltrane influences, adding a Trane-ish cry and modal scales to his woody tone. Brashear played on a laid-back Wyatt Ruther album, *Easy Living with the Ruther IV*, recorded in Vancouver, British Columbia, in 1972. He sounded somewhat tired in this performance. When he died, in 1973, the *Seattle Post-Intelligencer* acknowledged him as "one of the really great local jazz talents."

The bass player in the Poop Deck band was already well-known to Seattleites through his work with Ray Charles. Since the McSon Trio days, Milt Garred had, like Pony Poindexter, spent time in prison because of his drug addiction. Garred was in and out of jail throughout the 1950s and 1960s, drinking heavily when he was trying to get off heroin, notoriously as unreliable as he was brilliant—but, along with Chuck Metcalf, he continued to be the bass player of choice for anyone in town really serious about jazz. A 1972 private recording made at Seattle Center showed Garred to have kept intact his big, boomy sound and elastic attack, while becoming even more adept at weaving a line through the harmony. Garred died in 1978.

Working with Milt and Bill Richardson at the Poop Deck was Jerome Gray, then known as Jerry, who had gotten started at the Lake City Tavern. Gray is an enigma. Reputed by musicians to be the best pianist who ever played in

Jerry Gray, 1962.

Seattle, Gray retreated from playing in public in 1970. When Gray was a child, his right hand had been burned in an accident, and the fingers were webbed together. To compensate, he developed his left hand to phenomenal proportions, deciding he was going to be the next Art Tatum. He became an even more powerful player when he had his right hand operated on, around 1960.

A 1964 recording revealed Gray as a supremely logical, swinging player with crisp execution and drive, who means everything he plays and plays everything he means. In 1965 he arranged and played on a lovely album of standards for Joni Metcalf, *Joni! Joni Metcalf Sings Porter and Ellington*, with Chuck Metcalf on bass and George Griffin on drums. The last gig listed locally for Gray was in December 1969, at the Doubletree Inn, near Sea-Tac Airport. "He quit drinking, smoking, and playing music in public all in the same day," recalled Metcalf. "It was like he walked through a door into a different life."

Gray's sudden exit from the jazz life was apparently an expression of his dissatisfaction with his own progress. "I came to the wrong town," Gray said in an interview with jazz critic Maggie Hawthorn. "Very few people here thought of themselves as going anywhere or doing anything particularly consequential. There was a kind of 'We're just folks' attitude here. It was disastrous for me." Gray retreated to his studio, where he wrote and published a series of method books. A slight, intense man with a cherubic face, he continued to wield a tremendous influence locally through his teaching, which was as much about method as a sort of counseling practice about focusing one's goals and life in the music business. Musicians from Diane Schuur to Wayne Horvitz took a lesson or two from this virtuoso pianist and theorist. Through the early 2000s Gray could be found about town, listening to the progress of his students in various clubs or catching the great piano players like Tommy Flanagan or Hank Jones when they came to town. In 2026 he was living in a retirement community in his hometown of Spokane.

All the activity in the late 1950s and early 1960s prompted bassist Chuck Metcalf to revive his career. Metcalf had been fairly quiet throughout the 1950s, raising a family and practicing architecture. In 1961 he joined white pianist Dick Palombi and Bill Richardson in a house trio at the Penthouse, a posh new club at First Avenue and Cherry Street. When the owner began to book name players such as Dexter Gordon, Harold Land, and Carmell Jones, the Palombi trio backed them up. In 1962 vocalist Anita O'Day hired the trio off the bandstand for a tour, which took Metcalf to Los Angeles, where he performed on television with Lou Rawls and played with Buddy Greco. Greco hired Palombi as his accompanist, which ended the pianist's career in Seattle, but Metcalf returned, working jazz and commercial gigs throughout the 1960s. In 1966, Metcalf and Lowell Richards and a group of other activists started the Seattle Jazz Society, and in 1969, Metcalf toured Vietnam with pianist Overton Berry. A long commercial gig in the summer of 1972 convinced Metcalf he needed to get away from Seattle if he wanted to pursue jazz seriously, so he moved to San Francisco, where he became a first-call sideman, playing with Eddie Henderson, Sonny Simmons, Woody Shaw, Charlie Byrd, and others, and recording with vocalist Mark Murphy, avant-garde drummer Doug Hammond, and a cooperative group called San Francisco Ltd.

In 1979, Metcalf moved to New York City. The next year he was hired by Dexter Gordon for a five-month tour of Europe and the United States, after which he returned to San Francisco. In 1982, Metcalf resumed his career in Seattle. With the exception of a two-year break in 1984–85, when he lived in Wales and Holland (and recorded with pianist Albert Sarko), Metcalf became a stalwart of the Seattle scene. In 1989 he released a CD of his own tunes, *Elsie Street*, in the hard-bop tradition he had learned as a young man, followed by *Live at the Zoo* in 1990, with post-bop saxophonist Bert Wilson, and *Help Is Coming* in 1992. In the mid-1990s Metcalf moved back to San Francisco, where he retired in 2011. Inducted in 1990 into the Seattle Jazz Hall of Fame in its first cohort, Metcalf died in 2012.

Metcalf was a solidly grounded, blues-based player whose style, knowledge, and dues-paying experiences on the road made him an elder statesman to whom local players turned for mentoring in the jazz life. His grasp of harmony and structure, particularly—perhaps a reflection of his architecture background—was a regular source of pleasure. In 1985 he was cited as one of the "bassists who have contributed to jazz music over the past 65 years" in Todd Coolman's book *The Bass Tradition*.

In 1962, Pete Barbas sold the Poop Deck. His nightclub had been part of a renaissance on the Seattle jazz scene as tourists and businesses rolled in with the World's Fair. The Penthouse, across First Avenue from where Al Pierre had held forth in the 1940s at the Union Club, began to bring in national acts every week. John Coltrane would eventually release an album that was recorded there, *Live in Seattle*. The Noplace, at Occidental Avenue and South Washington Street, operated from 1960 to 1962, featuring Gerald Brashear, Al Larkins, and Dave Coleman, among others. The Door, an espresso coffeehouse on Seventh Avenue, also became a destination for jazz fans, where Bill Ramsay, Chuck Metcalf, Bud Schultz, Elmer Gill, Floyd Standifer, and others performed. The Townhouse, at Denny Way and Stewart Street, served for a year or so as a favorite jamming spot as well. Between 1957 and 1963 nine Seattle clubs were presenting modern jazz—the Ebony, Flame, Mardi Gras, Dave's Fifth Avenue, Lake City Tavern, Pete's Poop Deck, the Noplace, the Door, and the Penthouse. (Another curious spot called Gabe's featured recorded jazz that fans could listen to through earphones.) Several clubs also opened to feature Dixieland, including Ronnie Pierce's establishment in Pioneer Square, the Roaring '20s club at the fairgrounds itself, and the New Washington Hotel, where Wingy Manone played. Bob Summerise, the disc jockey who had broadcast from the Flame, noted in his weekly column for the *Puget Sound Observer*: "The town may seem dead, but Seattle is one of the most active jazz cities on the West Coast."

Even with the bustling jazz activity of the 1960s, some national musicians continued to think of Seattle as a remote spot in the woods where they could recuperate from the trials and tribulations of the jazz life. So it was for the pioneering violinist Joe Venuti, who visited a friend in Seattle in 1957 and moved there permanently in 1963 to "dry out." In the bargain Venuti treated local audiences—who often had no idea who he was—to a steady diet of amazing swing violin and shenanigans until his death in 1978.

Other musicians played important roles in the burgeoning scene of the early 1960s as well. One was the white bassist Freddy Schreiber, a brilliant musician who grew up in Seattle and later toured and recorded with Cal Tjader, following in Buddy Catlett's footsteps. Schreiber's discovery early in life that he had a terminal liver disease seems to have given him a dark, upside-down humor that spilled into everything he did. After a *DownBeat* reviewer praised his playing at the expense of other players on Tjader's album *Saturday Night, Sunday Night at the Black Hawk*, Schreiber penned a retort, published in *DownBeat*, satirizing the inflated language of jazz critics: "I think [the reviewer] was very fair in putting down Cal and the other guys in the group," wrote the bassist, "but I really think he should have listened to me more carefully. Evidently he did not listen closely to my angular, probing lines and I am sure that not once did he take note of my relentless throbbing beat." "Freddy was so funny," recalled Elmer Gill, who worked with the bassist at Ivar's, after Jerry Gray left the gig. "Right up until he died, he never lost his sense of humor. He was in a wheelchair and I called him up and he said, 'Man, I sure hope you're not calling me up for a gig.' This was about a week before he died." Schreiber died in 1965.

Another important musician on the early 1960s scene was Don Lanphere's old friend from Wenatchee, white pianist Jack Brownlow, about whom Paul Desmond, Dave Brubeck's saxophonist, was once reported to have said, "If I could play the piano, I'd want to sound like Jack Brownlow." There was also Dick Palombi's vocalist, Teddy Ross, who hit town with ten cents in his pocket and wound up on Broadway, playing in the hit production *The Wiz*, then in the film *Arthur* (as the chauffeur). There was white comedian Pete Barbutti, a fine pianist in his own right, who cut his teeth on the Seattle scene during the World's Fair, then went on to Las Vegas and *The Tonight Show* as a comedian. Larry Rockwell, a bassist who worked with Sarah Vaughan, was also on the scene in the late 1950s. And of course, the bluesy Overton Berry, who as early as 1958 was playing with his trio at the Calypso and would serve as Diane Schuur's accompanist during her years of struggle in the 1970s and 1980s before becoming one of Seattle's favorite lounge pianists.

Pete Barbas had been prescient in seeing that the Skid Road area around Pioneer Square could eventually become a lively nightclub district. It was long after he "pioneered" the area that the city followed his lead. But Barbas benefited from another development, a shift in local attitude related to the coming of the World's Fair itself. Prior to the 1950s, Seattle was a town on the margins, and apparently quite happy about it. Old Seattleites—in fact, Northwesterners in general—took pride in their isolation and were almost pleased that no one knew much about them. There was a hidden quality to the place, and the natives liked to think of it as a secret. Beat writer Jack Kerouac captured this sense when he visited briefly on his way to work as a fire lookout in the Cascades, describing Seattle as the "City in the Shroud"—furtive, hidden by clouds—a little spooky, but quiet, meditative, and somewhat spiritual. It was precisely this hidden-away quality that allowed the pioneer-era bootlegging scene to flourish. Likewise, musicians who took part in these goings-on, as Jerry Gray has suggested, never imagined that what they were doing had any importance. Isolated in the northwest corner of the country, hidden by clouds, working in a market far from the pulse of things—New York, Los Angeles—they could carry on their work without anyone really paying any mind.

Sometime in the 1950s all of this changed. Seattle decided it wanted to be noticed. One of the first things it had to do to accomplish this was to shed the image of the pioneers', loggers', and Native Americans' town on the marshes of Elliott Bay it had been stuck with for almost a century and replace it with a more sanitized, forward-looking one. In 1951 the city started this process by replacing its traditional Potlatch Festival, during which Native Americans had gathered to trade and celebrate at various points around Lake Washington, with a Scandinavian festival based on a pirate theme. In keeping with the technology worship that had evolved around the Boeing Company and the Cold War, the festival planners plunked a hydroplane race in the middle of the event. Thus was born Seafair, which continues to this day as a source of great pleasure for children and old-timers and an annual embarrassment for sophisticates and newcomers.

Not long after Seafair was established, the city fathers also decided they wanted to have another fair, a big shindig that would show off their progressive and futuristic city. After many years of planning, Century-21, usually called the Seattle World's Fair, was mounted at the site of the old Civic Auditorium and Armory, both of which were converted and made part of a new civic garden christened Seattle Center. As a monument to technological futurism, the city built the Space Needle. It also invited the rest of the world in to look. Seattle's shroud was pierced.

This was a major psychological change for the city, a mood swing it hadn't known since the days of the AYP Exposition in 1909, and it closed the door forever on the innocent days of the after-hours scene on Jackson Street. Many old-timers resented the change, feeling that Seattle had been a better, less pretentious town when it was a private, unaffected affair. The curmudgeonly newspaper columnist Emmett Watson even founded a mock organization, Lesser Seattle, to commemorate his distaste for Seattle's newfound boosterism. Though Watson kept his tongue firmly in cheek, Lesser Seattle had about it a hint of Northwest truth in its parochialism and xenophobia. But the Northwest also has a genuine affection and nostalgia for such personal and human-scale activities as the scene that once flourished along Jackson Street, a scene that from the 1960s on would become increasingly invisible and forgotten, until finally it was buried, like the Potlatch Festival itself, except in the memories of those who had once been there.

11 Jackson Street

A Lost Legacy?

EVEN IF SEATTLE HAD BEEN of a mind to keep its shadow side exposed after the World's Fair, there were forces at work that would have prevented after-hours jazz from becoming a part of the program. In the mid-1960s, when rock music rose to dominate popular music, mainstream jazz nearly died out, not only in Seattle but all over the country. For almost a decade there wasn't any room for jazz in record stores, on the radio, or in nightclubs. In Seattle, Dave's Fifth Avenue had split its bookings from the start between rock and jazz; soon it went all rock. The Mardi Gras and Poop Deck closed in the early years of the decade, and the Penthouse folded in 1968. The other clubs that had risen around the ballyhoo of the beatnik era and the World's Fair, such as the Door and the Downbeat, also went dark.

Players who couldn't adapt to the new situation often retreated from the scene in despair or died of one form of frustration or another. Ernestine Anderson stopped performing. So did Buddy Catlett. Floyd Standifer and Jabo Ward became less active. Leon Vaughn stopped playing altogether. Bob Winn, opting for commercial music and steady work, moved to Honolulu. Traff Hubert hung it up. So did Major Pigford and Roscoe Weathers. Billy Tolles and Tommy Adams turned to rock, and Tommy died young. Cecil Young and Jimmie Rodgers had both died. Bill Richardson, Vernon Brown, Gerald Brashear, Winfield King, Milt Garred, and Al Larkins followed them to the grave at the end of that difficult era. For a decade the jazz musicians who survived were pushed aside, or forced to play more commercial music.

Just as the rock avalanche fell, a reform-minded city hall and a new King County prosecutor dealt the coup de grâce to the last vestiges of the "tolerance policy" and the culture of corruption that went with it. In 1967 a downtown-Seattle tavern owner complained to the FBI that the cops on the beat were trying to extort protection money from him. Over the next three years a series of investigations led to an exposé of the nasty system of police payoffs and graft that had supported Seattle's gambling, prostitution, and bootlegging for more than half a century.

It was not a pretty story. A 1970 federal grand jury, a King County grand jury, and subsequent trials revealed that the tolerance policy, while in itself a victimless crime that had allowed people to have a good time, also supported a system in which police officers—much like organized criminals—demanded protection money even from owners who had nothing to hide. Those who didn't "pay to stay," as the policy came to be called, were simply hounded out of business. (It was shown, for example, that the vice squad harassed gay bars, driving customers away, then demanded payments in exchange for allowing owners to reopen.) The exposé resulted in a departmental bloodbath.

Police chief Frank Ramon resigned in 1969 and the assistant police chief, M. E. "Buzz" Cook, was indicted and convicted of perjury the following year. Forty officers were shown to be on the take; fourteen resigned or took early retirement, including two assistant chiefs, two majors, one captain, three lieutenants, three sergeants, a detective, and two officers. Mobster Frank Colacurcio was convicted of racketeering. The King County grand jury and related trials netted more convictions, though a 1973 conspiracy indictment against a rogue's gallery of city fathers, including longtime King County prosecutor Charles O. Carroll, who had turned a blind eye to the tolerance policy for decades and was suspected of taking bribes from the pinball industry, turned up no convictions. City Council member Charles M. Carroll (no relation to Charles O.), credibly accused of collecting $300 a month in bribes in his capacity as licensing czar, got off scot-free as well when he was dropped from the conspiracy case. But the tolerance policy and Seattle's long history of police corruption had come to a decisive end. The city would be known henceforth as a model of clean governance.

When the tolerance policy officially collapsed, it was directly supporting only two after-hours clubs, the 605 and the New Chinatown, so the consequences for working jazz musicians were negligible. However, its timing, coinciding as it did with the rise of rock, contributed to a curious disjunction in local jazz history. For almost a decade there was so little local jazz played in Seattle that when the music finally did make a comeback, around 1976, the fans—and even many local musicians—had no idea Jackson Street had ever existed. Many Seattle musicians in the 1980s were not even aware that Quincy Jones, Ray Charles, or Patti Bown had worked in the same town they were scuffling in. Even fewer knew who Al Pierre or Bumps Blackwell were. It was as if the musical past, like the corruption that had supported it, had been expunged from the town's official history, like an unpleasant memory. The result was a jazz scene sadly cut off from its own past. Older Black musicians, in particular, who had participated in the lively Jackson Street era felt passed over when the jazz scene revived, somehow robbed of what should have been their own legacy.

But what was that legacy? With the Jackson Street era in full view, can it be said with any assurance that there is a relationship between the old scene and the present one? In short, does Seattle have a jazz "tradition"? Yes. Standifer, Catlett, Anderson, and Metcalf—among others—stood as living testimony to the continuity of such a tradition, and their musical heirs, players such as trumpeter Thomas Marriott, pianist Marc Seales, bassist Phil Sparks, and multi-instrumentalist Jay Thomas, continue that legacy today. A few musicians, such as vocalist Darelle Holden, drummer D'Vonne Lewis, and bassist Doug Barnett, even boast a direct lineage from Jackson Street giants.

But "tradition" means many things to many people. For some it means a consistent style, such as the ones formulated at various times in New Orleans, Kansas City, Chicago, or Detroit. In that sense Seattle does not have a "tradition" of playing in a specifically regional style. Significant regional styles usually come about when a particular player's approach is so compelling that others imitate it. Though there were strong, individual stylists on Jackson Street—Dick Wilson, Fred Greenwell, and Gerald Wiggins come to mind—their approaches did not dominate other players, perhaps because these potentially influential musicians didn't stay in town long enough. As a result, there is no significant historical Seattle style. However, there were stylistic connections between Jackson Street's bluesy bebop and the music that followed.

In Floyd Standifer's straight-ahead bop with a modal twist, one could hear echoes of Jackson Street shuffles and blues. In Buddy Catlett one heard the same solid time, big sound, and soulful values the bassist had when he was playing with Count Basie and Quincy Jones. In a more nostalgic vein, Catlett's Sunday-night jam sessions at Lofurno's restaurant in the late 1980s and early 1990s, according to people like Sonny Booker, were the last living vestige of the feeling that existed on Jackson Street so many years before, when instrumentalists and vocalists came by to jam and sing, and the feeling was easy and convivial. Jabo Ward's swing-to-bebop fire fit right into the Lofurno's scene. And Chuck Metcalf, though his roots lay more in the 1950s, still had that link to basic swing and blues feeling that can only have come from many nights at the Elks Club. In 1990, Ward, Standifer, Catlett, Elmer Gill, and a younger drummer named Patti Padden formed the Local 493 Reunion Band, commemorating the after-hours scene on Jackson Street. This began a rapprochement between Seattle's jazz past and present. It continued in the soulful blues and swing of players such as Marc Seales, Jay Thomas, and Thomas Marriott as well as the award-winning jazz bands mentored at Garfield High School by Clarence Acox and Roosevelt High School by Scott Brown.

One of the problems for Seattle in maintaining a consistent level of performance and style, however, has been that many of the city's best players tend to move away, as opportunities beckon from elsewhere. Chuck Metcalf, with a gentle skepticism, noted this even back in the late 1980s: "All of the real heavyweights, the people that really felt themselves to be talented and really had ambitions for themselves in the music business, man, they were out of here! Quincy Jones! Out of high school, *blam!* Patti Bown, the same way. Bill Crow went right to New York and became a success. [Bassist] Larry Rockwell went to New York. [Bassist] Freddy Schreiber went down to California and almost instantaneously was working with Cal Tjader. The really talented ones, except for Floyd and Jerry Gray and a few others, didn't stay." But Metcalf himself was one of the "really talented ones," and he stayed, at least off and on. And while there is some justification to his criticisms, in voicing them he slighted himself. Jackson Street didn't produce musicians to rival Dizzy Gillespie and Charlie Parker, true. But Jackson Street had so much when most people—even those who lived nearby—thought it had nothing at all that the point would seem to be its very existence and authenticity, not its competitiveness with the national scene. Besides, Jackson Street did nurture musicians such as Quincy Jones, Patti Bown, and Freddie Greenwell, whether they stayed in town or not. And time and time again, it connected with the national scene in a way that was productive both for locals and musicians on the larger stage.

A good illustration of this kind of interchange was the contribution of alto saxophonist Joe Brazil, who arrived from Detroit in 1961. Brazil was a better mover and shaker than he was a musician, but after working at the Mardi Gras with another Detroit emigrant who arrived the same year, vocalist Woody Woodhouse, and at the Poop Deck and the Penthouse, he established the Black Academy of Music (later renamed the Brazil Academy of Music) with the notion of passing on African American traditions to youngsters in the neighborhood. Milt Garred, Jabo Ward, Floyd Standifer, and others played and taught at the academy, and Brazil also collared name artists who came through town—including Dizzy Gillespie, Joe Henderson, and Stanley Turrentine—to come talk to the kids. Brazil hired a regular coterie of Black musicians, notably West Virginia trumpeter Ed Lee. Like so many players, Lee came to Seattle after serving in the Twenty-First US Army Band at Fort Lewis, in the mid-1960s. A tall, gentle, diffident man, Lee was not always high on the local jazz radar, but he made a steady contribution, often appearing in pit bands, including theatrical productions at the Seattle Rep, and playing with Brazil's quintet, Keith Baggerly's big band, Roadside Attraction, and bands led by drummer/teacher Clarence Acox. Lee preceded Acox as a music teacher at Garfield High School and also went on the road with Lou Rawls and the musical *Hair*. Lee died in 2011.

Lee was already a highly schooled musician when he met Joe Brazil. Other players who had less training but also blossomed in Brazil's orbit included self-taught guitarist George Hurst, whom Acox described as an "exceptional musician," and tenor saxophonist Omar Brown, who could be found in 1970 performing at A Contemporary Theatre with the Modern Jazz Orchestra. Other Black musicians, such as multi-instrumentalist Sam Chambliss and bassist Doug Barnett Jr. (the grandson of Powell Barnett), got some of their first chances at sight-reading big-band charts, arranging, improvising, and theory at the BAM. Brazil later recorded with John Coltrane in a marathon twelve-hour session, in Lynnwood, Washington, after Coltrane's live album was finished at the Penthouse. The tapes were issued on the LP *Om*. He also recorded Coltrane at the Penthouse playing one of only two live renditions of his masterpiece, *A Love Supreme*, which was released on CD in 2021.

Two young musicians who worked with Joe Brazil went on to prominent national careers. Bassist Rufus Reid lived in Seattle from 1966 to 1969, studying at Olympic College in Bremerton, Washington, and working in Seattle at Rosellini's Four-10 and at the Checkmate, a club opened in 1966 by Sonny Booker. As a kid, Carlos Ward played with vocalist Ron Holden, keyboard man Dave Lewis, and bandleader Terry Cruise, then came to international attention in the 1980s as the lead alto player with Abdullah Ibrahim's band, Ekaya. Ward, whose interests turned toward the avant-garde, often jammed at a coffeehouse called the Llahngaelhyn, just south of the University Bridge, run by an eccentric white pianist/bassist named Jerry Heldman.

A variety of important young musicians, including Ward, Larry Coryell, Ralph Towner, Walter Zuber Armstrong, David Friesen, and Ron Soderstrom learned to improvise free jazz there. Heldman admired Scott LaFaro and Gary Peacock, both bassists with a rhythmically sprung, guitar-like approach to the instrument, moving it away from timekeeping to an expressive, supple counterweave against the rhythmic line. (Peacock moved to Seattle in 1966 but was not fully active as a player until a decade later, when he joined the Cornish faculty; his influence on Heldman was through records.)

"The Llahngaelhyn had a very great influence on the music in this place," said white bassist David Friesen, who remembered jam sessions that went on all night at the club. The Llahngaelhyn scene is a kind of missing link in Seattle jazz history. For while it was a hotbed of avant-gardism and free jazz, the music played there also remained grounded in blues, bebop, and swing tradition. Part of the reason for this was that Heldman himself had spent time on the old after-hours scene, where he had developed a firm respect for tradition. Another reason may have been the earthy, no-nonsense nature of the Northwest itself. Unlike California, Washington never seems to have abandoned a fundamental sense of swing and blues, no matter how "cosmic" its music became. This respect for fundamentals carried over in the music of the Llahngaelhyn's heirs.

Probably the most obvious example can be found in white bassist Michael Bisio, whose quintet CD *In Seattle* made several critical top-ten lists in 1990. Bisio is a modern player with a Charlie Haden–like sound and a feeling for composition very much like Charles Mingus's. His music has an "inside/outside" feel, with a kind of moody space around a blues feeling in the line. He now lives in New York, where he plays and records with pianist Matthew Shipp. White trumpeter Ron Soderstrom, who spent his formative years at the Llahngaelhyn coffeehouse learning to play free jazz, worked with Bisio. There was a direct line between what was happening in Bisio's music and the aesthetics that evolved at Heldman's café. (Friesen, who heard *In Seattle* "blindfolded," agrees: "That record we just heard, with Ron Soderstrom? That's like a very reserved, very tame [version] of [the] playing that came out of the Llahngaelhyn.")

The more Northwest music one hears, the better this seemingly tenuous bridge holds up. No matter how "far out" musicians in the region seem to go, they are always anchored by a healthy conservatism regarding line, blues, and traditional jazz feeling. The result is a graceful balance of heaven and earth. This certainly applied to the saxophonist Denney Goodhew, an amazing musician who recorded with the late white trumpet player and composer Jim Knapp on the ECM label but retired from music for health reasons around 2015 and died in 2026. But it also felt accurate in the 1990s for Knapp himself; for the band of former Cornish students called Timebone (Briggan Krauss, Arnold Hammerschlag, and Aaron Alexander); the gentle, run-on compositions of the fine pianist Dave Peck; the steady time and linear inventiveness of pianist Marc Seales; the Bill Frisell–inspired sounds of guitarist Brad Shepik; the open, Paul Motian–like drumming of Mike Sarin; and the world fusion creations of the Big Daddy of all Northwest groups, Oregon. Today you can hear that same "inside-out" sound in the quartet comprised of Thomas Marriott, drummer John Bishop, bassist Jeff Johnson, and saxophonist Rick Mandyck, which plays in Pioneer Square.

It's possible the continuity between Seattle jazz and the Llahngaelhyn free-jazz sessions is more a matter of regional temperament than an actual passing of traditions across the decades. But one has to ask why this particular blend of utopianism and common sense, of cosmic searching and earthy humility, has evolved in this corner of the world. Linking it to Seattle's background in basic blues does not seem half so far-fetched as saying it is just a matter of coincidence. A more easily defended legacy of Jackson Street is the direct, firsthand influence the house-rocking music of Billy Tolles and Tommy Adams had on the "Northwest sound" of rockers such as the Wailers, the Kingsmen, and the Sonics. In the late 1950s and early 1960s white kids in the Northwest seized upon Black R & B with a manic, almost awkward ferociousness, epitomized by the Kingsmen's anthem "Louie Louie," the Frantics' "Werewolf," and later the Sonics' "Psycho" and "The Witch." Some of this music had a jazz flavor. The Dynamics (with Larry Coryell), for example, with its horn section and keyboard, showed the cool, loping influence of "chitlins jazz." The Frantics were influenced more by the twang guitar sound of Duane Eddy, but their records were straight blues structures.

White musicians such as Larry Coryell, who grew up in eastern Washington, emphasized that the cultural thrust of their music came from their admiration of Black style, as personified in local musicians. "The Black people were cool," said Coryell, who died in 2017. "They had a unified culture. There was so much more emphasis on feeling, and very fundamental respect for rhythmic principles." Black R & B musician Dave Lewis, with sidemen also comfortable in a jazz environment—saxophonist Barney Hilliard and drummer George Griffin, for example—plowed a deep groove between the genres. At his peak, Lewis was much admired by local jazz musicians for his technique as well as his soulful jazz licks. His tune "J.A.J.," also covered by the Kingsmen, was no rock cliché, but a real instrumental oddity, a series of descending seventh chords followed by a "circle of fifths" bridge. Members of the Wailers frequented the Flame, where Floyd Standifer was playing his version of a tune the rock band would later record, "Mau Mau." Mike Burke, drummer for the Wailers, cites Griffin as a major influence. Dave Holden, who had worked with Billy Tolles in the 1950s, teamed up with Gerald Frank at the Downbeat in 1961, playing jazz/rock piano. None of this early rock could have been made in this way in the Northwest if the players hadn't been getting firsthand exposure to jazz.

One of the most important new musical elements rock music brought to the front was the electric guitar and its various electronic effects. It is curious that two of rock guitar's most influential exponents—Larry Coryell and Jimi Hendrix—arose in Seattle, drew early ammunition from Jackson Street, and have significant ties to jazz. Hendrix, whose experiments with distortion and feedback on his albums *Are You Experienced?*, *Axis*, *Bold as Love*, and *Electric Ladyland* permanently altered the sonic landscape of both jazz and rock, was a third-generation Seattle artist. His grandparents, Nora and Ross Hendrix, had been stranded in town in 1911 while working in a vaudeville show. His father, Al, was an amateur tap dancer who, with Jimi's mother, became famous in the Black community as a competition jitterbugger. Jimi, who started playing guitar in 1957, was influenced as a youngster by a local white rhythm-and-blues guitarist named Joe Johansen, who was also helpful to Larry Coryell: "The thing that connected me and Jimi Hendrix was Joe Johansen. Joe was responsible for teaching me R & B tunes. Very simple."

Hendrix left Seattle in 1961 and toured as a yeoman rhythm guitarist with several Black bands, including the Isley Brothers and Little Richard and the Upsetters. In New York he was exposed to the downtown bohemia coalescing around folk-rock and Bob Dylan, and began to experiment with his sound. Apocryphal stories to the contrary, Hendrix had not developed even the germ of his distortion effects in Seattle. What Hendrix did derive from his local background was simple blues discipline and form, for which there were lots of able role models on Jackson Street. The audience at Birdland had been listening to good dance music since Billy Tolles and the Savoy Boys opened there in 1941. Ultimately that simple foundation was as important for Hendrix's development as the experimental sounds he later heard in New York and London.

It may also be that the easy interchange in Seattle between jazz, R & B, rock, and blues—and the relaxed mixing of the races—had some subliminal influence on Hendrix's open-mindedness toward experimental forms. Though Hendrix never showed any interest in straight-ahead bebop, his experiments with sound

The Rocking Kings, with Jimi Hendrix, guitar, Washington Hall, 1960.

and time later had a huge influence on such jazz artists as Gil Evans, Miles Davis, and the group Weather Report in the jazz/rock fusion movement. It's interesting to note that Larry Coryell, who arrived in Seattle four months after Hendrix left, was one of the prime movers in this fusion.

Coryell played with both jazz and rock musicians in Seattle, including Jimmy Hanna and the Dynamics, Overton Berry, Jerry Gray, and Chuck Mahaffay. One night in 1965, at the Black and Tan, Gene Harris, the pianist with the Three Sounds, encouraged Coryell to go to New York. Coryell drove cross-country in a Volkswagen Bug and didn't stop until he got to Manhattan. A year later, he recorded an album that brilliantly combined avant-garde improvisation with rock 'n' roll rhythms, called *Out of Sight*, with drummer Bob Moses and Portland saxophonist Jim Pepper—arguably the first jazz/rock fusion record ever made. Coryell brought not only a solid blues, rock, and jazz foundation from Seattle but a sense of cosmic yearning, which he attributed to the city's geographic kinship with Asia. Is it possible Hendrix absorbed the same feeling? Looking out across Elliott Bay, with Mount Rainier looming behind, Coryell remarked that he felt a sense of possibility when he lived in Seattle, engendered by the town's isolation and the Pacific Ocean. "Seattle is not the real America," he said. "America starts on the other side of that mountain."

Floyd Standifer echoed this sentiment in a similar assessment of Seattle's place in the big picture:

> Seattle serves a unique purpose. It's one of the loveliest incubators you'll ever run into. Seattle always was a place to get it together, or come off the road and reassess yourself. But you can't stay here, if you're going to make it big. You don't have the numbers, first of all. You don't have the market value.
>
> But this town will hook you. You'll always end up coming back. And the reason you come back is, the first thing you ever were was a human being. And it's the last thing you're ever going to be. This town allows you to do that. All that other stuff in between is just stuff that you learn to do. You're looking for someplace where life can mean something, you come here.

Coryell and Standifer were right about Seattle's human scale, natural beauty, and isolation, but the city's Jackson Street musicians have also had an impact around the world, the most far-reaching influence being that of Ray Charles, Bumps Blackwell, and Quincy Jones. The entire Motown movement was based on Charles's breakthroughs. Later he would leap more artificial boundaries, by recording the first country-music album by a Black artist. Later still, he broke out of the straitjacket of the "Black artist" realm altogether, becoming a nationally loved, mainstream icon.

Bumps Blackwell's contribution to this process—referred to as "crossing over" to the white market—is less well known but important. When Blackwell left Seattle in 1951, he went to Los Angeles, where he was hired as an A & R man by Specialty Records. Four years later, Specialty sent him to New Orleans to produce a record by an unknown artist named Richard Penniman. In "Little Richard," Blackwell finally found the target for his creative energy that he had been looking for. As the lyricist, songwriter, A & R man, or producer, Blackwell midwifed nearly all of Little Richard's important early records, which made him one of the fathers of rock 'n' roll. He was a pioneer in a more important sense too, in that he helped define the role of the rock producer, which has more to do with marketing and manipulating raw talent than it does with music per se. This is precisely what Blackwell did when he virtually created Richard's first hit, "Tutti Frutti," in New Orleans, by rewriting the lyrics and cajoling Richard into a relaxed mood that captured his freewheeling spirit on record. Blackwell also produced the first crossover gospel hit, Sam Cooke's "You Send Me," which helped establish the soul music trend.

Is it a coincidence that yet a third figure from Jackson Street, Quincy Jones, also wound up as a prime mover in "crossing over" Black music? Probably not. Duke Ellington, who hated such marketplace terms as "rock," "jazz," and "funk," once told Jones that he would be the one to "decategorize American music." In his work with Michael Jackson, movie scores (*Roots*, *The Color Purple*), and his 1989 CD *Back on the Block*, which proposes a unified musical lineage of jazz, R & B, funk, and rap, Jones seems to have taken on Ellington's compliment as something of a life assignment.

The crossover work of these three men—Bumps Blackwell, Ray Charles, and Quincy Jones—has a clear legacy in such Seattle performers as vocalist Diane Schuur and saxophonist Kenny G. Schuur's expressive and fluid style owes as much in spirit to Ray Charles as it does in fact to Dinah Washington. Kenny G's fusion of jazz technique with an R & B dance sensibility is as old as Quincy Jones. Seattle's crossover tradition is directly related to its racially positive atmosphere in the 1940s. There was not only an unusual level of tolerance and mixing between the races, but a sense of excitement and possibility, a feeling that the old hierarchies—call it "tradition," if you like—did not apply in this little corner of the world, that a person could live up to his or her potential without worrying about the world cutting it down. Time after time, players make a point of mentioning this mellow atmosphere.

Ray Charles noted in his autobiography that "Seattle . . . was very different, because when you went to the clubs, you saw everybody—white, black—it didn't make any difference, people were just there! In Florida . . . if you worked in a white club, it was a white club, and that was that. It was new to me to go someplace and everybody was just loose and free." Whereas Detroit had riots, in Seattle a racial "incident" was news. Men like Quincy Jones and Billy Tolles grew up thinking that they could conquer the world. Likewise, Bumps Blackwell assumed that success was his for the taking, that he could take his "Junior Band" to an exclusive white district like Broadmoor or to the Trianon Ballroom.

In 1983, Charles, Jones, and Blackwell celebrated their mutual background in a fiftieth birthday party for Quincy Jones, held at the Paramount Theater. One of the highlights was a tongue-in-cheek performance of the old Jackson

Street warhorse “Big Fat Butterfly.” When Quincy and Ray and Bumps started in on those silly lyrics—“The chick was high, / As a butterfly,” they cracked up laughing, and all their old friends and compatriots in the audience laughed along with them. For a brief moment the old Jackson Street scene was alive in the room.

And then it was gone.

SELECTED DISCOGRAPHY

BY KEN WILEY AND PAUL DE BARROS

This discography is organized by artist, name of the band (if different from artist name), album title, date, the label, catalog, and in some cases individual song titles. Album titles are italicized, song titles enclosed in quotation marks. Album titles released under another artist's name or by another group, but which feature the artist in question, are listed in roman. Releases cited are not necessarily in print.

ANDERSON, ERNESTINE

Hot Cargo (1958). Mercury MG 20354.
Moanin' Moanin' Moanin' (1960). Mercury MG 20582.
Hello Like Before (1977). Concord Jazz 31.
Big City (1983). Concord Jazz 214.
When the Sun Goes Down (1984). Concord Jazz CCD 4263.
Be Mine Tonight (1986). Concord Jazz CCD 4319.
Now and Then (1993). Qwest Records 9-45249-2.
Blues, News & Love News (1996). Qwest Records 9-45900-2.
A Song for You (2008). HighNote HCD 7187.
Ernestine Anderson Swings the Penthouse (2015). HighNote HCD 7273.

BAILEY, MILDRED

Harlem Lullaby (1933). Academy Sound and Vision CD AFA 6065.
Squeeze Me (1936). Affinity CD AFS 1013.
Benny Goodman and His Orchestra. *Roll 'Em*, Vol. 1 (1939). CBS 460062-2.
The Complete Columbia Recordings of Mildred Bailey (2000). Mosaic Records MD10-204.

BISIO, MICHAEL

In Seattle (1987). Silkheart SHLP-107.
Michael Bisio and Kirk Knuffke. *Row for William O.* (2016). Relative Pitch Records RPR1043.
Travel Music (2020). MJB 3455.
Matthew Shipp. *New Concepts in Piano Trio Jazz* (2023). ESP-Disk 5085.

BLACKWELL, BUMPS

Little Richard. *18 Greatest Hits* (1966–57). Rhino Records RNCD 76899 (Blackwell, producer).

BOWN, PATTI

Patti Bown Plays Big Piano (1958). Columbia CL 1379.
Gene Ammons Quartet. *The Gene Ammons Story: Gentle Jug* (1962). Prestige P 24079.
Bill Coleman. *The Great Parisian Session* (1960). Polydor 837235-2.
See Quincy Jones, *Live at the Alhambra '60* and *The Birth of a Band.*

BRADLEY, OSCAR

Benny Carter and His Orchestra. *Coleman Hawkins / Benny Carter* (1948). Forlane UCD 19011.

BRASHEAR, GERALD

See Wyatt Ruther, *Easy Living with the Ruther IV.*
See Cecil Young, *Concert of Cool Jazz* and *Jazz on the Rocks.*

BRAXTON, BOB

"Summertime." Debut 1506.

BRAZIL, JOE

John Coltrane. *Om*, Parts 1 & 2 (1966). Impulse! AS9140.
James Moody. *The Teachers* (1970). Perception PLP6.
Roy Ayers. *Mystic Voyage* (1976). Polydor PD6067.

BURKE, CEELE

Louis Armstrong and His Sebastian New Cotton Club Orchestra. *Louis Armstrong: St. Louis Blues* (1980). CBS 467919-2.

CATLETT, BUDDY

Here Comes Buddy Catlett (2004). Pony Boy PB50141-2.

Frank Foster. *Basie Is Our Boss* (1963). Argo/Cadet LP717.

Louis Armstrong and His All-Stars (1966). Mercury 6499366.

Count Basie Orchestra. *The Count Basie Years* (1973). Roulette RE 102.

Count Basie Orchestra. *On My Way & Shoutin' Again* (1962). Verve MV 2647 IMS.

Count Basie Orchestra and Frank Sinatra. *Sinatra-Basie: An Historical First* (1988). Reprise FS 1008.

Bill Coleman. *The Great Parisian Session.* Polydor 837235-2.

See Quincy Jones, *Live at the Alhambra '60*, *The Birth of a Band*, and *I Dig Dancers.*

CHARLES, RAY

Maxin Trio et al. *Early Years* (1947–61). Jazz Archives No. 7, CD ZET 707.

Spotlight on Ray Charles (1960–?). Design Spotlight Series DLP-146.

The Genius of Ray Charles (1959). Atlantic SD 1312.

Genius Plus Soul Equals Jazz (1961). Impulse.

The Very Best of Ray Charles (2000). Rhino R2 79822.

COLEMAN, DAVE

Freddie Slack. *Riffette* (1942). Capitol.

T-Bone Walker. "I Got a Break Baby" and "Mean Old World." *The Complete Recordings* (1942). Mosaic MD6-130.

Willie Smith. *September in the Rain* (1946). Keynote.

Billie Holiday. *Billie Holiday and Her All Stars* (1946). Verve 841434-2.

COLTRANE, JOHN

Live in Seattle (1971). Impulse! GRD-2-146.

A Love Supreme: Live in Seattle (2021). Impulse! B00342290-02.

CORCORAN, CORKY

Sounds of Jazz Volume One: Corky (1957). Celestial 1.

Corky Corcoran Plays Something (1971). R.C.S. Records (RCS 2555).

Corky Corcoran and His Orchestra. *Jazz Club: Piano* (1945). Verve 840032-SJLP-1.

Corky Corcoran and the Seattle Strings. *The Sound of Love* (1957). Epic LN 3319.

Lionel Hampton All-Stars. *Stardust* ("Just Jazz" sessions) (1947). MCA Records MCA-198.

Harry James and His Orchestra. *The Best of the Big Bands* (1959). LRC Records CDC 8518.

CORYELL, LARRY

Free Spirits. *Out of Sight and Sound* (with Jim Pepper) (1967). ABC 593.

Larry Coryell and Emily Remler. *Together* (1985). Concord CCD 4289.

Shlomo Bat-Ain Group. *Distant Echoes* (1986). VeraBra Records CDVBR 2018-2.

Don Lanphere Larry Coryell (1990). Hep CD 2048.

Jimmy Hanna and the Dynamics. *Memory Bank* (1983). Bolo BSLP-8003.

See Chuck Mahaffay, *Seattle Beat* and *The Girl from Ipanema.*

CROW, BILL

From Birdland to Broadway (1995). Venus TKJV 19003.K.

Stan Getz. *Plays* (1952–54). Verve 833 535-2.

Gerry Mulligan. *Live in Boston at Storyville* (1956). Pacific Jazz PJ-1228.

Gerry Mulligan. *Newport Jazz Festival* (1958). CBS 88605.

Milt Jackson with the Quincy Jones Orchestra. *The Ballad Artistry of Milt Jackson* (1959). Atlantic 7567-82269-2.

Gerry Mulligan and the Concert Jazz Band. *Live at the Village Vanguard* (1960). Verve V-8396.

Gerry Mulligan. *Night Lights* (1963). Phillips PHM 200-108.

CRUSE, JUANITA

Juanita! (1960). Gene Norman Presents GNP51.

DARENSBOURG, JOE

Kid Ory's Creole Jazz Band (1945). Exner 3 and 4.

Kid Ory's Creole Jazz Band (1945). Decca 25133 and 25134.

Redd Foxx & His Ding Dong Daddies, original cast. (1946).

Kid Ory's Creole Jazz Band (1950). Columbia 38955, 38956, 38957, and 38958.

Kid Ory at the Beverly Tavern (1951). Sounds 1208.

Teddy Buckner and his Dixieland Five (1955). Gene Norman Presents GNP-11.
See John Wittwer [Trio].

DOLPHY, ERIC
At the Five Spot, Vols. 1–2 (1960). Prestige 7826.
Last Date (1965). Limelight 86013.

ELLINGTON, DUKE
Seattle Concert (1952). Victor WM-1002.

FRIEL, NEIL
Si Zentner (1965). RCA LPM/LSP3484.
Woody Herman. *Concerto for Herd* (1967). Verve V6-8764.

FRIESEN, DAVID
Color Pool (1975). Muse MR5109.
Triple Exposure (2016). Origin 82723.
Testimony (2020). Origin 82809.
David Friesen and John Stowell. *Through the Listening Glass* (1978). Inner City Records IC 1061.
Mike Nock Quintet. *Climbing* (1979). Tomato 2696502.
Mal Waldron–David Friesen Duo. *Dedication* (1985). Soul Note SN 1178.

GARRED, MILT
Maxin Trio et al. *Early Years* (1947–51). Jazz Archives No. 7, CD ZET 707.
See Corky Corcoran, *Sounds of Jazz.*

GILL, ELMER
"Lullaby of Birdland," "September Song," "Swedish Gumbo." Celestial EP001.
Elmer Gill Trio (1968). Aragon ASL201.
A Few of My Favorite Things (1976). Rada RST 1119.
I Can't Hear for Listening (1981). Intermodal IPLJ8200.
Three Generations of Jazz: Live in Switzerland (1988). Jam for Breakfast JFB110.

GOODHEW, DENNEY
First Avenue. *First Avenue* (1980). ECM 1194(2301194).
Rich Halley. *Multnomah Rhythms* (1981). Avocet P-100-1.
Ralph Towner. *Lost and Found* (1995). ECM 1563.

GRAY, JEROME
See Joni Metcalf, *Joni! Joni Metcalf Sings Porter and Ellington.*

GREEN, MILT
"My Last Affair." Linden 16.

GRIMES, HERMAN
Duke Ellington. *Duke Ellington* (1947). Columbia CL2522.

HAYES, CATHI
It's All Right with Me (1960). HiFi R416.
See The Signatures, *The Signatures Sign In* and *Prepare to Flip.*

HELDMAN, JERRY
See David Friesen, *Color Pool.*

HENSON, JULIAN
See Milt Green, "My Last Affair."

HENDRIX, JIMI
Are You Experienced (1967). Reprise RS6261.

HODGES, DEAN
See Joni Metcalf, *Ringaround.*
See Don Lanphere, *Stop.*

HOGAN, GRANVILLE "G.T."
Ahmad Khatab Salim and His Orchestra. *Blues Suite* (1958). Savoy SV 0142 (MG121132).
Cal Massey Sextet. *The Jazz Life* (1961). Candid CCD 79019.

HUBERT, TRAFF
See Cecil Young, *Concert of Cool Jazz* and *Jazz on the Rocks.*

JOHNSON, BILLY
See Roscoe Weathers, *Rosco* [*sic*] *Weathers: His Sterling Flute & Piccolo.*

JONES, GAYLORD
See Corky Corcoran, *Sounds of Jazz.*

JONES, QUINCY
Art Farmer Septet. *Plays the Arrangements and Compositions of Gigi Gryce and Quincy Jones* (1953–54). Original Jazz Classics OJC-054(P7031).
Dizzy Gillespie and His Orchestra. *Jazz Club: Big Band* (1956). Verve 840030-2.
The Birth of a Band (1959). Emarcy Jazz Series 818 177-1.
Live at the Alhambra '60 (1960). JMY 1004-2.
I Dig Dancers (1961). Mercury 20612.

JONES, QUINCY (*continued*)
Back on the Block (1989). Qwest Records 926 020-1.
Q's Jook Joint (1995). Qwest Records 9362-45875-2.
Michael Jackson, *Thriller* (1982). Epic QE 38112 (Jones, producer).

KELLY, RED
Chubby Jackson Big Band. *New York City 1949* (2014). Uptown UPCD 27.75.
Dick Collins. *Horn of Plenty* (1954). Victor LJM1019.
The Modest Jazz Trio (with Jim Hall). *Good Friday Blues* (1960). Pacific Jazz PJ(ST)10.
See Ramsay/Kleeb Big Band. *'Red' Kelly's Heroes.*

KENNY G
Jeff Lorber. *Wizard Island* (1979). Arista AL9516.
Kenny G (1982). Arista AL9608.
Breathless (1992). Arista 07822-18646-2.

KNAPP, JIM
First Avenue. *First Avenue* (1980). ECM 1194(2301194).
Jim Knapp Orchestra. *It's Not Personal, It's Business* (2021). Origin 82834.

LANPHERE, DON
First Sessions (1949). Prestige PCD 24114-2.
Gene Roland. *The Band That Never Was* (1950). Spotlite SPJ141.
From 'Out of Nowhere' (1982). Hep Records 2019.
Stop (1983). Hep Records 2034.
Don Lanphere–Larry Coryell (1990). Hep CD 2048.

LEVITT, ROD
Dizzy Gillespie and His Orchestra. *Jazz Club: Big Band / Jazz Club: Trumpet* (1956–57). Verve 840030-2/840038-2.
The Dynamic Sound Patterns of the Rod Levitt Orchestra (1963). Riverside 9471.
Insight (1965). RCA Victor LPM-3372.

LEWIS, DAVE
"David's Mood" and "Little Green Thing." *The History of Northwest Rock*, Vols. 1 and 2, respectively (1976, 1980). The Great Northwest Music Company GNW 4008 and 4008.

MAHAFFAY, CHUCK
Chuck Mahaffay and the Individuals. *Seattle Beat* (1962). Capitol Custom SLP 1002.
Chuck Mahaffay and the Individuals. *The Girl from Ipanema* (1964). 21 Records L2101.

MANCUSO, GUS
Introducing Gus Mancuso (1956). Fantasy LP 3233.
Music from New Faces (1957). Fantasy LP 3282.

MAY, CHARLIE
All Star Big Band Plays the Arrangements of Gaylord Jones (2000). Pony Boy Records PB50126-2.

MCKEE, GARCIA
Maxin Trio et al. *Early Years* (1947–51). Jazz Archives No. 7, CD ZET 707.

METCALF, CHUCK
Doug Hammond. *Reflections in the Sea of Nurnen* (1972). Tribe.
Elsie Street (1989). BopWare BW101.
Mark Murphy. *Stolen Moments* (1978). Muse MCD 5102.
Bert Wilson. *Live at the Zoo* (1990). 9 Winds NWCD 0138.
Chuck Metcalf Octet. *Help Is Coming* (1992). BopWare BW102.
See Joni Metcalf, *Joni! Joni Metcalf Sings Porter and Ellington.*
See Ernestine Anderson, *Swings the Penthouse.*

METCALF, JONI
Joni! Joni Metcalf Sings Porter and Ellington (1965). Camelot.
Ringaround (1982). Ringaround 2330.

MEYERS, VIC
Various Artists. Ragtime 1: The City, Vic Meyers and His Orchestra, "Springtime Rag" (1971). Folkways RBF17.

MONTGOMERY, MONK
The Mastersounds. *The King and I* (1957). World Pacific Records PJM-405.
The Mastersounds. *A Date with the Mastersounds* (1960). Fantasy 3316.

MOORE, PHIL
Phil Moore and the Phil Moore Four. *The Chair Song* (ca. 1945). Soundie. http://www.jazz-on-film.com.
Phil Moore and the Phil Moore Four. *She's a Rank Chick* (1946). Musicraft 15076.
Phil Moore and the Phil Moore Four. *You Talk Holes in My Clothes* (1946). Black and White 827.

Don Elliott. *Don Elliott Accompanied by Phil Moore and His Orchestra* (1957). ABC-Paramount ABC 190.

MORTON, JELLY ROLL

"Seattle Hunch." *Giants of Jazz: Jelly Roll Morton* (1929). Time-Life Records 19STL-J07.

OREGON

Oregon (1983). ECM 1258(811711-1).
45th Parallel (1989). Portrait OR 44465.

PALOMBI, DICK

See Ernestine Anderson, *Swings the Penthouse.*

PAYNE, STAN

Billie Holiday. *Billie Holiday with Frankie Newton and His Orchestra* (1939). Storyville SLP 4002.

PEACOCK, GARY

Albert Ayler. *Ghosts* (1965). Freedom AL 1000.
Allen Youngblood. *Selah* (1984). Griot 7771.
Jay Clayton. *Live at Jazz Alley* (1987). ITM Records ITMP 970065.
Quartett. *No Secrets* (1988). New Albion Records NA 017 CD.
Paul Bley–Gary Peacock Duet (1989). Owl Records 058 CD.
Gary Peacock, Keith Jarrett, and Jack DeJohnette. *Standards Vol. 1* (1983). ECM 1255.

PECK, DAVE

See Bud Shank, *Tales of the Pilot.*
Out of Seattle: Live at Jazz Alley (2002). Let's Play Stella LPS2002-01.
Good Road (2005). Let's Play Stella LPS2005-01.
Modern Romance (2010). Let's Play Stella LPS2010-01.

PERCIFUL, JACK

Harry James and His Orchestra. *Jazz Club: Big Band* (1968). Verve 840030-2.
Charlie May. *Relaxing with Charlie May* (2005). Pony Boy PB50118-2.

POINDEXTER, PONY

Gumbo! (1963). Prest PR16001.
Jon Hendricks. *A Good Git-Together* (1959). World Pacific Jazz 1283.
Wes Montgomery. *Montgomeryland* (1959). Pacific Jazz Records PJ-5.
Lambert, Hendricks, and Bavan. (1963). RCA LSP-2635.
Alto Summit. (1968). MPS 15192.

RAGLIN, ALVIN "JUNIOR"

Duke Ellington. "Black, Brown and Beige." *At His Very Best* (1944). RCA Victor LPM-1715.
Al Casey. *Al Casey–Sid Catlett Quartet* (1945). Saga 6925AG.
Duke Ellington and His Orchestra. *Liberian Suite* (1947). CBS 66607.

RAINY CITY JAZZ BAND

Rainy City Jazz Band (1947). Exner 5, 6, and 7.

RAMSAY, BILL

Frank Wess Orchestra. *Entre Nous* (1991). Concord Jazz CCD-4450.
Ramsay/Kleeb Big Band. *'Red' Kelly's Heroes* (1997). CARS CP-0010.
Seattle Repertory Jazz Orchestra, *SRJO Live* (2002). Origin 82399.

REID, RUFUS

Perpetual Stroll (1980). Theresa TR111.
Quiet Pride: The Elizabeth Catlett Project (2014). Motema Music MTM-114.
See Jimmy Rowles, *I Remember Bebop.*

REILLY, DEAN

Vince Guaraldi. *Vince Guaraldi Trio* (1956). Fantasy LP3225.
Earl Hines. *Fatha Plays Fats* (1956). Fantasy LP 3-217.

RICHARDSON, BILL

See Ernestine Anderson, *Swings the Penthouse.*

ROWLES, JIMMY

Stan Getz. *Plays* (1952–54). Verve 833 535-2.
Billie Holiday. *Billie Holiday: Stormy Blues* (1955). Verve VE2-2515.
Gerry Mulligan. *Gerry Mulligan Meets Ben Webster* (1959). Verve MGV-8343.
I Remember Bebop (1977). Columbia C2-35381-2.
The Peacocks (1977). Columbia PC34873.
Jimmy Rowles Plays Duke Ellington and Billy Strayhorn (1981). Columbia FC37639.
Music's the Only Thing That's on My Mind (1981). Progressive 7009.

RUBY, GREG

Syncopated Classic: Greg Ruby & the Rhythm Runners Play the Lost Work of 1920's Seattle Jazz Musician Frank Waldron (2017). GRM 003.

RUTHER, WYATT

Chico Hamilton. *Quintet* (1959). Warner Bros. WB(S)1344.
Easy Living with the Ruther IV (1972). Van-Los Music VLM-3605.
Fraser McPherson. *Fraser: Live at the Planetarium* (1975). Concord CJ-92.
Louise Rose. *Live at the Belfry* (1978). Iona IRS78-026.

SCHREIBER, FREDDIE

Cal Tjader. *Saturday Night, Sunday Night at the Black Hawk* (1962). Verve 8459.

SCHUUR, DIANE

Deedles (1984). GRP 1010.
Timeless (1986). Gramavision GRP-D-9540.
Diane Schuur and the Count Basie Orchestra (1987). GRP GR-1039
Friends for Schuur (2000). Concord CCD-4898-2.

SEALES, MARC

See Don Lanphere, *From 'Out of Nowhere.'*
Marc Seales with Ernie Watts. *People & Places* (2025). Origin 82930.
New Stories. *Circles by Hounds* (1994). Origin 82356.

SHANK, BUD

Bud Shank and Michel Legrand. *The Windmills of Your Mind* (1969). World Pacific ST20157.
Bud Shank and Shorty Rogers. *California Concert* (1985). Contemporary C14012.
Tales of the Pilot (1990). Capri 74025-2.

THE SIGNATURES

Prepare to Flip (1959). Warner Bros. WS 1353.
The Signatures Sign In (1959). Warner Bros. WS 1250.

SOUDERS, JACKIE

Jackie Souders and His Orchestra (1926–27). "By the Alamo" and "Every Little Thing," Columbia 837-D; "Gonna Get A Girl" and "Maybe Sometime," 906-D.

STANDIFER, FLOYD

How Do You Keep the Music Playing (1996). Nightflight.
Floyd Standifer and the Pampas Quartet. *Scotch and Soda* (2004). Pony Boy Records PB50143-2.
Northwest Jazz Sextet. *Journey Without Maps* (1979). Stan Keen Productions 7902100-S.
See Quincy Jones, *Live at the Alhambra '60* and *The Birth of a Band.*

STENTZ, CHUCK

Ray Borden. *Boston Bust Out* (1947–48). Hep 13.
Nat Pierce and His Orchestra (1948). Zim 1005.

STENTZ, JAN

Profile (1984). BAM J1002.

THURLOW, JANET

Charles Mingus. *The Complete Debut Recordings* (1953). Debut 12-DCD-4402-2.
Lionel Hampton and His Orchestra. "I Can't Believe That You're in Love with Me." MGM 10979.

TURAY, AL

Corky Corcoran. *Sounds of Jazz Volume One: Corky* (1957). Celestial 1.
See Milt Green, "My Last Affair."

TURNHAM, FLOYD

Maxine Sullivan (1939). Victor 26237; Victor 26260.
T-Bone Walker. "T-Bone Blues" (1940). *The Complete Recordings.* Mosaic MD6-130.
Les Hite. "Jersey Bounce" (1942). Hit 7001.
Gerald Wilson and His Orchestra (1945). Excelsior 122, 123, 127.
Joe Liggins and the Honeydrippers. *1990 Specialty Records Compilation* (1990). SP 7006.

VENUTI, JOE

Eddie Lang and Joe Venuti. *Stringing the Blues* (1927–32). Columbia C2L 24.
Joe Albany. *Joe Albany + Joe Venuti* (1974). Horo HDP 42.

WARD, CARLOS

Don Cherry. *Relativity Suite* (1973). JCOA Records JCOA 1006.
Rashied Ali Quartet. *New Directions in Modern Music* (1973). Survival SR104.
Abdullah Ibrahim. *Water from an Ancient Well* (1986). Black-Hawk BKH 50207-1 D.
See John Coltrane, *A Love Supreme: Live in Seattle.*

WEATHERS, ROSCOE

Bob Keene and His Orchestra. *Stringin' Along* (1957). Andex LP3001.

Rosco [sic] *Weathers: His Sterling Flute & Piccolo*. Bezel Records RWS 101/102.

WIEDOEFT, HERB

Jesse Stafford and His Orchestra (1928). The Old Masters 19.

WIGGINS, GERALD

Les Hite. "Jersey Bounce" (1942). Hit 7001.

Chris Woods. *Quartet* (1976). Black & Blue 33100.

Major Holley. *Featuring Gerry Wiggins* (1977). Black & Blue BLA CD 233074.

Live at Maybeck Recital Hall, Vol. 8 (1991). Concord Jazz CCD-4450.

Soulidarity (1995). Concord Jazz CCD-4706.

See Gus Mancuso, *Introducing Gus Mancuso*.

WILLIAMS, CLARENCE

Luke Jones. *The Compete Recordings 1946–1949* (1996). Blue Moon BMCD 6012.

WILLIAMSON, EVELYN

Lionel Hampton. *The Complete Lionel Hampton Victor Sessions 1937–1941* (2007). Mosaic MD5-238.

WILSON, BERT

Bert Wilson and Rebirth. *Kaleidoscopic Visions* (1982). AuRoar AU-003.

Bert Wilson and Rebirth. *Endless Fingers* (1997). Arabesque Jazz AJ0123.

WILSON, DICK

Andy Kirk and His Clouds of Joy. *Walkin' & Swingin'* (1936–41). Affinity AFS 1011.

Six Men and a Girl. *Mary Lou Williams Blues* (1940). Varsity 8193.

Six Men and a Girl. *Scratchin' the Gravel* (1940). Varsity 8190.

WINN, BOB

Bob Winn and Paul Madison. *Honolulu Sax Players* (1989). First Break Records FB 7005.

WITTWER, JOHN

John Wittwer Trio (1944). Exner 1 & 2.

Rags Stomps and Blues (1947). Jazz Man 18, 19, 20.

YOUNG, CECIL

Jazz on the Rocks (1951–52). Audio Lab 1516.

Cecil Young Quartet. *Concert of Cool Jazz* (1951–52). King LP 295-1.

Cecil Young Quartet (1955). Gene Norman Presents EP 102.

NOTES

Quotations attributed in the text to a speaker listed under "Oral History and Interviews" in "Sources" are understood to be drawn from that speaker's oral history and are not cited here. In cases where it is not clear which oral history a quotation or fact is drawn from, the interview is cited, using the name of the interview subject. Other citations are the names of authors of books or other printed matter, also listed by category in "Sources." In the case of an author with multiple bibliographic entries, the publication date of the relevant work is given in parentheses.

KEY
NW Ent = *Northwest Enterprise*
P-I = *Seattle Post-Intelligencer*
S. Times = *Seattle Times*

INTRODUCTION

On the pulse of jazz across the country: Schuller (1989).

Washington's Black historian: Mumford (1980, 1986).

CHAPTER 1. "SEATTLE HUNCH"

Jelly Roll Morton probably played Seattle more than once. He was reported to be "on his way to the Entertainer's Club, Seattle," on 31 July 1920 and was remembered to have been in Seattle in June 1920 by Don Pasquall (Gushee 1985, 1989). Merle I. Smith says her brother saw Morton play at the Black and Tan in the "late 1920s." Joe Darensbourg, the great Creole clarinetist who moved to Seattle in 1929, asserts that he worked with Morton there as well, though it was probably earlier. The reference to Holden is from Lomax and from Russwurm. Morton's aggregate time in the Northwest is from Pastras. Entertainer's Cabaret ad is from *Cayton's Weekly*, 3 Jan 1920.

Phil Moore on "the pimps and the whores": Sewald.

On Seattle's "Skid Road" (including *McClure's* quote): Mumford (1980); Morgan.

Manuel Lopes, Earl Russell "Noodles" Smith, and early Black settlement: Mumford (1980).

"a lot of mother wit": Wright.

Black population statistics: Q. Taylor.

Noodles's nickname and background: Rowell; Williamson & Royal; Darensbourg; E. Gayton.

Dumas Club: Address, date, and band, printed invitation, Black Heritage Society of Washington State Collections; years open, Williams obituary, undated newspaper clipping, Mary Elizabeth Adams scrapbook. In 1946, Noodles Smith opened another outlet called the Dumas Café, at 1040 South Jackson Street, managed for three years by his nephew Robert Wright. It was still in business in 1951.

Whang Doodle Orchestra engagements: Keller; *Seattle Star*, 23 Feb 1910 and 4 Feb 1914; *P-I*, 11 Jul 1919.

The Alhambra: Harrison.

"black and tan": Kenney.

Reb Spikes date: McCarthy.

Twelfth and Jackson neighborhood description: Rowell.

Characterization of Noodles Smith: *S. Times*, 15 Apr 1952.

New Harlem: *NW Ent*, 8 Mar 1934; club theme song, Wright (OAHC); rumor about Vic Meyers, Charles Lewis (OAHC).

Little Harlem Beer Tavern opening: *NW Ent*, 28 Jun 1934.

Noodles Smith: cars, houseboat, real estate, Wright.

Emma Gayton on Burr Williams: Rowell, E. Gayton & Clayborn.

Zelma, Elbe, and Noodles quote: Williamson & Royal.
East Madison neighborhood: Mumford (1980).
"There were parts of the city": H. Cayton.
LeEtta King quote: Mumford (1986).
On theater segregation: Q. Taylor.
Kenmore Park picnic: *Enterprise*, 3 Jul 1930.
Frank Waldron: Ruby & de Barros; Merle I. Smith letter.
Waldron in Tacoma, song publications, Seattle bands: Ruby & de Barros.
Personnel of the Odean Jazz Orchestra: Charles Adams, trumpet; Archie Jackson, piano; Francis King, violin; Ralph Gibbs, drums and vibes; and (later) Ralph Stephens, drums.
Gertrude Harvey Wright: Keller.
Powell Samuel "Shorty" Barnett background: Mumford (1980); D. Barnett II.
AYP Exposition: P. Barnett. The Seattle Symphony Orchestra played a symphonized rag at the AYP Exposition. By this time, according to Merle I. Smith (letter), several local composers, all white, had published rags, including Bernard Brin, Frederick Irwin, and Warren Camp.
Barnett and Local 458: Keller.
Anti-Black union violence: After Black workers came to Franklin to work in the mines, Mumford (1980) reports that a mysterious fire killed thirty-seven men, half of them Black.
Lacy's Dixieland Band: Droker (1981).
Classical musicians in Seattle: Armbruster.
Nora and Ross Hendrix date: Henderson.
Freddie Keppard: *S. Times*, 25 Oct 1914.
Use of word "jazz" and early dissemination of jazz: Stoddard (1982) writes: "I have long held the notion that black people in America and black music, such as jazz, were so widely scattered that it makes little sense to try to pin-point the music's geographical origin, much less, as some researchers have done, to try to identify a particular person like Buddy Bolden or Jelly Roll Morton as the source of the music. Rather, it is more likely the music was as widespread as blacks were and that the development of jazz took place over many years, in different places, and involved many people."
The Bobby Hayes group featured Howard Patrick (piano), who wrote "Sweet Daddy," Rhinehart (banjo), Zimmermacher (cornet)—also said to be "renowned in California"—and O'Brien (trombone).
Lillian Smith performances and biography: *Cayton's Weekly*, 8 Jun 1918; *Seattle Star*, 1 Jun 1927.

CHAPTER 2. THE JAZZ AGE

Antisaloon movement and liquor legal history: N. Clark (1965).
"The illegal stuff . . .": Stockley, *S. Times*, 29 Mar 1970.
Highway 99 roadhouses: Blecha & Holden.
Varsity Vagabonds: Foy.
Cotton Club: *NW Ent*, 5 Feb 1931.
Police Chief Forbes quote: *S. Times*, 23 Mar 1931.
Mud wrestlers and other nightclub details: Foy.
Johnny Reddin quote: *S. Times*, 22 Mar 1970.
Arrests in Seattle: *S. Times*, 2 Jan 1924.
The bartender known as "Doorbelly": Darensbourg.
Roy Olmstead: *S. Times*, 3 Jul 1973.
On meeting Louis Armstrong: D. Holden tape recording.
Oscar Holden: Morton comments, Lomax; biographical information, Holden family; Vancouver Prohibition jazz scene, Russwurm, Miller; move to Seattle, Givens.
Doc Hamilton's Barbecue Pit: Broderick (1959); Rochester; "Black Prince," *NW Ent*, 1 Jan 1931; Darensbourg, chapter 4, "There's Never Been a Town Like Seattle"; security system, *S. Times*, 7 Jan 1929; "big overcoat": Charles Lewis; raid, *S. Times*, 28 Jul 1924; Terry Pettus comment, Emmett Watson, *S. Times*, 24 Jan 1984; "chickens" quote and Sheriff Harry Lewis story, *S. Times*, 25 May 1931; "I ask you," *S. Times*, 29 Jan 1932.
Early acts billed as jazz: Kolb and Dill: *P-I*, 12 Sep 1919; Tom Brown, *P-I*, 21 Sep 1919; Sophie Tucker, *P-I*, 4 Nov 1917; Rudy Wiedoeft, *P-I*, 3 Dec 1917; Fanchon and Marco, *P-I*, 20 Jun 1920.
Tom Brown: This was not the same Tom Brown as the white New Orleans trombonist famous for being the first to use the word "jazz"—or "jass"—to describe his music, in Chicago, in 1915. That Tom Brown returned to New Orleans, where he opened a music shop and played locally until his death in 1958. However, that Tom Brown also led a group in 1916 in New York called "the Five Rubes," so whoever was leading the "Rube Jay Jazzers" in 1920 in Seattle probably had a good idea who the earlier Tom Brown was.
Vaudeville-cum-jazz: One such act that got started in Seattle was the white banjo player Eddie Peabody, who went on to considerable fame in the swing era.

In 1926, Peabody put together an act at the Fifth Avenue Theatre that remained popular there throughout his career.

Sid Hall Orchestra: *S. Times*, 12 May 1925.

Mamie Smith: *P-I*, 29 Apr 1923.

Buffano quote: *S. Times*, 1 Mar 1928.

Jazz Investigator: *S. Times*, 14 Jun 1921. "Jazz, Like Music of the Savage, Harms Nervous System, Says Doctor."

Spokane music professor: *S. Times*, 5 Feb 1925.

Madge Cayton: *Cayton's Monthly*, 1 Feb 1921.

Buck Clayton on Harper and Fain: Clayton.

Maryland Tavern raid: *S. Times*, 2 Jan 1928.

Two Pals ads: *NW Ent*, 3 Jul 1942.

Joe Darensbourg particulars: Darensbourg.

Gerald Wells: origins, Stoddard (1982), Bobrow; birthplace, death certificate; Local 493 location, Keller; in general, Stoddard (1982), McCarthy.

Garfield Ramblers particulars: E. Gayton, L. Gayton.

Quincy Jones on Evelyn Bundy: S. Taylor.

Jimmy Adams performances: *NW Ent*, 6 Apr 1931 and 18 Aug 1932; suicide, P. Johnson (1988), *NW Ent*, 27 Nov 1937.

Creon Thomas: Henson.

Leonard Gayton's career: L. Gayton.

Hub of the Seattle jazz world: C. Taylor.

Edythe Turnham biography and other details: Placksin, Dahl, Turnham, Keller.

Location of the Kopper Kettle: E. Gayton.

Edythe Turnham's style: Williamson & Royal.

Frances Turnham: In the 1920s the beautiful Turnham married dancer Earl Robinson and formed a successful vaudeville team, Earl and Frances, which performed at New York's Apollo Theater.

Location of the Bungalow: Rowell.

Joe Bailey: Turnham.

Knights of Syncopation 1928 personnel: business card in Floyd Turnham's scrapbook.

Ellington quote: Turnham.

Vido Musso incident: Turnham scrapbook, undated article.

Britt Woodman collaboration: *Los Angeles Sentinel*, 1 Mar 1951.

Turnham replacing Hodges: On 1 Mar 1951 the *Los Angeles Sentinel* reported the story, describing Turnham as a "tall, talented, young gent with a pleasing personality. . . . He is a perfect replacement for Hodges, having a style all his own and often called the greatest young altoist in local swing circles."

Mildred Bailey biography and other details: Placksin, Dahl, McCarthy, Zwisohn, liner note by Don DeMichael, *Red Norvo*, and Townsend, liner note, *Mildred Bailey, Her Greatest Performances 1929–1946*; jobs in Seattle, *S. Times*, 13 Dec 1951 and 14 Dec 1954; national radio show, *DownBeat*, 1 Sep 1944 and 1 Feb 1945; *Time*, 20 Mar 1944.

Evelyn Williamson performances: *NW Ent*, 1 Oct 1931, 28 Sept 1933, 3 Aug 1933; Williamson & Royal; Johnson (1988).

Chinese Garden: Williamson & Royall.

Marion Fulmighter and "Princess" Belle: Darensbourg, Henson.

Bungalow burns down: *S. Times*, 6 Mar 1929.

Steamship lines: *S. Times*, 12 Jan 1926.

Lillian Goode: *NW Ent*, 28 Sep 1933.

Zelma Winslow: arrest, *NW Ent*, 14 Sep 1993; "could sing her butt off," Rowell; personality, P. Moore.

Eddie Rucker with Black and Tan Orchestra, and other details: McCarthy; Williamson & Royal.

"Baby" Borders: Black Birds of Paradise, McCarthy; Elite Social Club, *NW Ent*, 6 Aug 1931; Black and Tan, *NW Ent*, 13 Apr 1933; 1938 is the last gig noted by *NW Ent*; Detroit and Fulmighter details, Johnson; Chinese Garden arrest, Williamson & Royal.

Hong Kong Chinese Society Club: *S. Times*, 14 Feb 1931; Darensbourg; *S. Times*, 12 Feb 1931, *Seattle Star*, 12 Feb 1931; *S. Times*, 3 Mar 1931; *S. Times* 1 Jan 1933.

Louisa Hotel and Wah Mee history: "Discovery of Prohibition-era murals in Seattle building with long and varied history is reported on February 6, 2018," http://www.HistoryLink.org/20550; http://wikipedia.org/wiki/Wah_Mee_massacre.

Phil Moore: Moore, Sewald. Moore's Garfield High School transcript says he transferred in 1933 from Portland's Grant High School, which means he probably arrived in Seattle when he was sixteen years old, not thirteen. However, Darensbourg says he worked with Moore in 1931, so it's possible Moore spent summers in Seattle before joining his parents there full-time. First Black musicians, Feather (1962).

Wilbert Barranco in Oakland: *DownBeat*, 16 Dec 1949.

Jackie Souders: "in the college style," *S. Times*, 8 Feb 1925.

Del Monte Blue Dogs: 1928, 1929, and 1930 *Musicland* yearbooks, and *S. Times*, 25 Jul 1929.

Goodrich Silvertown Cord Orchestra: *S. Times*, 28 Feb 1926.

J & V Syncopators: *S. Times*, 17 Mar 1926.
Shorty Clough personnel and gig: 1929 *Musicland* yearbook.
Paul Clifford: Foy.
Virgil Ireland: Darensbourg.
Clarence Barney biography and details and date of Parker's Pavilion: letter to author by Harold Finch, Feb 1991.
Jules Buffano: "Mikado," *S. Times*, 28 Mar 1928; biographical details, *S. Times*, 29 Sep 1939.
Butler Hotel: description and history, *S. Times*, 14 Nov and 26 Nov 1927, 20 Jun 1962, and 30 Oct 1983; raids, *S. Times*, 10 Aug 1924 and following.
Vic Meyers: early life, *S. Times*, 19 Aug 1938; *Musicland* 6, no. 21 (1926); other biographical detail, N. Jones, Morgan; Winchell show, *S. Times*, 26 Mar 1937; raids on Alhambra and Butler, *S. Times*, 16 May 1922; interracial marriage, Morgan.
Hiram Gill elections: Morgan.
1923 Landes Ordinance: *S. Times*, 20 Feb, 20 Nov, and 1 Apr 1923.
"Moral menace": *S. Times*, 31 Oct 1929.
"How Dry I Am": *S. Times*, 14 Nov 1927.
"Jazz and whoopee": *S. Times*, 20 Apr 1931.
Paul Whiteman: *Musicland*, 25 Apr 1930; and *S. Times*, 20 Mar 1930, and 6, 8, 9, and 13 Apr 1930.

CHAPTER 3. COMBOS AND DIVES

Depression in Seattle: Sale.
Blue Rose: Henson.
Julian Henson's style: Rowles.
Princess Belle: origins, Darensbourg.
Duke Turner: Stoddard (1982).
Japanese businesses: Booker; Reddick; Chin.
Filipino population: Q. Taylor.
Filipino bands: Keller.
Club Rizal: *NW Ent*, 22 Dec 1943.
Tokiwa Hotel and life along Jackson Street: Henson.
Darensbourg hard-luck story: Darensbourg.
Tootie Boyd: Ewing; Johnson.
Earl Whaley: at Broadway Hall, *NW Ent*, 29 Sep 1932; to China, Johnson.
Gene Coy: "first harbinger" conclusion based on *NW Ent* listings, Turay, Johnson; background before reaching Seattle, McCarthy.
Walter Page and John Lewis on Gene Coy: "Walter Page's Story as Told to Frank Driggs," *Jazz Review* 1, no. 1 (1958).
Dick Wilson: joins Gene Coy, McCarthy, Johnson; biography, Chilton, Darensbourg; D. Anderson apprenticeship, Mary Elizabeth Adams scrapbook, E. Gayton; return to Seattle, flyer from Gaylord Jones archive; death, McCarthy says tuberculosis, Darensbourg says syphilis.
Alvin "Junior" Raglin: Williamson & Royal; at the Congo Club, Johnson; at the Ubangi Club, Johnson; "one bitch of a guitar player," Turay; two-necked guitar, Henson; biography after Seattle, S. Dance (1970), Ulanov; Seattle engagement, M. A., *S. Times*, 16 Dec 1941; pictured in *Life*, 2 Sep 1944; Three Deuces engagement, *DownBeat*, 3 Jun 1946.
Gerald Wells at the Hi-Hatters: *NW Ent*, 21 May 1931.
Black migration: Reddick.
Interracial crowds on Jackson Street: Robert Wright, OAHC (1975).
411 Club: Johnson, Turay, Rowles.
Ubangi: description and entertainers, Rowell; closure, *NW Ent*, 25 Feb 1938; Marshal Royal said that Coreen Gibson, whose style was popularized by the white singer Ella Logan, developed a family act at the Ubangi that also included an older brother who started the dance craze "Peckin'," a big hit for Benny Goodman and Harry James.
Little Harlem Beer Tavern: *NW Ent*, 28 Jun 1934.
Congo Club description: Johnny Reddin, *S. Times*, 10 Mar 1963; Johnson.
Herman Grimes: early life, Darensbourg; Green Dot and Dutchman Tavern, Johnson, Bobrow; Ellington tenure and recordings: Mascagli, *Duke Ellington's Story on Records*.
Green Dot: Palmer Johnson, *NW Ent*, 30 Nov 1933.
Chinese Garden: Louie.
"Poor man's playground": *NW Ent*, 12 Oct 1933.
State Theatre, Cocoanut Grove, Lyons' Music Hall, and Virginian: Foy.
Shanghai jazz scene: in general, Johnson, Clayton; Whaley's imprisonment and so forth, Driggs letter to author, 22 Mar 1991; Department of State letter, Mary Elizabeth Adams; prison camp, Power.
Wayne Adams and Palmer Johnson's career after Shanghai: Johnson; Power.

CHAPTER 4. SWINGMANIA

Gaylord Jones's early career: G. Jones.
Husky Hot Club formation: *The Daily*, 2 Mar 1939 and following.

Norm Bobrow conversation with university president: Bobrow.
Trianon opening and description: *S. Times*, 19 and 21 May 1927; Harris on "future wives and husbands," D. Young, *P-I*, 26 Oct 1975; and *P-I*, 27 Apr 1985; Skreen, *S. Times*, 9 Nov 1975; "Trianon Saturday Night," Newsletter, 15 Feb 1941.
Card game anecdote: Ramage.
Black revues: *S. Times*, 13 Aug 1933, 20 Feb 1935, and 25 Aug 1937.
Les Hite: *NW Ent*, 16 Nov 1934.
First Ellington appearance: *S. Times*, 13 May 1934.
Lionel Hampton: *S. Times*, 15 Aug 1986.
Glen Gray: *S. Times*, 3 Aug 1937.
Finnish Hall: *S. Times*, 29 May 1924; 1934 Ellington show and other listings, *NW Ent*.
Tommy Dorsey: D. Young, *P-I*, 26 Oct 1975.
First swing concert: Gil Brown, *Seattle Star*, 5 Feb 1940.
"Fraught with significance": *The Daily* article from G. Jones archive.
Lionel Hampton concert: M.A.A., *S. Times*, 2 Dec 1940.
Fats Waller story: Bobrow, and *S. Times*, 11 Jul 1941.
Corky Corcoran: "ask my mother" and baseball story, Radke; fights and bus story, R. Kelly.
Woody Herman quote: Herman.
Charlie Blackwell: Hunziker.
Trianon segregation: D. Young writes: "For years, a Seattle city ordinance and the mind-set of John Savage kept black customers out of the Trianon." He then quotes Harris: "It was just the plain truth that if black people and white people were together at a dance there would be fights." "Spook nights" and Hampton incident, Bown and *NW Ent*, 29 Nov 1940. An attorney's search of Seattle's law library turned up no "mixed dancing" ordinance, which would have been contrary to state law, in any case.
"Black Laws" and Public Accommodations Act: Mumford (1980). During the 1940s the Black population of the state increased dramatically, from 7,424 to 30,691.
Redlining: N. Clark (1976).
"Peanut Heaven": Mumford (1986).
Black population: Reddick.
Boeing hiring policy: N. Clark (1976).
"Separate but equal": Droker (1976); *NW Ent*, 19 May 1943.
"Whites only": *NW Ent*, 23 Jun 1943.
Bremerton housing: N. Clark (1976).
Navy commander: *NW Ent*, 4 Apr 1943.
Grill Cafe: *NW Ent*, 9 Dec 1942.
Madrona Theatre: *NW Ent*, 16 Dec 1942.
Pacific Foundry Company: *NW Ent*, 19 May 1943.
Fort Lawton riot: Mumford (1986). See N. Clark (1976); Droker (1976); and Reddick on race relations in the West.
Local 493: Siegl.
Gerald Wells details: Emmett Lewis.
Al Pierre's early life: Spearman; Stoddard (1982, 1970); Darensbourg.
Duke Turner quote: Stoddard (1982).
Union Club description: W. Brown, 22 Aug 1989.
Pierre band's repertoire: Ward.
Al's Lucky Hour: Spearman.
Vernon Brown origins, early bands: *P-I*, 1 Oct 1966; Vaughn; Russell; W. Brown, 22 Aug 1989.
Connection to Al Pierre: W. Brown, 22 Aug 1989.
Buck Clayton anecdote: Clayton.
Clarence Williams: Armbruster; Dietsche. Luke Jones, who led the sessions with Williams on vocals, had another Seattle connection, having played in Shanghai, China (with Buck Clayton) during the same period Palmer Johnson played there with Earl Whaley.
Terry Cruise birth place: Local 493 roster; Ward.
Jabo Ward background, technique, and early career: Ward; Ward, chronology of engagements.
Dee Dee Hackett and Russell Jones: Johnson, B. Russell (6 Apr 1989), McCarthy; Hackett biography, Hackett Papers, OAC; first Seattle performance, *NW Ent*, 21 Sep 33; Stockton, *Stockton Independent*, 11 May 1935; San Francisco, *California Eagle*, 3 Apr 1941; back in Seattle, *NW Ent*, 24 Jan 1945.
***S. Times* review of Russell Jones:** 13 Oct 1943.
Lack of recreational facilities: Rowell, E. Gayton & Clayborn.
Eighth Avenue ordinance: *S. Times*, 16 Jul 1934.
Petition for Black dance hall: *S. Times*, 8 Nov 1939.
License granted: "An unwritten but rigid policy of the City Council forbidding cabarets east of Eighth Avenue in the Central portion of the city was relaxed yesterday to give Seattle's Negro community a dine-and-dance establishment at the Savoy Ballroom," *S. Times*, 19 Feb 1946.
Billy Tolles background, Savoy Boys: Tolles; Manning; Pigford; Booker.
Sonny Booker background: Booker.
Major Pigford career: Pigford.

Shift in mood and music styles postwar: Barrington; Tolles.

CHAPTER 5. ERNESTINE ANDERSON AND THE FIRST BEBOPPERS

Description of the Jackson Street area: composite from Greenwell (1990); W. Brown, 22 Aug 1989; Vaughn; Wiggins.

"Tolerance policy": Chambliss; Pigford; A. Hilbert; Bayley; "Chinese lottery," Booker.

"It's an old, old story": Walter C. Woodward Jr., *S. Times,* 30 Jun 1940.

"Russian John" Lasso: *S. Times*, 16 Dec 1961; Graf; Foy.

410-B Tavern: *S. Times*, 4 and 6 Aug 1941.

"Out of bounds area": *P-I*, 17 May 1943.

Seattle's racial tolerance, interracial marriage: E. Gayton.

Early Ernestine Anderson: E. Anderson.

Boatley with Kirk: McCarthy.

Basin Street speakeasy: location, Washington State Archives, Puget Sound Regional Branch; lottery, description of club, hours, A. Hilbert; Harold Curry, idiosyncratic dancers, Vaughn; Sammy Davis, Emmett Lewis, and Lillian Buford. Gorilla Jones, https://en.wikipedia.org/wiki/Gorilla_Jones. The address 413 South Maynard Avenue was reassigned to the Bush Hotel after the Olympus Hotel was demolished, hence some confusion today. But according to Washington State archival records, the club was in the Olympus. In a twist of fate highlighting a dark intersection of two marginalized communities, Lee also benefited indirectly from the Japanese incarceration of 1942, which allowed him to acquire the Olympus Hotel business upstairs as well as the Atlas Café, across the street, from their imprisoned Japanese American owners, according to *NW Ent*, 22 May 1942.

Quotes about Ernestine's sound: Q. Jones (1989).

Central Avenue: Gordon; Jack's Basket Room, E. Anderson.

Charlie Parker quote: Q. Jones (1989).

First bebop records: Hubert.

Janet Thurlow background, sound, career: Hampton; Poindexter; first press, undated press clipping, Thurlow scrapbook, quite possibly from Norm Bobrow's Northwest Jazz Letter, ca. 1949; band personnel, Cleveland, Gilles; performance with Quincy Jones, *S. Times*, 30 Aug 1951.

Jazz at the Philharmonic (JATP): origins, *DownBeat*, 1 Jan 1946; first Seattle shows, *Clef*, Jun 1946; *S. Times*, 29 Apr 1946.

Description of Roscoe Weathers: Standifer. Weathers's departure from McShann is noted in *Northwest Herald*, 4 Dec 1945. McShann himself has confirmed in a conversation with the author that Weathers played in his band. However, Weathers insisted that he had played with McShann when Bird was also in the band, and Wyatt Ruther says Weathers once showed him a photograph of McShann's band with Parker in the saxophone section. No discographies, personnel listings, recordings, or photographs bear this out.

Billy Tolles update: Tolles.

Kenny Dorham on Combo Clash: Tolles.

Early Pony Poindexter: Poindexter; Buford; Ernie Lewis; E. Anderson.

Gerald Wiggins: Wiggins; Greenwell; Ernie Lewis.

Juanita Cruse: liner notes, *Juanita!* (1960).

Wanda Brown: W. Brown, 21 Feb, 22 Aug, and 16 Sep 1989.

Description of New Orleans Club: Friel.

Evening with Billie Holiday: E. Anderson places this at the China Pheasant.

Wyatt "Bull" Ruther: Ruther.

Gene Ramey quote: S. Dance (1970).

Narcolepsy: Boas; Wiggins.

Adolphus Alsbrook's late career: "Adolphus Alsbrook," 2016, Wikipedia, https://en.wikipedia.org/wiki/Adolphus_Alsbrook.

Description of Washington Social Club: Bown (1987); E. Anderson; W. Brown, 22 Aug 1989; Sy Groves, Tolles; and *S. Times*, 1 Sep 1951.

Membership cards: *S. Times*, 10 Feb 1965.

Floor show: Perkins.

Vernon "Pops" Buford biography: V. Buford & L. Buford.

Al Hickey's early life: Hickey.

Jive Bombers background: Kopstein.

Jive Bombers personnel: Moton.

Lester Young: Jive Bombers, *S. Times*, 5 Feb 1948; at Washington Social Club, Buchmann-Moller.

Wardell Gray anecdote: Hickey.

CHAPTER 6. THE NEXT GENERATION

Chino Pozo: The reference is correct. Chano Pozo, the original Cuban drummer in Gillespie's band, was killed on 2 December 1948, and the little-known Chino took his place.

Gary Steele on Gillespie band performance at the Senator: Steele.

Quincy Jones on Gillespie, biography, early career: Unless otherwise noted, the majority of the quotations from Jones in this chapter are from these interviews in 1989 and 1990. Recollection of Gillespie band members at Washington Social Club and why he missed the show are from 1989 and 1990 interviews.

Charlie Taylor biography and band: C. Taylor; Bumps Blackwell Junior Band, C. Taylor.

Robert A. "Bumps" Blackwell: early life, Penn, Nite, White; *Ceremony in Swing*: *NW Ent*, 1 Dec 1939; assessment of musical ability, Charles & Ritz, Catlett, Gill.

Holiday: *S. Times*, 8 Feb 1949.

Cole: *NW Ent*, 2 Jul 1947.

Jordan: *NW Ent*, 12 Jan 1949.

R & B groups: all *NW Ent.*

Forty-First Infantry Division Band, Washington National Guard Band: "blow their nose," Blackwell; *S. Times*, 1 Oct 1947.

Gus Mankertz: Q. Jones; Standifer; Hawthorn (1983); *Seattle Spectator*, 4 Nov 1949, 2 Dec 1949, and 27 Apr 1960.

***Four Winds Suite*:** *The Spectator*, 19 Oct 1950.

Jones/Hampton story: composite from Q. Jones, Hickey, and Thurlow. Hampton's recollections, in *Hamp*, particularly Jones telling him he wanted to be a millionaire, are erroneous.

"Quincy Jones, Musical Prodigy": *The Spectator*, 19 Oct 1950.

Jones recorded with Hampton on a New York session in May 1951 that included "Hannah, Hannah," "Shalom, Shalom," "Eli, Eli (Part l)," and "Eli, Eli (Part 2)." A live concert recording in August 1961 in Malibu features "Flyin' Home," "Autumn in New York," "How High the Moon," "Out of Breath," and "Hamp's Boogie Woogie."

Skinner: Q. Jones (1989).

Jones/Thurlow at Trianon: Thurlow.

Resentment in the Hampton band: Thurlow.

Jones's family situation: Bown.

"Stone out of the ghetto": Jones as quoted in *S. Times*, 6 Mar 1983.

Patti Bown hailed as a prodigy: *S. Times*, 26 Aug 1949, and *The Spectator*, 1 Jun 1950.

Balliett on Patti Bown: *New Yorker*, 16 Jul 1979.

Patti Bown biography: Bown.

Myrtle Francois: *Pacific Leader*, 19 Nov 1954.

***Free and Easy* background and disaster:** Jablonski; Catlett.

Music as shapes: *Life*, Dec 1984.

CHAPTER 7. WHITE BOPPERS AND IVY LEAGUERS

First "modern" big band in Seattle: Pierce's, as Manning, Pierce, and Kimball all assert.

Ronnie Pierce's "dream band": Pierce band photo.

Social change: "atomic note," R. Kelly, 23 May 1989; "Bop was frantic," Pigford.

Woody Isbell, mentioned briefly in Ross Russell's biography of Charlie Parker, also performed at the Players Club, according to Manning.

New Chinatown details: T. Woo; opening date: *International Examiner*, 15 Jan 1987; Kimball. Catlett may be confusing the kitty at the New Chinatown with the one at the Black and Tan, which Phil Moore described exactly as Catlett describes this one. Club owner Danny Woo's daughter, Teresa Woo, who worked at the restaurant, does not remember the kitty Catlett describes either.

Notorious bebopper Don Lanphere: *Jazz Journal*, Feb 1987; Ramsey.

Wayne "Buzzy" Bridgeford: R. Kelly, 23 May 1989; Bridgeford's Getz gig: "Norm Bobrow Jazz Letter #1."

Neil Friel background, early years, late career: Friel.

Darryl Harpa: El Rancho gig: Stetler; identity as old Hamilton place, Blecha & Holden.

Fred Greenwell: Jimmy Zito, *DownBeat*, 14 Jan 1948.

Jazz loft on Sixth Avenue: Smith quote, Stephenson.

OWL Party ticket: According to Rick Anderson, in the *P-I*, 4 Nov 1976, OWL Party nominees received a quarter of a million votes, 3 percent of the total vote.

Red Kelly: *Jazz Record* 1944, 1945; Darensbourg; Crow (1990).

Johnny Reddin on the China Pheasant: *S. Times*, 10 Sep 1945.

Jack Perciful: Schuller (1989); Perciful.

Annex Sessions and scene: Mahaffay, "U of Washington Crew Bop Pioneers," *DownBeat*, 15 Jul 1949; Kimball; Kimball curriculum vitae.

Bill Crow: Crow interview; Crow (1990).

Joni Metcalf liner quote: *Joni Metcalf* (1969).

CHAPTER 8. "STRAIGHTEN UP AND FLY RIGHT"

Blue Rose: opening date, *NW Ent*, 16 Nov 1933.

Bob Braxton: *Billboard*, 17 Dec 1949.
Bowman, Darensbourg.
Big Lewis: E. Anderson.
Milt Green and the 908 Club: pool hall on Union, B. Moore.
Ruby Bishop: *S. Times*, 27 Jun 2019; BlackPast.org.
Merceedees Walton: Blecha (2016); *P-I*, 13 Apr 1952.
Ray Charles's arrival in Seattle: M. Jones's account jibes with McKee's but differs considerably from Charles's own story in *Brother Ray*, in which McKee plays no role in Charles's first night in town.
"I didn't know anyone" and "The entertainment business": Charles & Ritz.
Black Elks Club dates: *Cayton's Weekly*, 1 Nov 1919; *NW Ent*, 6 Jan 1943.
Black population: Q. Taylor.
Delridge Housing Project: Q. Taylor.
LeEtta King quote: Mumford (1980).
Powell Barnett quote: P. Barnett.
"virtually parodies of gospel songs": Woodfin.
"French and Be-Bop": *NW Ent*, 16 Jun 1949.
Charles's heroin use: Charles & Ritz.
Charles's blindness: According to records of the St. Augustine State School for the Blind, Charles was "totally blind" by the time he was six years old (Charles himself said seven). However, the expression "totally blind" is a technical term meaning the inability to read the printed word under any circumstances, even with visual aids. "Most blind people have *some* vision," according to Mary Jane Dillon, public information officer for the Florida school.

CHAPTER 9. JACKSON STREET GLITTERS, THEN GOES DARK

Cecil Young: Young at Yale, *DownBeat*, 15 Jun 1951; at the Elks, Hubert; fast tempos, Friel.
Breakfast show: Others place these shows at Basin Street, though Bobrow is conflating Cecil Young's reign at the 908 with events of an earlier period. Both Basin Street and the 411 had closed by the time Young came to town.
Ralph Gleason quote about Gerald Brashear is reported by Bobrow.
Rodgers's demise: Friel.
Jackson Street Community Council: *S. Times*, 21 Jul 1946.
Raids: Yukon Club, *S. Times*, 19 Jul 1947; Clover Club, *S. Times*, 3 Oct 1947; Rocking Chair, *S. Times*, 27 Dec 1947; Basin Street, *S. Times*, 12 Jun 1948; 166 arrested, *S. Times*, 8 Oct 1949.
Gambling profits: Chambliss.
Washington Social Club: *NW Ent*, 16 and 17 Sep 1950.
Sy Groves's advertisement addressed to Charles O. Carroll: Bayley.
"The one thing which bothered me": Charles & Ritz.
Magician's Club: Armbruster.
Frank Sugia: *S. Times*, 4 May 1972.
Dorsey: Skreen.
Second Herd: Herman reports in *Woodchopper's Ball* that he was inspired to form the Second Herd after hearing ex-Seattleite Phil Moore in a Hollywood club.
"1951 Orchestra Cavalcade": *S. Times*, 27 May 1951.
Stan Getz arrest: *S. Times*, 15 Feb 1954.
Charlie Parker story: Bobrow. Bobrow drove Bird from the Evergreen Ballroom, outside Olympia (where Bird performed on the same bill with Chet Baker and Dave Brubeck), to Seattle, then billeted him in his Seattle apartment. Parker spent the afternoon in the bar downstairs. The Seattle show was 31 October 1953, at the Metropolitan Theatre. Parker seemed destined never to give a solid performance in Seattle. His first confirmed appearance, on a 16 November 1948 Jazz at the Philharmonic session at the Moore Theatre, suffered from an inappropriate rhythm section, according to pianist Ken Boas. Saxophonist Don Lanphere recalled a later concert with Erroll Garner, when Bird played well (Lanphere). Lanphere was probably recalling an all-star show headlined by Stan Kenton at the Civic Auditorium on 24 February 1954 featuring Parker, Garner, June Christy, Dizzy Gillespie, Lee Konitz, and Candido. Critic Lou Guzzo of the Seattle *P-I* agreed with Lanphere, writing in his review that Parker "redeemed himself admirably for a shaky appearance recently at the Metropolitan."
Eric Dolphy: service dates, Simosko & Tepperman.
Tommy Adams: Not all rock drummers agree with Holden's assessment. Mike Burke, drummer with the legendary Tacoma band the Wailers, says he did not know of Tommy Adams in the 1950s.
Elmer Gill and the Question Marks: Not the same band as Billy Tolles's Four Question Marks.
Parker's Ballroom: Blecha (2023).
Union merger: Siegl.
John Wittwer's reference to "steal a march" on San Francisco stems from a 1956 refusal by Local 6 in

San Francisco to merge Black and white locals, *Musicland*, 7 Dec 1956.

Count of Black locals: Ernie Lewis.

AFM count of mergers nationally: Siegl.

Mayor Clinton: *S. Times*, 24 Jul 1956, reports closing of club. Standifer tells the story of the photo with ax.

Black "bottle clubs" succumbed: The Blue Note closed in 1958, when the unions amalgamated, according to Metcalf and Keller, but the *S. Times* of 19 Jan 1959 notes that the club was raided as late as this date.

CHAPTER 10. AFTER THE BOTTLE CLUBS CLOSED

Horace Henderson: Schuller (1989) notes that Henderson recorded the Wingy Manone riff that later became Glenn Miller's smash hit "In the Mood" as early as 1931, on *Hot and Anxious*.

Buddy Catlett: The Basie recording Catlett refers to in his quote was made by Joe Boles. Wynton Marsalis quote: *S. Times*, 16 Nov 2014.

Ernestine Anderson audition for Lionel Hampton: Charles had left Seattle, and his trio had dissolved before 1952. It's likely McKee and Anderson are recalling an earlier incident.

Hampton on the Potomac: "getting upstaged," E. Anderson. For a somewhat different account of this famous incident, see Crow (1990).

Anderson in the press: John Voorhees article: *P-I*, 28 Sep 1953; Ralph Gleason quote, Gleason; John S. Wilson, *New York Times*, 24 Aug 1958; John Tynan, *DownBeat*, 18 Sep 1958; "best-kept secret," *Time*, 4 Aug 1958.

Pony Poindexter: As for the "secret indictment," Poindexter was reading about the famous Kefauver hearings in San Francisco.

Poindexter's arrest and parole information: Seattle Police Department.

Patti Padden quote: Padden, conversation with author, Jun 2007.

Skating rink referred to in Standifer quote: The building is the same as the Savoy Ballroom, which later became Birdland.

Jay McNeely made a tape at Birdland in 1957 that was released as an LP; McNeely also recorded his only hit, "There Is Something on Your Mind," in West Seattle.

First rock 'n' roll record: according to Pete Blecha, Seattle rock historian.

Lake City Tavern bookings: Lake City Tavern, program, Seattle, 18 Aug 1955.

Kenneth Patchen: flyer, Maggie Hawthorn Archive.

Beat-era styles moved north to Seattle: Rosen.

Seattle Jazz Society founders: Seattle Jazz Society, membership brochure, 1966.

Bob Summerise: *Puget Sound Observer*, Aug 1958.

Freddy Schreiber: Schreiber's retort, *DownBeat*, 13 Sep 1962; "so funny," Gill.

CHAPTER 11. JACKSON STREET: A LOST LEGACY?

FBI, departmental bloodbath: Chambliss, Bayley.

Frank Colacurcio was sentenced in 1978 to thirty-six years for income tax evasion. Lofurno's restaurant closed in July 1993.

Best players moving away: Metcalf.

Ed Lee bio: *S. Times*, 8 Jun 2011; Earshot Jazz, Jun 1991.

George Hurst: Acox.

Michael Bisio: National Public Radio Jazz Critics Top 10 (1990).

Influence on "Northwest sound" of rockers: Seattle rocker "Little Bill" Engelhart, who had the 1959 hit "I Love an Angel," acknowledged in an interview that Black R & B players such as Tommy Adams had a "tremendous influence" on the early rock scene. Engelhart.

Bumps Blackwell and Little Richard, including "Tutti Frutti" story: White.

Blackwell, Jones, and Charles concert: Hawthorn, *Seattle Weekly*, 9 Mar 1983; "Quincy Jones: A Seattle Celebration," 50th Birthday Party program, Seattle, 11 Mar 1983.

SOURCES

ORAL HISTORIES AND INTERVIEWS

Recordings of the following oral histories and interviews are accessible to the public at the Ethnomusicology Archives, Suzzallo Library Special Collections, University of Washington, Seattle, Washington; and Paul de Barros Seattle Jazz Oral History Collection, Archives West. Interviews were with the author unless otherwise noted.

Alcivar, Bob. 17 June 1989. Transcript.
Anderson, Ernestine. Interview with Sandra Burlingame, 22 October 1988. Transcripts.
Anderson, Ernestine. Interview with author, 10 October and 15 November 1989. Transcripts.
Barbas, Pete. Interview with Ken Maffit, 9 July 1989. Tape recording.
Barrington, Pete. 20 May 1990. Tape recording.
Boas, Ken. 18 November 1989. Transcript.
Bobrow, Norm. 5 July, August, and 16 September 1989. Transcripts.
Booker, Quentin "Sonny." Interviews with Sandra Burlingame, 31 October 1988 and 23 May 1989. Transcripts.
Bown, Patti. 18 October 1987 and 5 April 1989. Transcripts.
Brazil, Joe. 3 October 1989. Transcript.
Brown, Wanda. Interviews with Ted Dzielak, 21 February and 22 August 1989. Transcripts.
Brownlow, Jack. Interview with Adam Woog, 26 September 1989. Transcript.
Buford, Vernon "Pops," and Lillian Buford. 2 June 1989. Tape recording.
Catlett, George "Buddy." 9 and 23 November 1988. Transcripts.
Charles, Ray. 11 April 1991. Transcript.
Cleveland, Jimmy. 30 November 1989. Tape recording.
Coleman, Dave. Interview with Sandra Burlingame, 1 November 1988. Transcript.
Coryell, Larry. 29 August 1989. Transcript.
Crow, Bill. 11 November 1989. Transcript.
Davis, Ralph. 22 March 1989. Tape recording.
Foy, Jack. 2 December 1989. Transcript.
Friel, Neil. 2 June 1989. Transcript.
Friesen, David. 20 September 1989. Transcript.
Gatewood, Donald. 5 September 1989. Tape recording.
Gill, Elmer. 23 October 1988. Transcript.
Gilles, Jim. Interview with Lynn Darroch, 22 October 1989.
Greenwell, Fred. Interview with Jim Wilke, 31 January 1988. Transcript.
Greenwell, Fred. 24 April 1990. Tape recording.
Hatfield, Ernie. 18 May 1987. Tape recording.
Hayes, Cathi. 20 April 1990. Tape recording.
Heldman, Jerry. 21 December 1989. Tape recording.
Henson, Julian. 20 January 1991. Tape recording.
Hickey, Al. Interview with Lynn Darroch, 24 June 1992. Tape recording.
Hilbert, Al. 16 August 1989. Tape recording.
Holden, Dave. 12 April 1991. Tape recording.
Holden family (Grace, Bob, Jimmy, and Leala). Interview with author and Ted Dzielak, 4 June 1989. Transcript.
Hubert, Traff. Interview with Jim Wilke, 21 March 1989. Transcript.
Johnson, Palmer. Interviews with author and Jim Wilke, 20 November 1988; 16 October, 23 October, 4 November, 26 November, and 17 December 1989. Transcripts.
Jones, Gaylord. 24 March and 24 April 1989. Transcripts.
Jones, Melody. Interviews with Susan Golden, 10 January 1988 and 8 November 1989. Transcripts.
Jones, Quincy. 5 December 1989. Transcript.
Jones, Quincy. 17 August 1990. Tape recording.
Keen, Stan. Interview with Mark Solomon, 29 August 1988. Transcript.
Kelly, Red. 23 May and 5 June 1989. Transcripts.
Kimball, Kenny. Interviews with Ken Maffit, 19 February and March 1989. Transcripts.
Lanphere, Don. Interviews with Joe Murphy, 14 September and 28 September 1988. Transcripts.

Lewis, Emmett. Interview with Ted Dzielak and Marianne Jones, 7 October 1989. Transcript.
Lewis, Ernie. 15 December 1990. Tape recording.
Mahaffay, Chuck. Interviews with Mark Solomon, 2 October and 8 November 1989. Transcripts.
Mancuso, Gus. 2 December 1989. Transcript.
Manning, Don. Interview with Lynn Darroch, 30 September 1989. Transcript.
McKee, Garcia. 17 March 1991. Tape recording.
Metcalf, Chuck. Interviews with Mark Solomon, September 1988. Transcript.
Montgomery, Buddy. 1 June 1990. Tape recording.
Morehouse, Rollie. Interview with Ken Maffit, 26 September 1989. Transcript.
Ostransky, Leroy. 7 July 1989. Tape recording.
Perciful, Jack. Interviews with Keith Raether, 11 September, 15 September, and 19 September 1989. Transcripts.
Perkins, Zenobia. 16 June 1989. Tape recording.
Pierce, Ron. Interviews with Ken Maffit, 14 May and 16 May 1989. Transcripts.
Pigford, Major. Interview with Ted Dzielak, 24 January 1989. Transcript.
Ramage, Chet. 9 May 1990. Tape recording.
Ramsay, Bill. Interviews with Joe Murphy, 9 March and 18 April 1989. Transcripts.
Reid, Rufus. 8 September 1988. Transcript.
Reilly, Dean. 20 May 1990. Tape recording.
Rowell, Bruce, Emma Gayton, and Oscar "Buster" Clayborn. 28 August 1990. Tape recording.
Rowles, Jimmy. 1 December 1989. Transcript.
Russell, Bob. Interviews with Ted Dzielak, 7 March and 6 April 1989. Transcripts.
Ruther, Wyatt. 18 May 1990. Transcript.
Standifer, Floyd. 27 September and 18 October 1988. Transcripts.
Steele, Gary. Interview with Rick Leppanen, 23 September 1989. Transcript.
Stentz, Chuck. Interview with Joe Murphy, 6 September 1989. Transcript.
Stetler, Dave. Interview with Joe Murphy, 13 December 1989. Tape recording.
Taylor, Charles. Interviews with Ted Dzielak, 29 December 1988 and 10 February 1989. Transcript.
Thurlow, Janet. 30 November 1989. Transcript.
Tolles, Billy. 30–31 January 1990. Tape recording.
Turay, Al. Interview with Ted Dzielak, 8 February 1989. Transcript.
Turnham, Floyd. 3 December 1989. Transcript.
Vaughn, Leon. 21 September and 27 September 1989. Transcripts.
Ward, Jabo. Interview with Joe Murphy, 27 January 1989. Transcript.
Wiggins, Gerald. 4 December 1989. Transcript.
Williamson, Evelyn, and Marshal Royal. 11 April 1991. Tape recording.
Winn, Bob. Interview with Adam Woog, May 1989. Transcript.
Wittwer, John. Interviews with Pete Leinonen, 27 November 1989 and 28 June 1990. Transcripts.

ADDITIONAL INTERVIEWS

Interviews with the author unless otherwise noted.

Acox, Clarence. 20 January 2026.
Anderson, Don. 1992.
Barnett, Doug, II. 19 January 1988.
Barnett, Doug, III. 18 January 1988.
Barnett, Powell. Interview with Richard Berner, 1967. University of Washington Northwest Collection. Transcript.
Blackwell, Robert A. "Bumps." Interview with Roberta Penn, 5 December 1983. Tape recording.
Brown, Wanda. 16 September 1989.
Burke, Mike. 2 April 1993. Telephone conversation.
Dillon, Mary Jane. 8 August 1991. Telephone conversation.
Dugan, Bob. 1993. Telephone interview.
Eckstine, Ed. 24 January 1990.
Engelhart, "Little" Bill. 26 July 1993.
Ewing, Vivian. Interview with Ted Dzielak, 18 August 1989.
Gayton, Emma. Interview with Ted Dzielak, 2 March 1989.
Gayton, Leonard. Interview coordinated by Esther Mumford. King County Black Oral History Project, Oral History Collection, Washington State Archives, Olympia. Transcript.
Gillespie, John Birks "Dizzy." 4 September 1989.
Graf, Bob. 9 November 1989 and February 1991.
Gray, Jerry. Interview with Maggie Hawthorn. Maggie Hawthorn Archive, Music and Art Division, Seattle Public Library. Transcript.
Hilbert, George. 26 April 1991.
Hunziker, Bill. 15 July 1991.
Johnson, Palmer. 10 January 1990.
Kelly, Bev. 26 April 1991.

Lewis, Charles. Interview coordinated by Esther Mumford. Washington Oral/Aural History Project (OAHC), Special Collections, Suzzallo Library, University of Washington. Transcript. 1975.
Montgomery, Monk. Interview with Maggie Hawthorn. Smithsonian Collection.
Moore, Bernard. 19 March 2025. Telephone conversation.
Moton, John. Interview with Ted Dzielak, 9 October 1990.
Padden, Patti. June 2007. Telephone conversation.
Pierce, Ron. 3 May 1991.
Pierre, Neva. 1 May 1991.
Radke, Fred. 4 May 1991.
Spearman, Johnnie. 14 June 1992.
Standifer, Floyd. 28 August 1992.
Stentz, Jan. 11 July 1991.
Taylor, Shelley. 3 May 2026. Email interview.
Thomas, Marvin. 29 February 2020.
Woo, Teresa. 20 June 2024.
Wright, Robert. Black Oral History Project, 1975–76, Bicentennial Oral History Program, Washington State Archives, Digital Archives, http://www.digitalarchives.wa.gov. Accessed 1 August 2025.

BOOKS

Allen, Linda. *Washington Songs and Lore.* Spokane: Melior, 1988.
Anderson, Martha. *Black Pioneers of the Northwest.* Seattle: By the author, 1980.
Armbruster, Kurt E. *Before Seattle Rocked: A City and Its Music*. Seattle: University of Washington Press, 2011.
Avery, Mary W. *Washington: A History of the Evergreen State*. Seattle: University of Washington Press, 1965.
Barney, Bigard. *With Louis and the Duke*. New York: Oxford University Press, 1986.
Barto, Harold, and Catherine Bullard. *History of the State of Washington.* Boston: D. C. Heath and Co., 1947.
Bayley, Christopher T. *Seattle Justice: The Rise and Fall of the Police Payoff System in Seattle*. Seattle: Sasquatch Books, 2015.
Blecha, Peter. *Stomp and Shout: R&B and the Origins of Northwest Rock and Roll*. Seattle: University of Washington Press, 2023.
Blecha, Peter, and Brad Holden. *Lost Roadhouses of Seattle*. Charleston, SC: History Press, 2022.
Broderick, Henry. *Early Seattle Profiles.* Seattle: Dogwood Press, 1959.
Bruyninckx, Walter. *60 Years of Recorded Jazz, 1917–1977.* Mechelen, Belgium: By the author, 1978–83.
Büchmann-Moller, Frank. *You Just Fight for Your Life: The Story of Lester Young*. New York: Praeger, 1990.
Cayton, Horace R. *Long Old Road.* Seattle: University of Washington Press, 1970.
Chambliss, William. *On the Take.* Bloomington: Indiana University Press, 1978.
Charles, Ray, and David Ritz. *Brother Ray.* New York: Dial Press, 1978. Reprint, New York: Warner, 1979.
Charters, Samuel B., and Leonard Kunstadt. *Jazz: A History of the New York Scene.* New York: Doubleday, 1962. Reprint, New York: Da Capo Press, 1984.
Chew, Ron. *My Unforgotten Seattle.* Seattle: University of Washington Press, 2020.
Chilton, John. *Who's Who of Jazz.* New York: Time-Life Records, 1978. Seattle: International Examiner Press, 2001.
Chin, Doug. *Seattle's International District: The Making of a Pan-Asian American Community.* Seattle: University of Washington Press, 2001.
Clark, Norman H. *The Dry Years: Prohibition and Social Change in Washington.* Seattle: University of Washington Press, 1965.
Clark, Norman H. *Washington: A Bicentennial History.* New York: Norton, 1976.
Clayton, Buck, assisted by Nancy Miller Elliott. *Buck Clayton's Jazz World.* New York: Oxford University Press, 1987.
Collier, James Lincoln. *Benny Goodman and the Swing Era.* New York: Oxford University Press, 1989.
Coolman, Todd. *The Bass Tradition.* New Albany: J. Aebersold, 1985.
Crow, Bill. *Jazz Anecdotes.* New York: Oxford University Press, 1990.
Crowther, Bruce. *Gene Krupa: His Life and Times.* New York: Universe Books, 1987.
Dahl, Linda. *Stormy Weather: The Music and Lives of a Century of Jazz Women.* New York: Pantheon Books, 1984.
Dance, Helen. *Stormy Monday: The T-Bone Walker Story.* Baton Rouge: Louisiana State University Press, 1987.
Dance, Stanley. *The World of Count Basie.* New York: Scribner, 1980.
Dance, Stanley. *The World of Duke Ellington.* New York: Scribner, 1970; New York: Da Capo Press, 1980.
Dance, Stanley. *The World of Swing.* New York: Da Capo Press, 1974.

Darensbourg, Joe (as told to Peter Vacher). *Jazz Odyssey.* Baton Rouge: Louisiana State University Press, 1987.

Dietsche, Robert. *Jump Town: The Golden Years of Portland Jazz 1942–1957.* Corvallis: Oregon State University Press, 2005.

Driggs, Frank. "Andy Kirk's Story." In *Jazz Panorama.* Edited by Martin Williams. New York: Collier, 1964.

Driggs, Frank, and Lewine Harris. *Black Beauty, White Heat: A Pictorial History of Classic Jazz 1920–1950.* New York: Morrow, 1982.

Dryden, Cecil. *Dryden's History of Washington.* Portland, OR: Binfords and Mort, 1968.

Eckland, K. O. *Jazz West.* Carmel-by-the-Sea, CA: Cypress, 1986.

Elliott, Eugene Clinton. *A History of Variety-Vaudeville in Seattle.* Edited by Glenn Hughes. Seattle: University of Washington Press, 1944.

Feather, Leonard. *Encyclopedia of Jazz.* New York: Bonanza Books, 1962.

Feather, Leonard. *Encyclopedia of Jazz in the Sixties.* New York: Bonanza Books, 1961.

Feather, Leonard, and Ira Gitler. *Encyclopedia of Jazz in the Seventies.* New York: Horizon Press, 1976.

Ficken, Robert E., and Charles P. LeWarne. *Washington: A Centennial History.* Seattle: University of Washington Press, 1988.

Giddins, Gary. *Celebrating Bird.* New York: Beach Tree Books (Morrow), 1987.

Goldman, Albert. *Elvis.* New York: McGraw-Hill, 1984.

Gordon, Robert. *Jazz West Coast.* London: Quartet Books, 1986.

Hampton, Lionel, with James Haskins. *Hamp.* New York: Warner Books, 1989.

Handy, D. Antoinette. *Black Women in American Bands and Orchestras.* Metuchen, NJ: Scarecrow Press, 1981.

Handy, D. Antoinette. *The International Sweethearts of Rhythm.* Metuchen, NJ: Scarecrow Press, 1983.

Hawes, Hampton, and Don Asher. *Raise Up Off Me.* Coward, McCann & Geoghegan, 1974. Reprint, New York: Da Capo Press, 1979.

Henderson, David. *'Scuse Me While I Kiss the Sky: The Life of Jimi Hendrix.* New York: Doubleday, 1978. Reprint, New York: Bantam Books, 1981.

Herman, Woody, and Stuart Troup. *The Woodchopper's Ball.* New York: Dutton, 1990.

Hinton, Milt, and David Berger. *Bass Line: The Stories and Photographs of Milt Hinton.* Philadelphia: Temple University Press, 1988.

Horricks, Raymond. *Quincy Jones.* New York: Hippocrene Books, 1985.

Jablonski, Edward. *Harold Arlen: Happy with the Blues.* New York: Doubleday, 1961.

Jones, Nard. *Seattle.* New York: Doubleday, 1972.

Keller, David. *The Blue Note: Seattle's Black Musicians' Union: A Pictorial History.* Pullman, WA: By the author, 2024.

Kenney, William Howland. *Chicago Jazz.* New York: Oxford University Press, 1993.

Kernfeld, Barry, and Stanley Sadie, eds. *The New Grove Dictionary of Jazz.* New York: Grove's Dictionaries of Music, 1988.

Klinkowitz, Jerome. *Listen: Gerry Mulligan.* New York: Schirmer Books, 1991.

Korall, Burt. *Drummin' Men.* New York: Macmillan, 1990.

Lomax, Alan. *Mr. Jellyroll.* 1950. Reprint, Berkeley: University of California Press, 1973.

Lyons, Len. *The Great Jazz Pianists: Speaking of Their Lives and Music.* New York: Quill, 1983.

Mascagli, Luciano, Liborio Pusciteri, and Giovanni Volonte. *Duke Ellington's Story on Records.* Vol. 1946–50. Milan: Musica Jazz, 1972.

McCarthy, Albert. *Big Band Jazz.* New York: Putnam, 1974.

Miller, Mark. *Such Melodious Racket: The Lost History of Jazz in Canada.* Toronto: Mercury Press, 1997.

Mingus, Charles. *Beneath the Underdog.* New York: Alfred A. Knopf, 1971.

Morgan, Murray. *Skid Road.* New York: Viking Press, 1951.

Moritz, Charles, ed. "Jones, Quincy Delight." *Current Biography* (1977).

Mumford, Esther. *Seattle's Black Victorians 1852–1901.* Seattle: Ananse Press, 1980.

Mumford, Esther. *Seven Stars and Orion.* Seattle: Ananse Press, 1986.

Newell, Gordon, and Joe Williamson. *Pacific Coast Liners.* Seattle: Superior, 1959.

Nite, Norm N. *Rock On: The Illustrated Encyclopedia of Rock n' Roll*, Volume 1: *The Solid Gold Years.* New York: HarperCollins, 1982.

Pastras, Phil. *Dead Man Blues: Jelly Roll Morton Way Out West.* Berkeley: University of California Press, 2001.

Placksin, Sally. *American Women in Jazz.* New York: Wideview, 1982.

Poindexter, Pony. *The Pony Express: Memoirs of a Jazz Musician.* Frankfurt, Germany: j.a.s. publikationen, 1985.

Ramsey, Doug. *Jazz Matters*. Fayetteville: University of Arkansas Press, 1989.
Reisner, Robert George. *Bird: The Legend of Charlie Parker*. New York: Citadel Press, 1962.
Rosen, Gerald. *Mahatma Gandhi in a Cadillac*. Berkeley: Frog Books, 1995.
Ruby, Greg, and Paul de Barros. *Frank D. Waldron: Seattle's Syncopated Classic*. Seattle: Greg Ruby Music, 2017.
Russell, Ross. *Bird Lives*. 1972. Reprint, London: Quartet Books, 1988.
Russell, Ross. *Jazz Style in Kansas City and the Southwest*. 1971. Reprint, Berkeley: University of California Press, 1973.
Sale, Roger. *Seattle Past to Present*. 1976. Reprint, Seattle: University of Washington Press, 1978.
Schuller, Gunther. *Early Jazz*. New York: Oxford University Press, 1968.
Schuller, Gunther. *The Swing Era*. New York: Oxford University Press, 1989.
Shapiro, Nat, and Nat Hentoff, eds. *Hear Me Talkin' to Ya*. 1955. Reprint, New York: Dover, 1966.
Simon, George. *The Big Bands*. New York: Schirmer Books, 1981.
Simosko, Vladimir, and Barry Tepperman. *Eric Dolphy*. New York: Da Capo Press, 1979.
Smith, Merle Irene. *Seattle Had a Tin Pan Alley, Too!* Seattle: By the author, 1989.
Southern, Eileen. *The Music of Black Americans*. New York: Norton, 1971.
Stearns, Marshall. *The Story of Jazz*. New York: Oxford University Press, 1956.
Stephenson, Sam. *The Jazz Loft Project: The Photographs and Tapes of W. Eugene Smith from 821 Sixth Avenue, 1957–1965*. New York: Alfred A. Knopf, 2009.
Stoddard, Tom. *Jazz on the Barbary Coast*. Chigwell, Essex: Storyville, 1982.
Taylor, Quintard. *The Forging of a Black Community: Seattle's Central District from 1870 Through the Civil Rights Era*. Seattle: University of Washington Press, 1994.
Ulanov, Barry. *Duke Ellington*. New York: Creative Age Press, 1946.
Unterbrink, Mary. *Jazz Women at the Keyboard*. Jefferson, NC: McFarland, 1983.
Waldron, Frank. *Syncopated Classic*. Seattle: By the author, 1924.
White, Charles. *The Life and Times of Little Richard*. New York: Harmony Books, 1984.
Williams, Martin. *Jelly Roll Morton*. New York: A. S. Barnes, 1962.
Williams, Martin, ed. *Jazz Panorama*. New York: Collier, 1964.
Woodfin, Henry. "Ray Charles." In *Jazz Panorama*, edited by Martin Williams. New York: Collier, 1964.

DAILY NEWSPAPERS
(Multiple References)

The Daily (University of Washington). 1 March 1939; 2 June 1939; 21 April 1964; 22 January 1969.
New York Times. 18 November 1980; 13 January 1986; 22 September 1989.
Seattle Post-Intelligencer. 15 November 1896–11 March 1983.
Seattle Times. 23 November 1901–November 2014.

DAILY NEWSPAPERS
(Single Reference)

[Seattle] *International Examiner*, 15 January 1987.
[Seattle] *Pacific Leader*. 19 November 1954.
[Stockton] *Stockton Independent*, 11 May 1935.
Anderson, Rick. "The Owl Party Tweaks Political Noses." *P-I*, 4 November 1976.
Gleason, Ralph. "A Growing Jazz Singer Searches for Her 'Touch.'" *San Francisco Chronicle*. 10 October 1957.
Guzzo, Lou. "Kenton Show Moves at a Steady Pace." *P-I*, 25 February 1954.
Hilburn, Robert. "So Long, 'Tutti-Frutti,' Hello, God." *Los Angeles Times*, 16 August 1981.
Newell, Berniece E. "Originator of 'Jazz' in 347th Orchestra." *Trench and Camp*, 25 November 1917.
Skreen, Chet. "Seattle-Tacoma's Big Ballroom Days." *Seattle Times*, 9 November 1975.
Winslow, Valerie. "Palmer Johnson Is 'Cooking' in Bellevue." *Bellevue* [WA] *Journal-American*, 28 January 1977.
Young, Dick. "The Trianon Ballroom Proudly Presents." *P-I*, 26 October 1975.

PERIODICALS AND MAGAZINES

California Eagle [Los Angeles], 1926–1943.
Cayton's Monthly. 1 February 1921.
Cayton's Weekly [Seattle]. 1 September 1917–21 February 1920.
DownBeat. 1 January 1942–21 April 1964.

Earshot Jazz [Seattle]. 1984–2025.
The Enterprise [Seattle]. 18 September 1925; 30 April 1926; 3 July 1930.
Musicland [Journal of Seattle Musicians' Union Local 76]. 1926–1957.
Northwest Enterprise [Seattle]. 1 January 1931–28 December 1950.
Northwest Herald [Seattle]. 5 January 1944–18 December 1946.
Puget Sound Observer [Seattle]. 27 March 1957–23 April 1958.
Seattle Republican. August 1909–August 1920.
Seattle Star. 1910–31.
The Spectator [Seattle University]. 4 November and 2 December 1949; 30 March, 27 April, 1 June, and 19 October 1950; 13 January 1965.

PERIODICAL AND MAGAZINE ARTICLES

"Bass Fiddler Junior Raglin." *Life*, 25 September 1944.
Blecha, Peter. "Merceedees (1913–2000)." History.Link.org, 2016.
Burnett, Stan. "Seattle JAZZ Scene." *Columns*, April 1957.
Douglas, Patrick. "The Gaytons." *Seattle*, January 1969.
Driggs, Frank. "Walter Page's Story as Told to Frank Driggs." *Jazz Review*, November 1958.
Droker, Howard. "On the Pay Streak at the Alaska-Yukon-Pacific Exposition." *Portage*, Summer 1981.
Droker, Howard. "Seattle Race Relations During the Second World War." *Pacific Northwest Quarterly*, October 1976.
Evans, Gary. "Don Lanphere." *Saxophone Journal*, November/December 1988.
"Floyd Turnham and Britt Woodman with Duke Band." *Los Angeles Sentinel*, 1 March 1951.
Giddins, Gary. "Joe Venuti: A Penchant for Mayhem." *Village Voice*, 28 August 1978.
Givens, Linda Holden. "Oscar William Holden: Seattle's Patriarch of Jazz Through the Eyes of a Granddaughter." 2 June 2015. https://www.historylink.org/File/11074.
Gushee, Lawrence. "New Orleans–Area Musicians on the West Coast, 1908–1925." *Black Music Research Journal* 9, no. 1 (1989).
Gushee, Lawrence. "A Preliminary Chronology of the Early Career of Ferd 'Jelly Roll' Morton." *American Music* (Winter 1985).
Harrison, Ashley. "The Story of Seattle's Black and Tan Club and Those Who Owned It." *South Seattle Emerald*, 15 May 2018. https://southseattleemerald.org/arts-culture/2018/05/15/the-story-of-seattles-black-and-tan-club-and-those-who-owned-it.
Hawthorn, Maggie. "Fifty Years of Quincy Jones." *Seattle Weekly*, 9 March 1983.
Kopstein, Jack. "The Jive Bombers." February 25, 2010. https://www.militarymusic.com/blogs/military-music/13515817-the-jive-bombers.
Lees, Gene. "Fiddler Joe." *Jazzletter*, September 1988.
Lunn, Chris. "Jack Perciful." *Victory Music*, April 1989.
"The Maestro Behind Michael Moves on to New Challenges." *Life*, December 1984.
Morris, Maine. "The Northwestern Picture." *Clef*, June 1946.
"Out of Nowhere." *Jazz Journal*, February 1987.
Penn, Roberta. "Robert 'Bumps' Blackwell." *The Rocket*, April 1986.
Power, Desmond. "Jazz in Occupied China: Black Jazzmen at the Japanese Prison Camp in Weihsien, China During World War II." BlackPast.org. 29 August 2012. https://blackpast.org/global-african-history/jazz-occupied-china-black-jazzmen-japanese-prison-camp-weihsien-china-during-world-war/.
Reddick, L. D. "The New Race Relations Frontier." *Journal of Education Sociology*, November 1945.
Rochester, Junius. "Doc Hamilton; King of Seattle's Speakeasy Living." *Seattle Weekly*, 2 February 1983.
Russwurm, Lani. "The Origins of Jazz in Vancouver." *Past Tense: Fragments of Vancouver History and Reflections Thereon*. 11 November 2015. https://pasttensevancouver.wordpress.com/2015/11/11/the-origins-of-jazz-in-vancouver/.
"Spinning Wheel Cabaret, Seattle." *Billboard*, 17 December 1949.
Stoddard, Tom. "Al Pierre's Bands (Revisited and Revised)." *Storyville*, April–May 1970.
"Turnham Band Clicks." *California Eagle*, 12 August 1948.
Umphrey, Wallace. "New Orleans in Seattle." *The Jazz Record*, December 1944.
Wittwer, John. "A Tribute to Joe Darensbourg." *The Jazz Record*, September 1945.

PAMPHLETS, LINER NOTES, PROGRAMS, PRIVATE PUBLICATIONS, EPHEMERA, AND UNPUBLISHED AND MISCELLANEOUS MATERIAL

Adams, Mary Elizabeth. Scrapbook. University of Washington Special Collections.

Black Heritage Society of Washington State Collections. https://www.bhswa.org/wordpress/collections/.
Blackwell, Robert A. "Bumps." Press biography.
Blackwell's Academy of the Performing Arts. Press package.
Bobrow, Norm. "Jazz Letter #1."
Bown, Patti. Résumé.
Broderick, Henry. Pamphlet. "Prohibition." Seattle: Dogwood Press, 1968. Seattle Public Library Northwest Collection.
Catlett, George "Buddy." Press biography.
DeMichael, Don. Liner note. *Red Norvo* (Giants of Jazz Series) (1980). Time-Life STW14.
Driggs, Frank. Letter to author. 22 March 1991.
Exner, Frederick B. Liner note. *Kid Ory, b/w Johnny Wittwer* (1945). Exner 1 and 2.
Finch, Harold. Letter to author. February 1991.
Gray, Jerry. Letter to author. 20 February 1988.
Hackett, Gertrude "Dee Dee." Biography. Hackett Family Papers. Online Archive of California (OAC). http://oac.cdlib.org.
Jones, Quincy. Press biography. Quincy Jones Productions.
Kenneth Patchen Poetry and Jazz Reading. Flyer. Maggie Hawthorn Archive, Seattle Public Library.
Kimball, Kenny. Curriculum vitae.
Kimball, Kenny. Letter to author. 11 February 1991.
Lake City Tavern. Program. Seattle. 18 August 1955.
Louie, Laurence. *Biography of Charlie Louie*. 2025.
Metcalf, Joni. Liner note, *Joni Metcalf* (1969). 21 Records 21-L-106.
Moore, Phil. "Things I Forgot to Tell You." 22 April 1986. Phil Moore Collection. Black Film Center & Archive, Indiana University Digital Collections. https://digitalcollections.iu.edu/collections.
Northwest Jazz Workshop. Charter document. 1 June 1956.
"Quincy Jones: A Seattle Celebration." 50th Birthday Party. Program. Seattle. 11 March 1983.
Ron Pierce band. Photograph caption.
Ruther, Wyatt. Résumé.
SeaFair Jazz Festival. Program. 5 August 1956.
Seattle Jazz Society. Membership brochure. 1966.
Seattle Jazz Society. Newsletter. June and December 1966; November and December 1976.
[Seattle] Local 493. Union roster. 14 January 1958. American Federation of Musicians Local No. 76 Archive.
Sewald, Ronda L., transcriber. "Portland/Seattle Trip." 9 April 1978. Phil Moore Collection. Black Film Center & Archive, Indiana University Digital Collections. https://digitalcollections.iu.edu/collections.
Siegl, Eleanor. "The Amalgamation of the Colored and White Musicians' Unions in Seattle." Term paper (University of Washington). 1966. American Federation of Musicians Local 76 Archive.
Smith, Merle I. Letter to author. 15 April 1990.
Townsend, Irving. Liner note. *Mildred Bailey, Her Greatest Performances 1929–1946*, Vols. 1–3 (1981). Columbia JC 3L 22.
"Trianon Saturday Night." Newsletter. 15 February 1941.
Turnham, Floyd. Chronology of engagements.
Turnham, Floyd. Press biography.
Ward, Jabo. Chronology of engagements.
Zwisohn, Laurence J. Pamphlet. "Bing Crosby: A Lifetime of Music." Palm Tree Library, Los Angeles.

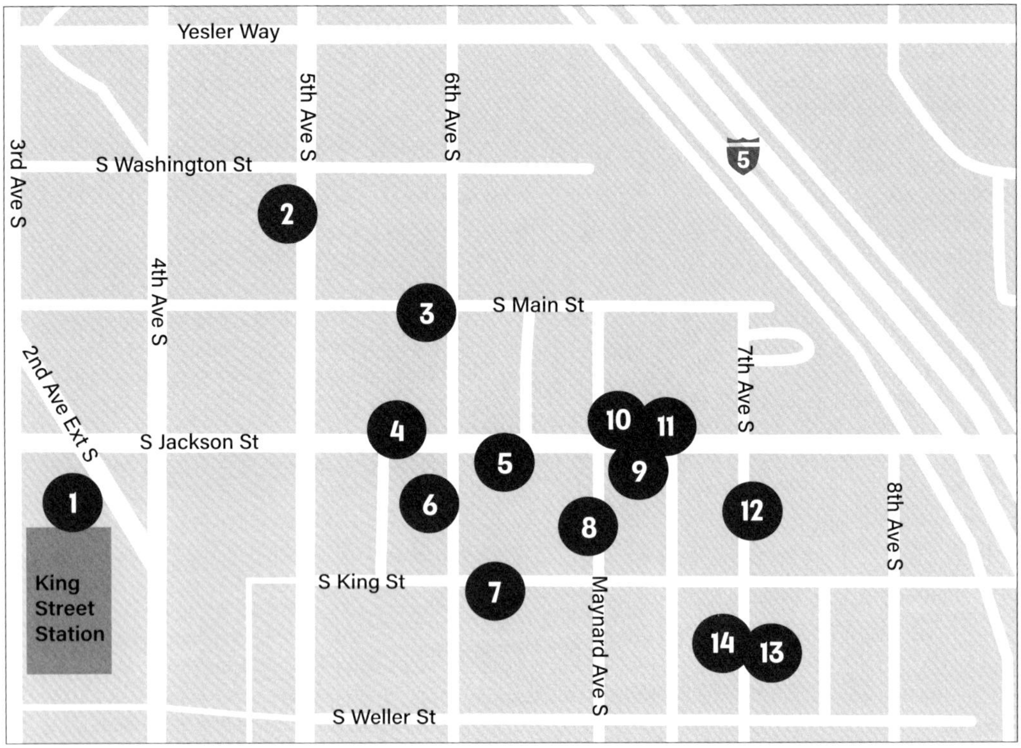

SEATTLE'S HISTORIC JAZZ DISTRICT, WEST OF I-5

1 KING STREET STATION

Jazz was brought to Seattle by Black musicians, many of whom arrived by train. Railroad porters and waiters were also customers for the night-spots and social clubs along Jackson Street. For a while, a club on the corner of Twelfth Avenue South and South Jackson Street (the Black and Tan) was even known as the "Colored Waiters, Porters, and Cooks Club." Today the station is home to several arts organizations.

2 THE DUMAS CLUB

Black people were not welcome in downtown establishments, so forward-thinking members of the Black community formed social clubs of their own. In 1912 entrepreneur Earl Russell "Noodles" Smith and his partner, Burr "Blackie" Williams, opened the Dumas Club, the first documented site of jazzlike music being played by local musicians in Seattle.

3 THE NEW CHINATOWN

Danny Woo, a longtime Chinatown–International District entrepreneur and descendant of one of the district's most prominent Chinese pioneers, opened this restaurant in 1940 at the northwest corner of Sixth Avenue South and South Main Street. It was known for its extremely late hours; the music often didn't start till after midnight and ended at dawn. The New Chinatown could serve five hundred people at banquets.

4 THE EBONY CAFÉ

People used to line up around the corner to get into the Ebony Café in the 1950s to hear the early "Jam for Breakfast" set, the brainchild of vibist, pianist, bandleader, and former Lionel Hampton sideman Elmer Gill (1926–2004). The Ebony was in the Governor Building, one of two beautifully ornamented, white structures along South Jackson Street built by the Rainier Heat & Power Company.

5 THE GREEN DOT

Though a Washington Federal Bank and its parking lot now occupy this corner, the Welcome Hotel used to house the Green Dot here. Opened in 1933, it was a tiny barber shop with a secret nightclub in back. Pianist Palmer Johnson (1907–1996), who played solo piano here in 1941, recalled that the place also doubled as a "bookie joint" (for betting on horse races).

6 THE 411 CLUB

In 1938 pianist Palmer Johnson was a regular at the 411 Club, usually playing with bassist Junior Raglin, who later toured and recorded with Duke Ellington. On Sundays horn players often dropped by to jam. One was Tacoma tenor saxophonist Corky Corcoran, who once got the best of the great Ellington saxophonist Ben Webster at the jam session.

7 RIZAL HALL

In the 1920s and '30s, the block of South King Street between Sixth Avenue South and Maynard Avenue South teemed with Filipino cafés, social clubs, and labor contract offices. Rizal Hall was a particularly lively spot, where jazz bands and community orchestras performed for dancing and listening.

8 BASIN STREET

Down a steep staircase in the basement of the now demolished Olympus Hotel, which stood where Hing Hay Park is today, Basin Street opened its doors in 1939. Basin Street featured jazz, booze, and gambling twenty-four hours a day. An up-and-coming teenage singer from Garfield High School, Ernestine Anderson, played some of her first gigs at Basin Street.

9 THE TOKIWA HOTEL

According to influential pianist Julian Henson, musicians working in the district sometimes rented rooms for a dollar or two a week at the Tokiwa. "My dad was a bartender at the 411 Club, so he had a lot of friends," recalled Henson. "Every once in a while, I'd go in there and he'd say, 'Kid, you doin' all right?' And he'd hand me a ten. Hell, that'd pay my room rent for a month."

10 THE CONGO ROOM

Like the Ebony, the Congo Room was also located in one of the elegant white buildings erected by the Rainier Heat & Power Company. The club was a "blind," which meant that the store in front was a cover for the real action in back, where there was a horseshoe-shaped bar, a ballroom, and gaming tables.

11 THE BLACK ELKS

In 1948 Ray Charles (1930–2004) played his first regular Seattle gig at the Black Elks Club. The club was upstairs, where patrons were greeted by a large stuffed elk; inside, barbecue sandwiches and drinks were on offer, and if you knew whom to ask, a taste of opium tea. Pianist Cecil Young (1920–ca. 1975), a hot modernist from the East Coast, also played the Black Elks.

12 GOLDEN WEST HOTEL

The Golden West Hotel was operated from 1920 to 1927 by Noodles Smith, who also owned the Coast Hotel with his wife Elbe. The Coast and the Golden West welcomed people of color, who were barred from downtown hotels. Several clubs flourished in the Golden West in the 1920s and '30s, including the Little Harlem Beer Tavern and the Ubangi.

13 THE CHINESE GARDEN

Charlie Louie opened this popular establishment on December 21, 1929, offering food, music, drink, and gambling to an enthusiastic Jazz Age clientele. Louie featured the best musicians in town, including pianists Palmer Johnson and Phil Moore and saxophonists Frank Waldron and Dick Wilson.

14 THE CLUB ROYALE

By far the most elaborately decorated nightclub in the district, the Club Royale boasted beautiful stylized murals on either side of a stairwell that led down to the venue. Opened in the summer of 1930, the Club Royale was colloquially known as the Bucket of Blood, though it was not particularly violent. Clarinetist Joe Darensbourg (1906–1983) recalled playing here with Seattle saxophonist Gerald Wells.

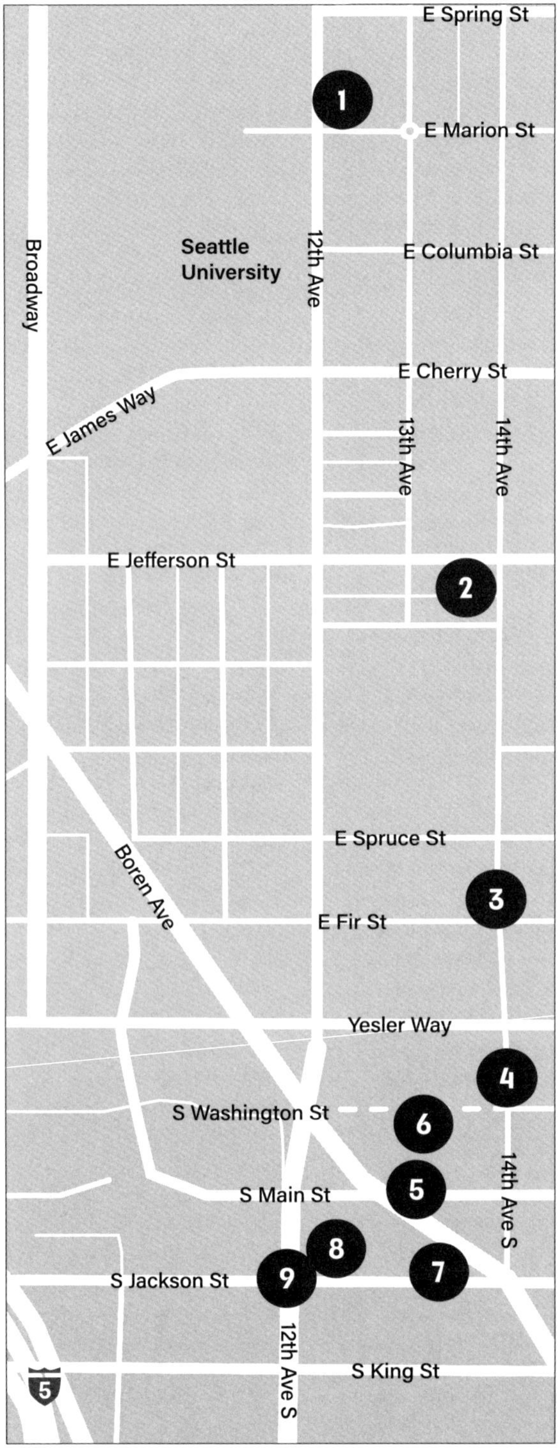

E Spring St
1
E Marion St
Seattle University
Broadway
12th Ave
E Columbia St
E Cherry St
E James Way
13th Ave
14th Ave
E Jefferson St
2
E Spruce St
Boren Ave
3
E Fir St
Yesler Way
4
S Washington St
6
5
14th Ave S
S Main St
8
9
7
S Jackson St
12th Ave S
S King St
5

SEATTLE'S HISTORIC JAZZ DISTRICT, EAST OF I-5

1 DOC HAMILTON'S BARBECUE PIT (AKA 908 CLUB)

Doc Hamilton's Barbecue Pit, which opened in 1924, was Seattle's elegant Prohibition counterpart to Harlem's Cotton Cub. Rich white patrons, sometimes including the mayor, rolled up out front in limousines and were greeted by a doorman wearing an admiral's uniform. Inside, they found liquor, gambling, and the best barbecue in town, with Doc himself turning the spit in a white chef's apron. By the 1940s, Dick Ruffin and Nixie Smith rechristened the place as the 908 Club, often presenting the great pianist Cecil Young.

2 THE BLUE NOTE

The final headquarters of the Black Musicians Local 493, the Blue Note served triple duty as union office, social club, and nightspot. The venue hosted sessions where name players showed up to jam, relax, and meet the locals. Floyd Standifer remembered meeting Duke Ellington saxophonist Johnny Hodges there, as well as Count Basie arranger Thad Jones. The floor tiles featured a blue pattern shaped like an eighth note.

3 WASHINGTON HALL

Washington Hall was the first Seattle venue to host a local group billed as a jazz ensemble. On June 10, 1918, Miss Lillian Smith's Jazz Band performed a Grand Benefit Ball here to raise money for the NAACP. Over the years, the stage has hosted Danish and Yiddish theater, Filipino Youth Club dances, boxing matches, hip-hop, avant-garde performance art, and plenty of jazz, blues, and rock 'n' roll, including one of Jimi Hendrix's first bands, the Rocking Kings.

4 THE ROCKING CHAIR

The Rocking Chair was the most exclusive of all the Seattle after-hours clubs and also sparked the career of its most famous citizen—Ray Charles. Known then as R. C. Robinson, the blind singer/pianist came to Seattle from Tampa, Florida, in 1948, when he was seventeen years old. Before he left Seattle in 1950, he commemorated the club with a single, "Rocking Chair Blues."

5 THE ENTERTAINER'S CABARET

Bailey Gatzert Elementary School and its playfield occupy what used to be a grid of four separate blocks, where the Entertainer's Cabaret, Finnish Hall, and the Rocking Chair featured music and dancing. In August 1920, the great New Orleans pianist and composer Ferdinand "Jelly Roll" Morton played the Entertainer's Cabaret, later called the Cotton Club and Sessions Playhouse.

6 FINNISH HALL

Behind the Entertainer's was Finnish Hall. From 1931 through 1956, swing fans jitterbugged on the grand hall's maple dance floor to the strains of Black big bands led by everyone from Louis Armstrong and Erskine Hawkins to Fletcher Henderson and Jimmie Lunceford.

7 BESSIE YOUNG'S BOARDING HOUSE

Before the Civil Rights Act of 1964 opened downtown hotels to all, touring Black artists often stayed at Bessie Young's Boarding House, a handsome Victorian building that stood where a parking lot is today. One longtime resident at Bessie Young's was saxophonist, trumpeter, and music teacher Frank Waldron, who taught Seattle's young musicians from the 1910s to the 1950s.

8 THE TWO PALS

Popular vocalist Dee Dee Hackett often sang at the Two Pals, located in an old wooden building that also housed a big-time gambling spot next door, the Main Event, and Noodles Smith's Hill Top Tavern. During World War II, owner Charlie Beale ran a weekly ad encouraging folks to come on down to the Two Pals to buy a war bond.

9 THE BLACK AND TAN

The Black and Tan, the most famous of all the Jackson Street venues, also lasted the longest, from 1920 to 1969, from the Jazz Age to the Motown era. Ray Charles and Garfield High School students Quincy Jones and Ernestine Anderson played here, as did local organ maestro Dave Lewis ("Little Green Thing"). The name refers to a venue where races mix in harmony, a major feature of the Jackson Street nightlife district.

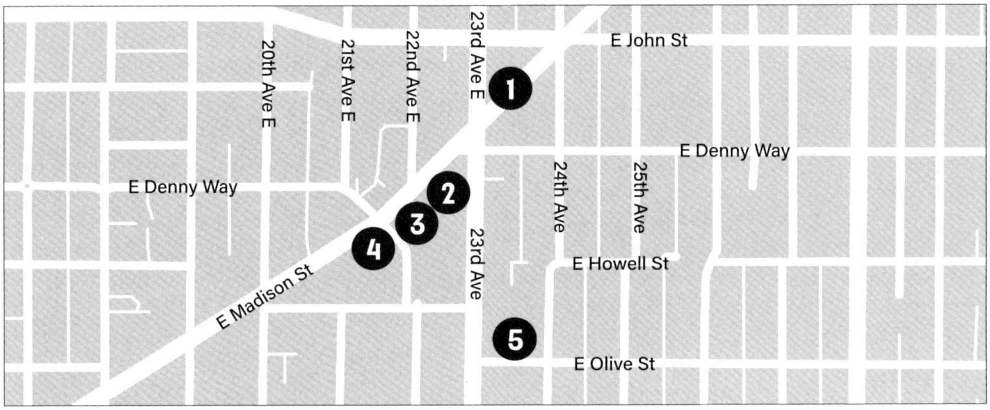

EAST MADISON STREET AREA

1 THE WASHINGTON EDUCATION AND SOCIAL CLUB

Quincy Jones hung out here as a high schooler to catch Ray Charles and other acts such as T-Bone Walker, Guitar Slim, and Cab Calloway. Quincy was amused by the place's hifalutin name, which owner Sirless Groves attached to his large, upstairs jazz mecca to convince authorities it was okay to sell hard liquor to "members." (In fact, anyone could get a membership card.) The great tenor saxophonist Lester Young played an extended gig here in 1948, and young Ernestine Anderson could also be found on the bandstand. The club ran from 1944 to 1951. The two-story building still stands.

2 BUMPS BLACKWELL'S BUTCHER SHOP

In the 1940s Robert "Bumps" Blackwell worked as a butcher here at the Madison Street Market, and he also ran an ad hoc music agency over the counter. "On any given day," recalled trumpeter Floyd Standifer, "you could walk over there and there'd be a whole bunch of people, most of them musicians, standing around at the meat counter."

3 THE MARDI GRAS

Known in 1927 as the Kopper Kettle, this venue reopened in 1936 as the Mardi Gras, a cozy tavern and restaurant. During World War II it became a notoriously disorderly dive, but in 1950 it reemerged under owner Wilmer Morgan as a classy steakhouse with cocktails and first-rate jazz. The great California alto saxophonist Pony Poindexter played here regularly in the 1950s, as did Seattle saxophonists Jabo Ward and Gerald Brashear. In the 1960s, Joe Brazil made the Mardi Gras his home base. The venue has since been demolished.

4 BIRDLAND (AKA SAVOY BALLROOM, EASTSIDE HALL)

This hallowed East Madison hall, now torn down, was exhibiting silent films as early as 1926 as the Gala Theatre. Local promoter Lemuel Honeysuckle converted it in 1941 into the Savoy Ballroom, where Billy Tolles debuted the Savoy Boys and stamped the place as Seattle's premiere spot for hip Black music. Known as Eastside Hall from 1951 to 1955, it was reinvented again by Wilmer Morgan as Birdland, which nurtured the career of Seattle keyboard ace Dave Lewis and also hosted touring Black R & B artists such as Hank Ballard, James Brown, and Big Jay McNeely.

5 EAST MADISON YMCA

Originally a modest wooden structure, the East Madison YMCA became a hot spot for jazz in the '40s with its all-ages Friday night dances. Garfield High School singer Ernestine Anderson fondly remembered meeting local musicians like trumpeters Sonny Booker and Quincy Jones, as well as bandleader Bumps Blackwell and pianist and vocalist Ray Charles, at the Y. Trumpeter Floyd Standifer, whose father preached at a church nearby, also found his jazz posse here. The modern building was constructed in 1965.

METHODOLOGY AND ACKNOWLEDGMENTS

IN 1987, WHEN KJRIS LUND, THEN EXECUTIVE DIRECTOR OF THE KING County Arts Commission, heard I was interested in researching jazz in Seattle, she suggested I contact Charles Payton at the Cultural Resources Historic Preservation Program to see about funding for oral history interviews. That was the beginning of *Jackson Street After Hours*. I want to thank Kjris for encouraging me at that time and, later, for guiding me through the political maze of Washington State Centennial funding. Without her help, it's doubtful this project would have gotten off the ground. I also owe many thanks to Charles for his contacts and moral support, and to Charlotte Jacobs at the King County Centennial Commission for sticking by the project.

Before continuing with the long list of generous people and institutions that helped make this book a reality, a note about its methodology and background may be useful. Most of the long quotations in the book are excerpted from the oral histories noted above. Interviews were conducted following guidelines set out by Willa Baum in *Oral History for the Local Historical Society* and *Transcribing and Editing Oral History*. Interviewees ranged historically from the late Floyd Turnham, who performed with his mother Edythe's band in Seattle in 1927, to post–World War II musicians such as Floyd Standifer and Chuck Metcalf, all of whom were still performing when the first edition was published in 1993. In choosing interview subjects, I leaned heavily toward the Black community, since Black musicians had most often received the least recognition. (Musicians referred to in the text are Black unless otherwise identified.) I interviewed musicians who went on to national acclaim, such as Quincy Jones and Patti Bown, but also those whose impact was local, such as Gus Mancuso and Julian Henson. Sessions were also taped with nightclub owners, bartenders, and others who had some direct involvement with the scene. Of eighty-three interviews, I conducted more than half; the others were done by volunteers, most of whom were associated with Seattle's Earshot Jazz Society, which initially sponsored the project by serving as its fiscal agent.

The project was originally intended as a modest volume of transcripts of selected oral histories tied together loosely with narrative material. As the research progressed, however, I became increasingly disenchanted with oral history as an exclusive or primary research tool. It left too many holes. The period before 1927, for example, was impossible to document through interviews, since none of the original players were still alive. Some of the best bebop players—Gerald Brashear, Milt Garred, and Cecil Young—had also died. Few subjects were able to provide an overview of economic, social, or racial conditions, or specific dates when important events occurred. In late 1988, making use of a generous grant from the King County Centennial Commission, I expanded the project to its present, more ambitious scope—a book documenting the roots of jazz in Seattle, using printed materials and secondary interviews as well as the oral histories. I employed a research assistant, Ted Dzielak, to comb through African American newspapers in the University of Washington Library's Special Collections Department and began to supplement the interviews with other resources, such as material from the *Seattle Times*, local histories, and general jazz histories and autobiographies. Among the most precious sources of material were private collections of scrapbook memorabilia and photographs shared by interview subjects. To all of those musicians, I extend my deep gratitude.

To Quincy Jones, for giving this project his time and credibility, and for convincing R. C. that it was worth his time, I offer thanks as well. I also thank the Black Heritage Society—Ralph Hayes, Joe Warner, Jim Yarbrough, and particularly historian Esther Mumford, who generously shared information, leads, and her meticulous sense of scholarship. To the late Al Smith, who not only offered his collection of vintage photographs but arranged several important interviews, many thanks as well.

I could not have found a more dedicated, thorough, and enthusiastic research assistant than Ted Dzielak. I thank him now for the many hours he spent in libraries, making lists, photocopying, and compiling information; for the grant proposals he wrote to support the project; and for the stimulating conversations we had over two years as the concept for the book took shape. I also thank research aides Paul Titialii and Mike Galligan, and Jane Peck at the Cornish College of the Arts for providing those aides through a credit program.

My grateful appreciation also goes out to Bill Crow, who not only endured an entire oral history interview by telephone but donated valuable research from the Institute for Jazz Study at Rutgers University in Newark, New Jersey. Thanks also to Kevin Whitehead for assistance in several research matters and for his critical reading of the manuscript, and to Floyd Standifer for his guidance in the early stages of the project, access to rare tapes, and a critical reading. My deepest appreciation goes to Audrey Houck of the *Seattle Times* library, for her patient assistance; to Julia Braun and Chet Ramage of the American Federation of Musicians Local 76, for theirs; and to the Tacoma, Portland, Los Angeles, and San Francisco union locals for various other information. For help in various other ways, thanks also to Merle I. Smith, Norm Bobrow, Linda Allen, Traff Hubert, Frank Driggs, Jerry Gray, Judy de Barros, Lawrence Gushee, Lola Pedrini, Ken Wiley, John McDonough, Jan Stentz, Roberta Penn, Al Hendrix, Don Duncan, and Mark Troxel.

Oral history is an art form in itself, and I would have been poorer for not having consulted at length with Dan Morgenstern of the Institute for Jazz Study and Bob Rusch of *Cadence*. Thanks to both of them and to oral historians Peter Heffelfinger of Anacortes, Washington, and Sharon Boswell of the Washington State Oral History Society. The oral histories themselves were conducted by a patient cadre of inquiring souls, to whom I am grateful: Ted Dzielak, Kate Smith, Ken Maffit, Joe Murphy, Adam Woog, Sandy Burlingame, Mark Solomon, Jim Wilke, Lynn Darroch, Susan Golden, Marianne Jones, Keith Raether, Rick Leppanen, and Pete Leinonen.

And to the transcribers who patiently took each word off the tapes, thank you as well: Jeff Kahrs, Karen Rahl, Sandra Burlingame, Beatriz Pascual, Nancy Slote, Mark Troxel, Susan Golden, Aleta Ashlock, Carmen Jones, Julie Johnson, Carolyn Mandile, Linda Grotefendt, Evelyn Roehl, Marcia Haines, Sarah Wilson, Jerry Alexander, Gwen Gottberg, Lara Morrison, Mary Scott, Marlene Stone, Hap Hanchett, Delva Earl, and Rick Huey. Thanks also to Ron Hall for coordinating volunteer transcribers; Phyllis Hatfield for the loan of a transcribing machine; Nola Freeman for guidance in working with seniors; Jim Wilke for his special help on the Palmer Johnson interview; the Refugee Women's Alliance for the loan of tape recorders; Caren Adams, Earshot Jazz, KPLU-FM, and United Way for helping provide volunteer transcribers; and Joe Canale of Acoustic Imports for his technical assistance.

Gracious thanks to those who offered support and help in other areas: Julie Niebuhr Eulenberg, *Alaska Airlines Magazine*, and Peter Davenport, for sticking by the project in its difficult "horse latitudes."

Thanks to Nick Allison for his judicious and sensitive editing and for taking on this project when he had so many other things to do; likewise to designer Art Chantry, whose love of Northwest music shines through on every page of the first edition. Thanks to the folks at Earshot Jazz, who supported this project after I left the organization, not only with operational funds but with moral support, volunteer help, and a spur-of-the-moment subsidy for plane tickets to interview Ray Charles.

Thanks to all the generous funders and friends who have supported *Jackson Street* through grants to Earshot as an organization and to Eduardo Calderón and myself as individual artists: Seattle Arts Commission, King County Arts Commission, Tacoma Arts Commission, Washington State Arts Commission, Washington Commission for the Humanities, Artist Trust, Allied Arts, King County Centennial Commission, King County Cultural Resources Historic Preservation Program, Court Productions, the Alpac Corporation, Washington Mutual Savings Bank, Paul Fishburg, Barbara Erwine, and Whit Symmes.

Thanks to my family for enduring the long hours, days, weeks, months, and years this project demanded. And, finally, to all the musicians and others who took the time out to be interviewed and share their scrapbooks and memorabilia for this project—thank you.

For the University of Washington Press, second edition of *Jackson Street After Hours*: deep thanks to my agent Anne Depue and University of Washington Press director Nicole F. Mitchell for making this update possible and to UW editorial, design, and production manager Jennifer L. Comeau, assistant editor Emily Feng, art director Katrina Noble, and publicity manager Molly Woolbright for helping make it happen; to Midori Okazaki and Emily Venemon of the Washington State Archives, Puget Sound Regional Branch; Laurence Louie; San Francisco Bay Area jazz writer Andy Gilbert and Celia Jackson, Oakland Public Library; the Museum of History and Industry, especially MOHAI digital image technician Aurora San Miguel; Meaghan B. Kahlo, Seattle Public Schools Records and Archives; Stephanie Johnson-Toliver, president of the Black Heritage Society, and the rest of the Jackson Street Jazz Trail Committee; Wing Luke Museum; Earshot Jazz; Tanya Woo; Pete Leinonen; Gary Hammon; Maia Santell; Greg Ruby; Ken Steiner; Peter Vacher; David Keller; and Bruce Heather.

ILLUSTRATION CREDITS

Every effort has been made to contact copyright holders for their permission to reprint illustrations in this book. The author and publisher would be grateful to hear from any copyright holder who is not here acknowledged and will undertake to rectify any errors or omissions in future printings or editions of this book.

Page 14 Courtesy of the Washington State Archives.
Page 15 Property of the Black Heritage Society of Washington State, Inc.
Page 16 Courtesy of the Washington State Archives, Puget Sound Regional Branch.
Page 21 Property of the Black Heritage Society of Washington State, Inc.
Page 24 Courtesy of Emma Gayton.
Page 25 Courtesy of Georgia Turnham.
Page 28 Courtesy of MOHAI, PEMCO Webster & Stevens Collection, 1983.10.8221.1.
Page 29 Courtesy of Al Hendrix.
Page 30 Courtesy of the Hogan Archive of New Orleans Music and New Orleans Jazz, Tulane University.
Page 32 Courtesy of the Duncan P. Schiedt Photograph Collection, Archives Center, National Museum of American History, Smithsonian Institution.
Page 35 Courtesy of MOHAI, PEMCO Webster & Stevens Collection, 1983.10.4584.1.
Page 37 Courtesy of Grace Holden.
Page 49 Courtesy of Emma Gayton.
Page 54 Courtesy of Shelley Taylor.
Page 56 Property of the Black Heritage Society of Washington State, Inc.
Page 57 Courtesy of Georgia Turnham.
Page 60 Courtesy of John McDonough.
Page 63 Property of the Black Heritage Society of Washington State, Inc.
Page 72 Courtesy of MOHAI, Seattle Post-Intelligencer Collection, 1986.5.35776.2.
Page 80 Courtesy of the Washington State Archives, Puget Sound Regional Branch.
Page 82 Courtesy of Vivian Ewing.
Page 85 Courtesy of Emma Gayton.
Page 87 Courtesy of MOHAI, Al Smith Collection, 2014.49.14.006.05.
Page 89 Photo by Al Smith.
Page 96 Courtesy of MOHAI, PEMCO Webster & Stevens Collection, 1983.10.1775.
Page 97 Courtesy of Gaylord Jones.
Page 98 Courtesy of the Washington State Archives, Puget Sound Regional Branch, with additional thanks to Laurence Louie.
Page 100 Courtesy of Palmer Johnson.
Page 103 Courtesy of Palmer Johnson.
Page 107 Courtesy of Gaylord Jones.
Page 108 Courtesy of Norm Bobrow.
Page 109 Photo courtesy of MOHAI, Al Smith Collection, 2014.49.14.047.09. Posters courtesy of Don Lanphere.
Page 111 Courtesy of MOHAI, Al Smith Collection, 2014.49.006.027.0073.
Page 112 Courtesy of MOHAI, Al Smith Collection, 2014.49.002.028.0103.
Page 113 Courtesy of Gaylord Jones.
Page 114 Courtesy of Gaylord Jones.
Page 116 Courtesy of Al Turay.
Page 117 Courtesy of Gaylord Jones.
Page 119 Courtesy of Dave Stetler.
Page 122 Courtesy of MOHAI, Al Smith Collection, 2014.49.14.006.06.
Page 127 Courtesy of the Tacoma Public Library, TPL-038, Chapin Bowen Photographs, Northwest Room at Tacoma Public Library.
Page 129 Courtesy of Wanda Brown.
Page 130 Courtesy of Bob Russell.
Page 132 Courtesy of Don Glenn.
Page 136 Courtesy of MOHAI, Al Smith Collection, 2014.49.14.007.12.
Page 138 Courtesy of Don Glenn.

Page 139 Courtesy of MOHAI, Al Smith Collection, 2014.49.002.034.0150.
Page 143 Courtesy of the Washington State Archives, Puget Sound Regional Branch.
Page 144 *Left*, courtesy of Billy Tolles. *Right*, courtesy of MOHAI, Al Smith Collection. 2014.49.13.12.01.
Page 145 Courtesy of MOHAI, Al Smith Collection. 2014.49.13.12.02.
Page 155 Courtesy of MOHAI, Al Smith Collection, 2014.49.29.09.01.
Page 158 Courtesy of Vernon Buford.
Page 159 Courtesy of MOHAI, Al Smith Collection, 2014.49.16.031.09.
Page 165 Courtesy of the family of Janet Thurlow.
Page 170 Courtesy of Wanda Brown.
Page 179 Courtesy of Wanda Brown.
Page 181 Courtesy of Wanda Brown.
Page 188 Courtesy of Dave Bradford.
Page 190 Courtesy of Garfield High School.
Page 191 Courtesy of Charles Taylor.
Page 198 Courtesy of Charles Taylor.
Page 199 Courtesy of Buddy Catlett.
Page 206 Mercury Records.
Page 212 Courtesy of MOHAI, Seattle Post-Intelligencer Collection, 2000.107.025.15.01.
Page 224 Courtesy of the Washington State Archives, Puget Sound Regional Branch.
Page 230 Courtesy of Bill Crow.
Page 237 Courtesy of Fred Greenwell.
Page 239 Courtesy of Fred Greenwell.
Page 240 Courtesy of Fred Greenwell.
Page 243 Courtesy of Red Kelly.
Page 253 Photo by DeWayne Sharp. Courtesy of Chuck Mahaffay.
Page 258 Courtesy of Chuck Metcalf.
Page 262 Courtesy of MOHAI, Al Smith Collection, 2014.49.14.001.02.
Page 263 Courtesy of MOHAI, Seattle Post-Intelligencer Collection, 2000.107.174.16.01, photo by Stuart B. Hertz.
Page 264 Courtesy of MOHAI, Al Smith Collection, 2014.49.16.040.11.
Page 265 Courtesy of Chuck Mahaffay.
Page 267 Courtesy of Elmer Gill.
Page 272 Courtesy of Melody Jones.
Page 278 Courtesy of MOHAI, Al Smith Collection, 2014.49.15.108.06.
Page 280 Courtesy of Melody Jones.
Page 282 Reprinted from the *Northwest Enterprise.*
Page 294 Courtesy of Traff Hubert.
Page 295 Courtesy of Traff Hubert.
Page 303 Courtesy of Dave Stetler.
Page 306 Peter Blecha Collection / Northwest Music Archives.
Page 318 Courtesy of the Seattle Municipal Archives, #63759, Series 2613-07.
Page 334 Mercury Records.
Page 341 Photo by Harold Kaminske. Courtesy of Chuck Mahaffay.
Page 349 Courtesy of Noreen Coleman.
Page 352 Courtesy of Pete Barbas.
Page 353 Photo by Egill Gustafson.
Page 355 Courtesy of Chuck Mahaffay.
Page 369 Courtesy of Al Hendrix.

INDEX

Page numbers in *italics* refer to illustrations

ABOUT THE AUTHOR

Erika Schultz

PAUL DE BARROS, RECIPIENT OF THE 2025 Jazz Journalists Association Lifetime Achievement award and a 2003 inductee into the Seattle Jazz Hall of Fame, has written about jazz for *DownBeat* magazine and *The Seattle Times* since 1982. In 1984, he cofounded the Seattle nonprofit Earshot Jazz. For two decades he taught jazz history, including several years at the University of Washington. His work has appeared in *The San Francisco Chronicle, The Washington Post, The Philadelphia Inquirer,* and *The Los Angeles Times.* He is the author of *Shall We Play That One Together? The Life and Art of Jazz Piano Legend Marian McPartland.*

Palmer Johnson and Russell Jones
To Be at Palomar Theater
Week Starting May 10

MOORE THEATRE
ITURBI
PIANISTIC GIANT
"His success is of the Paderewski order."—N. Y. Journal.
SAT. EVE., APR. 6
87c to $2.88 . Seats Now

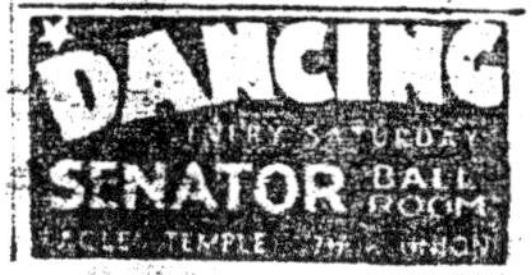

Chief to
Why
Chinese
Up Bo

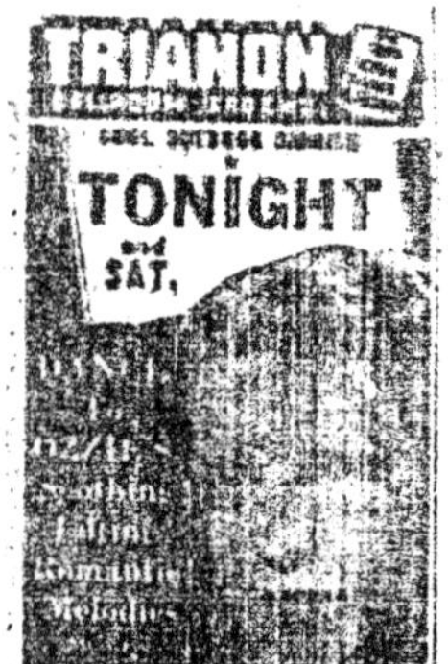

FRANK D. WALDRON'S
SYNCOPATED CLASSIC
For C Melody and Alto Saxophone With Piano Acc.
Two Classic Solos
Seven Original Syncopated Novelty Solos
Fifty One Jazz Breaks and Endings

Instructions on how to
Slap Tongue, Flutter Tongue, Laugh, Squeeze, Etc.
as performed by WALDRON himself. The biggest value ever offered to Saxophonists

Published by
The Waldron School of Saxophone & Trumpet
1242 JACKSON ST. SEATTLE, WASH.

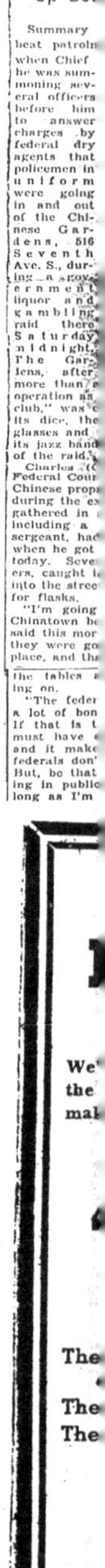

Bill Crammatte Again Presents
The BEST
DIXIELAND JAZZ
that you've heard here in years.
DON ANDERSON'S Truly Great
SEATTLE RHYTHM KINGS
For your DANCING and LISTENING Pleasure
TRIANON BALLROOM
FRIDAY, APRIL 6
3rd & Wall 9 to 1 $1.25 Inc. Tax
This Same Band S.R.O. at Lake City Tavern Every Wednesday

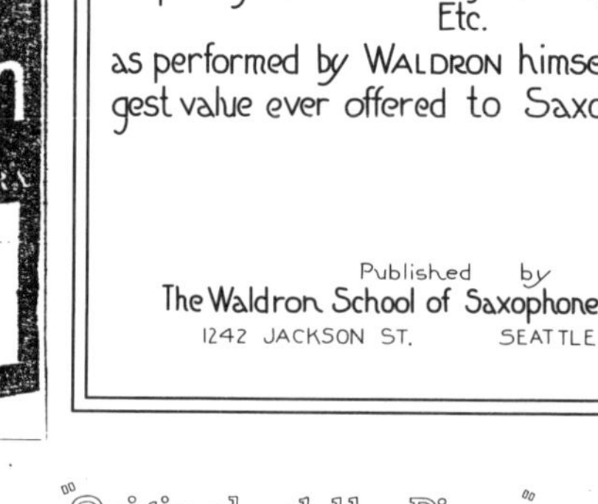